# A Guided Tour of the United States Economy

# A Guided Tour of the United States Economy

## Promises among the Perils

Edward L. Whalen

QUORUM BOOKS
Westport, Connecticut • London

**Library of Congress Cataloging-in-Publication Data**

Whalen, Edward, 1936–
A guided tour of the United States economy : promises among the perils / Edward L. Whalen.
p. cm.
Includes bibliographical references and index.
ISBN 1–56720–426–0 (alk. paper)
1. United States—Economic conditions—1945– I. Title.
HC106.5.W483 2002
330.973'092—dc21 2001031892

British Library Cataloguing in Publication Data is available.



Library of Congress Catalog Card Number: 2001031892
ISBN: 1–56720–426–0

First published in 2002

Quorum Books, 88 Post Road West, Westport, CT 06881
An imprint of Greenwood Publishing Group, Inc.
www.quorumbooks.com

Printed in the United States of America

The paper used in this book complies with the Permanent Paper Standard issued by the National Information Standards Organization (Z39.48–1984).

10 9 8 7 6 5 4 3 2 1

# Contents

# Exhibits

# Preface

Some books begin with an introduction; others with a foreword. This one begins with a "Forward!" It is intended as a word of encouragement for readers setting out to discover how the economy works.

Have you ever purchased a piece of assemble-it-yourself furniture? You get it home. Dump out all the pieces. Some big. Some small. Some familiar. Some peculiar. And then attempt to put them together. And finally resort to the instructions.

What follows is intended as a set of instructions—not on how to assemble a piece of furniture but rather on how to measure economic activity, to understand the national income and product accounts and how they fit with other economic statistics.

Like assembling a bookcase, we have to first get out all the pieces, examine them, determine their relationship to one another, and begin a process of assembly. In the end everything should snap together. No missing parts. None left over. What we have as a result in this instance is a device for assessing economic performance, determining those factors that are important and those that are trivial, and—most entertaining—developing a basis for evaluating ridiculous public statements by just about everyone with an ax to grind: politicians (especially), but also news media pundits, business and labor "leaders," interest group representatives, and the list goes on.

To say that I have spent a lifetime writing this book would be somewhat of an hyperbole. However, its genesis goes back a long way. A number of important events occurred in the year 1958. For me those important events included my graduation from Indiana University with a baccalaureate degree in economics. Commencement for me marked the beginning of my working life, which, aided by a doctoral degree in economics from Princeton University, has been viewed from the perspective of an economist. Now after forty years, the career phase of my life is ending. A review, therefore, of what has happened to the economy of the United States over those two score years seems appropriate.

My predilection for measurable facts and a quantitative approach has led to my selecting the national income and product accounts along with related business, commercial, and financial statistics as vehicles for describing the changes that have occurred over the forty years from 1959 to 1999. Had my career been ending rather than beginning in 1958, such a review would have been impossible. Forty years of such statistics did not exist in 1958. Even if they had, the effects of the Great Depression of the 1930s, World War II, and the extended recovery period that followed it would have distorted their interpretation. The span of time following 1958 has been fortuitously free of such massive disruptions characterizing the forty years that preceded it.

During such a period of relative calm (and even during so-called interesting times), reflections on economic data may not appear particularly exciting. We follow such statistics on a day-to-day, month-to-month, quarterly, and annual basis. The changes seldom are striking. Even when they are, delay in the availability of data frequently makes them less useful and interesting. We already know what has happened without the numbers.

However, viewed from a forty-year perspective, the changes appear dramatic! When I graduated in 1958, gross domestic product stood at around $500 billion. In 1999 it had risen to over $9 trillion. That's an increase of over 18 times! Reviewing those numbers in a moment of reflection led me to believe that their detailed examination and elucidation in an organized fashion could be exciting, interesting, and educational—to me at least. So at the outset my exploration has been to satisfy a personal curiosity. How could I have been so oblivious, so asleep, to the magnitude of the changes going on around me? Why didn't someone in 1958 point out what possibilities lay ahead? Those numbers reveal how far we have come.

Although the progress that has been made and the prosperity that has resulted are unimaginable by 1958 standards, the act of accomplishment was not accompanied by sensations of exhilaration or spasms of enthusiasm. There seemed to be too much to worry about. The Cold War and threat of nuclear annihilation, the Vietnam Conflict, exhaustion of fossil fuels, spread of new diseases in a more mobile world, terrorist attacks (domestic and foreign), and plenty of others subdued tendencies to celebrate. Those items all fall within an economist's category of exogenous factors—events separate from the economy. But the economy produced its own worries: remembrance of the Great Depression made every pause in economic growth seem like the beginning of a plunge into an abyss; every spurt seemed as if it might be a dash to economic disruption. Price inflation, unemployment, declining productivity, competitiveness in international markets, stagflation, the national government deficit, deficits in the U.S. balance of payments, social security and Medicare solvency—if not one, then another—always were before us.

In this book, as we view U.S. economic performance through the lens provided by national income and output statistics, we shall see that none of the economic obstacles have constituted permanent barriers to economic growth and prosperity. The remarkable progress brought about by a free-enterprise market-oriented economy operating in a context of political stability, rule of law, and private property rights has enabled those impediments to be addressed. Moreover, there is no reason that such progress will not continue to serve us well in addressing future problems. The nation should not be so preoccupied with possible problems as to not look beyond current horizons. Potential and promise rather than perceived perils should serve as guides in the future.

Much of the information presented in this book is the product of the unstinting labors and talents of a veritable legion of anonymous librarians at the Fondren Library of Rice University and of the Houston Public Library. There seemed to be no fact—however obscure—that they could not ferret out. Ever pleasant and eager to help, they are a credit to their profession.

This book would be longer, contain superfluous material, and be less focused if it were not for the editorial assistance of Eric Valentine, publisher of Quorum Books. His suggestions, encouragement, and prompt responses to my many questions are much appreciated. Greenwood Publishing Group copy and production editor Bobbie Goettler helped me bring the manuscript into alignment with the publisher's standards and ably guided me through the intricate publishing process. Daughter-in-law Haley B. Whalen provided further editorial assistance. Her comments vastly improved my grammar and sentence structure.

A special note of thanks is due to my wife, Joan. Not only has she been willing to share our marriage with this effort, but also she told all our friends and acquaintances that I was writing a book. After so much publicity, I had no alternative but to follow through with the endeavor. Moreover, far and away above the call of duty, she read my manuscript through from start to finish, checking out every detail and helping to point out sections that were unclear. That someone with a background in biology found it understandable should encourage those who are not familiar with national income and output statistics. Her efforts caught a lot of errors. If any are left, assign blame to me. I am used to it.

# 1

# The Journey Begins

We are going to embark on a journey to explore the economy of the United States. How big is it? How are the products and services we consume produced? How is income distributed among households and individuals? Where in the United States are incomes highest? Who does the consuming? The saving? The investing? Why are taxes so high? What does the government do with all that money? Why do other countries sell more to us than we sell to them? Is social security going bankrupt? Those are some of the tourist attractions that we shall visit.

Our curiosity will lead us to examine the economy's structure, operations, and performance at a particular moment of time and its changes over time. What industries have become more important in the U.S. economy? Is government taking over a larger and larger share of the nation's output? Are people's incomes rising or shrinking relative to corporate profits? Is income becoming more or less equally distributed? Those and other questions will be addressed in the course of our journey through time during a forty-year period from 1959 through 1999.

Why select that particular time period? Data availability constitutes one factor guiding the decision. The beginning year, 1959, currently is the earliest year for which consistent time series have been issued. The time of this writing is the year 2000. Five years must elapse until all data for a particular year have been collected and have been incorporated into the national statistics. Estimates for 1999, the last year of our time series, are available, but as yet they are not quite complete. They are like lettuce salads before dressing is added—suitable for consumption but susceptible of improvement with further processing.

While data availability seems like a necessary condition for our analysis, it may not seem very satisfying. Happily, however, the period from 1959 to 1999 appears to be ideally suited to use national income statistics as a device to understand and describe economic activity over an interval of time. The Great Depression of the 1930s, whose advent corresponded to early development of the national income and product statistics, and the federal government's response to the catastrophe dominated that decade, distorting usual economic relationships. World War II, followed soon after by the Cold War and Korean Conflict, held sway over the 1940s. Reconstruction of Europe and resumption of normal international trade relationships were not completed until the late 1950s. Consequently, only in the past forty years has economic activity been able to operate in an environment not disrupted by overwhelming exogenous events.

Is this trip necessary? Thomas Jefferson argued that educated citizens are essential to preserving a democracy. He observed,

> In every government on earth is some trace of human weakness, some germ of corruption and degeneracy, which cunning will discover, and wickedness insensibly open, cultivate, and improve. Every government degenerates when trusted to the rulers of the people alone. The people themselves therefore are its only safe depositories. And to render them safe, their minds must be improved to a certain degree. This indeed is not all that is necessary, though it be essentially necessary.[1]

Today there is a lot more to be educated about than in Jefferson's time. Dire warnings from politicians, businessmen, labor leaders, experts, and pundits about the fate of our economy bombard us daily. As if their bad news is not enough, they also utter proposals to correct or ameliorate their crises of the moment. Understanding the magnitudes involved in a context of the overall economy can help distinguish in that barrage between important and trivial concerns, between what makes sense and nonsense.

Our examination of economic data over a forty-year time span will show that the U.S. economy has performed spectacularly. Despite fear mongers' emphasis on perils ahead and at every turn, the country has prospered. The output of goods and services produced *per person* in 1999 is more than double what it was in 1959. That is spectacular! In 1959 few, if any, pointed out the future's promise. Many pointed out its perils. Forty years of evidence suggests that in the future we should be as much concerned with the nation's promises as with its perils. Indeed, failure to look beyond possible perils may result in lost opportunities.

Fear mongers might be inclined to take credit for our good fortune by maintaining that if they had not sounded an alarm, various disasters would have occurred. If so, they have performed a service. Like all of us, however, fear mongers have agendas too. Warnings of awful consequences can also serve to keep things desired by others from happening and to direct resources and events to favor the alarmists.

The real credit for our improved and improving standard of living belongs to our market-oriented economic system—a market system sustained by and sustaining an environment of political stability, a rule of law under which all men (and more recently women, too, of course, naturally) are equal, and the institution of private property.[2] Those traditions and customs—market orientation, orderly government, rule of law, and private property—in happy and reinforcing combination guide us to this marvelous existence.

A stable government assures people that the rules of the game will not change precipitously. The legal system is designed to treat all equally. Individuals—weak and poor as well as strong and rich—have the same rights before the law. Private property rights entitle people to own and use what they work to create.[3] The market mechanism rewards people according to their productivity. Under such an incentive system, as Adam Smith observed,

> every individual necessarily labours to render the annual revenue of the society as great as he can. He generally, indeed, neither intends to promote the public interest, nor knows how much he is promoting it. . . . He intends only his own gain, and he is in this, as in many other cases, led by an invisible hand to promote an end which was no part of his intention. Nor is it always the worse for society that was no part of it. By pursuing his own interest he frequently promotes that of the society more effectually than when he really intends to promote it. I have never known much good done by those who affected to trade for the public good.[4]

Out of perceived self-interest, we are driven to a frenzy of collective productive activity! The effort is not to keep body and soul together. Starvation does not threaten. Our standard of living exceeds the subsistence level by a wide margin. Indeed, it exceeds that margin so substantially that a case can be made that food intake has become excessive. Recent medical guidelines released by the federal government indicate that 55 percent of the U.S. population is overweight![5] Oops, another peril.

The market-driven economy is largely self-governing and self-directed. Indeed, von Mises observed,

> In an economic order based on private ownership of the means of production the market is the focal point of the system. The working of the market mechanism forces capitalists and entrepreneurs to produce so as to satisfy the consumer's needs. . . . If they are not equal to this task . . . other people who know better how to serve the consumer will replace them. Within the market society the working of the price mechanism makes the consumer supreme. . . . They determine directly the prices of consumers' goods, and thereby indirectly the prices of all material factors of production and the wages of all hands employed.[6]

Since no major-domo is in charge to ask how the economy operates, we have to discover it for ourselves.

## PLOTTING OUR JOURNEY

After a brief review of the history of the development of national accounting, we will examine characteristics of the four sectors of the economy: the household, government, rest-of-the-world, and business sectors. This chapter concludes with a preview of the major economic accounting aggregates.

The next four chapters deal with sources and uses of personal income. We can relate to personal income and outlays. Our common experience helps us make the distinction between how we measure our income and how our nation's bookkeeper—the Bureau of Economic Analysis of the Department of Commerce—measures it. Moreover, personal income and outlays comprise most of gross domestic product. Chapters 2 and 3 focus on accounting concepts and data for 1999. Chapter 3 concludes with a look at personal saving and investment, an exercise that requires integrating financial data from the nation's central banker, the Board of Governors of the Federal Reserve System, with the national income and product accounts.

Chapters 4 and 5 look at changes in personal income and outlays from 1959 to 1999. Statistics of income from the Internal Revenue Service help assess the distribution of income among individuals and the burden of the personal income tax. In chapter 5 assessing the growth in real personal consumption expenditure requires recognition of price inflation and introduction of price indexes. Trends noted and discussed include the declining share of personal income accounted for by salaries and wages and personal saving, and the rising shares of government transfer payments to persons, contributions to social security, and personal income taxes.

The government sector receives scrutiny in the next two chapters. In chapter 6, after reminding ourselves why this sector even exists, we examine state and local government revenues and expenditures. Once again, Federal Reserve System data are invoked to examine the composition of the saving and investment activities of state and local government. The next chapter follows a similar pattern for the national government. Chapter 7 concludes by bringing all levels of government together in the form in which they usually are found in summaries of the national income and product accounts.

Balance of payments accounts supply data for examining the components of U.S. exports and imports and our major trading partners in 1999. Those data are then reconciled to the national income and product accounts to construct an analysis of changes in the U.S. international financial position from 1959 to 1999. The effect of recent trade deficits on currency exchange rates and on the composition of foreign investment in the United States concludes chapter 8 and its treatment of the rest-of-the-world sector.

Last but not least comes business, the sector producing all those goods and services we consume, invest, and sell to the rest of the world. This sector is populated not with people but with business enterprises: proprietorships, partnerships, and corporations. To become acquainted, we first get an idea of the population: their number, their size, and their profitability. Corporations receive most of the attention since they account for 89 percent of all business receipts. Statistics of income data supplied by the Internal Revenue Service provide a basis for examining their distribution of assets, business receipts, and profitability. Input-output analysis and Department of Commerce data are used to link transactions in intermediate goods among firms to the final goods and services that consumers, government, and the rest of the world buy.

Chapter 10 brings together data from the four sectors to produce gross domestic product and related economic aggregates. Armed with those statistics, we now are in position to assess the performance of the U.S. economy: its real growth, productivity, price inflation, changes in its components, and geographic distribution.

Chapter 11 provides a glance behind. Each decade witnessed events that significantly changed gross domestic product and other national economic statistics. Included among them were Medicare and Medicaid in the 1960s, crude oil prices and stagflation in the 1970s, monetarism and government deficits in the 1980s, the stock market boom and dwindling personal saving in the 1990s. Mingled with the events are trends: rapid labor force growth (a product of Baby Boomers and an increasing proportion of women working outside the home), rising costs of medical care, and an increasing share of government expenditures in the form of social security and other transfer payments to persons constitute examples. Where will it end?

Chapter 12 concludes with a look ahead and a projection of gross domestic product to the year 2040. Social insurance programs (social security and Medicare) and their deficits figure prominently in the estimates. Are they in peril? Is disaster around the corner? Read on and discover!

## OUR VEHICLE FOR DISCOVERY

Our principal vehicle for exploration will be the national income and product accounts (NIPA) prepared and published by the Bureau of Economic Analysis of the U.S. Department of Commerce, which states, "This system of integrated, double-entry accounts provides a comprehensive and unduplicated measure of economic activity within a consistently defined framework. Thus the NIPA's—together with the industry, wealth, and regional accounts—can be used to trace the principal economic flows among major sectors of the economy."[7] NIPA statistics are presented in over 100 tables, and our inquiry will necessitate visiting many of them.

Despite the explanatory power of the NIPA, they do not take us everywhere we want to go. Consequently, we shall rely also on flow of funds accounts of the Board of Governors of the Federal Reserve System, the international transactions tables and input-output accounting data assembled by the Bureau of Economic Analysis, and statistics of income data prepared by the Internal Revenue Service. Those sources will be integrated with the NIPA to provide a comprehensive and consistent picture of the U.S. economy.

Before proceeding with the detail, some background information appears helpful. An historical approach seems best. How did national income and product accounting get started? Let's begin at the beginning.

## ACHIEVEMENT OF THE CENTURY

Compared to business accounting whose origins date back to the time of the Italian Renaissance in the 1300s, accounting for the economy is of recent origin. Much of its development occurred in this century.[8] Someone had to develop a system to measure economic activity, and the Department of Commerce receives (and takes) much of the credit. After completing a review of its work over the past 100 years, the department declared that the NIPA was "its achievement of the century."[9]

Prior to World War I, individual investigators sporadically attempted estimates of the nation's total output. With the war effort and a need to estimate the nation's war materiel producing capacity, groups such as the National Industrial Conference Board, the National Bureau of Economic Research, and the Federal Trade Commission undertook the effort more intensely. Efforts continued into the 1920s, but even by the end of the decade, time-series estimates on a current basis were not available.

Then came the stock market crash in October of 1929, followed by the Great Depression. People knew that production of goods and services had fallen drastically, but no one could tell by how much. To find an answer the Senate, on June 8, 1932, passed a resolution instructing the Department of Commerce to prepare for the Congress a report on national income for 1929, 1930, and 1931. The requested report, the product of an effort directed by Simon Kuznets of the National Bureau of Economic Research under Department of Commerce auspices, was submitted to the Senate on January 4, 1934. For that work and his subsequent contributions to studies of national income, business cycles, and economic growth, Simon Kuznets was awarded the Nobel Prize in economics in 1971.

Even though the latest data contained in the report were two years old, it represented a pioneering advance in national income accounting. Encouraged by its success, the project continued throughout the 1930s. This period witnessed rapid development of terminology, definitions, monthly and quarterly estimates, and many of the other concepts and practices taken for granted by most people today. Paralleling the empirical work came advances in macroeconomic theory that provide a framework for the collection, organization, and presentation of data. John Maynard Keynes' *The General Theory of Employment, Interest and Money*, published in 1936, in particular, influenced the definition and categorization of national income and product.

With World War II came economic recovery and a new set of problems whose resolution was assisted by the availability of national income and product information. Price inflation replaced price deflation. Shortages replaced excess productive capacity. National income and product estimates provided a basis not only for overall resource planning but also for controlling inflation. Using national income and product information, investigators calculated an inflation gap, the difference between potential real output of goods and services relative to projected aggregate demand. Those calculations in turn provided decision makers guidance in determining monetary and fiscal policy designed to effectively constrain civilian demand.

The United States was not alone in its efforts to develop national income and product accounts. The United Kingdom Treasury, assisted by John Maynard Keynes, completed its first analysis of national income in 1941.[10] As World War II drew to a close, collaboration with Canada and the United Kingdom intensified. Under United Nations auspices, the effort became an international one. In 1947 the United Nations issued a report, *The Measurement of National Income and Construction of Social Accounts,* that identified five major aggregates:

- National income,
- Gross national product,
- Net national product,
- Personal income, and
- Disposable income.[11]

Those aggregates, with their definitions little changed, are in use today. Only gross domestic product—which has replaced gross national product as the featured aggregate in the United States and most other countries—is omitted from the list.

The national income and product accounts underwent further refinement in the early 1950s when the United Nations published reports defining a system of five national accounts for sectors of the economy.[12] As with the definition of national aggregates, the system of national accounts has withstood the test of time and remains largely intact to form the framework for national income accounting.

In any new area of endeavor, a number of independent approaches frequently emerge. Such was the case for national income accounting. Efforts to measure economic activity on a national scale and to examine relationships among economic sectors were not confined to the national income and product accounts. During the 1930s Wassily Leontief, a Harvard economist, pioneered in the development of input-output analysis, a matrix arrangement showing what industrial sectors produced intermediate goods and what sectors used them to produce final products for consumption, investment, and export to the rest of the world. Morris Copeland of the National Bureau of Economic Research developed data on financial relationships through a flow-of-funds analysis identifying those sectors issuing financial instruments and those holding them. Raymond Goldsmith, a Yale economist, produced estimates of national wealth and constructed a national balance sheet based on a perpetual inventory method of estimating the nation's stock of capital.[13]

Until the 1950s those approaches were independent of one another. That decade marked efforts to integrate them. The national income and product accounts continued to occupy center stage as a source of economic information. In the 1960s input-output analysis, flow-of-funds analysis, and balance-of-payments information were integrated with the national income accounts in the United

States. Further refinements followed in response to new national economic policy concerns. As observed by the Department of Commerce in its review of a century of accomplishment, "In the late 1960's and 1970's, accelerating inflation prompted the development of improved measures of prices and inflation-adjusted output. In the 1980's, the internationalization of trade in services led to expansion of the estimates of international trade in services in the NIPA's."[14]

In 1968 the United Nations published a revised system of national accounts integrating stocks and flows and making provisions for income distribution statistics, balance sheets, and reconciliation accounts.[15] Further refinements since then include moves toward standardization of definitions and concepts with other international organizations such as the International Monetary Fund and World Bank and with nation states. More recently, the Commission of the European Communities, the International Monetary Fund, the Organization for Economic Co-operation and Development, the United Nations, and the World Bank issued a new guide for countries to follow in preparing estimates of their national accounts.[16] It updates the 1968 system of national accounts and brings them into alignment with other international standards for measuring balances of payments, employment, and government revenues and expenditure.

This brief review of the development of the national income and product accounts suggests that the concepts, definitions, and estimates we often take for granted are not immutable. Not so long ago, they did not exist. Analysts involved in their evolution had to create them. Concepts, definitions, and estimates that proved useful were retained; those that did not were abandoned. Only gradually did a standardized, comprehensive, and logical approach to measuring relevant aggregates of economic significance and showing the structure of the economic system emerge. The framework and processes used to prepare estimates of national income and output will continue to evolve in response to changing conditions and new questions that require new answers.

## ECONOMIC SECTORS

The total output of a nation's economy conceivably could be constructed by adding up all the market transactions of individual parties in the country. However, the detail underlying the total would be too great to tell us much about relationships among individual transactors. Fortunately, many of the transactors are similarly organized, share common goals, engage in comparable transactions, and behave in a like manner in response to changes in economic conditions. In the case of personal income, for example, we often can treat all the households, individuals, and people-serving nonprofit institutions as a group without making distinction among them.

Accordingly, dividing the economy into four sectors has been adopted as a standard for constructing the national income and product accounts. The four sectors are:

- Households,
- Business,
- Government, and
- Rest of the world.

Economists assume that all human beings engage in rational, purposeful activity. Von Mises observed, "Whatever people do in the market economy, is the execution of their own plans. In this sense every human action means planning."[17] Although individual perspectives differ, members of at least three of the four sectors are judged to share common goals.

### Household Sector

Households are assumed to possess as their objective maximization of satisfaction and well being from the consumption of goods and services given a limit on resources (e.g., income) available. Maximizing a household's satisfaction can present a challenge. A single individual may fail to maximize his or her satisfaction because of incomplete information as to prices and product quality. A decision once made, however, is rarely subjected to self-criticism. For households consisting of related family members and any unrelated persons sharing the same living quarters, satisfaction maximization becomes vastly more complicated. It's Sunday afternoon, quality time together! Your wife wants to see a matinee. You want to go fishing. The kids want to watch television. For whatever resources are to be expended, someone's (perhaps everyone's) satisfaction is not going to be maximized. In a functioning family unit, however, the objective somehow is approximated.

### Business Sector

Ascribing to business maximizing satisfaction as a goal does not seem appropriate. Instead, economists assume that businesses are in business to maximize profits. In order to do so, they produce goods and services of the kind, design, and quality that prospective purchasers desire, in a manner that minimizes production costs, and at quantity that is economically efficient. When those conditions are satisfied, the largest difference between total revenue from the sales of a firm's output and the total cost of production results. Unlike satisfaction and a feeling of well being from consumption of goods and services, use of generally accepted accounting principles enables profit to be measured with a high degree of precision and in a manner that invites comparison of performance among firms. Consequently, profit maximization has proved to be a powerful motivation to producers of goods and services, making them exquisitely sensitive to consumer demand, quick to develop new products, and innovative in finding efficient ways of producing them.

**Government Sector**

Some would ascribe to government the goal of seeking to maximize social welfare.[18] Unlike profit maximizing, however, such a goal is not readily subject to measurement. Maximizing social welfare is akin to household maximization of satisfaction. Even in a closely knit family unit, working out compromises among individuals' preferences proves to be imprecise and imperfect. The problem is more vastly complicated when reaching such compromises for an entire society.

In business the bottom line gives a clear and immediate message about how a firm and the individuals within it perform. Profit is quantifiable. Costs and revenues from which it is determined are quantifiable. In many cases results can be attributed with accuracy to particular groups or even individuals within an organization. In government maximizing social welfare lacks that objectivity. How many politicians and bureaucrats ask themselves at the end of each day how much they contributed to social welfare? Even if they did, how would they know? Would their colleagues care? More likely, getting reelected and advancing in pay grade provide guidance to their actions.

However imperfect, social welfare maximization as government's role is unlikely to be replaced. It is too convenient. Accepting social welfare maximization as government's goal legitimizes its role in income redistribution. Our examination of personal income will provide ample evidence of the magnitude of that activity. But not everyone is enthusiastic about that goal. Author Ludwig von Mises states, "[Government] Planners sometimes describe their proposals as measures to combat poverty and want. The description is ambiguous. All economic policies are designed as remedies for poverty. Laissez faire too is a method of abolishing poverty. Both history and economic theory have demonstrated that it has been more successful than any other policy."[19]

Governments do have a unique role in the provision of public goods and services. Public goods are not subject to the usual discipline of the market. When they are provided, anyone or everyone enjoys their benefits without obligation to pay for them. Consequently, businesses rarely find providing public goods and services profitable or even feasible. The Constitution of the United States assigns responsibility for a number of such goods and services to the federal government: national defense; international relations; regulation of commerce; the postal service; issuing of currency and coin; enactment, enforcement, and interpretation of laws and regulations; naturalization of citizens; sponsorship of research; and patent protection. Such functions as police and fire protection, road and highway maintenance, public health, education, and welfare comprise the public goods and services undertaken by state and local governments.

**Rest-of-World Sector**

The rest-of-the-world sector represents a residual resulting from the other three sectors seeking achievement of their goals. The results also are influenced by the actions of other countries attempting to attain their goals. Of course, countries in the rest of the world have their households, businesses, and governments that may or may not operate in an environment as congenial as ours. In any event David Ricardo demonstrated that those transactions that do occur voluntarily among nations tend to serve their mutual advantage.[20]

## THE SUMMARY ECONOMIC ACCOUNTS

As in business accounting, all the national income and product accounts use a double-entry system to record entries. The five summary accounts corresponding to the economic sectors used to prepare aggregate statistics for the United States are:

- National income and product account,
- Personal income and outlay account,
- Government receipts and expenditure account,
- Foreign transactions account, and
- Gross saving and investment account.

The household, government, and foreign sectors of the economy appear to have been provided with an account. Where is one for the business sector? Business sector transactions are embedded primarily in the national income and product account. The business sector produces most of the economy's output of final goods and services. Since that information is recorded in the national income and product account, the business sector's transactions are recorded there.

Our approach will vary a bit from that framework. The business sector will have its own account. The approach facilitates presenting relationships among the sectors in a symmetrical way and showing their relationship to input-output analysis. Besides, as the site for most of the economy's productive activity, the business sector surely deserves equal treatment with the other three sectors.

Our treatment of saving and investment represents a further departure from the standard structure. Rather than constructing a single saving and investment account for all sectors, a separate account will be developed for each of them. Once again, this approach serves to make relationships among sectors clearer. For the moment, obtaining a general perspective of the five accounts seems appropriate.

### National Income and Product Account

Sales of output for *final* goods and services constitute the national income and product account's sources of funds. Sources match outlays exactly. Business outlays consist of employee compensation, rent, interest, dividends, taxes, and other costs incurred in the production process. The household sector contributes to output of *final* goods and services only modestly: just "services rendered by paid household workers and services rendered by nonprofit institutions serving households."[21] The compensation paid to household workers determines the value attributed to their services. A similar technique is used to estimate government's contribution to the national output of *final* goods and services. Compensation paid to government employees is used in determining the value of public services provided by them.

Note the emphasis placed on *final* goods and services in the above paragraph. Products produced for consumption by households and government, for export, or for sale to business as productive capital to produce future goods and services are classified as final goods. What else is there? Intermediate goods and services. Intermediate goods and services are those used in the process of production to produce other goods and services. In many cases a product's classification depends on who buys it and how it is used, not what it is. A kilowatt of electricity used to light a bulb in your living room is considered to be a final product. (In personal consumption expenditure, it is classified as a service.) An identical kilowatt sold to the local grocery or used to power an electric motor driving a press in a printing company would be classified as an intermediate product. A pickup truck sold to your grandmother who is going to use it to drive to church on Sunday and haul her groceries would be considered a final good; an identical make and model sold to a local construction firm would be considered an intermediate good.

*An Illustration of Final Goods.* To define the distinction between final and intermediate goods and services is one thing; to understand how the distinction is made is another. Perhaps an example will help. You purchase a loaf of bread for 89 cents. The production account for the business sector will include your purchase of the bread, but it will NOT include the grocer's purchase of the loaf from the baker AND the baker's purchase of flour from the miller AND the miller's purchase of wheat from the farmer who grew the grain, even though they all may have occurred during the same time period. Including them would overstate the goods and services available for their ultimate use either as consumable items or as investments to produce yet more goods and services.

Your expenditure is income to the grocer. The grocer's purchase of bread constituted income for the baker. The baker's purchase of flour provided income to the miller. And so on to the farmer who sold the grain. Thus it is that the dollar value of sales of final goods and services equals income paid to the factors of production that produced them.

An illustration is presented in Exhibit 1.1. It should be recognized as an outrageously simplified version of what really happens behind the scenes when you purchase that loaf of bread. First, we're going to assume that only five parties are involved in the series of transactions leading up to your purchase: the farmer, the miller, the baker, the grocer, and you, the consumer. The farmer does not own the land he tills; he pays rent. Similarly, the miller, baker, and grocer do not own the facilities in which they operate; they all pay rent. They all have borrowed money for the equipment they use; they all pay interest on those borrowed funds. Those assumptions are in place to make explicit the payments that are made for the use of the factors of production used to produce bread.

**Exhibit 1.1**
**Example of Effect on the National Income and Product Account of Production and Purchase of Loaf of Bread**

| Item | Farmer | Miller | Baker | Grocer | Total |
|---|---|---|---|---|---|
| Sale of Product | $ (0.27) | $ (0.41) | $ (0.73) | $ (0.89) | |
| Purchase for Resale | - | 0.27 | 0.41 | 0.73 | |
| **Value Added** | $ (0.27) | $ (0.14) | $ (0.32) | $ (0.16) | **$ (0.89)** |
| | | | | | |
| Labor Compensation | $ 0.18 | $ 0.08 | $ 0.21 | $ 0.11 | *$ 0.58* |
| Rent | 0.04 | 0.01 | 0.02 | 0.02 | *0.09* |
| Interest | 0.03 | 0.02 | 0.06 | 0.01 | *0.12* |
| Income of Owner | 0.02 | 0.03 | 0.03 | 0.02 | *0.10* |
| **Total Expenses** | $ 0.27 | $ 0.14 | $ 0.32 | $ 0.16 | *$ 0.89* |

Wages, salaries, and fringe benefits paid to employees appear as employee compensation. The farmer may or may not have hired hands. Nevertheless, employee compensation is imputed for the farmer—the wages and benefits a person of comparable skills would earn performing that work.

In Exhibit 1.1, sales of each producer's product appear as negative numbers. For each of the producers, it is income and a negative sign is assigned to distinguish it from the other numbers that are expenses. The income of the owner/operator can be considered a reward for management, for organizing the running the enterprise, for taking risk. Typically, it is determined as the difference between income from sale of the product and the other expenses. Consequently, as a residual, under certain conditions (unfortunate from the standpoint of the owner/operator), when total expenditure exceeds or equals sales income, it can be negative or zero.

Value added is the difference between the sale of the product and the cost of the goods purchased for resale. For the farmer, to get the process going without further complication, we assume the seeds are in the ground already and nothing is purchased for resale. For further simplification we ignore other inputs, supplies like fertilizer, fuel, electricity, and other supplies and expenses going into the production process.

We start the process with a farmer. He sells the wheat that eventually becomes a loaf of bread for twenty-seven cents. With those twenty-seven cents, he pays for the labor, land, equipment, and management that were required to produce the wheat. A miller who buys the wheat for twenty-seven cents grinds it into flour. As flour, the miller is able to sell the wheat to a baker for forty-one cents. His processing has increased the value of the wheat by fourteen cents. With those fourteen cents, he pays for the factors of production required to produce the flour. A baker turns the flour into bread. He bought the flour for forty-one cents and sells it to a grocer in the form of bread for seventy-three cents, thus adding thirty-two cents in value. As with the farmer and the miller, he uses the thirty-two cents to pay his factor inputs. The grocer does not change the bread but moves it to a place and at a time where and when you find it convenient to make your purchase. For all that has gone before, you pay the grocer eighty-nine cents. Your eighty-nine pennies are shown in Exhibit 1.1 within the small rectangle. The bread cost the grocer seventy-three cents; he sold it to you for eighty-nine cents. Thus, his services have added sixteen cents to his purchase from the baker. With those sixteen cents, he pays for his factor inputs.

Note that each producer's payments to his inputs to the production process equal his value added. The difference between what the purchased material cost and what the raw materials cost determines what is available to pay the factors of production for their role in processing the output.

The column on the far right sums the entries for all the parties to the transaction. The sum of the values added equals the consumer's price of the product. They not only are equal; they are equivalent! The sum of the amounts paid by the producers in the form of employee compensation, rent, interest, and profit equals the final price of the product. The number shown in bold represents the number that would appear as a source of funds in the production account of the business sector. The numbers in italics represent the numbers that would appear as uses of funds in that account.

*Components of the National Income and Product Account.* Exhibit 1.2 provides an overview of the major components of the national income and product account. In addition, the other four accounts are shown along with their total amounts to give an idea of their relative magnitudes. In accordance with the double-entry system, sources of funds appear on the right, and uses of funds appear on the left for each of them. Total sources and uses of funds appear at the bottom of each account, and sources equal uses in all instances.

For the national income and product account, the bottom line is labeled *Gross Domestic Product.* It amounts to $9,299 billion in 1999. The Department of Commerce defines gross domestic product as "the market value of goods and services *produced by labor and property located in the United States*."[22] Under that definition the output of an automobile plant owned by a Japanese firm but located in Kentucky gets counted in gross domestic product. Similarly, wages paid to a farm worker in California who is a resident of Guatemala are recorded as on the use-of-funds side of the account as part of gross domestic income. *Gross Domestic Income* is conceptually equivalent to gross domestic product; however, in Exhibit 1.2, it amounts to $9,371 billion–$72 billion more. In practice, gross domestic product differs from gross domestic income. They are derived independently from different sources of information that are less than perfect, but the statistical discrepancy is relatively small.

In addition to gross domestic income and product, other major national income and product aggregates appear on the left-hand side of the account. *Gross National Income* represents the "market value of the goods and services *produced by labor and property supplied by U.S. residents*."[23] In 1999 it amounts to $9,360 billion. Dividends paid to a U.S. resident by a Canadian mining company that strikes it rich in the frozen wastelands will be recorded in gross national income but excluded from gross domestic product. For the same reason,

**Exhibit 1.2**
**Overview of National Income and Product Accounts, 1999**

| Uses of Funds* | | Sources of Funds* | |
|---|---|---|---|
| **National Income and Product Account** | | | |
| National Income | 7,470 | | |
| Net National Income | 8,199 | | |
| Gross National Income | 9,360 | | |
| Gross Domestic Income | 9,371 | | |
| Gross Domestic Product | $ 9,299 | Gross Domestic Product | $9,299 |
| **Personal Income and Outlay Account** | | | |
| Disposable Personal Income | 6,638 | | |
| Taxes, Outlays, & Saving | $ 7,790 | Personal Income | $7,790 |
| **Government Receipts and Expenditure Account** | | | |
| Government Outlays | $ 2,788 | Government Receipts | $2,788 |
| **Foreign Transactions Account** | | | |
| Receipts from Rest of World | $ 1,296 | Payments to Rest of World | $1,296 |
| **Gross Saving and Investment Account** | | | |
| Gross Investment | $ 1,646 | Gross Saving | $1,718 |
| | | Statistical Discrepancy | (72) |

* Amounts in $ Billions for 1999.

*Source*: U.S. Department of Commerce. Bureau of Economic Analysis. "Selected NIPA Tables." *National Accounts Data*. 8 Aug. 2000: Tables 1.9, 2.1, 3.1, 4.1, & 5.1. 9 Sep. 2000. <http://www.bea.doc.gov/bea/dn1.htm>.

dividends paid by a U.S. corporation to a resident of a foreign country is excluded from gross national income but included in gross domestic product. Of the two measures, gross domestic product and gross national income, the former ranks as the more commonly cited measure of aggregate output and income throughout the world.

*Net National Income*, amounting to $8,199 billion in 1999, falls short of gross national income. The difference is an allowance for consumption of fixed capital. As plant and equipment are used in producing goods and services they wear out or become obsolete. Net national income recognizes that deterioration in the capital stock; the gross aggregates do not. Working up the left-hand column of the account, we come to *National Income*. Amounting to $7,470 billion, it is least in dollar amount but first on the list. It measures the amounts paid to factors of production supplied by U.S. citizens, such as employee compensation, rent, interest, dividends, and profits.

### Personal Income and Outlay Account

The personal income and outlay account shows *Personal Income* on the right as a source of funds totaling $7,790 billion for 1999. On the left appears an identical amount for the uses of personal income. *Disposable Personal Income*, $6,638 billion, is the difference between personal income and what we pay the government and appears on the left-hand side also. Now, we have now accounted for and defined all the major aggregates mentioned in our review of the history of the development of the national income and product accounts.

### Government Receipts and Expenditures Account

As its name implies, the government receipts and expenditures account deals with the sources of funds for and their uses by the government sector. Taxes provide most of government receipts. Total outlays include expenditures, consisting of government employee compensation, consumption of goods and services, interest payments, and money the government gives away. If payments exceed receipts, or vice versa, a deficit or surplus entry assures that sources and uses match. In Exhibit 1.2, the final entry for the government receipts and expenditures account totals $2,788 billion.

### Foreign Transactions Account

The last entry on the right-hand side of the foreign transactions account is labeled "Payments to the Rest of the World" even though the right side of the account—as with all the other accounts—represents sources of funds. From the perspective of the foreign transactions account, payments to foreigners by U.S. citizens, governments, and firms constitute a source of funds. Receipts to U.S. entities from foreigners are entered on the left-hand side of the account as a use of funds. Both receipts and payments balance to $1,296 billion in 1999. Sources of funds for the foreign transactions account include imports of goods and services, payments of interest and dividends to foreigners holding securities issued by U.S. entities, and transfer payments to foreigners. Exports of goods and services and receipts from foreigners of dividends and interest for U.S. investments abroad make up the uses of funds. Sources and uses are made equal with a balancing entry, net foreign investment. It is included on the right-hand side as a payment to the rest of the world. As we shall see, currently that figure is negative and has been for a long time. Its negativity results mainly of the excess of U.S. imports of goods over exports.

### Gross Saving and Investment Account

The gross saving and investment account consolidates saving and investment for the other sectors. Personal saving, a use of funds in the personal income and outlay account, becomes a source here. It is combined with retained earnings of the business sector and government surpluses (or deficits).

As shown in Exhibit 1.2, *Gross Investment* amounts to $1,646 billion; *Gross Saving* amounts to $1,718 billion. They don't balance! Arghh! Fortunately, allowance for a *Statistical Discrepancy*, $72 billion—the same difference (approximately) between gross domestic income and gross domestic product—brings them into equality. Investment in facilities, machinery, and equipment by business and infrastructure by government exemplify uses of funds summarized in the gross saving and investment account.

## AN OVERVIEW

Each account's sources of funds equal its uses of funds. Since the rest of the world is included (and since interplanetary trade does not yet exist), the accounting structure defines a closed system. One account's uses of funds constitute sources of funds for the others, and vice versa.

Gross domestic product, amounting to $9.3 trillion, can be considered the most general and encompassing of the national aggregate statistics. As a portion of that aggregate, the personal income and outlay account looms large: its sources and uses of funds, amounting to $7.8 trillion, equal more than 80 percent of gross domestic product. Moreover, its bottom line exceeds national income's $7.5 trillion figure. Examination of just personal income and outlays appears to explain most of what the NIPA is about.

A look at the government, foreign, and saving-and-investment accounts gives cause to pause, however. With personal income their bottom lines far exceed gross domestic product. Clearly, the aggregation process entails more than a simple combination of the accounts. In order to understand that process, an in-depth investigation of all accounts is required.

Starting with ourselves—persons and households—seems like the best way to approach the national income and product accounts. Consequently, we shall begin with the national income statistic called the *Personal Income and Outlay Account*.

## NOTES

1. Thomas Jefferson, *Notes on the State of Virginia* written in the year 1781; somewhat corrected and enlarged in the winter of 1782, for the use of a foreigner of distinction, in answer to certain queries proposed by him, 2nd ed. (Philadelphia: 1794) 216, American Antiquarian Society, *Early American Imprints* 1639–1800 (Worchester, MA: Readex Microprint, 1960) Evans number 27162.

2. Tom Bethell, *The Noblest Triumph: Property and Prosperity through the Ages* (New York: St. Martin's Press, 1998) 19.

3. John Locke, *Two Treatises on Government*, 3rd ed. (London: 1698) Book 2, Chapter 5, 185. *Early English books* (Ann Arbor, MI: University Microfilms International, 1978): 793:25.

4. Adam Smith, *An Inquiry into the Nature and Causes of the Wealth of Nations* (Hartford, 1818) Book IV, Chapter 2, p. 319, American Antiquarian Society, *Early American Reprints*, 2nd series (New York: Readex Microprint, 1980): 45724.

5. Marlene Cimons, "Are You Overweight?" *Runner's World* 34.1 (January 1999): 36–37.

6. Ludwig von Mises, *Omnipotent Government, The Rise of the Total State and Total War* (New Haven: Yale University Press, 1944) 49.

7. U.S. Department of Commerce, Bureau of Economic Analysis, *National Income and Product Accounts of the United States, 1929–94*, vol.1 (Washington, DC: U.S. Government Printing Office, April 1998) M-1.

8. Much of the following is based on Carol S. Carson, "The History of the United States National Income and Product Accounts: The Development of an Analytical Tool," *The Review of Income and Wealth* 21. 2 (June, 1975): 153–81.

9. U.S. Department of Commerce, Bureau of Economic Analysis, "GDP: One of the Great Inventions of the 20th Century," *Survey of Current Business* (January 2000): 1.

10. Richard Ruggles, "National Income Accounting, *The History of Accounting, An International Encyclopedia,* eds. Michael Chatfield and Richard Vangermeersch (New York and London: Garland Publishing, Inc., 1996) 427.

11. Richard Stone, "Definition and Measurement of the National Income and Related Totals," Appendix to *Measurement of National Income and the Construction of Social Accounts*, Studies and Reports on Statistical Methods, no. 7 (Geneva: United Nations, 1947).

12. United Nations, *A System of National Accounts and Supporting Tables* (New York: United Nations, 1952 and 1953).

13. Chatfield 428–29.

14. "GDP: One of the Great Inventions of the 20th Century," *Survey of Current Business* (January 2000): 7.

15. United Nations, *A System of National Accounts and Supporting Tables*, Studies in Methods, Series F, no. 2, Revision 3 (New York: United Nations, 1968).

16. United Nations, System of National Accounts 1993 (New York: United Nations, 1993).

17. Ludwig von Mises, *Planned Chaos* (Irvington-on-Hudson, NY: The Foundation for Economic Education, Inc., 1947) 29.

18. W. Keith Bryant, *The Economic Organization of the Household* (New York: Cambridge University Press, 1990) 1.

19. Mises, *Omnipotent Government* 426.

20. David Ricardo, *Principles of Political Economy and Taxation*, 1st American ed. (Georgetown, DC: 1819), American Antiquarian Society, *Early American Reprints*, 2nd

Series (New York: Readex Microprint, 1981): 49280.

21. U.S. Department of Commerce, Bureau of Economic Analysis, *An Introduction to National Economic Accounting*, Methodology Paper No. 1 (Washington, DC: U.S. Government Printing Office, 1985): 8.

22. *National Income and Product Accounts of the United States, 1929–94* M-1.

23. *National Income and Product Accounts of the United States, 1929–94* M-1.

# 2

# Getting Personal

Choosing among the four sector accounts of the national income and product accounts (NIPA) is like choosing among one's children. Choices and judgments are difficult. However, if pressed to choose which of the four sector accounts is most important, my choice would have to be the personal income and outlay account. One reason for the selection—a dispassionate one—is its size. We already have seen that in dollar terms it is the largest of the four. The second reason—a personal one—is that we are in it. Your income and expenditure—assuming you are a resident of the United States—and mine are recorded in that account.

Although personal income and outlays should be familiar to us, the concepts, organization, and conventions developed by the Bureau of Economic Analysis (BEA) of the Department of Commerce and associated with the personal income and outlay account itself present challenges to understanding. We will find that by the time we complete study of that account, we will have covered most of the technical aspects of the NIPA. The patterns here are repeated in the other accounts, often in a simpler context.

Because of its importance and complexity, four chapters are devoted to the personal income and outlay account. In this chapter we will examine sources of personal income and the amounts of each for 1999. The content of chapter 3 deals with uses of personal income for the same year. NIPA statistics provide opportunities to inspect in great detail the goods and services that persons consume. It concludes with bringing sources and uses together and includes treatment of personal saving and investment. That treatment requires us to incorporate flow-of-funds data into our analysis.

With concepts and magnitudes of the components of sources and uses of personal income in 1999 as background, chapters 4 and 5 investigate how they have changed during the forty-year period from 1959 and, whenever possible, why they have changed. We will see that not many events have changed significantly how personal income is used, but those that do occur deserve careful consideration. Chapter 4 provides an opportunity to explore how personal income is distributed among states and persons. The latter adventure introduces us to statistics of income prepared by the Internal Revenue Service from individual income tax returns. Chapter 5 includes adjustments for changes in prices that occur over time and an examination of changes in the composition of personal consumption expenditure.

## DEFINITION OF PERSONS

Personal income conjures up images of people receiving paychecks. However, persons whose income makes up personal income include more than just folks. In addition to households and individuals, it includes nonprofit institutions that primarily serve individuals, private noninsured welfare funds, and private trust funds. Examples include trade unions and professional associations, educational institutions, foundations for education and research, and religious and welfare organizations. They provide such functions as medical care, private education and research, and religious and welfare services.[1] In most cases, when dealing with personal income and its uses, reference only to walking and talking persons suffices. Occasionally, however, we have to remember those artificial beings whose economic actions affect the personal income and outlay account.

## CATEGORIES OF PERSONAL INCOME

Most people earn most of their income by working for others. The income they receive comes in the form of salaries and wages. Some people may work for themselves as sole proprietors of a business. Whatever they receive from the sales of their business outputs after expenses are paid becomes their income. Those who own property that is in productive use earn rent. Owners of corporate stock receive dividends (when and if corporations declare them). Lenders receive interest from their debtors. Finally, old folks receive social security checks, a prime example of transfer payments.

Although you might not relish the task, you can imagine someone adding up all those sources of income for all the people and families in the United States to arrive at a national estimate of personal income. Actually, the BEA keeps track of total salaries and wages, other income from employment, proprietor's income, rental income, dividends, interest, receipts of transfer payments from business and government, and deductions for our contributions for social insurance. In addition, it records the personal income taxes that we pay, our outlays for personal consumption expenditures, interest payments, and transfers abroad, and how much we save. It makes available detailed data on personal consumption expenditures, breaking them down into over a hundred products and services—everything from how much we spend for electricity for our homes to our purchases of flowers, seeds, and potted plants. How does the BEA manage to amass all that data?

### Sources of Data

Within the Department of Commerce, the BEA undertakes the task of preparing the national income and product statistics. The Bureau collects relatively few of the numbers that go into the accounts but rather relies mostly on other federal government agencies for data gathering. Major contributors to that effort include the Department of Commerce's Census Bureau, the Department of Labor's Bureau of Labor Statistics, the Department of the Treasury's Internal Revenue Service, the Department of Agriculture, and the Office of Management and Budget in the Executive Office of the President. The BEA casts its net widely, however, and information is obtained from state governments, industry trade associations, and nonprofit institutions. Sources cited range from the renowned Board of Governors of the Federal Reserve System to the less well-known American Kennel Club and to the even more generally recognized National Football League.

Government agencies and others collect data in the normal course of their business. For example, the Social Security Administration can be expected to have a pretty good fix on contributions to federal social insurance programs. If it does not, a crisis concerning the social security program may arrive sooner than we think. Other numbers have to be "manufactured" through regular censuses and sample surveys. Data on manufacturing activity fall into that type of information.

Where the BEA obtains its data and how it handles them may change over time. New sources emerge; existing ones change or cease to become available. New processing techniques and refinements develop. Adoption of such changes is not trivial for it often requires revising not only current year and recent estimates but also a series of estimates over an extended prior period of time.

Most recently, for example, in April 2000, the BEA reported personal income to be $7,791.8 billion for 1999. In August 2000 it reported a figure of $7,789.6 billion for 1999 personal income.[2] The difference between the two numbers results from the eleventh comprehensive revision of the NIPA. It reflects changes in definitions and classifications, in newly available and revised data sources, and new and improved statistical methodologies.[3] The changes affect estimates dating in some instances as far back as 1929. The data used here are based on the eleventh comprehensive revision.

### Access to Data

Personal income and the other national income and product statistics are widely cited in government publications and in pronouncements by public officials. Newspapers, television, radio, and magazines often feature commentary on the latest figures. Where does the media get its numbers?

Those numbers—frequently accompanied by an interpretation—generally appear first in regular and occasional press releases and monthly in the *Survey of Current Business* issued by the BEA. Some data series are available annually, some quarterly, and some monthly. Like many private enterprises and ourselves, the Internet has touched the BEA, and ready access to national income and product statistics in machine-readable form has been greatly facilitated. Two Web sites deserve special mention.

- The BEA Web site at <http://www.doc.bea.gov> presents summary NIPA estimates, selected articles from the SURVEY OF CURRENT BUSINESS, and the monthly news releases for gross domestic product (GDP) and for personal income and outlays.
- The Web site of the Department of Commerce's STAT-USA provides the monthly news releases of GDP and on personal income at the time of the releases, the underlying detail NIPA tables, and the complete issues of the SURVEY.[4]

A subscription service, STAT-USA can be accessed at <http://www.stat-usa.gov>. Other products that can be purchased from the BEA include printouts, diskettes, and CD-ROMs.

## PERSONAL INCOME CATEGORIES AND CONCEPTS

Exhibit 2.1 provides a summary of personal income in 1999 for people and nonprofit people-serving entities. The first column in Exhibit 2.1 displays dollar amounts of the components of personal income in billions of dollars. The second column contains percentages of total personal income accounted for by each component. Percentages are shown to the nearest whole percent. That convention usually will be followed in subsequent tables. Although showing percentages to the nearest whole percent results in occasional rounding errors, greater precision seems unwarranted and often obscures significant differences among the parts of an aggregate. Although amounts change from year to year (and from quarter to quarter and month to month, for that matter), their relative size—namely, percentages—tends to be more stable over time. Percentages do change, of course, and such changes can be significant, but they generally occur more slowly.

Exhibit 2.1 contains an entry you will not find in the published NIPA series: *Gross personal income*. I created it! It shows what personal income would be if *Personal contributions for social insurance* were not deducted from the earnings of employed and self-employed persons. Those "contributions" are a tax and as such belong with other taxes as an outlay of, not a deduction from, income. But in the NIPA convention they are deducted, and the result is *Personal income*, \$7.8 trillion. Treatment of personal contributions for social insurance is not the only instance of peculiarities in the presentation of NIPA data that we shall encounter.

To assume that presentation of data by either the public or the private sector is neutral with respect to the aim of the presenting entity assumes too much. Self-interest and profit motives rampant in the private sector engender a healthy

**Exhibit 2.1**
**Personal Income, 1999**

| | 1999 Amounts in $ Billions | Percent of Total |
|---|---|---|
| Wages and salaries | $ 4,470.0 | 55 |
| Other labor income | 501.0 | 6 |
| Proprietors' income with IVA and CCAdj* | 663.5 | 8 |
| Rental income of persons with CCAdj* | 143.4 | 2 |
| Personal dividend income | 370.3 | 5 |
| Personal interest income | 963.7 | 12 |
| Transfers | 1,016.2 | 13 |
| **GROSS PERSONAL INCOME** | **$ 8,128.1** | **100** |
| Personal contributions for social insurance | (338.5) | (4) |
| **TOTAL PERSONAL INCOME** | **$ 7,789.6** | **96** |

* IVA: inventory valuation adjustment; CCAdj: capital consumption adjustment.

*Source*: U.S. Department of Commerce. Bureau of Economic Analysis. "Selected NIPA Tables." *National Accounts Data*. 8 Aug. 2000: Table 2.1. 9 Sep. 2000. <http://www.bea.doc.gov/bea/dn1.htm>.

skepticism of facts presented by individual and business interests. Skepticism encourages us to examine the data for ourselves and draw our own conclusions. The vague motivations of the public sector should not lull us into a sense of credulity. Political agendas can be every bit as compelling as profit motives in influencing how data are presented. NIPA data, like any other set of facts, can be presented in various ways, sometimes to reveal and at other times to mask developments in the economy of interest to the public.

Aside from addressing possible connivances, introduction of *Gross personal income* provides a basis for calculating the relative importance of the various sources of income that make up the $8.1 trillion figure. As shown in the right-hand column of Exhibit 2.1, the largest share, 55 percent, goes to *Wages and salaries*, the income persons employed by others receive. Closely related to their wages and salaries is *Other labor income*, 6 percent. Income of self-employed persons, *Proprietors' income*, accounts for an additional 8 percent. Taken together, those three components, representing income generated mainly from labor, comprise a little over two-thirds of gross personal income. The remaining one-third is divided among four components, of which *Transfers* is largest at 13 percent,. It is followed closely by *Personal interest income*, 12 percent.

The shares of the other two, *Personal dividend income* and *Rental income of persons*, dwindle to single digit percentages.

In a market economy, computing personal income appears—in concept, at least—easy. You just add up the amounts that persons—people and people-serving nonprofit institutions—earn. However, some income people earn does not involve market transactions. Implicit rent earned by homeowners on their dwellings provides a familiar example. Some people rent their dwellings; others own them. If a homeowner were to sell his or her dwelling and begin renting, national income would increase because previously unrecorded income would become a market transaction. The BEA insulates estimates of national income and product from the accidents of home ownership by imputing rental income to those who own their homes. In the course of our closer examination of the eight components of personal income, we will encounter more imputations of income calculated by the BEA.

Not all personal income generated through activities that do not involve market transactions is recognized. For example, if you live in a city and raise a vegetable garden or gather apples from a fruit tree in your backyard, you generate in-kind income for yourself. The economic significance of implicit rent and fresh garden veggies pale beside another major omission: the economic value of women working in the home as housewives. Ignoring their contribution has resulted in an understatement of the nation's output. As a greater proportion of women have become engaged in employment outside the home in the past forty years, growth in national output has been overstated because of that omission.

### Wages and Salaries

As the most common form of income for most households and individuals, *Wages and salaries* account for almost $4.5 trillion, over half of *Gross personal income*. Unlike the amount on your paycheck or dollars you receive from a paymaster, that figure includes employee contributions to social insurance.

An income statistic as large as $4.5 trillion deserves closer inspection. Exhibit 2.2 provides a more detailed look at wages and salaries. The figures show that the United States is not entirely a market economy driven by private interests. At $3.7 trillion, wages and salaries of *Private industries* account for most of the total—84 percent. However, wages and salaries of *Government* (federal, state, and local) account for $724.4 billion, 16 percent—nearly one dollar in six. The private industry category is broken down further by type of business. The payroll of *Corporations* accounts for 69 percent of total personal income. Left over after corporations' 69 percent and government's 16 percent is the remaining 15 percent for *Other private businesses*, *Households*, *Nonprofit institutions*, and the *Rest of the world*. The *Rest of the world* appears as a negative $5.4 billion. Salaries and wages paid by foreigners to U.S. persons are less than the amounts we pay them. Consequently, the number is negative. Households pay to other households $11.1 billion, mainly for domestic service. The payroll of nonprofit

**Exhibit 2.2**
**Wage and Salary Disbursements, 1999**

| | 1999 Amounts in $ Billions | Percent of Total |
|---|---|---|
| **Private industries** | **$ 3,756.1** | **84** |
| Corporations | 3,082.1 | 69 |
| Other private business | 326.2 | 7 |
| Households | 11.1 | 0 |
| Nonprofit institutions | 336.7 | 8 |
| **Government** | **724.4** | **16** |
| General government | 652.2 | 15 |
| Government enterprises | 72.2 | 2 |
| **Rest of the world** | **(5.4)** | **(0)** |
| **TOTAL WAGE & SALARY ACCRUALS** | **$ 4,475.1** | **100** |
| Unpaid wage accruals | (5.2) | (0) |
| **WAGE & SALARY DISBURSEMENTS** | **$ 4,470.0** | **100** |

*Source*: U.S. Department of Commerce. Bureau of Economic Analysis. "Selected NIPA Tables." *National Accounts Data*. 8 Aug. 2000: Tables 1.14, 2.1 & 5.1. 9 Sep. 2000. <http://www.bea.doc.gov/bea/dn1.htm> And "'Annual Only' NIPA Tables." *National Accounts Data*. 30 Aug. 2000: Table 1.15 & 6.3B. 5 Sep. 2000. <http://www.bea.doc.gov/bea/dn1.htm>.

institutions exceeds that of other private business. Not-for-profit health care establishments, private colleges and universities, and religious organizations account for much of that figure.

Not all those salaries and wages have been paid. From accrued wages and salaries, the unpaid portion, $5.2 billion, is deducted. Only the paid portion is included in personal income, a peculiar accounting convention that will come back to haunt us clear to the end of our journey exploring the NIPA.

The distinction between wages and salaries received for personal income and wages and salaries earned does make some sense. Most individuals and households do not consider the amount of compensation earned between payroll dates as a significant asset. However, the distinction made by the BEA seems to me to be exceedingly fine. The adjustment is a minor one. Wages and salaries accrued but not paid amount to only $5.2 billion, one-tenth of 1 percent of total accruals of $4,475.1 billion. Most people do not account for inventory valuation adjustments, capital consumption adjustments, and imputed interest in calculating their income, but they are included in calculation of personal income.

Given the current convention, *Wages and salaries* in Exhibit 2.1, therefore, represent actual disbursements to employees. They include commissions, tips, and bonuses, in-kind remuneration, and voluntary contributions to deferred compensation plans. The Bureau of Labor Statistics contributes mightily by tabulating estimates of wages and salaries of employees covered by state unemployment insurance. Those estimates include employees in most industries and state and local governments. The Department of Agriculture provides estimates for farm income; the Railroad Retirement Board, for railroad transportation. The Office of Personnel Management and the Office of Management and Budget generate respectively the information on which federal civilian and military wages are based.

Not all those salaries and wages are paid by direct deposit, checks, or dollars and cents. Buried in the figures are three forms of in-kind compensation:

- Food provided to service men and women by the U.S. military and to employees by some employers,
- Clothing allowances for military personnel, and
- Lodging provided to employees by some businesses.

Although market transactions do not take place in those instances, the BEA estimates an imputed value for them and includes it under wages and salaries. They are not exactly equivalent to monetary compensation, however. The food may not please your palate, the clothing may not fit, and the lodging may not be decorated to your taste. Army chow, fatigues, and barracks come to mind as examples. Moreover, they are forms of income that have to be used to be earned. Saving such income is not possible. The distortion, however, is a minor one. Those three adjustments add $11.3 billion to wages and salaries, a lot of money to most of us but relatively insignificant compared to total wages and salaries, $4.5 trillion.

### Other Labor Income

As shown in Exhibit 2.1, $501.0 billion—6 percent of *Gross personal income*—takes the form of *Other labor income*. Like wages and salaries, persons who work for others receive it, and together the two aggregates account for 61 percent of total income. Exhibit 2.3 provides a display of the components of *Other Labor Income*. It is divided into three major parts: *Pension and profit-sharing plans*, *Private welfare funds*, and *Other labor income*.

*Pension and profit-sharing plans* account for $169.6 billion and make up 34 percent of *Other labor income*. Government contributions to its employees' retirement plans, $109.2 billion, exceed those of the private sector, $60.4 billion, by a wide margin. The difference seems more striking in the light of Exhibit 2.2, which shows that government employees' wages and salaries are less than one-fifth of those of private sector employees. Private sector employer contributions to old-age and survivors insurance, which is compulsory rather than elective as it is for government, account for part of the discrepancy. Even with that allowance, however, government pension programs appear to be relatively generously funded.

**Exhibit 2.3**
**Other Labor Income, 1999**

| | **1999 Amounts in $ Billions** | | | **Percent of Total** | | |
|---|---|---|---|---|---|---|
| **Pension and profit-sharing plans** | | | **$ 169.6** | | | **34** |
| Private pension & profit-sharing | | $ 60.4 | | | 12 | |
| Government employee retirement | | 109.2 | | | 22 | |
| **Private welfare funds** | | | **328.4** | | | **66** |
| Group insurance | | $292.0 | | | 58 | |
| Group health insurance | $280.2 | | | 56 | | |
| Group life insurance | 11.8 | | | 2 | | |
| Workers' compensation insurance | | 34.5 | | | 7 | |
| Supplemental unemployment insur. | | 1.9 | | | 0 | |
| **Other labor income** | | | **3.0** | | | **1** |
| **TOTAL OTHER LABOR INCOME** | | | **$ 501.0** | | | **100** |

*Source*: U.S. Department of Commerce. Bureau of Economic Analysis. "'Annual Only' NIPA Tables." *National Accounts Data*. 30 Aug 2000: Table 6.11C. 5 Sep. 2000. <http://www.bea.doc.gov/bea/dn1.htm>.

Employer payments to *Private welfare funds* constitute the largest share of *Other labor income*, $328.4 billion, 66 percent. Employers may reward employees for their efforts by payments to private group health and life insurance plans, privately administered workers' compensation plans, and supplemental unemployment benefit plans. *Group insurance*—medical and life together—accounts for 58 percent of other labor income. *Group health insurance* premiums, $280.2 billion, overshadow the $11.8 billion in premiums for group life insurance. *Workers' compensation insurance*, at $34.5 billion, overshadows the $1.9 billion for *Supplemental unemployment insurance*. If you remember only that *Other labor income* includes employer payments for pensions and group health insurance, you will have accounted for 90 percent of the total.

Current estimates of employer costs of pension and profit-sharing plans come from the Bureau of Labor Statistics or Internal Revenue Service tabulations of business tax returns. The Bureau of Labor Statistics also furnishes the basis for estimating employer costs for group medical programs. Premiums for group life insurance and the employers' share come from trade association sources.[5] The Census Bureau surveys of state and local government retirement programs provide the source for their costs. Other sources involved in contributing components of other labor income include the Health Care Financing Administration and the Social Security Administration.

*Other* in *Other labor income* is used to account for yet other rewards for human exertion. Familiar to many people are fees received for serving on juries and as witnesses. The fees go into *Other*. If a justice of the peace marries you, the fee you pay goes there too. Collectively, those odds and ends add up to an impressive $3 billion but amount to only 1 percent of the total.

### Proprietors' Income

*Proprietors' income* comes next on our list of personal income components (Exhibit 2.1). If you serve on a board of directors of a company and are not an employee of that corporation, the fees you receive are treated as proprietors' income. If you are self-employed, and your receipts exceed your expenses, you pay yourself. The category, proprietor's income, contains those net earnings. The BEA adjusts your estimate of what you earned before including it in aggregate personal income. For reasons to be described later, BEA substitutes its own estimate for your calculation of depreciation expenses and adjusts income for changes in the value of your inventory. If you are not engaged in a financial business, interest income drops out (but is added back as interest income of persons). A comparable adjustment is made for dividends. Unless you are in a real estate business, rental income is moved too. Family farms constitute another exception.

In Exhibit 2.4, *Proprietor's Income* is divided into two categories: *Farm* and—for want of a more descriptive term—*Nonfarm*. *Farm Income* accounts for only $25.3 billion, 4 percent of the $663.5 billion total, making one wonder why such a distinction is made. Different treatment of *Farm Income* from that of other sole proprietorships provides one reason.

The Department of Agriculture reduces farmers' gross cash receipts generated from such sources as market sales, inventory change, and government payments, and adjusted for nonmonetary incomes by production expenses to estimate *Farm Income*. Family farms frequently are organized as proprietorships. But there are exceptions, and that estimate is adjusted for corporate farm income obtained from Internal Revenue Service tabulations. Internal Revenue Service tabulations also provide a basis for estimating nonfarm proprietors' income.

For farmers living on a farm in their own home, proprietors' income is increased by a BEA estimate of the imputed value of the rent that would have been made on a comparable rented dwelling. Some farmers also produce food and fuel that they consume. The value of those products less an estimate for the materials and services used to produce them is included in farm income. Together *Goods produced for on-site consumption* amount to a "mere" $500 million, less than 2 percent of $25.3 billion in 1999 farm income.

Despite the small size of the imputations, they provide an opportunity to illustrate the process used to estimate imputed income. Farm *Goods produced for on-site consumption*, $500 million, reflects the price you would pay for the goods if you bought them at a roadside stand. The price does not represent a farmer's income, however. *Intermediate production costs*, $300 million, were incurred to produce the goods: for example, seeds, fertilizer, pesticides, as well

**Exhibit 2.4**
**Proprietors' Income, 1999**

| | 1999 Amounts in $ Billions | | | Percent of Total | | |
|---|---|---|---|---|---|---|
| **Farm Income** | | | **$ 25.3** | | | **4** |
| Capital consumption adjustment | | | (8.3) | | | (1) |
| Farm income without imputations | | | 33.1 | | | 5 |
| Farm products consumed on farm | | | 0.2 | | | 0 |
| Goods produced for on-site consumption | | $0.5 | | | 0 | |
| Intermediate production costs | | (0.3) | | | (0) | |
| Imputed rent income for owner-occupied housing | | | 0.3 | | | 0 |
| Estimated space rent | | $6.6 | | | 1 | |
| Deductions | | (6.3) | | | (1) | |
| Intermediate costs | $(1.0) | | | (0) | | |
| Capital consumption allowance | (3.8) | | | (1) | | |
| Indirect bus. tax & nontax lia. | (0.9) | | | (0) | | |
| Net interest | (0.6) | | | (0) | | |
| **Nonfarm Income** | | | **638.2** | | | **96** |
| Inventory valuation adjustment | | | (1.4) | | | (0) |
| Capital consumption adjustment | | | 52.7 | | | 8 |
| Nonfarm income without imputations | | | 579.4 | | | 87 |
| Margins on owner-built housing | | | 7.5 | | | 1 |
| | | | - | | | |
| **TOTAL PROPRIETORS' INCOME** | | | **$ 663.5** | | | **100** |

*Source*: U.S. Department of Commerce. Bureau of Economic Analysis. "Selected NIPA Tables." *National Accounts Data*. 8 Aug. 2000: Table 1.14 & 2.1. 9 Sep. 2000. <http://www.bea.doc.gov/bea/dn1.htm>. And "'Annual Only' NIPA Tables." *National Accounts Data*. 30 Aug. 2000: Table 8.21. 5 Sep. 2000. <http://www.bea.doc.gov/bea/dn1.htm>.

as labor. The difference between those costs and the gross value of the products constitutes the farm's income, $200 million.

The process is a bit more complex in the case of *Imputed rent income* on a farmers' owner-occupied dwelling. *Estimated space rent*, $6.6 billion, represents an estimate of the amount of rent farmers would pay if they were tenants in their place of residence. That gross rent would be offset by costs incurred in making the dwelling available. *Intermediate costs*, $1.0 billion, include such expenses as cleaning and maintenance, insurance, legal and other professional fees, repairs, and supplies. *Capital consumption allowance*, $3.8 billion, reflects the property's reduction in value resulting from fair wear and tear. Property taxes constitute a prime example of items making up the $900 million of *Indirect business taxes and nontax liability*. Imputation of net interest, $600 million, reflects a further attempt by the BEA to insulate the NIPA from accidents of institutional arrangements.

Some farmers owe money on their homes. Others own them debt free. Farmers in identical circumstances except for a difference in their amount of debt would show different amounts of rent income. To bring the amount of rent in each case into equality, the BEA assumes that a mortgage exists on the entire amount of the value of the dwellings in both cases and calculates interest paid as an additional offset to gross rent.

Nonfarm proprietors' income without imputations amounts to $579.4 billion. Like its farm counterpart, it undergoes adjustments. After all adjustments are made, nonfarm proprietors' income becomes $638.2 billion. The *Inventory valuation adjustment* (IVA) is a negative $1.4 billion. Generally withdrawals from inventory are recorded at original cost. In a time of rising prices, their value and thus the cost of production is understated, and net income is overstated. The IVA corrects for that cost understatement. The *Capital consumption adjustment* adds $52.7 billion to *Nonfarm income without imputations*. Proprietor depreciation allowances on plant and equipment exceed BEA estimates of consumption of fixed capital and thus result in an apparent understatement of income on their income tax returns. (Surprise!) The capital consumption adjustment adjusts nonfarm proprietors' income more to the BEA's liking. Note that the capital consumption adjustment for farms is negative, suggesting that farmers, in the BEA's opinion, fail to fully account for the wear and tear on their plant and equipment.

*Nonfarm income* includes an imputation on *Margins on owner-built housing*. If you build your own home, your act of courage should result in a lower cost than if you had built it through a contractor. Whether you know it or not, the BEA imputes the difference between your cost and the value of the house and adds it to proprietors' income. In 1999 that adjustment amounted to $7.5 billion—once again, small relative to the $663.5 billion total for proprietors' income.

## Rental Income of Persons

If you rent real property to others, your income belongs here. Rental income of persons also includes royalties people receive from patents, copyrights, and rights to natural resources, which the Internal Revenue Service tabulates from amounts reported on individual income tax returns. Some people own dwellings that they live in; others own dwellings that they rent out. In the view of the BEA, both sets of owners receive income in the form of housing, although only renters engage in actual market transactions. To put numbers in tune with its view, the BEA imputes a figure for rent owners would have paid if they had rented and puts it under rental income of persons in a manner similar to that used to calculate rental income of owner-occupied farm housing. For 1999 the figure amounts to $132.8 billion. Tenant-occupied nonfarm housing, $49.2 billion, reflects an approximation to the value of market transactions.

**Exhibit 2.5**
**Rental Income of Persons, 1999**

| | | 1999 Amounts in $ Billions | |
|---|---|---|---|
| **Rental Income** | | | **$ 191.0** |
| Nonfarm housing | | $ 181.9 | |
| Owner occupied | $132.8 | | |
| Tenant occupied | 49.2 | | |
| Farms owned by nonoperator landlords | | 6.5 | |
| Nonfarm nonresidential properties | | 2.6 | |
| **Capital consumption adjustment** | | | **(56.0)** |
| **Royalties** | | | **8.4** |
| **TOTAL RENTAL INCOME OF PERSONS** | | | **$ 143.4** |

*Source*: *U.S. Department of Commerce. Bureau of Economic Analysis. "Selected NIPA Tables." National Accounts Data. 8 Aug. 2000: Table 2.1. 9 Sep. 2000. <http://www.bea.doc.gov/* bea/dn1.htm>. And "'Annual Only' NIPA Tables." National Accounts Data. 30 Aug 2000: Tables 8.15 and 8.18. 5 Sep. 2000. <http://www.bea.doc.gov/bea/dn1.htm>.

Every ten years the Census Bureau conducts a survey of housing and residential finance. That sample of housing stock and average annual rent is used to conjure up rental income estimates not only for owner-occupied but also for tenant-occupied housing. For years between the decennial census, estimates are developed from surveys conducted by the Census Bureau every other year on housing stock and average annual rent or on the number of households from the Census Bureau's monthly population survey and the Bureau of Labor Statistics' consumer price index for rent.

Exhibit 2.5 provides one version of the components that make up the $143.4 billion in rental income of persons. *Owner-occupied nonfarm housing rental income*, $132.8 billion—an imputed figure—accounts for most of *Nonfarm housing*. Rent earned on the family farm by folks who moved to the city to make their fortunes and now lease it to others appears as a $6.5 billion figure in *Farms owned by nonoperator landlords*. *Nonfarm nonresidential properties* amounting to $2.6 billion include the rental value of buildings and equipment owned and used by nonprofit institutions serving individuals. The BEA adjusts all those figures downward by a $56.0 billion *Capital consumption adjustment* to recognize depreciation of structures and equipment in terms of current prices. Most people's accounting records record historical costs and do not allow for depreciation expressed in terms of current prices.

**Exhibit 2.6**
**Personal Dividend Income, 1999**

| | 1999 Amounts in $ Billions | | Percent of Total | |
|---|---|---|---|---|
| **Domestic industries** | | **$ 328.9** | | **89** |
| Manufacturing | $ 77.8 | | 21 | |
| Other goods producing | 24.8 | | 7 | |
| Distributive | 90.7 | | 24 | |
| Service | 135.6 | | 37 | |
| **Rest of the world** | | **41.8** | | **11** |
| Receipts from rest of the world | $ 76.3 | | 21 | |
| Payments to rest of the world | (34.5) | | (9) | |
| **Net corporate dividends** | | **$ 370.7** | | **100** |
| Dividends paid to government | | (0.4) | | 0 |
| **PERSONAL DIVIDEND INCOME** | | **$ 370.3** | | **100** |

*Source*: U.S. Department of Commerce. Bureau of Economic Analysis. "Selected NIPA Tables." *National Accounts Data*. 8 Aug. 2000: Tables 2.1 and 3.1. 9 Sep. 2000. <http://www.bea.doc.gov/bea/dn1.htm>. And "'Annual Only' NIPA Tables." *National Accounts Data*. 30 Aug. 2000: Table 6.20C. 5 Sep. 2000. <http://www.bea.doc.gov/bea/dn1.htm>.

### Personal Dividend Income

Corporations—some of them, at least—pay dividends to their stockholders. Dividend payments to persons appear as *Personal dividend income*. The total amount shown in Exhibit 2.1, $370.3 billion, includes dividend payments from foreign as well as domestic corporations. Exhibit 2.6 shows that *Domestic industries* dividends account for $328.9 billion or 89 percent of *Personal dividend income*. Net dividends from corporations in the *Rest of the world* amount to $41.8 billion, 11 percent. Note that this amount is a net figure. Foreign dividends are shown net: what we pay them is deducted from what they pay us. Foreign corporations actually pay $76.3 billion in dividends to U.S. stockholders, but U.S. corporations pay $34.5 billion to stockholders in the rest of the world. Like the rest of the world, dividends for each domestic industry are shown net. Some corporations receive dividends as well as pay them, and the figures reflect the difference between payments and receipts.

We also see in Exhibit 2.6 what industries produce those dividends for their stockholders. *Service* industries provided the largest share of domestic dividends, $135.6 billion, 37 percent. Dividends from finance, insurance, and real estate amounting to $100.8 billion accounts for most of that $135.6 billion. *Distributive* industries—transportation and trade—pay the second largest dividend amount, $90.7 billion, and *Manufacturing*, $77.8 billion, follows them. Dividends for the *Other goods producing* industries—agriculture, mining, and construction—at $24.8 billion are less than a third of those of *Manufacturing.*

All four sectors together with the rest of the world corporations generate $370.7 billion in dividends, but not all of those dividends are included in personal income: $400 million is received by the government sector. The small amount of total dividends paid to government suggests that federal, state, and local governments are not heavy investors in the stock market. Despite all the news media interest in the stock market, a glance at Exhibit 2.1 reminds us that a relatively small portion of the total income people receive—just 5 percent—comes from *Personal dividend income.*

### Personal Interest Income

*Personal interest income* at $963.7 billion (12 percent of *Gross personal income*) is over twice the size of dividend income. However, unlike dividend income that approximates amounts persons actually receive, most people are not aware of 44 percent of the interest income the BEA attributes to them. Of the $963.7 billion, $421.1 billion takes the form of imputed interest income. First, let's deal with the more familiar form of interest income: monetary interest paid to persons.

Persons receive interest income from businesses, the rest of the world, the government, and other persons. Checking and savings accounts, government and corporate bonds, and loans made by individuals exemplify assets that earn interest. For business, government, and the rest of the world, net monetary interest—the difference between interest receipts and interest payments—amounts to $347.8 billion, 36 percent of the $963.7 billion in personal interest income. As shown in Exhibit 2.7, the business sector's net interest payments, $176.1 billion, represent the difference between two substantial amounts, $1.7 trillion in payments and $1.5 trillion in receipts. The magnitude of those numbers indicates that businesses do a lot of borrowing and lending among themselves.

Internal Revenue Service tabulations of business tax returns—adjusted for inaccurate reporting and conceptual differences—provide a basis for calculating the other interest components of net interest paid by business. To estimate net interest for the rest of the world, the BEA conducts its own surveys of direct investment income and relies on Treasury Department surveys of portfolio income.

According to the BEA, two categories of financial institutions pay imputed interest income to persons: financial intermediaries (banks, credit agencies, and investment companies) and life insurance companies. Even though they may not know it, *Financial intermediaries* pay $342.8 billion in imputed interest. Not all of the imputed interest goes to persons: in 1999 $72.0 billion went to other businesses, $16.4 billion to the rest of the world, $1.4 billion to the federal government, and $9.2 billion to state and local government.

**Exhibit 2.7**
**Personal Interest Income, 1999**

| | 1999 Amounts in $ Billions | | Percent of Total | |
|---|---|---|---|---|
| **Paid by business** | | **$ 624.2** | | **65** |
| Business net monetary interest | | 176.1 | | 18 |
| Paid | $ 1,709.9 | | 177 | |
| Received | (1,533.8) | | (159) | |
| Business net imputed interest | | 448.1 | | 46 |
| Paid by financial intermediaries | $ 342.8 | | 36 | |
| Received from financ'l intermediaries | (72.0) | | (7) | |
| Paid by life insurance companies | 177.3 | | 18 | |
| **Rest of world net interest** | | **$ (117.0)** | | **(12)** |
| Monetary interest paid | $ 134.4 | | 14 | |
| Monetary interest received | (235.0) | | (24) | |
| Imputed interest received | (16.4) | | (2) | |
| **Paid by government** | | **$ 261.8** | | **27** |
| Federal | | 264.7 | | 27 |
| Monetary interest paid | $ 281.8 | | 29 | |
| Imputed interest received | (15.7) | | (2) | |
| Imputed interest received | (1.4) | | (0) | |
| State & local | | (3.0) | | (0) |
| Monetary interest paid | $ 75.1 | | 8 | |
| Imputed interest received | (68.9) | | (7) | |
| Imputed interest received | (9.2) | | (1) | |
| **Paid by persons** | | **194.8** | | **20** |
| **PERSONAL INTEREST INCOME** | | **$ 963.7** | | **100** |

*Source* : U.S. Department of Commerce. Bureau of Economic Analysis. "'Annual Only' NIPA Tables." *National Accounts Data* . 30 Aug. 2000: Table 8.20. 5 Sep. 2000. <http://www.bea.doc.gov/bea/dn1.htm>.

Imputed net interest paid to persons by life insurance companies (and noninsured pension plans) constitutes another major source of income, $ 177.3 billion. It represents the investment earnings of those entities, and the BEA attributes those earnings to policyholders and plan participants. Unlike imputed interest paid for services furnished without charge by financial intermediaries that are offset by counterentries in personal consumption expenditure, imputed interest from life insurance carriers and noninsured pension plans contribute to personal saving.[6]

As a result of all those interest rate imputations, $421.1 billion of the $963.7 billion in *Personal interest income* takes a form that persons do not see. Those imputations represent services furnished without payment to depositors and investors by financial institutions. Have you noticed that the rate of interest you earn on your deposit at a bank is less than the rate of interest it charges on a loan? So has the BEA!

It imputes an interest payment based on the difference between what banks, insurance companies, and credit unions earn on your deposits and insurance premiums and what they pay out. Also added to interest income are services implicitly provided by domestic dealers who make markets in securities. Rather than charge for their services, they sell securities they hold to clients at a higher price than their purchase price.

What do those imputations attempt to achieve? Let's say that you have saved $1,000. You deposit it in a savings account of your local bank, the East Bank of Ohio. On your deposit you earn 5 percent interest. The bank in turn takes the $1,000 and lends it to someone else named Frank N. Stine and charges him 10 percent. Essentially, through the financial intermediary of a bank, you have loaned your $1,000 to Mr. Stine. You accept—at least tolerate—the lower return on your money because the bank incurs the cost (and risk) of lending to a particular individual. However, Mr. Stine (presumably) would have been equally happy to have borrowed directly from you had you been willing to handle the transaction yourself. (Maybe if you had known Mr. Stine's parents and knew that he came from a good family, you would have been happy to make the loan to him.) The BEA's adjustment makes estimates of personal income impervious to the way a loan is made.

Net interest payments by the rest of the world are negative. They are recipients of net interest! Foreigners hold more debt from the United States than our domestic holdings of foreign debt. As a result, more is paid to the rest of the world than the rest of the world pays to us.

Federal government net interest payments include the largest single source of net monetary interest. Monetary interest payments of $281.1 billion are offset by $15.7 billion in receipts for a net of $266.1 billion. With an imputed interest offset of $1.4 billion, the figure becomes $264.7 billion. A look at state and local government reveals a startling contrast. State and local government net monetary interest payments amount to only $6.2 billion. They are more than offset by imputed interest of $9.2 billion. The federal government's sizeable interest payments result from its large outstanding debt. On the other hand, as a group state governments usually maintain surpluses. What do they do with the extra funds? They often buy federal government notes, bonds, and other evidences of debt. Hence, some of the $68.9 billion in state government interest receipts comes from the federal government. The BEA obtains those figures for federal and state interest payments from government and regulatory reports.[7]

*Interest paid by persons*, $194.8 billion, constitutes the last component shown on Exhibit 2.7. It accounts for 20 percent of personal interest income and is not a net figure. Since persons both receive and pay the interest, netting the figure would cause it to disappear.

**Exhibit 2.8**
**Transfer Payments to Persons, 1999**

| | 1999 Amounts in $ Billions | | | Percent of Total | | |
|---|---|---|---|---|---|---|
| **From government** | | | **$ 986.5** | | | **97** |
| Social Security (OASDHI) | | $588.0 | | | 58 | |
| Government unemployment benefits | | 20.3 | | | 2 | |
| Veterans benefits | | 24.3 | | | 2 | |
| Family assistance | | 17.8 | | | 2 | |
| Other government transfers | | 336.1 | | | 33 | |
| **From business** | | | **29.7** | | | **3** |
| Insurance payments to persons | | $ 16.4 | | | 2 | |
| Automobile insurance | $13.3 | | | 1 | | |
| Medical malpractice insur | 3.1 | | | 0 | | |
| Donations | | 9.1 | | | 1 | |
| Other | | 4.2 | | | 0 | |
| **TOTAL TRANSFER PAYMENTS** | | | **$ 1,016.2** | | | **100** |

*Source*: U.S. Department of Commerce. Bureau of Economic Analysis. "Selected NIPA Tables." *National Accounts Data*. 8 Aug. 2000: Table 2.1. 9 Sep. 2000. <http://www.bea.doc.gov/bea/dn1.htm> And "'Annual Only' NIPA Tables." *National Accounts Data*. 30 Aug. 2000: Table 8.16. 5 Sep. 2000 <http://www.bea.doc.gov/bea/dn1.htm>.

### Transfer Payments to Persons

Transfer payments to persons represent income households and individuals receive for which no contribution to current output of goods and services is required. Reference once again to Exhibit 2.1 shows that after wages and salaries receipt of *Transfers*, amounting to $1.0 trillion, is the second largest single component of personal income—13 percent of the total.

Exhibit 2.8 provides additional detail about this major component of personal income. Transfer payments come from two economic sectors: government and business. Private business distributes $29.7 billion in transfer payments, but compared to government they are relatively insignificant, just 3 percent of *Total transfer payments*. Business transfer payments are derived from Internal Revenue Service tabulations of business tax returns. Despite their small size, business transfer payments are not without interest. As shown in the table, they consist primarily of payments for personal injury claims where automobile insurance claims clearly outstrip those of medical malpractice insurance. *Donations* amount to $9.1 billion. A corporation's gift to, say, a local YMCA will be included in that total. The *Other* category consists of income taxes paid by domestic business on income earned abroad.

Government transfers account for 97 percent of all transfer payments. *Social security* alone accounts for 58 percent of the grand total. It encompasses:

- Old age, survivors, and disability insurance (OASDI),
- Hospital insurance (the H in OASDHI), and
- Supplementary medical insurance.

*Other government transfers* amounting to $336.1 billion constitutes another major category accounting for 33 percent. It includes such programs as

- Medical care,
- Railroad retirement benefits,
- Workers' compensation,
- Food stamps, and
- Educational assistance.

The remaining 6 percent is distributed among three programs: *Government unemployment benefits*, *Veterans benefits*, and *Family assistance*.

As a result of all of those programs, about one dollar in every eight earned by those who contribute to the production of goods and services is transferred to others who currently are making no contribution to national output. Is that fair?

One of the great strengths of a market-oriented economic system is that it provides individuals with incentives to maximize their productivity and thus their incomes. Some are more successful than others. Some are unable to compete. Disparities of income result. The market mechanism simply does not address those inequalities.

You work hard; you produce something useful; you're rewarded. Your income matches your productivity (almost). Why not exactly? Karl Marx, the author of *Das Kapital* is not considered a friend of market-oriented economies, but he did us a favor by pointing out weaknesses of the capitalistic system and proposing what he considered a better alternative. In the twentieth century his propositions led to experiments with communism as a form of economic organization. As vehicles for economic progress, they have not proved successful; however, Karl had a vision, an attractive and beautiful ideal. He proposed a system in which goods and services produced by a society would be distributed according to the dictum, "From each according to his ability, to each according to his needs."[8] That inspirational principle, alas, dampens individual incentives to be productive. Under such a system, if one individual fails to exert himself to the utmost, aggregate production of goods and services will be diminished relatively little. His share of the output—and everyone else's—will be imperceptibly reduced. The discovery of one is equally discoverable by all. When all behave rationally collective output diminishes. The appeal to social justice conflicts with the drive to greater and greater productivity. How a pie is sliced influences the size of the pie.

Through their governments the people of the United States have made a collective decision to strike a balance between the two opposing objectives. Some may think one dollar in eight is too large; others may consider it too small. Those who believe it to be too large recognize that confiscating a portion of people's income for other purposes tends to dampen their incentives to be productive. Those pressing for larger transfers assign high priority to alleviating the blight of poverty and its consequences in the midst of plenty. The push and shove of the differing viewpoints produced in 1999 the balance seen here. Transfer payments as a percent of personal income—13 percent—represent, if you will, our compassion index at that point in time.

### Personal Contributions to Social Insurance

Those transfer payments are not achieved without a price. As shown in Exhibit 2.1, a substantial portion of that price takes the form of *Personal contributions for social insurance*. With respect to social insurance, "contribution" is a euphemism. It carries a much more pleasant connotation than "taxes," but really a tax is what it is. Most employees do not see the money that pays their contribution to social insurance. Their employers automatically deduct employees' contribution from their pay. Self-employed persons and others participating in the programs also contribute, and they have ample opportunity to feel the pain.

Social insurance payments provide funding for the following federal government programs:

- Old-age, survivors, and disability insurance (social security),
- Hospital insurance,
- Supplementary medical insurance,
- Unemployment insurance,
- Government employee retirement programs,
- Railroad retirement,
- Veterans life insurance, and
- Temporary disability insurance.

Exhibit 2.9 displays distribution of "contributions" to those programs in terms of dollar amounts and their percentage share of the total. The first three items on the list account for 99 percent of total social insurance contributions. Great passions may be attached to the others, but they are rounding level concerns.

All the contributions totaling to $338.5 billion are subtracted from rather than added to the preceding figures in Exhibit 2.1. The difference between that number and all the preceding entries produces the $7.8 trillion estimate for *Personal Income*.

**Exhibit 2.9**
**Personal Contributions to Social Insurance, 1999**

| | 1999 Amounts in $ Billions | | | Percent of Total | | |
|---|---|---|---|---|---|---|
| **Federal social insurance funds** | | | **$ 336.6** | | | **99** |
| OASDHI | | $314.2 | | | 93 | |
| Employees | $281.5 | | | 83 | | |
| Self-employed | 32.7 | | | 10 | | |
| Supplemental medical insurance | | 20.3 | | | 6 | |
| State unemployment insurance | | - | | | | |
| Railroad retirement | | 1.4 | | | 0 | |
| Veterans life insurance | | 0.7 | | | 0 | |
| **State and local social insurance funds** | | | **1.9** | | | **1** |
| **TOTAL PERSONAL CONTRIBUTIONS** | | | **$ 338.5** | | | **100** |

*Source*: U.S. Department of Commerce. Bureau of Economic Analysis. "'Annual Only' NIPA Tables." *National Accounts Data*. 30 Aug. 2000: Table 3.6. 5 Sep. 2000. <http://www.bea.doc.gov/bea/dn1.htm>.

Putting social insurance programs in the most favorable possible light is not limited to calling employee payments to them contributions. The way they are shown in the personal income and outlay account reflects that bias as well. Payments for social securities hardly differ from other expenses and as such belong as additions to outlays rather than as deductions from income. But showing contributions as outlays would place them in proximity to direct personal taxes and nontaxes and give away the pretense.

## CONCLUSION

Why do people in the United States work so hard? What do they receive for all their effort? The national income and product accounts statistic, personal income, provides a quantitative measure of their reward. It reflects many of the complexities and contradictions inherent in an economy blending private and public interest. Not all income is earned from private enterprise. Nearly a sixth of all wages and salaries is earned from government activities. Not all income is received in return for current contributions to production of goods and services. About one dollar in eight is received by persons through transfer payments for which productive activity is not required. About 4 percent of what people earn is involuntarily taken away for social insurance contributions. Although those exceptions have their effect, the balance is clearly tipped to reward the private sector for productive activity.

Although receipt of income represents an immediate reward for persons' productive effort, it is not the driving force. The real reward consists not of receiving income but of spending it. We shall examine the ultimate purpose in the next chapter.

## NOTES

1. U.S. Department of Commerce, Bureau of Economic Analysis, *Personal Consumption Expenditures*, Methodology Paper Series Number 6 (Washington, DC: U.S. Government Printing Office, 1990) 5.

2. U.S. Department of Commerce, Bureau of Economic Analysis, "Selected NIPA Tables," *National Accounts Data*, 21 Apr. 2000: Table 2.1, 6 May 2000. And 8 Aug. 2000: Table 2.1, 9 Sep. 2000 <http://www.bea.doc.gov/ bea/ dn1.htm>.

3. Brent R. Moulton and David F. Sullivan, "A Preview of the 1999 Comprehensive Revision of the National Income and Product Accounts: New and Redesigned Tables," *Survey of Current Business* (Sep. 1999): 15.

4. U.S. Department of Commerce, Bureau of Economic Analysis, *National Income and Product Accounts, 1929-94*, vol. 1 (Washington, DC: U.S. Government Printing Office, April 1998) M-19.

5. U.S. Department of Commerce, Bureau of Economic Analysis, "Updated Summary of NIPA Methodologies," *Survey of Current Business* (September 1998): 24.

6. *National Income and Product Accounts, 1929-94* M-7, M-9.

7. U.S. Department of Commerce, Bureau of Economic Analysis, *Personal Consumption Expenditure*, Methodology Paper Series Number 6 (Washington, DC: U.S. Government Printing Office, 1996) 17.

8. Karl Marx, "Critique of the Gotha Program," (1891) *The Marx-Engels Reader*, 2nd ed., ed. Richard Tucker (New York: W. W. Norton Company, 1978) 531.

# 3

# Where the Money Goes

The market mechanism rewards with earned income persons whose labor and ownership of productive resources contribute to the output of goods and services. But ultimately earning high income does not motivate people to produce goods and services. Consumption—satisfaction of their human needs and wants—constitutes the end purpose of economic activity. In a money-oriented market economy such as ours, we earn income to spend it.

Despite the separation enabled and required by specialization of labor and the institution of money, fundamentals remain. Consumption still constitutes the purpose of all productive activity. Over any interval of time, all income earned and its disposition match. Three things happen to the income we earn:

- We pay taxes.
- We buy goods and services.
- We save what is left over.

Virtually every person pays taxes and buys things. We all consume goods and services to sustain our existence. However, not every person—individual, household, or nonprofit organization serving people—manages to save each year. In any year some spend more than their income, but in the aggregate persons usually consume less than they receive in income.

The conceptual framework of the national income and product accounts (NIPA) preserves the equality between personal income and outlays. Not only does the NIPA define and show the sources of personal income, but it also records the three things that happen to the income we earn. Exhibit 3.1 displays those three things and some other items along with the estimates for 1999. This exhibit begins where we left off, with *Personal income* totaling $7.8 trillion for 1999.

**Exhibit 3.1**
**Uses of Personal Income, 1999**

| | | 1999 Amounts in $ Billions | | Percent of Total |
|---|---|---|---|---|
| **PERSONAL INCOME** | | **$ 7,789.6** | | **100** |
| Less: Personal tax and nontax payments | | 1,152.0 | | 15 |
| **DISPOSABLE PERSONAL INCOME** | | **$ 6,637.7** | | **85** |
| Personal outlays | | 6,490.1 | | 83 |
| Consumption expenditures | $ 6,268.7 | | 80 | |
| Interest paid by persons | 194.8 | | 3 | |
| Transfer payments | 26.6 | | 0 | |
| Personal saving | | 147.6 | | 2 |
| **TOTAL USES OF PERSONAL INCOME** | | **$ 7,789.6** | | **100** |

*Source*: U.S. Department of Commerce. Bureau of Economic Analysis. "Selected NIPA Tables." *National Accounts Data*. 30 Aug 2000: Table 3.4. 5 Sep. 2000. <http://www.bea.doc.gov/bea/dn1.htm>.

## PERSONAL TAX AND NONTAX PAYMENTS

Not all that personal income of $7.8 trillion consists of money that we can spend as we choose. Benjamin Franklin observed, "In this world nothing is certain but death and taxes."[1] The great sage and scientist of the nation's founding fathers may have observed today that taxes are more certain than death. Thanks to estate and inheritance taxes, we pay them not only as we live but also after we die.

The first entry under outlays of personal income—*Personal tax and nontax payments*—recognizes the inevitably of taxes. In 1999 it amounted to $1,152.0 billion. Although it is not the largest single use of personal income—thank goodness—it does account for about 15 percent of the total. Such a big number deserves a closer look.

Personal taxes include payments both to the federal government and to state and local governments. They include taxes paid by U.S. citizens on income, realized capital gains, and gifts. Personal taxes do not include estate and inheritance taxes—at least not any more. Effective with the 1999 comprehensive revision of the NIPA, those taxes are classified as capital transfers. Understanding the change in classification takes some effort. Brent R. Moulton and his associates at the Bureau of Economic Analysis (BEA) admit,

**Exhibit 3.2**
**Personal Tax and Nontax Payments, 1999**

| | 1999 Amounts in $ Billions | | | Percent of Total | | |
|---|---|---|---|---|---|---|
| **Federal** | | | **$ 902.2** | | | **78** |
| Income taxes | | $892.7 | | | 77 | |
| Nontaxes | | 9.5 | | | 1 | |
| **State and local** | | | **249.7** | | | **22** |
| Income taxes | | $194.8 | | | 17 | |
| Motor vehicle licenses | | 11.8 | | | 1 | |
| Other taxes | | 8.0 | | | 1 | |
| Nontaxes | | 35.1 | | | 3 | |
| Fines | $10.2 | | | 1 | | |
| Other | 24.9 | | | 2 | | |
| **PERSONAL TAX & NONTAX PAYMENTS** | | | **$ 1,152.0** | | | **100** |

*Source*: U.S. Department of Commerce. Bureau of Economic Analysis. "'Annual Only' NIPA Tables." *National Accounts Data*. 30 Aug 2000: Table 3.4. 5 Sep. 2000. <http://www.bea.doc.gov/bea/dn1.htm>.

The classification of a transaction as a capital transfer is sometimes difficult because a transaction may represent the acquisition or disposition of an asset to one party and disposable income to the other party. For example, estate and gift taxes are linked to the transfer of assets and therefore are capital transactions from the point of view of the household; however, from the government's point of view, these taxes represent funds that are available for spending and would be considered as current transactions. In general, BEA will follow international guidelines in which a transaction is classified as a capital transfer if it is viewed as a capital transaction by either party to the transaction.[2]

Reclassification of estate and inheritance taxes brings to mind the admonition of chapter 2 that the way the NIPA are presented is not necessarily a neutral presentation of the facts. The change, after all does reduce people's apparent tax burden. How handy! How much? As a result of the change in classification, $36.9 billion is dropped from the apparent tax rolls: $28.8 billion for the federal government and $8.1 billion for state and local government.[3] The tax bite of inheritance and estate taxes no longer appears in the NIPA.

Exhibit 3.2 shows that the federal government takes in $902.2 billion—slightly over three-fourths of the $1,152.0 billion bite of personal tax and nontax payments. Federal personal income taxes alone account for virtually all of that $902.2 billion total. *Nontaxes*, relatively inconsequential in amount, consist largely of fines and immigration fees.[4]

State and local governments pick up $249.7 billion, the rest of the total. As in the case of the federal government, *Income taxes* dominate state and local government's aggregate personal tax and nontax payments. *Motor vehicle licenses* add a discernible but decidedly lesser amount. *Other taxes* include hunting, fishing, and other personal licenses and contribute a negligible $8.0 billion (negligible on a national scale, that is). *Nontaxes* add more to state and local coffers than all the taxes other than personal income taxes. Donations and unclaimed bank deposits comprise most of the source of *Other* nontaxes.

The $1,152.0 billion of *Personal Tax and Nontax Payments* in 1999 represents money taken by federal, state, and local levels of government from those who earned income. Those taxes are not the only involuntary payment made to government units. Personal contributions for social insurance totaling $338.5 billion constitute another deduction. Together they amount to nearly $1.5 trillion dollars—19 percent of personal income. From an aggregate standpoint, the 19 percent suggests that persons devote over two months out of every year earning enough income to make payments to their federal, state, and local governments for personal taxes and nontaxes.

Alert readers will note that personal taxes do not include sales taxes and property taxes. Those taxes are levied on things rather than persons, and we will encounter them when we deal with sources of funds for the government sector. Their exclusion from personal taxes means that the tax burden is greater than the $1.5 trillion figure above implies.

In the events leading up to the independence of the United States from Great Britain, James Otis observed that there should be no taxation without representation.[5] Consequently, our form of government is representative. Payments that individually we involuntarily make to government are levies that collectively we sanctioned through our duly (not dully) elected representatives. Would those early patriots be surprised by cost of representative government?!

Following *Personal tax and nontax payments* on Exhibit 3.1 comes *Disposable personal income*, which is calculated as the difference between total personal income and personal tax and nontax payments. For 1999 *Disposable personal income* amounts to a little over $6.6 trillion dollars and represents the amount of income available to individuals for spending as they choose.

How sweet it is! Disposable personal income: the aggregate amount of income that we can spend as individuals for things we need and—helped by ample advertisements in newspapers and on billboards, radio, television, and even the Internet—for things we think we want. Or we can choose not to spend it—at least, for now. We can *save* disposable personal income. In Exhibit 3.1, those two choices appear as *Personal outlays* and *Personal saving*.

*Personal outlays* constitute the largest single use of personal income, $6.5 trillion or 83 percent of personal income in 1999. As a use of disposable personal income, outlays are by far a more popular option exceeding *Personal saving*'s $147.6 billion more than forty times.

## PERSONAL OUTLAYS

Exhibit 3.1 shows that personal outlays are divided into three parts:

- Personal consumption expenditures,
- Interest paid by persons, and
- Personal transfer payments to the rest of the world.

The category *Personal consumption expenditures* heads the list and totals $6.3 trillion, all but $221.4 billion of personal outlay's $6.5 trillion. One of the things that the earners of personal income do with their disposable personal income is consume goods and services, and of that they do a lot.

### Personal Consumption Expenditures

As a first step in appreciating the tabulation of personal consumption expenditures we should recall that "person" in personal income includes more than just people. Earlier we observed that it includes nonprofit institutions serving people as well as individuals and households.

Just like people, nonprofit institutions receive income in the form of sales of services to people, rent, dividends, interest, and transfers. And they spend it, too. Nonprofit institutions pay salaries and wages to people; buy goods and services from business, government, and the rest of the world; and make transfer payments. In the process of consolidating expenditures of people-serving nonprofit institutions with individuals to form personal outlays, the BEA cancels certain transactions. Purchases (sales) of nonprofit institution services by (to) individuals drop out along with transfers between the two entities. Compensation of employees—salaries, wages, and other compensation—does not cancel, however, since it reflects a market value for presumably productive activity.[6]

Purchases of new goods and services account for most of personal consumption expenditures. They include consumer goods produced in the rest of the world and imported for sale in the United States, as well as domestically produced goods since not everyone "buys American," an admonition virtually impossible to achieve and usually unwise. The following purchases that people make are *excluded* from personal consumption expenditures:

- *Purchases for business use.* For example, if you as a sole proprietor purchase a pickup truck for both personal and business use, the transaction would be included as a business expense.
- *Purchases from other individuals.* For example, the BEA ignores the glass of lemonade you buy from your neighbor's kid. However, payment for services rendered by household workers are included since, as in the case of people-serving nonprofit institutions, it represents value received from productive activity.
- *Purchases of structures, houses, mobile homes.* Since most buildings and dwellings last a long time, the BEA treats such purchases as investments and records them

elsewhere in the NIPA. Also treated as investments are purchases of equipment by nonprofit institutions serving primarily people.

- *Payments for public goods.* The BEA records consumer purchases of government goods and services primarily regulatory or administrative in nature or usually provided by nonprofit institutions as personal nontax payments. Your purchase of a fishing license or tuition payments to a public university gets placed in the personal tax and nontax payment category. When government-produced goods and services have their counterparts in the private sector, however, they become personal consumption expenditures. Your room and board charges at a public university's dormitory become part of personal consumption expenditures; likewise, your purchase of a postage stamp.
- *Finance charges.* Interest paid by persons includes finance charges.

In addition to new goods, persons also purchase used goods. The amount included in personal income is not the gross amount paid but only the net amount: the difference between its cost to the seller and the price you paid. Furthermore, only purchases of persons from the business sector, government, or the rest of the world are included. Transactions among persons cancel out in the consolidation process. For example, if you purchase from your neighbor his used car, personal income—the national aggregate, that is—is not affected. If you purchase a used car from a dealer, however, the dealer's margin and other costs associated with the transaction are included in personal consumption expenditures.

*Personal consumption expenditures*, accounting as they do for $6.3 trillion, constitute a huge aggregate. If you are curious about the composition of personal consumption expenditures, you will not be disappointed. The BEA produces not one but two approaches to classifying the components of personal consumption expenditures: by type of expenditure and by type of product. Personal consumption expenditures by type of expenditure is a twelve-category classification system that reflects the nature or purpose of the expenditure. Additional detail appears under each of the twelve categories. Personal consumption expenditures by type of product consists of three broad categories: durable goods, nondurable goods, and services. The details shown for by-expenditure type are rearranged to fit the by-product classification. The BEA publishes by-type-of-product data monthly and quarterly. By-type-of-expenditure data appear only annually. We will focus on personal consumption expenditures by type of product.

Exhibit 3.3 displays the three broad categories of personal consumption by type of product along with twenty-eight subcategories. The BEA publishes detailed personal consumption expenditures data for over 300 items.

*Durable goods* head our list but account for the smallest portion of *Personal consumption expenditures*, $761.3 billion—12 percent. *Nondurable goods* follow at $1.8 trillion, between two and two and a half times larger than durable goods. Last but certainly not least come *Services*, accounting for $3.7 trillion, well over half of *Personal consumption expenditures*.

**Exhibit 3.3**
**Personal Consumption Expenditures by Type of Product, 1999**

| | 1999 Amounts in $ Billions | | Percent of Total | |
|---|---|---|---|---|
| **Durable goods** | | **$ 761.3** | | **12** |
| Motor vehicles and parts | $320.7 | | 5 | |
| Furniture & household equipment | 288.5 | | 5 | |
| Ophthalmic & orthopedic appliances | 22.1 | | 0 | |
| Recreational equipment | 51.3 | | 1 | |
| Jewelry and watches | 48.8 | | 1 | |
| Books and maps | 29.8 | | 0 | |
| **Nondurable goods** | | **1,845.5** | | **29** |
| Food | $897.8 | | 14 | |
| Clothing and shoes | 307.0 | | 5 | |
| Gasoline, fuel oil, other energy goods | 142.7 | | 2 | |
| Tobacco products | 66.0 | | 1 | |
| Toilet articles and preparations | 57.5 | | 1 | |
| Semidurable house furnishings | 38.3 | | 1 | |
| Household supplies | 57.1 | | 1 | |
| Drug preparations and sundries | 136.8 | | 2 | |
| Nondurable toys & sport supplies | 63.1 | | 1 | |
| Stationery and writing supplies | 23.1 | | 0 | |
| Net foreign remittances | 1.6 | | 0 | |
| Periodicals and sheet music | 37.0 | | 1 | |
| Flowers, seeds, & potted plants | 17.5 | | 0 | |
| **Services** | | **3,661.9** | | **58** |
| Housing | $906.2 | | 14 | |
| Household operation | 360.2 | | 6 | |
| Transportation | 256.5 | | 4 | |
| Medical care | 943.6 | | 15 | |
| Recreation | 237.1 | | 4 | |
| Personal care | 70.1 | | 1 | |
| Personal business | 586.2 | | 9 | |
| Education and research | 148.9 | | 2 | |
| Religious and welfare activities | 170.2 | | 3 | |
| Net foreign travel | (17.0) | | (0) | |
| **TOTAL PERSONAL CONSUMPTION** | | **$ 6,268.7** | | **100** |

*Source*: U.S. Department of Commerce. Bureau of Economic Analysis. "'Annual Only' NIPA Tables." *National Accounts Data*. 30 Aug 2000: Table 2.6. 5 Sep. 2000. <http://www.bea.doc.gov/bea/dn1.htm>.

Those categories are not without economic significance. High consumer confidence tends to stimulate purchases of durable goods. Such goods yield their services over extended periods of time and often entail relatively significant expenditures. Their acquisition tends to diminish a purchaser's liquidity or involves borrowing. Only when future income seems assured and prospects for it becoming higher seem bright are persons disposed to incur the kind of change in financial circumstance involved in a major acquisition of durable goods.

In periods of low consumer confidence, purchases of durable goods tend to fall. Being durable, they last, and often purchases of new replacements can be deferred. Not everyone may be in a position to defer durable goods purchases, but in gloomy economic times those who can will exercise that option.

Nondurable goods and services are less susceptible to variation with changes in economic conditions. Abstention from consuming food, shelter, and clothing on a daily basis inflicts a real hardship on individuals and poses a near term threat to comfort, health, and life. Consequently, those items are less sensitive to changes in economic conditions. As we shall see, however, even within those categories degrees of urgency to consume vary among particular items.

The BEA defines durable goods as consisting of commodities that can be stored or inventoried and that have an average life of at least three years. The subcategory *Motor vehicles and parts* comprises $320.7 billion or 5 percent of the $6.3 trillion in personal consumption expenditures. New automobiles account for only $97.3 billion of the $320.7 billion. Other motor vehicles at expenditures of $119.9 billion constitute the largest item in that category. Has a pickup truck passed you lately—a new one? Used automobiles make up $58.7 billion in expenditures, suggesting the market for used automobiles is brisk––and the margin is substantial. Tires, tubes, accessories, and other parts complete the items included under *Motor vehicles and parts*.

At $288.5 billion in expenditures and 5 percent of personal consumption expenditures, *Furniture and household equipment* comes second after *Motor vehicles and parts* both on the list and in dollar amount among durable goods. Video and audio goods including musical instruments and computer goods at $99.1 billion make up the largest single item under that subcategory. Music teachers and sellers of television sets might find that information encouraging but misleading if they overlooked inclusion of computing equipment in the $99.1 billion for that particular set of durable goods. Computers, peripherals, and software account for $31.9 billion of that figure. Other *Furniture and household equipment* items include everything you can think of: kitchen and other household appliances, china, glassware, utensils, floor coverings, comforters, quilts, blankets, pillows, picture frames, mirrors, art products, portable lamps, clocks, writing equipment, and hand, power, and garden tools, refrigerators and freezers, cooking ranges, dishwashers, laundry equipment, stoves, room air conditioners, sewing machines, and vacuum cleaners.

The remaining four items are much smaller in dollar significance. Purchases of eyeglasses fall into the pretentiously named *Ophthalmic and orthopedic ap-*

*pliances*. Items comprising durable recreational equipment—such as jewelry, books, and maps—provide examples of products whose purchase often can be postponed when economic conditions become rough for consumers.

One does not have to be a friend of Sherlock Holmes to deduce that given the definition of durable goods, nondurable goods consist of those commodities having average lives of less than three years. Exhibit 3.3 provides a display of the major subcategories of nondurable goods along with their amounts and percents of personal consumption expenditures in 1999.

The *Food* category with $897.8 billion in expenditures constitutes the largest single nondurable goods subcategory. It consists mainly of purchases of groceries, alcoholic and nonalcoholic beverages, and purchased meals from retail, service, and amusement establishments, hotels, dining and buffet cars, schools, school fraternities, institutions, clubs, and industrial lunchrooms. Finding a meal anywhere else would be a challenge. But an imputed item, food furnished to employees, adds another $9.6 billion.

All the entries under durable goods reflect transactions that actually occur. They consist of observable and measurable market transactions. Goods change hands; sales are made; buyers and sellers engage in an exchange. In constructing the aggregate amount for personal consumption expenditures for nondurable goods and services, the BEA in addition inserts imputed transactions. Those inserts are designed to improve the extent to which the NIPA measure actual production of goods and services and remove the distorting effects of various institutional arrangements.

In our earlier discussion of personal income components, we noted that the BEA includes in wage and salary income an imputed value for food furnished employees (including the military) and in proprietors' income and an imputed value for food produced and consumed on farms. The system of double-entry accounting upon which national income accounting is based requires that imputation of income be matched with an equal imputation of consumption. The *Food* category includes those income imputation offsets.

Women's and children's clothing and accessories at $168.7 billion constitutes the largest item listed under *Clothing and shoes*. Men's and boy's clothing and accessories are just over half that amount. Those statistics seem to verify what could be concluded from simple observation of a crowd. Although some articles of clothing, accessories, luggage, and shoes last longer than three years, they are all lumped together as nondurable goods.

*Gasoline, fuel oil, & other energy products* appear next on our list. Keeping all those new and used automobiles, pickup trucks, sports utility and recreational vehicles running up and down the nation's highways prompted purchases of gasoline and oil amounting to $128.3 billion. A vast petroleum industry and its distribution network depend upon those purchases. Fuel oil and coal expenditures of $14.4 billion make up the rest of the $142.7 billion total for energy sources and suggest that many households do not rely on those sources of energy to keep their homes warm during the heating season.

The remaining items on the list of nondurables are smaller than the first three. With expenditures of $136.8 billion, only *Drug preparations and sundries* come close to food, clothing, and energy. That figure excludes drug preparations and related products dispensed by physicians, hospitals, and other medical services. Next comes *Tobacco products* huffing and puffing along at $66.0 billion (including attorneys' fees). Some habits are hard to break. *Nondurable toys and sports supplies*, offering an alternative form of recreation and means of relaxation, occupy $63.1 billion of consumers' nondurable expenditures. *Household supplies*, amounting to $57.1, include cleaning and polishing agents and paper products and enable housekeepers to make things clean, bright, and shining around the house. Expenditures for *Toilet articles and preparations* at $57.5 edge out (barely) household supplies. *Semidurable house furnishings* include such things as draperies, lampshades, brooms, and brushes that help absorb and banish the odor of tobacco smoke. *Net foreign remittances* amounting to $1.6 billion represent personal remittances in kind to nonresidents.

Services must be consumed at the time and place of purchase. While the definition seems clear, application is easier said than done. Certain services contain an inseparable goods component and vice versa. Whichever of the two components of a particular item predominates determines the category into which it falls. The *Food* industry, for example, includes restaurant meals as a nondurable good. However, substantial service is involved since most eating establishments do not allow their customers to wander into the kitchen and help themselves. Natural gas and electricity are classified as services, but something is coming through the pipes and wires. Exhibit 3.3 lists the major subcategories of services, their amounts, and their percentages of personal consumption expenditures.

*Housing* heads the list and at $906.2 billion accounts for 14 percent of all personal consumption expenditures. Imputations for owner-occupied nonfarm dwellings and for rental value of farm dwellings appear here and make up most of that $906.2 billion.

Utilities (electricity, gas, water, and other sanitation services) fall into *Household operation*. Collectively, utilities account for $214.5 billion of the $360.2 billion required to "keep the homes fires burning." Individually, they are surpassed by telephone and telegraph, with expenditures of $121.7 billion. Maintenance of appliances and house furnishings, moving and warehouse expenses, postage and express charges, and premiums for fire and theft insurance on personal property less benefits and dividends constitute other expenditures in that subcategory.

The cost of operating your automobile and buying an airline, bus, or train ticket adds to *Transportation*. It accounts for $256.5 billion of services purchased and is broken down into three subcategories: user-operated transportation, purchased local transportation, and purchased intercity transportation.

User-operated transportation, $205.5 billion, makes up most of the *Transportation* category. Caring for and finding a place to put the family buggy comprises most of that subcategory. Purchased intercity transportation constitutes $38.7 billion of *Transportation*, and airline travel dominates that subcategory.

Among purchases of services, *Medical care* looms as the largest single subcategory. At $943.6 billion, 15 percent, it takes up more than food, more than housing, more than any other major category of personal consumption expenditures. The cost of making sick people well and keeping dying people alive exceeds the entire amount people spend for all durable goods. Payments to hospitals and nursing homes account for nearly half of the total spent for *Medical care* and include current expenditures of nonprofit hospitals and nursing homes and payments by patients to proprietary and government hospitals and nursing homes. Health insurance is recorded under *Medical care* and consists of health, hospitalization, and accidental death and dismemberment insurance provided by commercial insurance carriers, and administrative expenses of nonprofit and self-insured health plans. Health insurance from commercial insurance carriers includes the amount of premium payments they receive but not all of it. Their premiums are recorded net of benefits and dividends paid by them.[7] If the benefits were not deducted, they would be double counted: once in the premiums and again as payments to medical care providers.

Although paying to get your radio or television set repaired may not seem like a form of recreation, the fun guys at the BEA consider it to be and place it in the *Recreation* subcategory. With an expenditure of only $3.9 billion, such repairs do not appear to be a very popular form of recreation. *Recreation* also includes admissions to motion picture shows, to legitimate theater, ballet, and opera, to professional and amateur athletic events and racetracks, and to entertainment of nonprofit institutions. The costs of the persons you see stumbling dazed and bewildered from sightseeing buses or following around tourist guides like chicks following a mother hen also are treated as a form of recreation. There too go payments to billiard parlors, bowling alleys, dancing, riding, shooting, skating, and swimming places, amusement devices and parks, golf courses, private flying operators, casino gambling, net receipts of lotteries, expenditures for purchases of such diversions as pets and pet care services, cable TV, film processing, photographic studios, sporting and recreation camps, and videocassette rentals.

Your expenditures for a hair cut, a shoeshine, cleaning your clothes, and joining a health club go into *Personal care*—just 1 percent of personal consumption expenditures. It includes watch, clock, and jewelry repairs, costume and dress suit rental, and miscellaneous personal services.

*Personal business* is a major expenditure item ranking in size only after *Medical care*, *Housing*, and *Food*. Bank service charges (including trust services and safe deposit rental) and brokerage and investment charges (including investment counseling) fall into this subcategory. *Personal business* also contains things you did not know you bought: imputations for the value of services furnished without payment by financial intermediaries ($243.8 billion, a figure we saw before in chapter 2) and the expense of handling life insurance. As with medical insurance, premiums for casualty insurance is recorded net of benefits and dividends paid by stock and mutual insurance companies. Those entries offset imputations to proprietor's income, rental income, and interest income noted in our discussion of personal income. One might expect that Funeral and burial expenses would be the last payment for *Personal business*, but it is followed by expenditures for trade unions and professional associations, employment agency fees, money order fees, spending for classified advertisements, and tax return preparation services.

Education and research get counted in *Education and Research*. For private institutions this category includes current expenditures (including consumption of fixed capital) less receipts—such as those from meals, rooms, and entertainment—that are accounted for in other classifications. Also deducted are expenditures for research and development financed under contracts or grants. Your payments for tuition at public institutions of higher education are not included in *Education and Research*. You already paid for public education student tuition—and a lot of other services—when you paid your personal tax and nontax payments to the government.

*Net foreign travel* is unique among the product categories shown in Exhibit 3.3 in that the amount is negative for 1999. Expenditures in the United States by nonresidents exceeded the amount U.S. citizens spent on travel abroad.

### Amassing Personal Consumption Expenditures Information

Before turning our attention briefly to the other two components of personal outlays, consideration of the manner in which the BEA goes about obtaining all the detail for personal consumption expenditures seems in order. Personal consumption expenditures in 1999 accounted for $6.3 trillion of $7.8 trillion of personal income. The aggregate is broken down into hundreds of different commodity and service groups, and yet the BEA does not intrude into our lives gathering the information. How does it accomplish that feat?

To assemble personal consumption expenditures in such detail, information from a multitude of government agencies and sources outside the public sector is required. Statistical reports from the Census Bureau provide sales data, cost of purchased goods for manufacturing and trade, and service industry receipts and expenses. Other government agencies report on such items as sales of electricity and fuel oil, receipts and expenses for higher education, prices paid by consumers, merchandise trade, and revenue from transportation services. Private sector sources cover such items as sales to persons of motor vehicles, tires, drugs, natural gas, gasoline and oil, water and sanitation services, transit service, brokerage and investment counseling, fabrics and yarn, expenses for life insurance, premiums and benefits for life insurance, and hospital and religious institutions' receipts and expenses.[8]

A complete assembly of data occurs only about every five years. Those "benchmark" years currently occur on those years ending in "2" or "7." On those years the Census Bureau conducts economic censuses that provide extensive data on agriculture, mining, construction, manufactured items, wholesale trade, retail trade, and on transportation and service industries. From those data the BEA develops input-output tables that show how much of each industry's output is used by other industries as input to produce their outputs, how much is exported, and how much is purchased by state and local governments and by consumers.[9]

For the years in between, the following data are missing for many of the commodities included in personal consumption expenditures:

- Detailed commodity shipments, revenues, and receipts that serve as a basis for identifying commodities purchased by persons and the amounts produced;
- Sales of wholesalers and retailers by merchandise line that enable converting establishment-industry data to a commodity basis; and
- Materials purchased by mineral, construction, and manufacturing establishments used to calculate the residual purchased by persons.

However, some commodities in personal consumption expenditures are purchased only by persons. Those commodities include:

- Food furnished employees (including military),
- Food produced and consumed on farms,
- Standard clothing issued military personnel,
- Rental value of owner- and tenant- occupied dwellings,
- Expenses of handling life insurance,
- Personal remittances in kind to foreigners,
- Expenditures abroad by U.S. residents,
- Expenditures in the U.S. by foreigners,
- Health insurance,
- Motor vehicles,
- Gasoline and oil,
- Tobacco products,
- Computers and peripheral equipment, and
- Reimbursement for government employee use of own motor vehicles.

For other commodities not limited to purchases only by persons, detailed information is available on an annual basis.

Estimates for all those items—many of which are imputed—are estimated directly on an annual basis, using a variety of source data. The last item on the list—reimbursement for government employee use of own motor vehicles—does not appear as an item on the list of personal consumption expenditures; it is recorded as a negative entry to purchases of used automobiles that offsets a positive entry for government purchases elsewhere in the NIPA.

Assembling personal consumption expenditures for many of the other commodities requires use of an estimating technique called the "retail-control method." From such sources as Census Bureau annual surveys of retail store sales, Federal Reserve Board data on retail sales of department stores, and trade association reports on their industry's receipts, estimates of expenditure by groups of businesses are obtained. Those totals then are distributed to commodities based on the proportions observed in the most recent Census Bureau economic census. The accuracy of such calculations depends on the validity of the assumption that those proportions remain constant over time.

Although long, the story about where the BEA obtains its data and how it puts them together to form personal consumption expenditures and personal income is far from finished. Annual estimates of personal income are published within a month after the end of the year. Those "advance" estimates are replaced with "preliminary" and "final" estimates in the following two months. But "final" is not final. Annual revisions of the NIPA usually occur each summer and cover the most recent year and the preceding two years. Every five years or so, comprehensive revisions of definitions, classifications, statistical methods, and the way the information is presented take place and result in further changes. As the preceding description indicates, our personal income figure of $7,789.6 billion is not an absolute measure; it's just an indicator subject to better information and methodologies.

### Interest Paid by Persons

People borrow money. When they do they are expected to pay the lender interest until they repay the principal amount. The category *Interest paid by persons* includes all interest paid by persons except mortgage interest. Mortgage interest is reflected in the rental income of persons.[10] If mortgage interest were included, the $194.8 billion figure shown in Exhibit 3.1 for *Interest paid by persons* would equal $495.1 billion.

### Personal Transfer Payments to the Rest of the World

At $26.6 billion *Transfer payments* to the rest of the world constitutes the smallest component of personal outlays in Exhibit 3.1. It represents personal remittances in cash and in kind to the rest of the world less such remittances from the rest of the world.[11]

## PERSONAL SAVING

Third, last, and least among the three components of outlays of personal income is *Personal saving*. Personal income minus personal tax and nontax payments and minus personal outlays consisting of personal consumption expenditures, interest paid by persons, and personal transfer payments to the rest of the world determines personal saving. Reference to Exhibit 3.1 shows that it amounts to $147.6 billion, 2 percent of personal income. What individuals think they save in the aggregate and what the BEA estimates as personal saving differ as a result of imputations. National statistics include the current saving of persons, private institutions serving primarily persons, life insurance companies, private noninsured welfare funds, and private trust funds.[12]

Although numerically small, personal saving manifests an economically significant phenomenon. No greater luxury exists than saving. For those who save it indicates that their immediate wants and needs are satisfied, that their means exceed their cravings. In a secular sense it represents satisfaction and contentment.

### Savers and Dissavers

Not everyone saves. Some people behave as if their cravings are limited; they are the savers. Others behave as if their cravings are immediate and inexhaustible. Their consumption expenditures exceed their income; they dissave. Some people with low incomes save; others with higher incomes borrow. People in identical circumstances with respect to possessions, wealth, and income differ in their saving habits. That difference is attributed to differences in their rates of time preference. Some people discount the future very heavily. They value consumption at some point of time in the future very little. They want satisfaction of their wants and needs now! Others value deferred consumption more highly and are said to have a lower rate of time preference.

Of course, an individual's rate of time preference changes with changing circumstances. Individuals of advanced age may avoid buying green bananas and eat dessert first at their meals. Prospects for future enjoyment in this world may seem rather uncertain. On the other hand, a younger person confident of many tomorrows may find postponing consumption a more reasonable proposition. Expectations of stability tend to lower rates of time preference and increase saving. What is true for individuals extends to groups. A society under threat of invasion and determined to resist will consume more than it produces—draw on prior accumulations of saving—as part of an all out defense effort. Impending catastrophe does not encourage thrift. Under threat of bankruptcy, frugality often does not characterize a firm's actions (especially by its management).

Despite all those differences in behavior, patterns of saving do show an orderly behavior. Generally speaking, those with high incomes save and save more than those with low incomes. Satisfying immediate needs is easier when possessing the means to acquire them. A higher income offers more opportunity for greater saving than a lower one.

### Accounting for the Effects of Saving

Saving may appear as a residual: what is left over after subtracting from personal income personal tax and nontax payments and outlays for personal consumption expenditures, interest payments, and transfers to the rest of the world. However, visualizing saving as a passive process consisting of wallet and coin purse leftovers misrepresents the reality. Saving entails action just as much as paying taxes and buying things. People choose to save and then as a result of those choices must decide the form saving will take.

When persons save, what they own (assets) increases and/or what they owe (liabilities) decreases. The difference between their assets and their liabilities constitutes their net worth (wealth). And their change in wealth over a fixed period of time is equivalent to saving—the difference between income and disbursements. So it is that the flow concepts of income, disbursements, and saving—which are defined over a specified period of time—are related to assets, liabilities, and wealth—stock concepts that exist at particular moments of time.

The relationship can be summarized in a series of simple equations. If we let

$Y$ represent income;
$T$ tax and nontax payments;
$C$ outlays for personal consumption expenditures, interest payments, and transfers to the rest of the world; and
$S$ savings,

then

$$S = Y - T - C.$$

Assets can be divided into two broad categories: financial assets—such things as currency and coin, checking and savings deposits, bonds, and common stocks—and tangible assets—automobiles, houses, buildings, machinery, equipment. Total assets equal liabilities plus wealth (or net worth). If we let

$FA$ for financial assets,
$TA$ for tangible assets,
$L$ for liabilities, and
$W$ for wealth,

we have

$$FA + TA = L + W$$

or expressing the relationship for wealth

$$W = FA + TA - L.$$

Since saving equals a change in wealth,

$$Y - T - C = S = \Delta W = \Delta FA + \Delta TA - \Delta L$$

where $\Delta$ represents "change in."

Exhibit 3.1 shows that in 1999 *Personal saving* amounted to $147.6 billion. Alternatively, one could say that personal wealth increased by that amount and then ask what effect the increase had on the holdings of financial and tangible assets of persons and their liabilities. The NIPA, however, are concerned with the output of goods and services and flows of income and disbursements. To answer questions about changes in assets and liabilities, we must look elsewhere.

### Flow-of-Funds Accounts

The Board of Governors of the Federal Reserve System compiles the flow-of-funds accounts of the United States that

> measure acquisition of physical and financial assets through the U.S. economy and the sources of funds used to acquire the assets. . . . The accounts encompass all net changes in financial claims or liabilities resulting from (1) current transactions in the economy, (2) the allocation of saving between investment in physical capital and investment in financial capital, and (3) decisions to change the composition of financial assets and liabilities.[13]

Happily, the data prepared by the Board of Governors are consistent not only internally but also with the NIPA published by the BEA.

Although the two accounting systems are consistent, certain differences in treatment affect the reconciliation of personal saving between them.

- Flow of funds considers household purchases of durable goods as expenditure for capital assets. The NIPA treats them as personal consumption expenditures even though durable goods—such as automobiles and household appliances—in most instances have useful lives of three or more years. The Federal Reserve takes a different tack and recognizes the durability of durable goods.
- Flow of funds treats wage accruals as part of the statistical discrepancy; NIPA records wage accruals explicitly.
- Flow of funds attributes ownership of government insurance and pension fund balances to households and individuals; the NIPA assigns them to the government sector.

Other differences in practice between the two accounting systems exist but do not involve reconciliation of personal saving. To this taxpayer any such differences between the two accounting systems appear likely to render more harm than good to the general welfare and understanding of economic relationships. Both systems attempt to estimate accurately different aspects of the same economic reality. The NIPA are akin to a statement of earnings in business accounting; flow-of-funds accounting relates to a balance sheet. Since construction of both is based on adoption of a standard set of conventions, no law of nature would be violated if common practices applied to each of them. Fortunately, from the information available, adjustments can be made to align the two systems. Without regard to the merit of the alternative practices, I have chosen to adapt flow-of-funds data to NIPA data rather than vice versa.

### Access to Flow-of-Funds Data

Work on flow-of-funds data began in 1947. Annual data were first published in 1955; quarterly data appeared first in August 1959. The Board of Governors of the Federal Reserve System—or rather their minions—draw flow-of-funds data from a wide variety of public and private reports and publications. Some of those sources are available only annually, requiring interpolation for quarterly data. Benchmark revisions are issued annually, usually in September.

**Exhibit 3.4**
**Personal Saving and Investment, 1999**

| | | | **1999 Amounts in $ Billions** | | | **Percent of Total** |
|---|---|---|---|---|---|---|
| **PERSONAL SAVING** | | | **$ 147.5** | | | **20** |
| Change in liabilities | | | 622.2 | | | 83 |
| Discrepancy | | | (19.6) | | | (3) |
| Gov't insur & pension fund adjustment | | | 3.8 | | | 1 |
| **CHANGE IN WEALTH & LIABILITIES** | | | **$ 754.0** | | | **100** |
| Change in Financial Assets | | | 491.7 | | | 65 |
| Change in Tangible Assets (Investment) | | | 262.4 | | | 35 |
| Capital expenditures | | 408.1 | | | 54 | |
| Residential | $ 349.4 | | | 46 | | |
| Nonprofit institutions | 58.7 | | | 8 | | |
| Consumption of fixed capital | | (145.7) | | | (19) | |
| Residential | $(111.7) | | | (15) | | |
| Nonprofit institutions | (34.0) | | | (5) | | |
| **CHANGE IN TOTAL ASSETS** | | | **$ 754.0** | | | **100** |

*Source* : Board of Governors, Federal Reserve System. "Z.1 Historical data." *Flow of Funds Accounts of the United States* . 15 Sep. 2000: Tables F.9 and F.100. 18 Sep. 2000. <http://www.bog.frb.us/releases/z1/current/data.htm>

Today, flow-of-funds data regularly appear in publications of the Board of Governors of the Federal Reserve System. Some information can be accessed from its Internet site *<http://www.federalreserve.gov/>*. The BEA also participates in disseminating flow-of-funds information. Both the Federal Reserve Web site and the Department of Commerce's STAT-USA contain historical data in machine-readable form.

### Saving and Flow-of-Funds Data for 1999

Changes in assets and liabilities that accompanied personal saving of households and nonprofit institutions primarily serving persons from the beginning to the end of 1999 appear in Exhibit 3.4. We begin with *Personal saving*, $147.5 billion.

Although in the aggregate households and nonprofit institutions saved, they also increased their liabilities. The *Change in liabilities* for 1999 amounted to $622.2 billion. Before adding saving (or change in wealth) to liabilities, we have to allow for errors and omissions in data sources. Flow-of-funds account data have to recognize a discrepancy relating to the household and nonprofit institution sector. The adjusting entry for *Discrepancy*, $19.6 billion, is a negative number. In addition, the *Government insurance and pension funds* of government employees are attributed to persons rather than to the governments under the flow-of-funds accounts conventions. That adjustment, $3.8 billion, is added to the sum of *Personal saving*, *Change in liabilities* and the *Discrepancy*. This arithmetic feat produces total *Change in wealth and liabilities* of $754.0 billion.

As Exhibit 3.4 shows, the total of changes in wealth and liabilities is accompanied by an equal total of changes in financial and tangible assets. Financial assets increased by $491.7 billion, and tangible assets increased by $262.4 billion. Households and nonprofit institutions expenditures for residential construction, plant, and equipment amounted to $408.1 billion—more than the *Change in tangible assets (Investment)*. The *Change in tangible assets* is shown net of *Consumption of fixed capital*, $145.7 billion. Note that the term "investment" is attached to the change in tangible assets. Individuals invest in both financial and tangible assets. Economists use the term "invest" in a more restrictive way, limiting it to acquisition of producers' plant and equipment and residential housing.

### A Balance Sheet for Households and Nonprofit Institutions

Exhibit 3.4 shows how aggregate financial and tangible assets change with liabilities and net worth. Changes in components of assets and liabilities represent changes to the balance sheet for households and nonprofit organizations during a quarter or a year, but they do not tell us what holdings existed at the beginning or end of a period. The Federal Reserve System provides that information on its Web site in connection with Z.1 releases of flow-of-funds data. A slightly abbreviated version of the information available in August 1999 appears in Exhibit 3.5. Since the balance sheet represents an estimate at a particular point in time—the end of the 1999 calendar year—reconciliation with the NIPA is neither conceptually nor practically possible. Consequently, no adjustments are made to the flow-of-funds data for differences between the two accounting systems.

*Assets. Total assets* held by households and nonprofit organizations amount to $49.2 trillion for yearend 1999. *Financial assets* at $35.3 trillion account for 72 percent of the total and are divided into three categories:

- Cash and cash equivalents,
- Credit market instruments, and
- Market-valued and other financial assets.

The third category, by far the largest at $28.8 trillion—58 percent of total assets, consists mostly of corporate stocks. The market value of corporate stocks comprises the $8.5 trillion in *Corporate equities* directly held by persons and nonprofit organizations. Corporate stocks are held indirectly through *Mutual fund shares*, *Life insurance reserves*, *Pension fund reserves*, and *Investment in bank personal trusts* and comprise a major portion of the $28.8 trillion in those assets. The value assigned to ownership of noncorporate business, farm business, and unincorporated security brokers and dealers constitutes the $4.6 trillion in *Equity in noncorporate business*. Security credit is included among the $0.7 trillion of *Other financial assets*.

Most liquid among the three categories is *Cash and cash equivalents*. In fact, included in its $4.2 trillion is $0.5 trillion of *Currency, checkable deposits, and other*. Money! Households settle virtually all market transactions with money even though it constitutes only 1 percent of their total assets. As we saw in Exhibit 3.1, personal income—and, therefore, its disposition—excluding imputations amounted to $7.8 trillion in 1999. That $0.5 trillion in checkable deposits and currency is kept busy clearing all those transactions.

Despite its importance for clearing transactions, money is not a very popular asset to hold since it earns little or no return. In times of rapid price inflation, the return on money can be negative as its purchasing value deteriorates. *Time and savings deposits* typically earn a higher interest return while offering the advantage of being readily convertible to money. Those advantages explain the willingness of households and nonprofit organizations to hold greater amounts of them, $2.9 trillion. *Money market fund shares*, $0.8 trillion, usually offer even higher returns, but their convertibility to money can be less convenient.

*Cash and cash equivalents* constitute 9 percent of total assets. *Credit market instruments*, at $2.4 trillion, account for around 5 percent. When issued, the rate of return on those assets typically exceeds those of income-earning time and saving deposits and money market fund shares. Between time of issue and time of maturity, credit market instruments can be converted to money but subject holders to market risk. Sellers may receive more or less than the amount paid for them. They also subject holders to default risk. An issuer may be unable to pay interest or the maturity value when due. *U.S. Government securities*—at $0.9 trillion—outdistance each of *Municipal securities* and *Corporate and foreign bonds* and are considered to be free of default risk by virtue of the government's ability to issue currency and coin—noninterest-bearing forms of debt. In time of rapid price inflation, that virtue can become a vice.

The replacement value of all the houses compacted in cities, sprawling across suburbs, and dotting the rural landscape—all the appliances and furnishing that fill them—all the automobiles and pickup trucks and vans and recreational vehicles that congest highways and byways—are embodied in the $13.8 trillion figure for *Tangible assets*. They are what you get for $13.8 trillion. Things for hurricanes and tornadoes to blow away, earthquakes to shake, and fires to burn plus traffic jams. Real estate holdings and equipment of nonprofit organizations contribute only $1.1 trillion to *Tangible assets*' $13.8 trillion total. Since the $13.8 trillion are based on flow-of-funds data rather than the NIPA, they represent their replacement value. Of the $13.8 trillion in *Tangible assets*,

**Exhibit 3.5**
**Balance Sheet of Households and Nonprofit Organizations, 1999**

| | 1999 Amounts in $ Trillions | | Percent of Total | |
|---|---|---|---|---|
| **Financial assets** | | **$ 35.3** | | **72** |
| Cash and cash equivalents | | 4.2 | | 9 |
| Currency, checkable deposits & other | $ 0.5 | | 1 | |
| Time & savings deposits | 2.9 | | 6 | |
| Money market fund shares | 0.8 | | 2 | |
| Credit market instruments | | 2.4 | | 5 |
| U.S. Government securities | $ 0.9 | | 2 | |
| Municipal securities | 0.5 | | 1 | |
| Corporate & foreign bonds | 0.7 | | 1 | |
| Other credit market instruments | 0.2 | | 0 | |
| Market-valued & other financial instruments | | 28.8 | | 58 |
| Corporate equities | $ 8.5 | | 17 | |
| Mutual fund shares | 3.0 | | 6 | |
| Life insurance reserves | 0.8 | | 2 | |
| Pension fund reserves | 10.0 | | 20 | |
| Investment in bank personal trusts | 1.1 | | 2 | |
| Equity in noncorporate business | 4.6 | | 9 | |
| Other financial assets | 0.7 | | 1 | |
| **Tangible assets** | | **13.8** | | **28** |
| Real estate | | 11.1 | | 23 |
| Households | $10.0 | | 20 | |
| Nonprofit organizations | 1.1 | | 2 | |
| Consumer durable goods & equipment | | 2.7 | | 5 |
| **TOTAL ASSETS, LIABILITIES & NET WORTH** | | **$ 49.2** | | **100** |
| **Liabilities** | | **6.8** | | **14** |
| Home mortgages | 4.5 | | 9 | |
| Consumer credit | 1.4 | | 3 | |
| Other liabilities | 0.9 | | 2 | |
| **Net Worth** | | **42.3** | | **86** |

*Source*: Board of Governors, Federal Reserve System. "Z.1 Historical data." *Flow of Funds Accounts of the United States*. 15 Sep. 2000: Tables B.100. 18 Sep. 2000. <http://www.bog.frb.us/releases/z1/current/data.htm>

*Consumer durable goods and equipment* make up $2.7 trillion—5 percent of total assets held by households and nonprofit organizations.

*Liabilities and net worth.* Liabilities and net worth equal total assets, $49.2 trillion. *Net worth*, at $42.3 trillion and accounting for 86 percent of the total, represents the wealth of households and nonprofit organizations. *Liabilities*, at $6.8 trillion, make up the rest. *Cash and cash equivalents* plus *Credit market instruments* together, about $6.6 trillion, come close to *Liabilities*. The highly liquid financial assets held by households and nonprofit organizations could almost pay off all that they owe. However, because the households and nonprofit organizations holding the assets are not the same ones that have incurred the debt, paying off the debt is unlikely to occur. The devil is in the details.

Most of the liabilities take the form of *Home mortgages* and *Consumer credit*—long- and short-term forms of debt, respectively. Together they amount to nearly $5.9 trillion of the $6.8 trillion. Many of the houses and consumer durable goods owe their existence to those two credit instruments. *Other liabilities* comprising the debt of households and nonprofit organizations include municipal securities and commercial mortgages of nonprofit organizations, bank loans other than home mortgages and consumer credit, other loans and advances, trade payables of nonprofit organizations, security credit, and deferred and unpaid life insurance premiums.

## CONCLUSION

In chapter 2 we examined the sources of $7.8 billion in personal income. In this chapter we have looked at how that $7.8 trillion of income is used. In 1999 most of it—80 percent—is used for personal consumption expenditures—purchases of durable and nondurable goods and services. Tax and nontax payments to the federal government and to state and local governments take care of another 15 percent. Those involuntary payments are made in addition to contributions for social insurance that are recorded as deductions from personal income. The 5 percent remaining goes to interest payments, remittances of transfers to residents of foreign countries, and saving.

A closer look at the phenomenon of saving led us to an examination of flow-of-funds data published by the Board of Governors of the Federal Reserve System. That information shows the interplay of financial flows, of capital expenditures for residential construction, plant, and equipment, and of wealth formation. Saving and an increase in wealth or net worth are synonymous. They occur when current income exceeds current expenditures. Alternatively, we could say that they occur when changes in assets (both financial and tangible) exceed changes in liabilities.

Assets and liabilities are balance sheet concepts. Unlike income and expenditure, they deal with stocks existing at points in time rather than flows through time. A look at the 1999 balance sheet for households and nonprofit organizations shows that claims against others—financial assets—constitute over 70 percent of total asset holdings. With the current value of physical assets—real estate, plant and equipment of nonprofit organizations, and consumer durable goods—total assets of households and nonprofit organizations amount to over $49 trillion. On the other side of the balance sheet, liabilities comprise about one-seventh of the $49 trillion total. The rest, over $42.3 trillion in 1999, represents the net worth or wealth of households and nonprofit organizations.

That net worth represents an accumulation of saving year by year. If annual saving had occurred at the 1999 rate of $147.5 billion, around 286 years would be required to accumulate $42.3 trillion. That takes us back to around 1713. However, the rate has been neither that large nor constant. Accumulation of $42.3 trillion in net worth dates back to the dawn of time.

Tracing wealth accumulation back to its origins appears a bit too ambitious. But we are about to examine what has happened to personal income and its uses over the past forty years.

## NOTES

1. Benjamin Franklin, "Letter to Jean Baptiste LeRoy" (13 Nov. 1789), *The Writings of Benjamin Franklin*, vol. 10, ed. Albert Henry Smyth (New York: Macmillan Co., 1907) 68–69.

2. Brent R. Moulton, Robert P. Parker, and Eugene Seskin, "A Preview of the 1999 Comprehensive Revision of the National Income and Product Accounts: Definitional and Classificational Changes," *Survey of Current Business* 79-8 (August 1999): 13.

3. U.S. Department of Commerce, Bureau of Economic Analysis, "'Annual Only' NIPA Tables," *National Accounts Data*, 30 Aug 2000: Table 8.29, 5 Sep. 2000 <http://www.bea.doc.gov/bea/dn1.htm>.

4. U.S. Department of Commerce, Bureau of Economic Analysis, *National Income and Product Accounts of the United States, 1929–94*, vol. 1 (Washington, DC: U.S. Government Printing Office, April 1998) M-9.

5. James Otis, *The Rights of the British Colonies Asserted and Proved* (Boston: Edes and Gill, 1764): p. 55, American Antiquarian Society, *Early American Imprints, First Series* (Worcester, Massachusetts, 1955–83): Microopaque number 9773. The sound bite, "No taxation without representation," generally is attributed to James Otis; however, he took eighty pages to make his case and even then didn't use the famous phrase. Before television the thought rather than a clever use of words evidently counted.

6. U.S. Department of Commerce, Bureau of Economic Analysis, *Personal Income Expenditures*, Methodology Paper Series Number 6 (Washington, DC: U.S. Government Printing Office, 1990) 6.

7. *Personal Income Expenditures* 4–5.

8. *Personal Income Expenditures* 4–5.

9. U.S. Department of Commerce, Bureau of Economic Analysis, *GNP: An Overview of Source Data and Estimating Methods*, Methodology Paper No. 4 (Washington, DC: U.S. Government Printing Office, Sep. 1987) 7.

10. *National Income and Product Accounts of the United States* M-8.

11. *National Income and Product Accounts of the United States* M-9.

12. *National Income and Product Accounts of the United States* M-9.

13. Board of Governors of the Federal Reserve System, *Guide to the Flow of Funds Accounts* (Washington, DC: Board of Governors of the Federal Reserve System, 1993) 7.

# 4

# Personal Income in Space and Time

Chapters 2 and 3 provided us with snapshots of personal income for a particular year. But national income and product statistics date back to 1929 and are prepared not only annually but also monthly and quarterly. In this chapter we will explore the time dimension of personal income and examine what has happened to it during the forty-year period from 1959 to 1999.

Our exploration of the time dimension of sources of personal income will show that while all components have increased, some have increased more than others. Growth in other labor income, transfer payments, and personal contributions for social insurance has been particularly rapid, leading us to examine some of the causes behind the numbers. How personal income is distributed geographically throughout the United States receives attention. For that investigation we the use personal income statistics prepared for each state in the aggregate and on a per capita basis. That examination leads to curiosity about the distribution of income among persons. To address that issue we have to step outside the national income and product accounts (NIPA) and turn to other data sources.

## SOURCES OF PERSONAL INCOME OVER TIME

While we may not expect personal income to change for any given year—although revisions often cause changes—we certainly expect it to change from year to year. Exhibit 2.1 provided us with a display of the sources of personal income in 1999. Exhibit 4.1 displays the same information along with personal income for 1959—forty years prior. A mere glance reveals that the figures for 1959 are much, much smaller than for 1999. *Personal income* in 1959 is a little more than one-twentieth of 1999's figure—a "mere" $394 billion compared with $7.8 trillion. Given such differences in magnitude, comparison of amounts is not going to be particularly informative.

**Exhibit 4.1**

**Personal Income, 1959 and 1999**

| | **1959 Amounts in $ Billions** | **Percent of Total** | **1999 Amounts in $ Billions** | **Percent of Total** | **Annual Percent Change** |
|---|---|---|---|---|---|
| Wage and salary disbursements | $ 259.8 | 66 | $ 4,470.0 | 57 | 7 |
| Other labor income | 13.4 | 3 | 501.0 | 6 | 9 |
| Proprietors' income with IVA and CCAdj | 51.8 | 13 | 663.5 | 9 | 7 |
| Rental income of persons with capital consumption adjustment | 15.2 | 4 | 143.4 | 2 | 6 |
| Personal dividend income | 12.6 | 3 | 370.3 | 5 | 9 |
| Personal interest income | 23.0 | 6 | 963.7 | 12 | 10 |
| Transfer payments to persons | 24.2 | 6 | 1,016.2 | 13 | 10 |
| Personal contributions for social insurance | (6.0) | (2) | (338.5) | (4) | 11 |
| **TOTAL PERSONAL INCOME** | **$ 394.0** | **100** | **$ 7,789.6** | **100** | **8** |

* IVA: Inventory valuation adjustment; CCAdj: Capital consumption adjustment.

*Source* : U.S. Department of Commerce. Bureau of Economic Analysis. "Selected NIPA Tables." *National Accounts Data* . 8 Aug. 2000: Table 2.1. 9 Sep. 2000. <http://www.bea.doc.gov/bea/dn1.htm>.

Comparison of the components of personal income for the two years on the basis of their percents of total offers a more promising approach. On that basis careful inspection reveals certain similarities and some differences worthy of comment. For both of the two years, *Wages and salary disbursements* constitute the largest component of the total; however, their relative importance has declined. In 1959 they accounted for 66 percent of total personal income; in 1999, 57 percent. *Proprietors' income* was relatively much more important as a source of personal income in 1959 than in 1999, having shrunk from 13 to 9 percent of the total. Is twilight falling on the small, independent businessperson? Another relative loser, *Rental income of persons*, declined from 4 to 2 percent.

As those three items have declined in relative size, the others have increased. *Other labor income* rose from 3 to 6 percent of the total. *Personal dividend* income shows a relative increase from 3 to 5 percent. The relative share of *Personal interest income* grew from 6 to 12 percent. The remaining two items—*Transfer payments to persons*, and *Personal contributions for social insurance*—grew significantly. For each of them their percents of the total more than doubled over the forty-year period.

Behind those changes in percentages relative to total personal income lie interesting tales.

## Accounting for Growth

Why did the percentages of some of the components of personal income relative to the total increase and others decline? An answer that begs the question but nevertheless deserves attention is that some components grew faster than others. And how can we measure growth over a forty-year period?

If measuring growth in total personal income is our objective, we can observe that total personal income has grown in forty years from $394.4 billion to $7,789.6 billion—an increase of $7,395.2 billion. One could say that growth averaged $185 billion a year. However, that approach does not do a very good job of describing what happened between 1959 and 1999. For the first ten years, from 1959 to 1960, actual growth per year averaged $39 billion a year, far short of the $185 billion. In the last ten years, actual growth averaged $319 billion annually, substantially more. Alas, not everything in the world is linear. A linear approach may provide satisfactory approximations over short intervals, but it clearly does not work very well over an extended time period.

Since a linear approach is unsatisfactory in this situation, we are driven to a somewhat more complicated exponential approach to growth measurement. An exponential approach is commonly encountered when calculating compound growth rates or compound interest rates.

How do you compute these rates? That question is best answered first by an illustration. Assume you invest $1,000 in a five-year certificate of deposit that earns 5 percent and that the interest earnings are automatically reinvested at the end of each year. At the end of the first year you will have

$$\$1{,}000 + \$1{,}000 \cdot 0.05 = \$1{,}000 \cdot (1 + 0.05) = \$1{,}000 \cdot (1.05).$$
$$= \$1{,}050.$$

At the end of the second year, you will have

$$\$1{,}050 + \$1{,}050 \cdot 0.05 = \$1{,}050 \cdot (1 + 0.05) = \$1{,}050 \cdot (1.05)$$
$$= \$1{,}102.50.$$

But

$$\$1{,}050 = \$1{,}000 \cdot (1.05)$$

So we have

$$\$1{,}050 \cdot (1.05) = \$1{,}000 \cdot (1.05) \cdot (1.05) = \$1{,}000 \cdot (1.05)^2.$$

For the end of the third year, the amount will be

$$\$1{,}000 \cdot (1.05)^3.$$

And so on until at the end of the fifth year the proceeds will be

$$\$1{,}000 \cdot (1.05)^5 = \$1{,}276.28.$$

Now suppose at the end of the five-year period you receive the \$1,276.28 and remember that you initially bought the certificate of deposit for \$1,000 but forget the rate of interest. You can state the result as

$$\$1{,}000 \cdot (1 + i)^5 = \$1{,}276.28$$

And solve for $i$

$$i = \sqrt[5]{\frac{1{,}276}{1{,}000}} - 1 = 0.05.$$

The average annual compound rate of interest in your certificate of deposit is 5 percent.

### Average Annual Growth Rate

We have not yet commented on the column labeled "Annual Percent Change" in Exhibit 4.1. Figures in that column describe with a single number the compound rate of increase that has characterized personal income and each of its components during the forty-year period.

Calculating those growth rates follows a pattern similar to that for calculating average annual compound rates of interest. For each of the items, its 1959 figure replaces the 1,000 in the denominator; its 1999 figure, the numerator; and 5 over the radical sign is replaced with forty. Of course, rearranging the numbers does not produce a solution, but thanks to calculators and computers, what formerly was a chore involving tables of logarithms now can be accomplished quite easily. The application of all that electronic activity produces the results appearing in the last column of Exhibit 4.1.

Total personal income increased at an average compound rate of 8 percent per year. Three of the eight sources of personal income did not maintain their 8 percent pace of increase: *Wages and salaries*, *Proprietors' income*, and *Rental income of persons*. Thus their shares of the total declined by the end of the forty-year period. The others, with growth rates greater than 8 percent, increased their shares. Three components of personal income:

- Personal interest income,
- Transfer payments to persons, and
- Personal contributions for social insurance

showed particularly robust growth averaging a compound rate of 10 percent or more per year.

### Accounting for Differences in Growth Rates

Mathematics invariably provides a self-contained answer for the changes in shares; however, it does not tell us what happened during the forty years to account for the differences. That kind of explanation will require examining the various components. Three components in particular will engage our attention: *Other labor income*, *Transfer payments to persons*, and *Personal contributions for social insurance*. Their rise in importance is a product of political rather than economic forces, and their rapid expansion suggests that behind each lies an exciting tale and ahead of each a day of reckoning.

*Other labor income*. As presented in Exhibit 4.1, other labor income shows an annual 9 percent growth rate over forty years. What has caused it to grow so rapidly? Exhibit 2.3 provided a breakdown of the components of other income for 1999. Exhibit 4.2 adds 1959 data to that display.

*Group health insurance*, in 1959 already the second largest component of employer contributions after *Pension and profit-sharing funds* and accounting for 23 percent of total other income, has grown at an astounding 12 percent per year over forty years. By 1999 *Group health insurance* accounts for 56 percent of the total. Its overwhelming growth has reduced the relative importance of all other components except for the *Government employees retirement fund*. Government contributions to publicly administered government employee retirement plans have held their own. With a 9 percent average annual increase, their percentage of the total has been maintained at 22 percent of *Other labor income*.

How is it that group health care insurance has become such an important part of other labor income? History provides an important perspective. It shows that a series of events often cascade from an incident little noticed at the time of its occurrence. If the federal government had adopted a different course, the phenomenon we observe with respect to other labor income might not have happened.

Scientific advances in the first quarter of the twentieth century led to improved medical care, greater reliance on hospitals to deliver technologically advanced treatments, and rising costs for patients. The Great Depression brought

**Exhibit 4.2**

**Other Labor Income, 1959 and 1999**

| | 1959 Amounts in $ Billions | Percent of Total | 1999 Amounts in $ Billions | Percent of Total | Annual Percent Change |
|---|---|---|---|---|---|
| **Employer Contributions** | **$ 13.3** | **100** | **$ 498.0** | **99** | **9** |
| Pension and profit-sharing funds | 4.8 | 36 | 60.4 | 12 | 7 |
| Government employees retirement funds | 3.0 | 22 | 109.2 | 22 | 9 |
| Private welfare funds | 5.6 | 42 | 328.4 | 66 | 11 |
| Group health insurance | $3.0 | 23 | $280.2 | 56 | 12 |
| Group life insurance | 1.0 | 7 | 11.8 | 2 | 6 |
| Workers' compensation | 1.4 | 11 | 34.5 | 7 | 8 |
| Supplemental unemployment | 0.1 | 1 | 1.9 | 0 | 7 |
| **Other** | **0.0** | **0** | **3.0** | **1** | **12** |
| **TOTAL OTHER INCOME** | **$ 13.4** | **100** | **$ 501.0** | **100** | **9** |

*Source*: U.S. Department of Commerce. Bureau of Economic Analysis. "'Annual Only' NIPA Tables." *National Accounts Data*. 30 Aug 2000: Table 6.11. 5 Sep. 2000 <http://www.bea.doc.gov/bea/dn1.htm>.

about a crisis for health care providers—as well as for a lot of other people. Hospitals and physicians found revenues dropping as patients no longer were able to afford the cost of treatment. The American Hospital Association responded with the formation of a nonprofit prepay plan called Blue Cross. The American Medical Association followed with Blue Shield. By enabling individuals and households to more easily afford their medical bills, the plans helped restore patient revenues, providing income security to health care providers and expense security for their customers. By the end of the 1930s, commercial indemnity insurance developed to supplement Blue Cross and Blue Shield. The next twenty years saw a rapid expansion of private medical insurance. But not without help from the federal government.

Circumstances during World War II played a role. Wage and price controls made life difficult for employers. Raising salaries to attract and retain employees in a time of labor shortage was not an option:

> Enter Henry Kaiser, whose West Coast armaments plants were losing key staff. Unable to offer pay increases, Kaiser asked the government to allow him to provide health care to his employees without taxing it as employee income. Eager to keep the Kaiser plants rolling, the government approved the request on an "experimental, temporary" basis. Not surprisingly, tax-free health benefits soon became universal and permanent, and the Kaiser loophole metastasized into Section 106 of the Internal Revenue Code.[1]

Today few question why employees are not taxed for employer-paid medical insurance premiums. What would have happened if the federal government had not granted that fateful exception? Would World War II have been lost? Does group health insurance inherently possess traits that naturally cause employees to prefer receiving their income in that form rather than cash over which they have discretion? Would medical care costs seem less like a "free" good if people paid for their insurance premiums with after-tax income?

The Internal Revenue Code goes to great lengths to insure that less obvious forms of personal income are fully taxed. An employee whose employer furnishes an automobile must keep meticulous records of its use for business and personal purposes to avoid possible intimidation by a zealous tax auditor. Distinction between personal and business expenses on travel arranged primarily for business purposes must be maintained. Nor are only white-collar employees subjected to such harassment. The Internal Revenue Service requires declaration of income received from tips by those performing well their generally menial service to others.

Because of the precedent and employer-paid premiums' peculiar exemption from personal income taxation, group health care insurance burgeoned, and third-party payment for medical services has become a norm. Under such a norm, usual market disciplines break down. Those who receive the service don't pay for it directly. Those who render the service and charge for it (the health care providers) and those who pay for it (the insurers) often have differing views on what the service is worth. Not being subject to customary budget constraints, the sick demand nothing but the best. With financing assured, health care providers are all too willing to provide it. It's like a smorgasbord: no one goes away hungry. All drinks are on the house; no one is left standing.

Those who would reform the health care system tend to overlook its supporting pillar: exemption of employer-paid medical insurance premiums. Elimination of tax breaks accorded employer-paid medical care insurance premiums accompanied by a corresponding reduction in overall tax rates is likely to result in a diminution of the dominance of group health insurance.[2] As employees made known their preferences, after-tax income would shift from a predetermined allocation for medical care to discretionary cash.

But that reform so far has not happened.

By 1960 medical insurance covered about 75 percent of the civilian population. Continuing sophistication of medical care caused costs to rise, and they in turn prompted increasing premiums. The percentage of those covered ceased to increase. The poor and the elderly were left without coverage. Then came the 1964 landslide victory of Lyndon B. Johnson as President of the United States, the Great Society program, and adoption of Medicare and Medicaid in 1965.[3] With the entry of those two programs on the national scene, the cost of health care skyrocketed. And so did group health insurance premiums as a component of other labor income. Once firms offered such programs to their employees, they were stuck with them and with largely involuntary increases in the cost of labor.

Employer contributions to group health insurance and government contributions to publicly administered employees retirement funds together have risen from 45 percent to 78 percent of other labor income. By 1999 the other five components are crowded into the remaining 22 percent.

*Transfer Payments to Persons.* The rate of growth in *Transfer payments to persons* has exceeded that of *Other labor income.* It has enjoyed a 10 percent average annual growth rate over the forty-year period. Exhibit 2.8 in chapter 2 showed us the composition of *Transfer payments to persons* in 1999. Exhibit 4.3 provides a somewhat different treatment and compares its composition in 1999 with 1959. When it comes to giving money away, government performance surpasses business by a wide margin. Government transfers to persons account for 95 percent of the $24.2 billion total in 1959 and 97 percent of the $1,016.2 billion total in 1999.

Transfers to persons from social insurance funds dominate the picture accounting for 62 percent of the total. With 42 percent of total transfers in 1959 and 37 percent in 1999, OASDI has increased at an annual growth rate of 9 percent and continues to constitute the largest single transfer payment; however, it has contenders in the high growth rate arena.

No percentage average annual rate of change is shown for *Hospital and supplementary medical insurance* (Medicare). It did not exist in 1959. Established in 1965, Medicare is a federal program for aged and disabled persons insured under the social security program. Since becoming operational in 1966, Medicare's benefit payments have expanded from nothing in 1959 to $208.1

**Exhibit 4.3**

**Transfer Payments to Persons, 1959 and 1999**

| | 1959 Amounts in $ Billions | Percent of Total | 1999 Amounts in $ Billions | Percent of Total | Annual Percent Change |
|---|---|---|---|---|---|
| **Social insurance funds** | **$ 15.0** | **62** | **$ 633.4** | **62** | **10** |
| Old-age, survivors, and disability insurance | $10.2 | 42 | $379.9 | 37 | 9 |
| Hospital & supplementary medical insurance | - | | 208.1 | 20 | |
| Other social insurance programs | 4.9 | 20 | 45.3 | 4 | 6 |
| **Veterans benefits** | **3.8** | **16** | **22.2** | **2** | **5** |
| **Public assistance programs** | **3.8** | **16** | **296.7** | **29** | **12** |
| Medical care | $ 0.5 | 2 | $189.0 | 19 | 16 |
| Other public assistance programs | 3.2 | 13 | 107.7 | 11 | 9 |
| **Other government transfers** | **0.4** | **2** | **34.1** | **3** | **12** |
| **Business transfers to persons** | **1.3** | **5** | **29.7** | **3** | **8** |
| **TRANSFER PAYMENTS TO PERSONS** | **$ 24.2** | **100** | **$ 1,016.2** | **100** | **10** |

*Source* : U.S. Department of Commerce. Bureau of Economic Analysis. "'Annual Only' NIPA Tables." *National Accounts Data* . 30 Aug 2000: Tables 3.12 and 8.16. 5 Sep. 2000. <http://www.bea.doc.gov/bea/dn1.htm>.

billion by the end of the period, enabling it to become the second largest single transfer payment at 20 percent of the total. Together, OASDI and Medicare transfer payments total $588.0 billion, of which over a third consists of Medicare payments. Considering that the old age, survivors, and disability insurance programs had a thirty-year head start, Medicare certainly has come a long way in a short period of time—both relatively and absolutely.

Medicare has a twin: Medicaid. It is included in *Medical care* under *Public assistance programs* in Exhibit 4.3. Although both Medicare and Medicaid share an enormous appetite for tax funds, they are not identical twins. Born at the same time in the federal government's fecund womb, Medicaid is not funded through the social security program. Feeding both from the same teat would produce an intolerable drain, an udder breakdown. With access to general revenue sources, Medicaid's $189.0 billion in transfer payments now ranks as the third largest transfer payment program, accounting for 19 percent of the total. It has become the largest program providing medical and health related services to the poor and covers eligible persons whose income and resources are limited.

In contrast to Medicare, an annual rate of growth of 16 percent from 1959 to 1999 appears in Exhibit 4.3 for *Medical care* (Medicaid). That is because states were already providing financial assistance for indigent medical care. Although born on the banks of the Potomac River, historical precedent explains why Medicaid is state administered and jointly funded by the federal government and the states. That a $1.5 billion expenditure by all states for indigent medical care in 1965 explains the administrative arrangement for $189.0 billion thirty-four years later shows that precedents can have a lot of leverage.

Although the Medicare and Medicaid programs started late, they got off to a robust start. In the thirty-three years from 1966 to 1999, they grew at an average annual rate of 16 percent. For the past ten years, however, growth rates have been constrained to the 9 to 10 percent range as managed care rationing helped contain costs.

Three programs—OASDI, Medicare, and Medicaid—account for 76 percent of all 1999 transfer payments—both government and business. For the other 24 percent, the list of programs is long and would be even longer when the "other" categories were broken out.

The growth in *Other social insurance programs* has been somewhat less robust, growing only at a 6 percent rate. As a result, its importance in the pantheon of government transfer programs (each sacred to someone) has declined from a magnificent 20 percent to a modest 4 percent. Included in that grouping are:

- Unemployment insurance,
- Railroad retirement,
- Pension benefit guarantee,
- Veterans life insurance,
- Military medical insurance,
- Workers' compensation, and
- Temporary disability insurance.

The last two on the list are state rather than federal programs, although they get help and hindrance—funding and regulations—from the national government.

Employment insurance programs consist of unemployment insurance, workers' compensation insurance, and temporary disability insurance. Like virtually all the other "little" transfer programs, their relative importance has shrunk as a result of the massive increases in the "Big Three."

Although accounting for only 2 percent of total transfer payments to persons in 1999, *Veterans benefits* appears in Exhibit 4.3 on a line of its own. Past glories account for its distinction now. In 1959 benefits to veterans accounted for 16 percent of total transfer payments. Thanks to the absence of major conflicts over the past forty years, the benefits seem to be fading away, like old soldiers.

*Medical care* accounts for most transfers from *Public assistance programs*. The $107.7 billion yet to be addressed in *Other public assistance programs* consists of a combination of both federal and state programs and include:

- Food stamp benefits,
- Supplemental security income,
- Earned income tax credit,
- Family assistance,
- Black lung benefits,
- Direct relief,
- General assistance,
- Energy assistance,
- Emergency assistance,
- Medical insurance premium payments paid on behalf of indigents, and
- Payments to nonprofit welfare institutions.

In 1959 such programs as food stamp benefits, black lung benefits, supplemental security income, direct relief, and earned income tax credit did not exist.

Food stamp benefits, a creation of the early 1960s, are intended to enable persons with little or no income to obtain a nutritionally adequate diet. At close to $15.5 billion in 1999, keeping people fed as compared to keeping them well seems like a bargain. And it's more of a bargain in 1999 than just a few years prior. In 1994 transfers in the form of food stamps peaked at $22.8 billion.

A larger amount, $31.1 billion, goes to supplemental security income. It was established in 1972 to provide income support to persons aged sixty-five or older, blind or disabled adults, and blind or disabled children. Since its inception, dollar amounts of transfers have risen relentlessly.

The earned income tax credit enables low-income taxpayers to claim a tax credit on their earnings. Although a tax credit reduces federal revenue, it is represented as a $25.7 billion payment in the NIPA. It got off to a later start than the preceding two programs but has surpassed Food stamp benefits and is gaining on Supplemental security income.

Tax credits dodge usual Congressional reviews associated with the appropriations process. In some circles such maneuvers make their outcomes suspect.

The Earned income tax credit (EITC) is one of those. That it amounts to $25.7 billion shows how determined individuals can be when avoiding federal income taxes. Qualification for the program does not seem easy or straightforward. According to the Internal Revenue Service, to claim the EITC you must meet all of the following rules:

- You, your spouse, and your qualifying child(ren) must each have a valid SSN that allows you to work.
- Your filing status must be married filing jointly, head of household, qualifying widow(er), or single.
- You are not filing Form 2555 or Form 2555-EZ (related to foreign earned income).
- Your investment income must be $2,350 or less.
- Your earned income and modified AGI must each be less than:
  $10,200 if you have no qualifying children, or
  $26,928 if you have one qualifying child, or
  $30,580 if you have more than one qualifying child.
- You (and your spouse if filing a joint return) are not a qualifying child of another person.
- Your child(ren) meet(s) the age, residency, and relationship tests for a qualifying child.
- Your qualifying child(ren) qualifies(y) only for you or your qualifying child(ren) also qualifies(y) for another person whose modified AGI is lower than yours.
- Your main home (and your spouse's if filing a joint return) has been located in the United States for more than half the year.
- You (or your spouse if filing a joint return) must be at least age 25 but under age 65 at the end of 1999.
- You (and your spouse if filing a joint return) cannot be claimed as a dependent on anyone else's return.[4]

To clear up any questions a respondent may have, fifty-three pages of explanation precede the checklist.

To a certified public accountant, determining his qualification should present only a mild challenge. But how many of them have incomes of less than $30,580? For typical high school and college dropouts flipping burgers, mowing lawns, or washing windows (or in the case of Bill Gates, running Microsoft), another challenge awaits after their mastery of qualification matters: figuring the amount of the tax credit. Probably in desperation, the Internal Revenue Service does offer to figure the credit. For those who persist and want to know in advance what benefits may result, it provides instructions. Everyone filing a federal individual income tax return—with or without an earned income tax credit—faces the same kinds of instructions and examples.

Family assistance amounting to $17.8 billion includes the aid to families with dependent children (AFDC) program. AFDC is a federal-state program that has been around since 1935. Under its provisions states receive federal general revenue appropriation for administration of approved programs. Beginning with 1996 *Family assistance* includes assistance programs operating under the Personal Responsibility and Work Opportunity Reconciliation Act of 1996.

The bills introduced in the House and Senate from which the Personal Responsibility and Work Opportunity Reconciliation Act of 1996 is derived carried a more lengthy title describing their authors' intentions:

> A bill to restore the American family, enhance support and work opportunities for families with children, reduce out-of-wedlock pregnancies, reduce welfare dependence by requiring work, meet health care needs of America's most vulnerable citizens, control welfare and medicaid spending, and increase State flexibility.

Brevity must have constrained them from mentioning a cure for acne and ingrown toenails. As sometimes happens, corrective action precedes rather than follows such legislation. Spending for food stamps and family assistance peaked in 1994 at $22.8 billion and $23.2 billion, respectively. While some may appreciate Congressional intentions, so much attention on such a small portion of a problem seems misplaced. Focusing effort on public welfare seems akin to repairing a leaky faucet on the Titanic on the evening of April 14, 1912. Congress appears unwilling and unable to deal with the massive intergenerational transfers from the working and well to the old and ill under social security, Medicare, and Medicaid entitlements. Perhaps what is needed is an AAWP to offset the lobbying pressures of the AARP.

Those preceding four programs account for $82.2 billion of the $107.7 billion in other public assistance programs in 1999. The remaining $25.5 billion is distributed among the remaining seven programs on the list. In many cases those programs are state-administered with funding in large measure from federal government support.

Some government transfer payments stem from programs that are related neither to social insurance nor to public assistance. They are placed under *Other government transfers* and collectively amount to $34.1 billion in 1999. The rather rapid growth of 12 percent a year this group of programs has enjoyed stems not so much from their individual good fortune but rather from additions to the list. Federal programs include:

- Payments to nonprofit institutions,
- Aid to students, and
- Payments for medical services for retired military personnel and their dependents at nonmilitary facilities.

State programs include:

- Education,
- Employment and training,
- Foster care,
- Veterans benefits,

- Alaska dividends, and
- Crime victim payments.

Humbling is the thought that each of those programs required determined legislators and/or congressmen to push through the legislative action that brought them into being. Zealous representatives of the people empowered to make the world a better place . . . for some at the expense of the many. Undoubtedly great effort was required to create those programs. The inertia of the status quo before such programs were established resisted change mightily. Only one thing exceeds that inertia: the inertia against eliminating existing programs.

*Personal Contributions for Social Insurance. Personal contributions for social insurance* in Exhibit 4.1 is the smallest of the three components of personal income that have grown at double-digit average annual growth rates over the past forty years. The smallest grower is also the fastest grower. Its rapid growth is a reminder that government does not create the resources that enable transfer payments. Through taxes, government takes from many persons to give to enough persons to insure continued support for its transfer programs.

Exhibit 4.4 gives us a glimpse at what has happened to the components of personal contributions for social insurance from 1959 to 1999. *Old age, survivors, disability and hospital insurance* (OASDHI) immediately draws our attention. Over the past forty years, it has increased at an average annual rate of 11 percent. All other components have increased at decidedly lower rates. OASDI alone accounts for the 10 percent growth rate in *Personal contributions to social insurance* over that extended period of time.

Given our earlier examination of OASDHI transfer payments, the growth rate of OASDHI contributions is not surprising. Moreover, the growth rate also is not sustainable! But actuaries, politicians, and pundits tell us it must not decline or just level off but increase ever more! How has the problem developed? A little bit of history will help.

The Social Security Act became law in 1935. Since that time it has been amended many times before and after 1959. In 1958 Congress increased the wage base from $4,200 to $4,800, provided for a tax rate increase to 2.5 percent in 1959, and added benefits for eligible dependents of disability beneficiaries. And so it has gone for most of the forty years since 1959: more benefits, larger wage base, higher tax rate. The 1960s saw substantial enhancement of the benefits derived from participation in OASDHI. In 1961 men became eligible for early retirement at age sixty-two with reduced benefits—an advantage that had been extended to women in 1956. Hospital insurance for the elderly, Medicare and Medicaid, was added in 1965. A 1972 amendment provided that beginning in 1975 benefits were to be automatically indexed to the consumer price index.[5]

All those goodies had to be paid for. What has happened to the wage base and employee compulsory "contribution" rate since 1959? At the beginning of the period, only OASDI existed. The contribution rate was 2.5 percent, and annual maximum taxable earnings stood at $4,800. In 1966 Medicare came into play with the same maximum earnings that in 1966 rose to $6,600. The total

contribution rate for Medicare and OASDI was set at 4.2 percent. Contribution rates and annual maximum taxable earnings then proceeded to rise, and by 1990 they stood at 7.65 percent and $51,300.
In 1991 Medicare's annual maximum taxable earnings stepped drastically ahead to $125,000, while OASDI's maximum rose more modestly to $53,400. More maximum taxable earnings increases followed each year. After 1994 no limit applied to maximum taxable earnings for Medicare. As of 1999 the maximum for OASDI stood at $72,600. No change in the contribution rate has occurred since 1990, however. It has been fixed at 7.65 percent.

An employed person earning the 1959 taxable earnings maximum, $2,500, paid $120 in social insurance contributions in 1959. In 1999, the same worker earning the 1999 taxable earnings maximum, $72,600 paid $6,458.70. A 2.5 percent "contribution" in 1959 has grown to a 7.65 percent "contribution" in 1999. While earnings were growing at an average annual rate of 7 percent, contributions were growing at a 10.5 percent average rate per year. For the social insurance funds, however, base and rate adjustments alone did not increase collections by 11 percent a year. In 1959 the wages of 27 percent of workers participating in the program exceeded the $4,800 ceiling; in 1997, with the ceiling at $65,400, only 6 percent did.[6]

To further increase aggregate contribution growth, coverage—the number of persons compelled to participate in the program—has increased. In 1998 coverage extended to about 148.5 million employed or self-employed workers—about 96 percent of all jobs in the United States.[7]

With the 1970s economic reality began to catch up with political opportunism. Fear of a cash shortfall in the social security trust funds developed in 1973 and prompted a six-month delay in implementing cost-of-living adjustments for benefit payments from January to June 1975. Cash shortage fears elicited escalation of both contribution rates and maximum annual earnings subject to the tax.[8]

The administration of Ronald Reagan marked an end to enthusiasm for social security benefit expansion and brought a hard look at the long-term solvency of the program. A modest rollback in a few selected benefits, basing cost-of-living adjustments on the lower of increases in prices or average wage rates, increasing the retirement age gradually from sixty-five to sixty-seven between the years 2000 and 2027, further rate and wage base increases, and a move from a pay-as-you-go basis to a trust fund approach to funding social security represented significant policy changes of the period.[9]

Despite an 11 percent growth rate in contributions to social security over the past forty years, actuarial studies tell us that we have not "contributed" enough:

> In the long range (i.e. the next 75 years) the difference between the summarized income and cost rates for the OASDI program is a deficit of 1.89 percent of taxable payroll based on the intermediate assumptions. . . . The assets of the combined OASI and DI trust funds are estimated to be depleted under present law in 2037.[10]

**Exhibit 4.4**

**Personal Contributions to Social Insurance, 1959 and 1999**

| | 1959 Amounts in $ Billions | Percent of Total | 1999 Amounts in $ Billions | Percent of Total | Annual Percent Change |
|---|---|---|---|---|---|
| **Federal social insurance funds** | **$ 5.9** | **98** | **$ 336.6** | **99** | **11** |
| OASDHI | 5.1 | 85 | 314.2 | 93 | 11 |
| Employees | 4.5 | 75 | 281.5 | 83 | 11 |
| OASDI | $4.5 | 75 | 218.0 | 64 | 10 |
| Hospital insurance | - | | 63.5 | 19 | |
| Self-employed | 0.6 | 10 | 32.7 | 10 | 11 |
| Supplementary medical insurance | - | | 20.3 | 6 | |
| State unemployment insurance | - | | - | | |
| Railroad retirement | 0.3 | 5 | 1.4 | 0 | 4 |
| Veterans life insurance | 0.5 | 8 | 0.7 | 0 | 1 |
| **State and local social insurance funds** | **0.1** | **2** | **1.9** | **1** | **8** |
| **TOTAL CONTRIBUTIONS** | **$ 6.0** | **100** | **$ 338.5** | **100** | **11** |

*Source*: U.S. Department of Commerce. Bureau of Economic Analysis. "'Annual Only' NIPA Tables." *National Accounts Data*. 30 Aug 2000: Table 3.6. 5 Sep. 2000. <http://www.bea.doc.gov/bea/dn1.htm>.

In other words, contributions from employers and employees right now need to be 1.89 percent higher than they are currently. When hospital insurance is included, add another 1.21 percent for a total of 3.10 percent.[11]

**Overview of the Components of Sources of Personal Income**

Exhibit 4.1 shows that property income—consisting of rent, interest, and dividends—starts the period accounting for 13 percent of total personal income and ends it with 19 percent. If property income's share has grown, then the share of labor and labor-related income has fallen. Exhibit 4.5 shows graphically the shifts occurring during the intervening years. Six charts appear in Exhibit 4.5. Horizontal axes measure years; vertical axes measure percent of personal income. The scales of the vertical axes have adjusted to capture the range of changes in percentages over the forty-year period for each of the sources. The components of personal income relating to labor income appear in the top row, and property income components are placed in the bottom row.

*Net wages and salaries* consist of *Wages and salaries* plus *Proprietors' income* less *Personal contributions for social insurance*. They represent what is left over after social security takes its toll. *Net wages and salaries* and the other sources of personal income are expressed as percentages of personal income for each of the years from 1959 to 1999. The drop is seen in the top left graph. *Net wages and salaries*, the amount of take-home pay (before personal income taxes) by the employed and self-employed, declined discernibly from almost 78 percent at the beginning of the period to around 61 percent in the early 1980s. The share of the pie going to workingmen and women became smaller over a twenty- to twenty-five-year period. Since then it has bounced around in the 60 percent to 62 percent range.

Such shifts do not occur without reason—or reasons. One possible explanation for the decline in the share of take-home pay as a percent of personal income is that salaries and wages do not constitute the only cost of labor to employers. Who pays for *Other labor income*? Employers. At the margin the value of labor's contribution to production is matched to labor cost. If labor costs in the form of *Other labor income* increases, employers will try to reduce other labor costs like *Wages and salaries*.

*Wages and salaries* and *Other labor income* are not the only costs associated with employment of labor as a factor of production. We already have noted that the fastest growing component of personal income over the past forty years has been *Personal contributions to social insurance*, rising from 2 percent to 4 percent of the total from 1959 to 1999. Growing right along with personal contributions has been *Employer contributions to social insurance*. Moreover, that is not the only government-imposed cost of labor. Included in businesses' calculus of labor costs are administrative burdens of complying with federal programs in the area of occupational safety and health and of affirmative action that were developed in the 1970s. More recently, day care has been added. In the United States companies with fifty or more employees are required by law to offer at

**Exhibit 4.5**

**Personal Income Sources as Percents of Total Personal Income, 1959 to 1999**

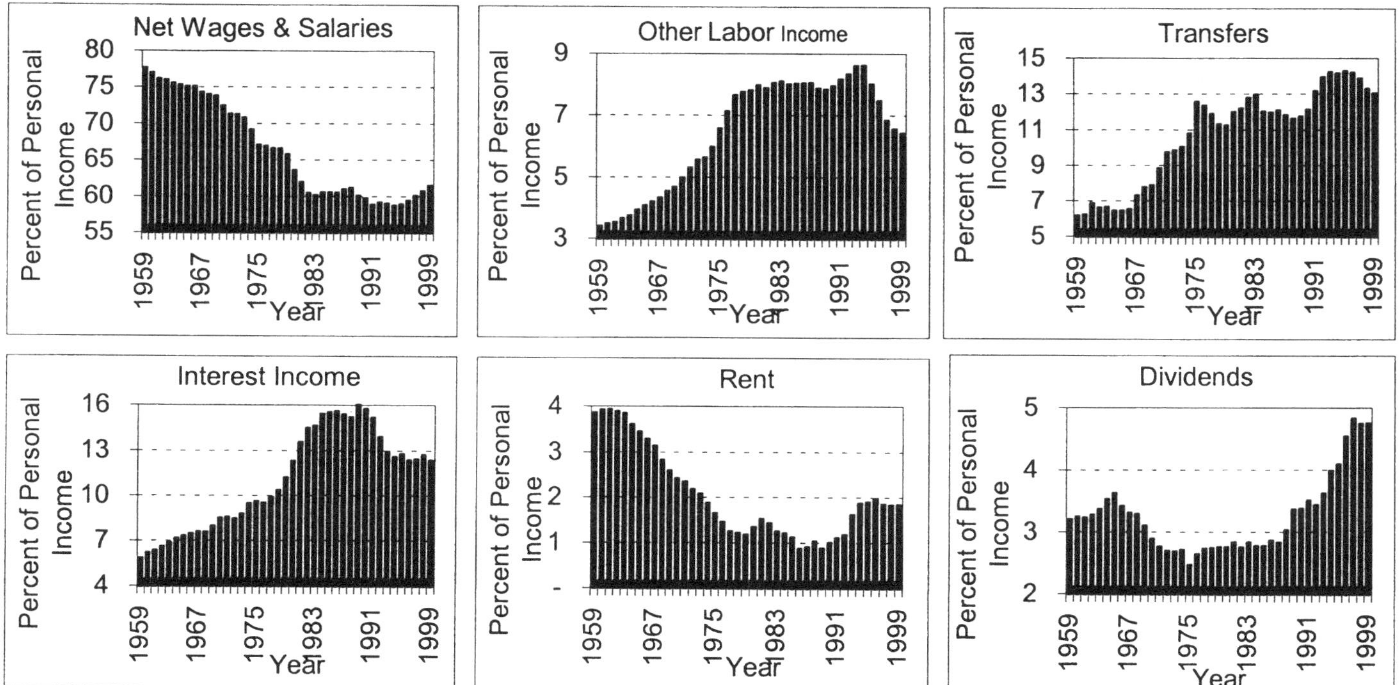


*Source* : U.S. Department of Commerce. Bureau of Economic Analysis. "Selected NIPA Tables." *National Accounts Data* . 8 Aug. 2000: Table 2.1. 9 Sep. 2000. <http://www.bea.doc.gov/bea/dn1.htm>.

least twelve weeks of unpaid leave to employees with a sick family member, a newborn infant, or a recently adopted child. And the list goes on and on.

In another context von Mises observed, "It is not in the power of governments to increase the supply of one commodity without a corresponding restriction in the supply of other commodities more urgently demanded by consumers. The authority may reduce the price of one commodity only by raising the prices of others."[12] So also, it can be said that when government increases one cost of labor, business will strive to achieve a corresponding reduction in other labor costs.

*Transfers* exhibit a generally rising share of personal income. Much of that rise can be attributed to Medicare and Medicaid. From the mid 1960s to the mid 1970s, medical costs rose sharply. Then came a period of about fifteen years when transfers accounted for roughly 11 to 12 percent of personal income. The early 1990s witnessed another surge in Medicare and Medicaid to 13 to 14 percent followed by another attempt at cost containment.

From the beginning of the period to the 1980s, the relative importance of *Rent* as a source of personal income declined. With greater price stability in the 1980s, its share increased somewhat, although the gains have not been continuous. After dropping to lows approximating 1 percent in the mid to late 1980s, rent's share has climbed to around 2 percent, still well below its share in the early 1960s.

The 1970s were a rough decade for dividend income. After contributing more than 3 percent to personal income in the 1960s, its share dropped to between 2 and 3 percent, hitting a low of 2.5 percent in 1975. Since the late 1980s, *Dividends* have shown a generally rising trend ranging between 4 and 5 percent by the late 1990s.

From the beginning of the period to the middle of the 1980s, *Interest income*'s share of personal income grew. Rising debt and rising interest rates accounted for the pattern. In the early 1960s the interest rate on ten-year U.S. Government bonds was around 4 percent. By the early 1970s it had risen to the 6 percent range. In 1981 the interest rate peaked at nearly 14 percent. From that high point it began, with interruptions, falling. By the early 1990s it averaged between 7 and 8 percent a year. With the 1990s have come further declines in the interest rate to between 5 and 6 percent in 1999.[13] With the decline has come a concomitant fall in the percentage of personal income accounted for by *Interest income* from 1989's high of 16 percent to 1999's 12 percent.

## DISTRIBUTION OF PERSONAL INCOME AMONG STATES

"Personal income in time and space" sounds like a title to a book or chapter. Here is where the title for this chapter originated. Having explored changes in personal income and its sources over time, we now turn our attention to its distribution geographically. The U. S. Department of Commerce prepares personal income statistics for the fifty states and the District of Columbia as well as for the nation as a whole.

### Inequality in Personal Income by State

*State personal income* totals $7,783.2 billion. The national estimate we have been using is $7,789.6 billion. The sum of the parts is smaller than that of the whole because estimates for states include only income of persons within their borders. Earnings of federal civilian and military personnel stationed abroad and U. S. residents employed temporarily abroad by U. S. firms are excluded. Different data sources and processing also affect results.

Personal income by state varies widely. Residents of Wyoming generate the smallest amount of personal income, just $12.7 billion; California, the largest, $991.4 billion. Examination of states in between shows that just a few states generate most of the nation's personal income. The personal income of four states,

- California, $991.4 billion,
- New York, $616.7 billion,
- Texas, $538.3 billion, and
- Florida, $419.8 billion,

account for one-third of the total. Add the personal income of four more states,

- Illinois, $377.7 billion,
- Pennsylvania, $343.1 billion,
- Ohio, $305.6 billion, and
- New Jersey, $289.5 billion,

and you account for half of the nation's personal income. The smallest eight states—one of which is not a state, the District of Columbia—by contrast account for less than 2 percent. The numbers suggest that the geographic distribution of aggregate personal income among states is very unequal.

### Personal Income and Disposable Personal Income

Total personal income is not the only economically significant statistic that varies from state to state. The amount that individuals and households are able to keep in the form of disposable personal income varies also. In chapter 3 we saw from Exhibit 3.1 that for the nation as a whole, tax and nontax payments account for 15 percent of personal income. Depending on the state, tax and nontax payment can vary from a low of 10 percent to a high of 19 percent.

The federal individual income tax is considered to be a "progressive" tax; that is, taxes assessed as a percentage of a person's income tend to rise as the amount of that income increases. For states the tax structure is mixed. Income taxes tend to be progressive in the sense just defined. Sales taxes are considered "regressive." Although the same rate applies to purchases, those with low incomes tend to spend a higher proportion of their income than those with high. Thus, they bear a higher proportion of a sales tax.

**Exhibit 4.6**
**State Per Capita Personal Income and Tax and Nontax Payments as Percents of Personal Income, 1999**

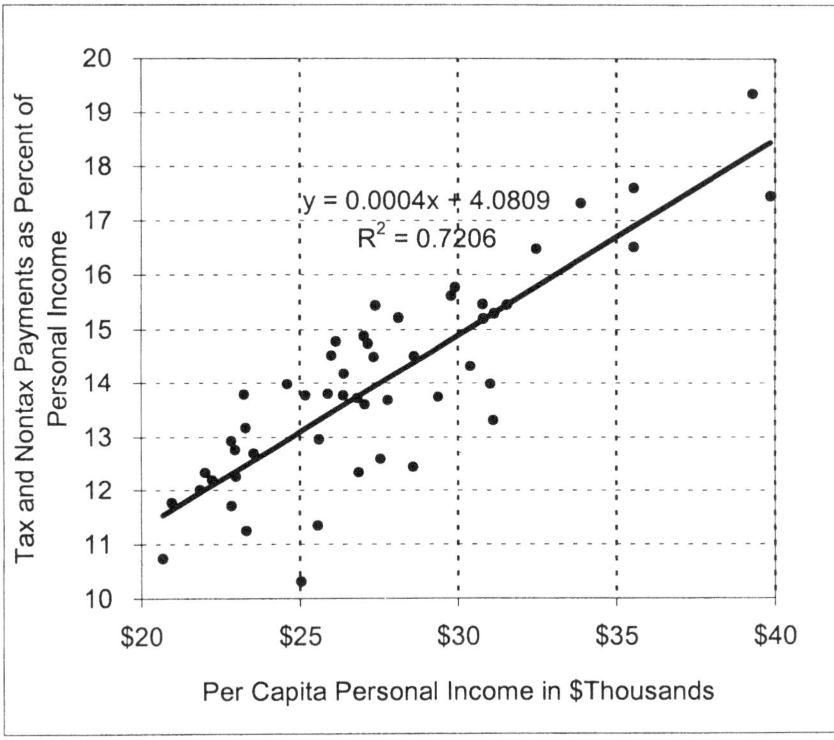


*Source*: U.S. Department of Commerce. Bureau of Economic Analysis. "Detailed annual State tables." *Regional Accounts Data*. 12 Sep. 2000: Tables SA1_5899, SA2_5899 and SA51_589. 22 Sep. 2000. <http://www.bea.doc.gov/bea/regional/spi/recent.asp>.

If the tax structure tends to be progressive, we might expect that a higher percentage of tax and nontax payments occurs in states with high per capita personal income. Exhibit 4.6 explores that possibility. *Per Capita Personal Income* is measured along the horizontal axis; the percent accounted for by tax and nontax payments, along the vertical.

The straight line drawn on the chart summarizes the relationship between *Tax and Nontax Payments as Percent of Personal Income* and *Per Capita Personal Income*. It is calculated as a least-squares regression line and is the only line that minimizes the sum of squares of the vertical distances between the line and the dots. The upward slope of the line indicates that as *Per Capita Personal Income* by state rises *Tax and Nontax Payments as Percent of Personal Income* rises. The value assigned to the line's slope suggests that each $1,000 increment in personal income increases the percentage of personal income taken away in tax and nontax payments by four-tenths of one percent. Since not all the dots fall on the line, it is not a perfect representation of the observed relationship between personal income and the percentage. The calculated relationship accounts for only 72 percent of the observed variation of disposable income as a percentage of personal income among the states.[14] Although average per capita personal income is a significant factor, other factors clearly play a role. Such possible factors include differences in states' tax structure, the size of their public sector relative to their personal income, and differences in the distribution of individuals' taxable income within states.

## DISTRIBUTION OF PERSONAL INCOME AMONG INDIVIDUALS

Other things being equal—as economists like to say (at least, this one)—a high income is better than a low one. Even better is an income that is higher than other people's income. Invidious comparisons are ignoble but irresistible. The satisfaction derived from a high income is diminished somewhat when everyone you know earns even more. In economic matters the principle of relativity differs from that of physics but exerts its influence on the universe of human relations.

We have seen how personal income is distributed among states. So, how is it distributed among individuals? We can't tell. Personal income is a *national* (or state) statistic. Although personal income provides total estimates of how much individuals, households, and nonprofit institutions serving people receive, it is not computed from a summation of each unit's income. It is an *estimate.* Many of its components are based on aggregates and information derived from surveys for which unit data are not available.

### Data Sources

To get an idea of how income is distributed among individuals, we have to turn to other statistical sources. Two sources of the distribution of income among households and individuals are available: (1) money income to families and individuals and (2) individual adjusted gross income. For our inquiry into the distribution of income among individuals and households, we will use individual adjusted gross income. But money income as a basis for analysis deserves comment.

The Bureau of the Census of the Department of Commerce has been collecting information on the money income received by families and individuals annually since 1947. Money income is based on interview samples of the population and differs from the concept of personal income used in the NIPA. It consists of money income (except for capital gains) before payment of personal income taxes, social security and Medicare taxes, and other deductions like union dues. Money income does not include receipts of such noncash benefits as food stamps, health benefits, and subsidized housing. As we observed based on the sources of personal income, since 1959 those transfer payments have become increasingly significant income sources.

The Internal Revenue Service (IRS) of the Department of the Treasury prepares annually distributions of adjusted gross income of persons based on a sample of individual income tax returns. For taxpayers familiar with preparing their individual federal income tax returns, differences between adjusted gross income and the concept of personal income readily come to mind. We are not taxed (yet) for the imputed income items the Department of Commerce calculates as it prepares the NIPA, although some zealous federal bureaucrat may be working on that project.

Adjusted gross income (AGI) amounted to $5,389.9 billion for 1998—the most recent year available. To reconcile that number, BEA begins with its personal income estimate for 1998, $7,391.0 billion, and deducts $2,611.8 billion for items not included in AGI. Examples include nontaxable transfer payments, other labor income, imputed income, and interest income on municipal bonds. Additions amount to only $1,305.6 billion, about half the deductions. Major additions include personal contributions for social insurance, net gains from the sale of assets, and taxable pension benefits.

Those subtractions and additions produce the Bureau of Economic Analysis's estimate of adjusted gross income: $6,084.8 billion. Comparison of the bureau's estimate with that of the Internal Revenue Service shows a significant margin of error, $695.5 billion. A 9 percent difference meets the test that 10 percent is close enough for government work, however. Some of the difference can be attributed to income earned by low-income individuals who are not required to file income tax returns, income not reported to the Internal Revenue Service that Bureau of Economic Analysis picks up in its preparation of personal income, sampling error, and just plain mistakes. According to Thae S. Park, "The AGI gap can be considered as a rough indicator of noncompliance with the Federal tax code."[15]

### Distribution of Adjusted Gross Income

Adjusted gross income from a sample of individual income tax returns prepared by the Internal Revenue Service provides a basis for constructing a distribution of income among persons and households in the United States. Those results are summarized in Exhibit 4.7. In 1999 individuals filed 124.7 million federal individual income tax returns. Those returns are divided into twenty-two groups based on the size of their adjusted gross income. Around 1 million returns report no adjusted gross income. They will be excluded from our analysis. Of the 123.8 million returns with adjusted gross income, 15 percent fall into the first four groups reporting adjusted gross income from a dollar to under $7,000. A study for 1993 showed that about half of all returns with adjusted gross income under $5,000 were filed by dependents of other taxpayers. The percentages of their total returns in each of the following groups are provided in the table along with cumulative percentages. The cumulative percentage shows, for example, that 32 percent of all returns report adjusted gross income of less than

**Exhibit 4.7**
**Individual Income Tax Returns and Adjusted Gross Income (AGI), before and after Income Tax, 1998**

| | Number of returns | | | Adjusted gross income or deficit | | |
|---|---|---|---|---|---|---|
| Size of adjusted gross income | Number in Millions | Percent of total | Cumulative Percent | Amount in $Billions | Percent of total | Cumulative Percent |
| **All returns, total** | **124.7** | | | **$ 5,389.3** | | |
| No AGI | 1.0 | | | (42.3) | | |
| $1 to $1,000 | 1.8 | 1 | 1 | 1.1 | 0 | 0 |
| $1,000 to $3,000 | 5.7 | 5 | 6 | 11.5 | 0 | 0 |
| $3,000 to $5,000 | 5.6 | 5 | 11 | 22.3 | 0 | 1 |
| $5,000 to $7,000 | 5.3 | 4 | 15 | 31.5 | 1 | 1 |
| $7,000 to $9,000 | 5.1 | 4 | 19 | 40.9 | 1 | 2 |
| $9,000 to $11,000 | 5.3 | 4 | 23 | 53.1 | 1 | 3 |
| $11,000 to $13,000 | 5.1 | 4 | 27 | 61.2 | 1 | 4 |
| $13,000 to $15,000 | 5.2 | 4 | 32 | 73.1 | 1 | 5 |
| $15,000 to $17,000 | 4.8 | 4 | 36 | 77.1 | 1 | 7 |
| $17,000 to $19,000 | 4.7 | 4 | 39 | 83.9 | 2 | 8 |
| $19,000 to $22,000 | 6.5 | 5 | 45 | 133.6 | 2 | 11 |
| $22,000 to $25,000 | 5.9 | 5 | 49 | 137.7 | 3 | 13 |
| $25,000 to $30,000 | 8.2 | 7 | 56 | 224.8 | 4 | 18 |
| $30,000 to $40,000 | 13.1 | 11 | 67 | 456.1 | 8 | 26 |
| $40,000 to $50,000 | 10.0 | 8 | 75 | 447.3 | 8 | 34 |
| $50,000 to $75,000 | 15.9 | 13 | 87 | 970.0 | 18 | 52 |
| $75,000 to $100,000 | 7.2 | 6 | 93 | 618.9 | 11 | 63 |
| $100,000 to $200,000 | - | 5 | 98 | 818.6 | 15 | 78 |
| $200,000 to $500,000 | - | 1 | 100 | 455.9 | 8 | 87 |
| $500,000 to $1million | - | 0 | 100 | 205.2 | 4 | 91 |
| $1million or more | 0.2 | 0 | 100 | 507.7 | 9 | 100 |
| **AGI returns over $0** | **123.8** | **100** | | **$ 5,431.7** | **100** | |

**Exhibit 4.7 (continued)**
**Individual Income Tax Returns and Adjusted Gross Income (AGI), before and after Income Tax, 1998**

| Total income tax | | | After tax adjusted gross income | | |
|---|---|---|---|---|---|
| Amount in $Billions | Percent of total | Cumulative Percent | Amount in $Billions | Percent of total | Cumulative Percent |
| **$ 783.9** | | | **$ 4,605.4** | | |
| 0.1 | | | (42.4) | | |
| 0.0 | 0 | 0 | 1.1 | 0 | 0 |
| 0.1 | 0 | 0 | 11.3 | 0 | 0 |
| 0.2 | 0 | 0 | 22.1 | 0 | 1 |
| 0.5 | 0 | 0 | 31.1 | 1 | 1 |
| 0.7 | 0 | 0 | 40.1 | 1 | 2 |
| 1.4 | 0 | 0 | 51.7 | 1 | 3 |
| 2.0 | 0 | 1 | 59.2 | 1 | 5 |
| 2.7 | 0 | 1 | 70.4 | 2 | 6 |
| 3.4 | 0 | 1 | 73.7 | 2 | 8 |
| 4.2 | 1 | 2 | 79.8 | 2 | 9 |
| 7.3 | 1 | 3 | 126.3 | 3 | 12 |
| 9.0 | 1 | 4 | 128.7 | 3 | 15 |
| 17.0 | 2 | 6 | 207.8 | 4 | 19 |
| 40.3 | 5 | 11 | 415.8 | 9 | 28 |
| 44.9 | 6 | 17 | 402.4 | 9 | 37 |
| 109.0 | 14 | 31 | 861.0 | 19 | 56 |
| 85.3 | 11 | 42 | 533.6 | 11 | 67 |
| 143.2 | 18 | 60 | 675.4 | 15 | 82 |
| 110.3 | 14 | 74 | 345.6 | 7 | 89 |
| 58.5 | 7 | 82 | 146.7 | 3 | 92 |
| 143.6 | 18 | 100 | 364.1 | 8 | 100 |
| **$ 783.8** | **100** | | **$ 4,647.8** | **100** | |

*Source:* United States. Department of Treasury. Internal Revenue Service. "Number of Individual Income Tax Returns, Income, Exemptions and Deductions, Tax, and Average Tax, By Size of Gross Income, Tax Years1996-98." 6 Jul 2000 *Individual Tax Statistics. Data by Size of Income*. 14 Jul 2000 <http://www.irs.ustreas.gov/plain/tax_stats/soi/ind_agi.html>.

$15,000; over half, of less than $30,000; and three-fourths, of less than $50,000. Just two percent of the returns show income of more than $200,000.

The second cluster of three columns in Exhibit 4.7 displays a similar set of data for adjusted gross income. When all 124.7 million returns are considered, adjusted gross income nets to almost $5.4 trillion. Excluding returns showing negative adjusted gross income brings the total to over $5.4 trillion. At the low end of the income scale—the top of the columns—the first four groups with adjusted gross income from $1 to under $7,000 and with 15 percent of returns together account for just 1 percent of total adjusted gross income. The next group, with adjusted gross income of $7,000 to under $9,000, accounts for 4 percent of the returns but only 1 percent of total adjusted gross income. The percentage of returns exceeds the percentage of gross income for all following groups until we get to returns with adjusted gross income greater than $40,000 and less than $50,000. At that point the percentage of returns, 8 percent, equals the percentage of income, 8 percent. At the upper end of the income scale—the bottom of the columns—the last three groups with adjusted gross income of $200,000 or more account for two percent of returns and 22 percent of total income. Is that fair?

Exhibit 4.8 displays graphically the relationship between number of returns and adjusted gross income. The vertical axis measures the *Cumulative Percentage of Adjusted Gross Income*. The horizontal axis measures *Cumulative Percentage of Number of Returns*. The curve traces out the observed relationship between the percentages of returns and income. The diagonal line illustrates complete equality in the distribution. The Gini coefficient, a measure of inequality represented by the area between the diagonal line and the curve, equals 0.57. If everyone received the same income, the coefficient's value would be zero. If one person received all income, it would register 1.0.

### Distribution of Federal Individual Income Tax

Mention already has been made of the federal income tax policy to burden higher incomes with a proportionately larger share of the cost of government. The third cluster of three columns in Exhibit 4.7 provides some insight into the degree to which that policy objective is realized. The third cluster provides data on amounts of income tax collected from each income group. The amount column shows that individual income taxes generated about $783.9 billion in federal government revenue. From returns with AGI, $783.8 billion was collected in 1998. Thirty-two percent—almost one-third—of all returns showing adjusted gross income under $15,000 and accounting for a 5 percent of adjusted gross income paid one percent of that $783.8 billion. As we trace down the columns of Exhibit 4.7, we can see that the share of total taxes paid is less than the share of total income until over 87 percent of the returns is accounted for. Those groups collectively receive 52 percent of the income but pay 31 percent of the tax. In a representative form of government, such tax breaks for so many—

**Exhibit 4.8**

**Adjusted Gross Income(AGI) before & after Federal Individual Income Tax, 1998**

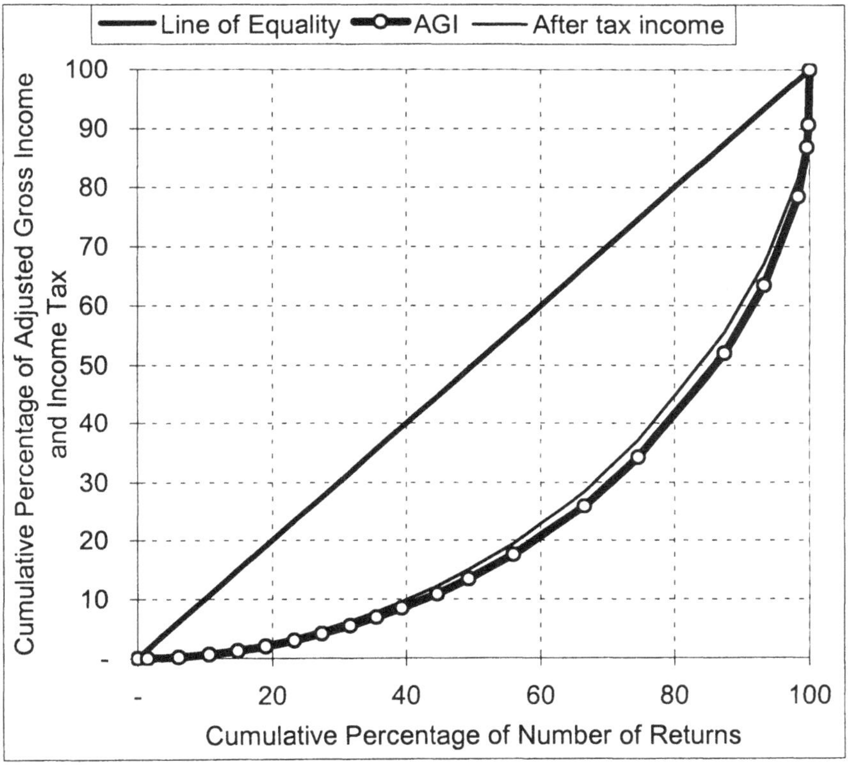


helped by a natural weakness for invidious comparisons—make acceptable to the masses a burden that otherwise would be intolerable.

Only for those returns with adjusted gross income from $75,000 to under $100,000 does the percent of taxes paid equal the percent of income. Taxpayers in that group accounted for 6 percent of the returns, reported 11 percent of total adjusted gross income, and paid 11 percent of the total income tax—an approximation to the situation if the federal government's income tax were collected in proportion to one's income. If you received 1 percent of the income, you would pay 1 percent of the tax; if you received 10 percent, you pay 10 percent.

At that break-even point, 93 percent of the returns account for 63 percent of total income and 42 percent of total taxes. From the remaining 7 percent of returns with 37 percent of the income, 58 percent is to be collected. The last three groups—just two percent of the returns—receiving only 22 percent of total income—pay 40 percent of federal individual income taxes. Is that fair?

**Distribution of After-Tax Adjusted Gross Income**

It would be a mistake to assume that the inequality of the distribution of adjusted gross income is reduced significantly by the difference in the distribution of tax collections. The effect of the disproportional increase in taxes for higher income groups on their net income is much more modest. Adjusted gross income totals around $5.4 trillion. Federal income taxes at $733 billion amount to 14 to 15 percent of that total. The fourth cluster of three columns in Exhibit 4.7 deals with adjusted gross income after the tax. The amount of after-tax AGI is computed as the difference between before-tax AGI and total income tax. Comparing the after-tax AGI amounts with that for AGI before tax in Exhibit 4.7 shows how slight the effect is.

The first four groups with the lowest adjusted gross income account for 1 percent of before-tax adjusted gross income. They account for 1 percent of after-tax adjusted gross income. Returns reporting adjusted gross income of less than $100,000 account for 52 percent of before-tax income and 67 percent of after-tax income. The top three groups with adjusted gross income above $200,000 account for 22 percent of before-tax income; 18 percent of after-tax income.

A graphic portrayal is presented in Exhibit 4.8. Although the after-tax curve is nearer to the diagonal line than the curve representing adjusted gross income before tax, it follows the before-tax curve very closely. The Gini coefficient is reduced from a before-tax figure of 0.57 to an after-tax 0.54.

For that slight modification in income redistribution, taxpayer-citizens in the United States are confronted with a voluminous and complicated tax code. For all but professional accountants and lawyers specializing in tax matters, it is essentially incomprehensible. Consequently, from 1959 to 1999 the cost to persons of preparing their tax returns has grown at an average annual rate of 12.6 percent per year.[16] In 1999 taxpayers paid $6.0 billion for tax preparation services—an expenditure of time and effort that adds little to citizens' happiness and well-being and much to grief and pain. What a waste (unless you are an accountant or tax lawyer)!

## CONCLUSION

From 1959 to 1999 personal income has changed significantly in amount and composition. In 1959 it amounted to less than $400 billion; in 1999, to nearly $7.8 trillion. Over the forty-year period, wages and salaries have dropped from around two-thirds of personal income to 57 percent. Take-home pay from wages and salaries has been squeezed by more rapid growth in other labor income, transfer payments, and personal contributions for social insurance.

The rise of other labor income, transfer payments, and personal contributions for social insurance stems largely from a common source: Medicare, a federal medical insurance program for aged and disabled persons insured under the social security program. With Medicaid, a companion federal medical insurance program also established in 1965 and providing medical and health related services to indigent persons, have come rapidly rising medical costs. Consequently, the associated rise in group health insurance premiums offered by employers as part of employee benefit packages and exempt from state and federal income taxes has come to dominate sources of other labor income and account for its rapid rise. Rapid growth in transfer payments reflects Medicare and Medicaid benefit distributions. Covering Medicare benefits has contributed to increases in personal contributions for social insurance. The promise of medical care for all carries with it the peril of enormous cost burdens.

Old Age, Survivors, and Disability Insurance (OASDI) constitutes the largest single component of Transfer payments and the largest item in Personal contributions to social insurance. Like Medicare, its growth rate over the forty-year period has contributed to the relative decline in take-home labor income. The promise of government-provided retirement benefits for all retirees carries with it the peril of heavy tax burdens on the working population.

Personal income is distributed unequally among states and among persons. When ranked in terms of personal income from largest to smallest, the smallest eight states account for only 2 percent of the nation's total personal income. One-third of the nation's personal income is found in just four states—California, New York, Texas, and Florida. Eight states account for nearly half. In those states resides nearly half of the nation's population as well.

Using adjusted gross income reported by the Internal Revenue Service for individual income tax returns, we find a similar pattern of inequality. In terms of before-tax adjusted gross income, 49 percent—nearly half—of the returns with the smallest income account for only 13 percent of total adjusted gross income. The 2 percent of the returns reporting the highest adjusted gross income account for 22 percent of the total. The federal individual tax structure is designed to extract a higher proportion of taxes from high incomes than from low. The 49 percent of returns with the smallest adjusted gross income pay only 4 percent of total taxes assessed. The 2 percent of returns with highest adjusted gross income pays 40 percent of the tax. Despite the disparity in tax collections, after-tax distribution of income closely follows the before-tax distribution. For the promise of more equal after-tax incomes, we trade the peril of a complicated income tax structure.

## NOTES

1. Michael Horowitz, "What do we do about Medicare?" *The American Enterprise,* (Jan./Feb. 1997): 21–22.

2. Horowitz: 21–22.

3. Kennett Lynn Simmons, *Managed Health Care: right idea—wrong rules*, diss., University of Texas at Austin, 1992.

4. United States, Department of the Treasury, Internal Revenue Service, "Publication 596 Earned Income Tax Credit for Use in preparing 1999 Returns," 12 Apr. 2000: 54, 8 Oct. 2000 <http://ftp.fedworld.gov/pub/irs-pdf/p596pdf>.

5. Max J. Skidmore, "Social Security in the United States," *Social Security Pro-*

*grams: A Cross-Cultural Comparative Perspective*, eds. John Dixon and Robert P. Scheurell (Westport, CT: Greenwood Press, 1995) 22.

6. Social Security Administration: 170.

7. United States, Social Security Administration, *Annual Statistical Supplement to the Social Security Bulletin, 1999* (Washington, DC: U.S. Government Printing Office, 1999): 37.

8. United States, Social Security Administration, *Annual Statistical Supplement to the Social Security Bulletin, 1996* (Washington, DC: U. S. Government Printing Office, 1996): 23.

9. John B. Williamson and Fred C. Pampel, *Old-Age Security in Comparative Perspective* (New York: Oxford University Press, 1993) 103.

10. United States, Board of Trustees, Federal Old-Age and Survivors Insurance and Disability Insurance Funds, *The 2000 Annual Report of the Board of Trustees of the Federal Old-Age and Survivors Insurance and Disability Insurance Trust Funds* (Washington, DC: US Government Printing Office, 2000): 3.

11. United States, Board of Trustees of the Federal Old-Age and Survivors Insurance and the Federal Disability Insurance Trust Funds and Board of Trustees of the Federal Hospital Insurance Trust Funds, *Status of the Social Security and Medicare Programs: A Summary of the 2000 Annual Reports* (Washington, DC: U.S. Government Printing Office, Apr. 2000): 7.

12. Ludwig von Mises, *Omnipotent Government, The Rise of the Total State and Total War* (New Haven: Yale University Press, 1944) 247.

13. Board of Governors of the Federal Reserve System, "Treasury constant maturities, 10-year," *Historical Data,* 18 Sep. 2000: H.15, 29 Sep. 2000 <http://www.bog.frb.us/releases/h15/data.htm>

14. The percentage is based on the coefficient of determination for the regression line.

15. Thae S. Park, "Comparison of BEA Estimates of Personal Income and IRS Estimates of Adjusted Gross Income: New Estimates for 1997 and Revised Estimates for 1959-96," Survey of Current Business (Feb. 2000): 14.

16. United States Department of Commerce, Bureau of Economic Analysis, "Underlying detail estimates for PCE, historical file," *State of the Nation Library*, 8 Sep. 2000: Table 206U, 8 Oct. 2000 <http://www.stat-usa.gov/online.nsf/NIPANav?OpenNavigator>.

# 5

# Personal Spending over Time

This chapter provides a second perspective on the dimensions of personal income. In chapter 4 we looked at sources of personal income over time and how personal income is distributed among states and among individuals. Here we will be engaged in a similar exercise as we examine uses of personal income—the other side of the earning-spending coin. That examination will lead us to consideration of price changes that have occurred during the period.

Price changes were not relevant when we were dealing with a single period or with the income side of personal income. What a dollar will buy in terms of goods and services, however, has changed over time and is changing now. Consequently, to see what has happened to a dollar's purchasing power we have to make allowances for changes in prices of goods and services. Price considerations become relevant when we want to use our income to satisfy wants and needs, when we step outside the realm of financial exchanges and trade dollars for goods and services, when dollars touch the "real" world. Price inflation (or deflation) adjustments are made not to personal income but to personal consumption expenditures and to disposable personal income, which—as we have seen and we will see again—is used largely to buy goods and services.

## OVERVIEW

In the previous chapter we observed that in absolute terms an enormous difference exists between *Personal income* in 1999 and 1959. As shown in Exhibit 4.1, *Personal income* in 1959 amounted to $394.0 billion; in 1999 it amounted to $7.8 trillion. The 1959 amount is one-twentieth of the 1999 amount. The difference in magnitudes is so vast that comparisons of the numbers become meaningless. The same problem arises in the case of uses of personal income. In the double-entry accounting world maintained by our national bookkeepers, total uses of personal income equal total sources of personal income. As is the

**Exhibit 5.1**

**Uses of Personal Income as Percents of Total Personal Income, 1959 to 1999**

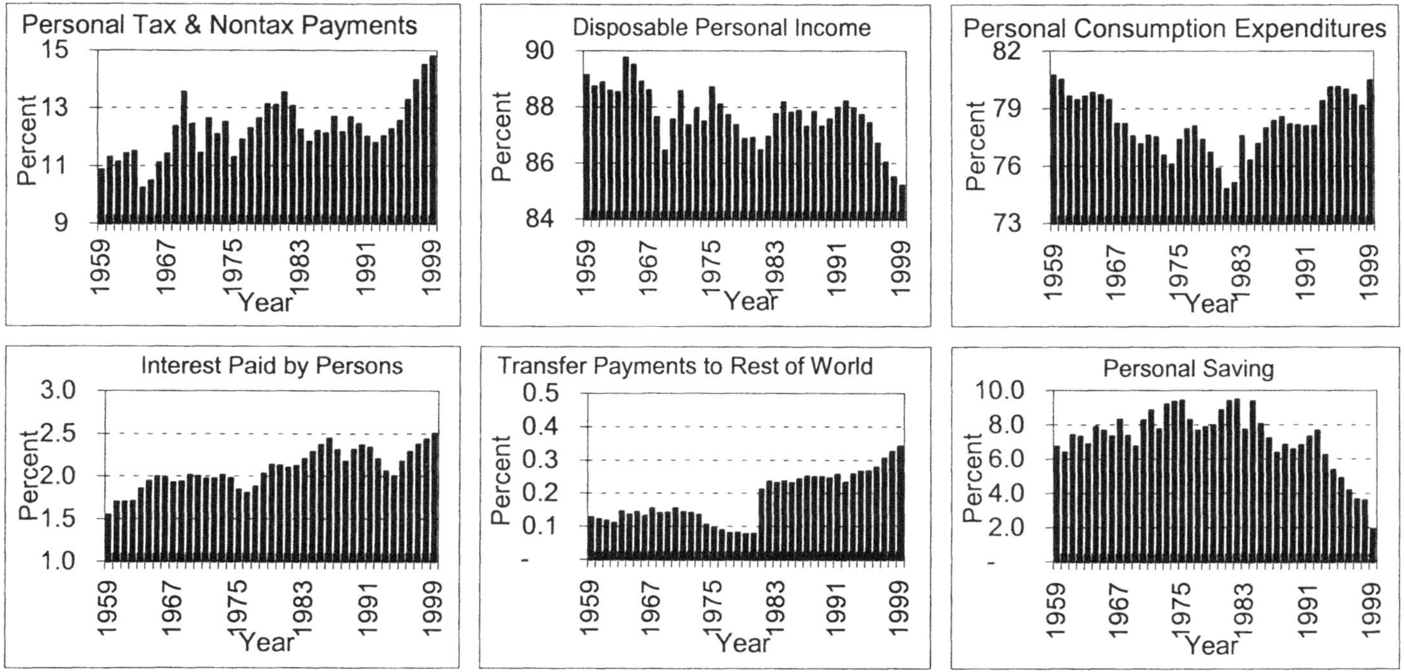


*Source* : U.S. Department of Commerce. Bureau of Economic Analysis. "Selected NIPA Tables." *National Accounts Data* . 8 Aug. 2000: Table 2.1. 9 Sep. 2000. <http://www.bea.doc.gov/bea/dn1.htm>.

case of comparisons of sources of personal income, comparisons of uses of personal income relative to the total do, however, provide meaningful information.

Exhibit 5.1 shows graphically the six groupings of personal income as percentages of the total. One chart is provided for each category. Horizontal axes mark the years from 1959 to 1999; vertical axes, percentages of total personal income. Note the range differences among the charts. The range for *Disposable Personal Income*, for example, extends from 84 percent to 90 percent. In the case of *Transfer Payments to Rest of World*, its low is zero and its high is one-half of one percent. A common scale for all would make detecting changes over time difficult for the smaller components.

*Disposable Personal Income* shows a relative decline during the forty-year period. In 1959 consumers kept $89.10 from every $100 of personal income. By 1999 their command of the discretionary portion of their personal income had fallen to $85.20. The highest retention rate occurs in 1964, $89.80. The lowest figure is the most recent, the latest development in an unrelenting decline beginning in 1993. The cause of the relative decline in personal income is not hard to find: *Personal Tax and Nontax Payments*. For virtually all working-age U.S. citizens, the tax burden has never been higher. In 1964, a time of the Cold War and increasing involvement in Vietnam, $10.20 would have been taken on average from each $100 of your personal income; in 1999, $14.80—a 45 percent increase! Where's the peace dividend?

Despite the incursions of government tax and nontax payments on personal income, *Personal Consumption Expenditures* begin and end the period at very close to 81 percent of personal income. As shown in the graph, consumption expenditures' share has not been constant, however. In 1981 it reached a low of 75 percent. That low point corresponds to a dip in disposable personal income and occurred at a time of sharp contraction in economic activity.

Of considerably less consequence is *Interest Paid by Persons*. In 1999 it reached a forty-year high, 2.5 percent. But that peak is only 2.5 percent! A combination of rising personal debt and rising interest rates accounts for the continuous increase since 1994. The first year of our series, 1959, marked the lowest percentage: 1.5 percent. Relatively, *Interest Paid by Persons*' growth has been more rapid than even *Personal Tax and Nontax Payments*.

*Transfer Payments to Rest of World* constitute another small use of personal income. In 1999 they reached their highest point, just 0.3 percent (3/10 of 1%). In 1981—the same year personal consumption expenditures take a dip—they register a surge from 0.1 percent to 0.2 percent.

One use of *Personal Income* remains, *Personal Saving*. During much of the period, *Personal Saving* as a percentage of *Personal Income* ranged above 6 percent. It began the period at 6.7 percent. The year 1982 marks its peak, 9.5 percent. Since 1992, when *Personal Saving* accounted for 7.7 percent of the *Uses of Personal Income*, it has been dropping. In 1999 *Personal Saving* reaches its lowest point, 1.9 percent. In 1999 the percentage for *Interest Paid by Persons* exceeded the percentage for *Personal Saving* for the first time.

Of the five uses, *Personal Consumption Expenditures* makes up by far the largest use. Next in significance comes *Personal Tax and Nontax Payments.* We will focus on those two and conclude with a look at *Personal Saving* in the course of our examination of changes in the pattern of uses of personal income over the past forty years.

## PERSONAL TAX AND NONTAX PAYMENTS

The composition of *Personal Tax and Nontax Payments* should be familiar. But not all the taxes you pay appear here. Conspicuously missing are sales and property taxes. They are not "personal" taxes. By tradition they are classified as "indirect" taxes, taxes on things rather than people. Being taxed on the things you buy and the property you own may feel just as personal as being taxed on your income, but the bookkeeping system just does not work that way.

Most income taxes are collected through withholdings. With the net drawn tight and given the government's eagerness for taxpayer dollars, taxpayers' money is taken away before they see it, making its burden invisible. As a form of federal income taxation, declarations and settlements have become relatively more important. Much of that increase can be attributed to quarterly tax payments and growth in property income as a share of personal income. Stiffer penalties for shortfalls in withholdings and quarterly payments have stimulated a compliant public to increase its overpayments causing refunds to increase relative to the total collected.

### Changes in Shares

In 1999, Federal tax and nontax payments accounted for 78 percent of the $1,152 billion total of federal, state, and local collections. Incredible as it may seem, formerly the federal government's share was even greater! In 1959, 90 percent! Federal personal tax and nontax payments have grown at 8 percent per year—close to the overall average in personal income. Payments to state and local governments, however, have exceeded that rate by a substantial margin with an 11 percent average growth rate. The appetite for taxpayer dollars at the state and local level has been stimulated in part by unfunded federal mandates and matching programs such as Medicaid. The 11 percent growth rate in state and local income taxes accounts for their rise in the share of total payments. Nontaxes increased more rapidly, but their small size contributes just an additional two percentage points to the state and local share.

Although governments favor income taxes, they are not popular with people. Author Barber Conable asserts, "Sixty to 65 % of the American public has identified the income tax as the one they really hate."[1] One reason for their distaste is the bite income taxes take. Perceptions and misconceptions provide other reasons. Both income taxes and OASDHI payments are withheld, blurring distinction between the two. Perceived unfairness and complexity are others. Low-income taxpayers feel the rich get by with paying little; the rich know they pay a lot. Responsiveness of the Congress to constituents' requests for exceptions because of their special circumstances results in complexity.

Despite the income tax's unpopularity all levels of government have come to rely on it as a source of personal tax and nontax receipts. Nevertheless, those other trivial taxes and nontaxes—accounting for 6 percent of direct levies for federal, state, and local governments combined—are in no danger of being phased out.

## Changes in Tax Burden

Taxpayers—at least this one—are less concerned about the composition of their tax and nontax payments and which level of government is collecting them than with the total amount extracted from their income. Exhibit 5.2 revisits in greater detail the chart for *Personal Tax and Nontax Payments* shown in Exhibit 5.1. The pattern of extraction for the federal government and for state and local governments is shown separately on Exhibit 5.2. The horizontal axis once again measures years; the vertical measures *Percent of Personal Income*, accounted for by *Personal Tax and Nontax Payments* and its components. The line closest to the horizontal axis represents *State and Local Income Tax Payments*. The line just above it represents the total of state and local income taxes and other personal tax and nontax payments they collect. With only a few modest perturbations, both lines show a steady year-by-year rise in percent taken from taxpayers' income.

Decidedly less steady is the pattern shown for *Federal Income Tax Payments*. In 1999 *Federal income tax payments* as a percentage of personal income stood at 11.6 percent. But that percentage is not the peak for the period. It reached its highest point in 1969 at 11.8 percent of personal income and a low point in 1964 at 8.9 percent. But those extremes have been followed by ups and downs in each following decade. What has caused the bumpy ride? Memories are short, but each originating event was hailed at the time as an historical, long-to-be-remembered accomplishment.

The so-called Kennedy tax cut produced the dip in 1964. President Kennedy had proposed the cut "to stimulate economic growth."[2] Legislation responding to that proposal was passed in the early days of the Johnson administration just as business activity was picking up. Inflationary pressures and the Vietnam Conflict prompted President Johnson's proposal for a Vietnam War surtax. His proposal resulted in a 10 percent across-the-board increase in income taxes retroactive to January 1968 and continuing to the middle of 1970. The action accounts for the peak in 1969.

Responding to a subsequent downturn in economic activity, President Richard Nixon called for a cut in individual taxes. The result was a law passed in 1971 that phased in tax rate reductions over a three-year period. Another counter-cyclical attempt occurred with 1975 legislation providing for tax cuts and introducing the earned income credit. In 1981 President Ronald Reagan proposed the first of a series of calls for legislation to reduce individual income

**Exhibit 5.2**
**Personal Tax and Nontax Payments as Percents of Personal Income, 1959 to 1999**

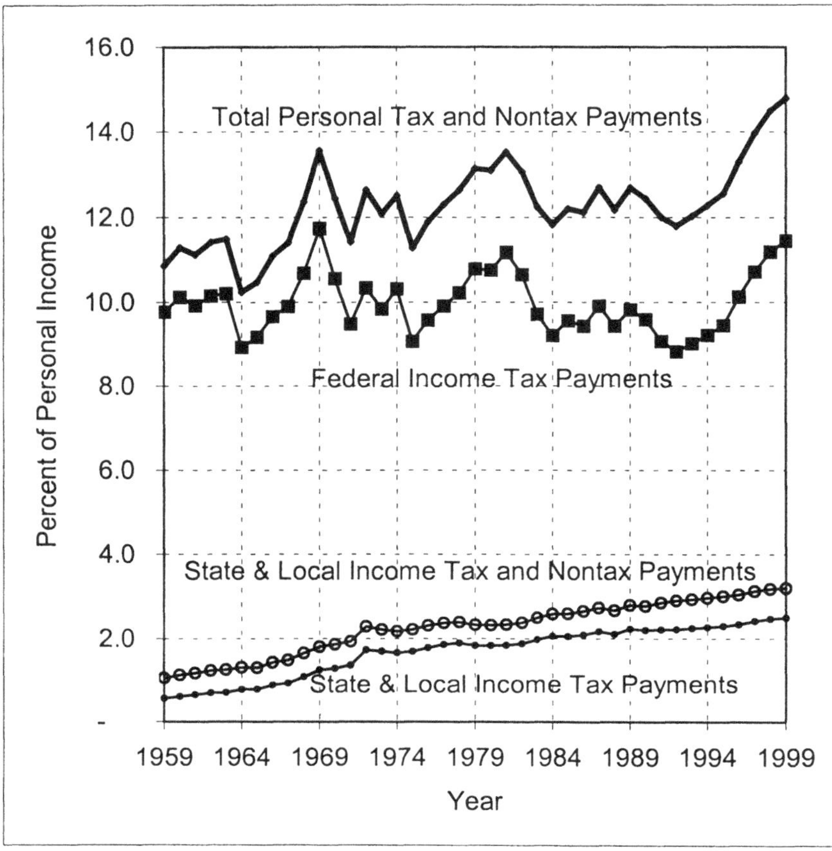


*Sources* : U.S. Department of Commerce. Bureau of Economic Analysis. "Selected NIPA Tables." *National Accounts Data* . 8 Aug. 2000: Tables 2.1, 3.1, 3.2, and 3.3. 9 Sep. 2000. <http://www.bea.doc.gov/bea/dn1.htm>.

taxes. The Economic Recovery Tax Act and successors "lowered marginal tax rates for individuals by 25 percent."[3]

One cannot help but notice that despite those series of tax cuts, the percent of personal income taken away by the federal income tax has been maintained and indeed has tended upward. The progressive nature of the tax rates accounts for the tendency. As incomes rise income taxes increase more than in proportion. That gimmick enables Washington politicians from time to time to announce tax cuts that really restore an earlier status quo. The situation was ameliorated somewhat during the Reagan-initiated tax-cut years with legislation tying income tax schedules to increases in the cost of living. Consequently, as the chart shows, the fluctuations have become less sharp. The tendency persists, however, because inflation accounts for only one of the two factors causing incomes to rise. Real economic growth per capita accounts for the other. Tying the tax schedule to per capita personal income would have removed a need for occasional "tax cuts." Then the tax-cut charade would end; federal government expenditure would increase in proportion to overall economic growth; and politicians would be required to call for increased taxes when they desire to increase the government's share of national output.

The bold line at the top of the graph traces the percentages of personal income taken away by total personal tax and nontax payments to federal, state, and local governments. Its movements up and down follow the gyrations of the federal individual income tax. State and local government personal taxes contribute to the upward trend.

## ACCOUNTING FOR CHANGES IN PRICES

Let us turn our attention to personal consumption expenditures. In 1959 personal consumption expenditures amounted to $318.1 billion; in 1999, to about $6.3 trillion. Like personal income, personal consumption expenditures in 1959 were around one-twentieth of their level in 1999. Before concluding that people forty years ago were impoverished and the standard of living in the United States then was equivalent to that of a third-world country today, we should adjust for population growth. During the period population grew from 178 million to 273 million, making 1959 per capita personal consumption expenditures about $1,800 and 1999, $23,000.

At about one-thirteenth of its level forty years later, per capita personal consumption in 1959 would be considered well below the poverty level today. What's misleading about the numbers? Comparing expenditure in 1959 with that of 1999 requires taking into account changes in prices before valid conclusions can be drawn. Prices have been and are changing all around us in usually unnoticed countless little ways.

### Recognition of Price Change over Time

Accounting for price changes is not necessary or appropriate in every case. In chapters 2 and 3, for example, we looked at the components of the sources and uses of personal income for a particular year; no adjustment was needed on that occasion. In chapter 4 we examined sources of personal income over time. Once again, taking into account price changes was unnecessary. Indeed, it was not appropriate, for adjustments for price changes are not applied to sources of personal income. However, they are applied to personal consumption expenditures for goods and services over time. Just looking at the level of expenditures is not enough. Until we allow for price changes, we can draw no conclusions about changes in the quantity of goods and services people purchased.

**Constructing Indexes of Price and Quantity**

In the 1920s Irving Fisher wrote a seminal work on price indexes.[4] It has guided analysis of the problem of appropriately taking account of price changes in the aggregate since that time. Price indexes provide measures of relative price change. He identified six types of index number formulae, tested hundreds of variations, and judged them according to two criteria: time reversal and factor reversal. By time reversal he meant that you should come to the same conclusion about relative price change for a group of goods and services regardless of whether you proceed from the past to the present or from the present to the past. By factor reversal index numbers should not change as a result of weighting prices with quantities of goods and services in different years.

As a result of his investigation, he defined as ideal a formula that takes the form for two adjacent years

For a price index of: $I_P = \sqrt{\frac{\sum P_1Q_0}{\sum P_0Q_0} \cdot \frac{\sum P_1Q_1}{\sum P_0Q_1}}$

And for a quantity index of: $I_q = \sqrt{\frac{\sum P_0Q_1}{\sum P_0Q_0} \cdot \frac{\sum P_1Q_1}{\sum P_1Q_0}}$

Where

*0* represents the beginning year and
*1* the ending year;
$Q_i$ quantities of the goods and services included in the group and
$P_i$ their respective prices in the *i*th year (either 0 or 1).

It looks complicated (and it is), but it satisfies the criteria.

When we are dealing with a single commodity or service, determining what is happening to prices and quantities becomes a straightforward exercise. If we know its prices and the amounts spent on it over a period of time, we can calculate what has happened to the quantity purchased. Similarly, if we know the quantities and total expenditures, we can calculate changes in prices. When confronted with two or more commodities or services, the situation becomes vastly more complicated. Over time prices of some items go up; some go down. So also with quantities. If we want an overall idea of what is happening to output or the general rate of inflation, a convention, a process—an agreed-upon procedure—has to be adopted. Each calculation method possesses certain advantages and disadvantages, and we want a method that yields consistent results.

If, for a bundle of products, you want to calculate a general index of prices, you have to adjust for changes in quantities. Similarly, calculating an overall index of output requires recognizing price changes. Getting a set of price and quantity indexes that ties to the overall levels of expenditure seems like a reasonable goal. Moreover, relative changes in output should be unaffected by which prices are selected as base. Likewise, relative changes in prices are independent of quantities. An illustration will help identify the problems and their resolution.

Exhibit 5.3 contains a presentation of illustrative price and quantity index calculations for two nondurable goods—purchased meals and gasoline—over a two-year period. The top rows of the table present hypothetical observed data. In the first year the average price of a meal is $10 and of a gallon of gasoline is $1.10. Quantities are in billions—22 billion meals and 100 billion gallons of gasoline—so total expenditures for those two items are $220 billion and $110 billion, respectively. In the second year the price of a meal rises to $11, and the price of a gallon of gasoline falls to $0.90. With quantities rising to 23 billion meals and 140 billion gallons, expenditures rise to $253 billion and $126 billion.

Adding prices or meals eaten and gallons of gasoline together to strike an average makes no sense. Expenditures expressed in the common denominator of dollars can be added, however, and we see that total expenditures in the first year amounted to $330 billion; in the second, to $379 billion. To the right of those two figures appears an index of expenditures using the first year as base. The index—114.85, calculated by dividing 379 by 330 and multiplying the resulting ratio by 100—indicates that expenditures from the first to the second year rose by about 15 percent.

If we want to calculate an index for prices in general, we have to hold quantities constant. We have a choice. We can use the first-year quantities as base and apply prices for the two years to them. Or we can use the second-year quantities. Does the choice make a difference? The following sets of calculations in the table suggest that it does indeed. When we use first-year quantities as base—22 billion meals and 110 billion gallons of gasoline—the resulting index—100.61—suggests that the general price level for those two commodities has increased very slightly. Using the second-year quantities as base—23 billion meals and 140 billion gallons of gasoline—produces an index of 98.70, indicating that prices declined.

Fisher's index dodges the question of which weights to use by incorporating both. He multiplies the two indexes together and takes their square root. His formula strikes an average—in this case, 99.65, the geometric mean of the two index numbers.

Similar sets of calculations appear in the lower half of the table for quantity indexes. The first adopts first-year price levels as the base—meals at $10 and gasoline at $1.10 a gallon—and results an index of 116.36, indicating an apparent overall quantity increase of over 16 percent; the second, using the second year—meals at $11 and gasoline at $0.90—results in 114.15, suggesting a 14 percent increase. Once again Fisher's index—115.25—strikes a compromise by taking the geometric mean of the two.

Whimping out and compromising offers more than the advantage of avoiding arguments. Multiplying the Fisher price and quantity indexes together results in an index for change in expenditure—114.85—that agrees with the observed data. Repeating the process for adjacent years creates a time series of price and

**Exhibit 5.3**
**Comparison of Price and Quantity Index Calculations**

| | First Year | | | Second Year | | | |
|---|---|---|---|---|---|---|---|
| **Commodities** | **Prices** | **Quantities** | **Expenditure** | **Prices** | **Quantities** | **Expenditure** | **Indexes** |
| **Observed Prices and Quantities** | | | | | | | |
| | $P_0$ | $Q_0$ | $P_0Q_0$ | $P_1$ | $Q_1$ | $P_1Q_1$ | |
| Meals | $10.00 | 22 | $220 | $11.00 | 23 | $253 | |
| Gasoline | $ 1.10 | 100 | 110 | $ 0.90 | 140 | 126 | |
| Total | | | $330 | | | $379 | 114.85 |
| **Price Index with First Year Quantity Weights** | | | | | | | |
| | $P_0$ | $Q_0$ | $P_0Q_0$ | $P_1$ | | $P_1Q_0$ | |
| Meals | $10.00 | 22 | $220 | $11.00 | | $242 | |
| Gasoline | $ 1.10 | 100 | 110 | $ 0.90 | | 90 | |
| Total | | | $330 | | | $332 | 100.61 |
| **Price Index with Second Year Quantity Weights** | | | | | | | |
| | $P_0$ | | $P_1Q_0$ | $P_1$ | $Q_1$ | $P_1Q_1$ | |
| Meals | 10.00 | | $230 | 11.00 | 23 | $253 | |
| Gasoline | 1.10 | | 154 | 0.90 | 140 | 126 | |
| Total | | | $384 | | | $379 | 98.70 |
| **Fisher Ideal Price Index** | | | | | | | 99.65 |
| **Quantity Index with First Year Price Weights** | | | | | | | |
| | $P_0$ | $Q_0$ | $P_0Q_0$ | | $Q_1$ | $P_0Q_1$ | |
| Meals | $10.00 | 22 | $220 | | 23 | $230 | |
| Gasoline | $ 1.10 | 100 | 110 | | 140 | 154 | |
| Total | | | $330 | | | $384 | 116.36 |
| **Quantity Index with Second Year Price Weights** | | | | | | | |
| | | $Q_0$ | $P_0Q_1$ | $P_1$ | $Q_1$ | $P_1Q_1$ | |
| Meals | | 22 | $242 | 11.00 | 23 | $253 | |
| Gasoline | | 100 | 90 | 0.90 | 140 | 126 | |
| Total | | | $332 | | | $379 | 114.16 |
| **Fisher Ideal Quantity Index** | | | | | | | 115.25 |

quantity indexes. The price indexes are based on a chain of quantity weights; the quantity indexes are based on a price-weighted chain. Hence, the term, chain-weighted indexes.

### Price and Quantity Indexes for Personal Consumption Expenditures

Despite the virtues of chain-weighted price and quantity indexes using the Fisher formula, until recently the national income and product accounts employed fixed-weighted price and quantity indexes to analyze price and output changes. As long as outputs remained relatively the same, distortions created were insignificant. Large shifts in petroleum prices in the 1970s and early 1980s and their concomitant effects on prices and outputs in the economy's energy sector introduced material errors. The 1980s also brought rapid expansion of electronic products—especially personal computers—accompanied by price cuts. The magnitude of those changes signaled a new era to the Department of Commerce and hastened its use of chain-weighted indexes. In 1995 the Department of Commerce adopted chain-weighted indexes using 1992 as the initial base year. More recently, 1996 has been adopted as the base year.

Exhibit 5.4 presents personal consumption expenditures (PCE) for 1959 and 1999 expressed in current dollar prices and adjusted for changes in the price level. Along with those two amounts, the price index is included as well. Personal consumption expenditures and other national income statistics that have been adjusted for price level changes often are referred to as "real," as in *real* disposable personal income or *real* personal consumption expenditures. Contrary to connotation, those price-adjusted series are not real but exist entirely as creations of an artificial calculating convention, an algorithm. Personal consumption expenditures that do result from actual transactions involving prices prevailing at the time and quantities of goods and services sometimes are called "nominal" personal consumption expenditures. The term suggests something trivial or not actual. No wonder people get confused with economic terminology.

In principle, if you know any two of the three items on Exhibit 5.4, you should be able to derive the third. For example, dividing the $318.7 billion PCE in current dollars by the PCE price index, 21.6, and multiplying by 100 should produce the $1,470.7 billion price-adjusted PCE for 1959. In practice the result is close, but because of rounding, no cigar. However, the differences are relatively small.

The average annual growth rate of personal consumption expenditures expressed in current-value dollars over the forty-year period is 7.74 percent. The *PCE Price Index* percent change is 4.02 percent; in *Price-Adjusted PCE* growth rate, the change is 3.57 percent. Adding the latter two percentages together to approximate 7.74 percent is tempting. The conceptually correct relationship is not additive but a multiplicative one that takes the form:

$$100\cdot(1+r_P)\cdot(1+r_Q)-100$$

**Exhibit 5.4**
**Personal Consumption Expenditures (PCE) in Current and Constant Dollar Value Amounts with Price Index (1996 = 100), 1959 and 1999**

| | 1959 Amounts in $ Billions | 1999 Amounts in $ Billions | Annual Percent Change |
|---|---|---|---|
| **PCE in Current Dollars** | **$ 318.1** | **$ 5,978.8** | **7.74** |
| Durable goods | 42.7 | 817.8 | 7.47 |
| Nondurable goods | 148.5 | 1,779.4 | 6.50 |
| Services | 127.0 | 3,390.8 | 8.77 |
| **PCE Price Index** | **21.6** | **104.8** | **4.02** |
| Durable goods | 42.0 | 93.1 | 2.01 |
| Nondurable goods | 24.6 | 103.7 | 3.66 |
| Services | 16.7 | 108.0 | 4.77 |
| **Price-Adjusted PCE** | **1,470.7** | **5,978.8** | **3.57** |
| Durable goods | 101.6 | 817.8 | 5.35 |
| Nondurable goods | 603.7 | 1,779.4 | 2.74 |
| Services | $ 758.8 | $ 3,390.8 | 3.81 |

*Source*: United States. Department of Commerce. Bureau of Economic Analysis. "Underlying detail estimates for PCE, historical file." *State of the Nation Library*. 8 Sep. 2000: Tables 206U, 207U, and 705U. 8 Oct. 2000 <http://www.stat-usa.gov/online.nsf/NIPANav?OpenNavigator>.

where $r_P$ stands for the *PCE Price Index* percent change (divided by 100), and $r_Q$ is the *Price-Adjusted PCE* growth rate (also divided by 100). Multiplication produces a closer approximation than addition. In this case the calculation yields 7.73. Compared with the sum of the rates for PCE price index and price-adjusted PCE index—7.59—the product of the two numbers is closer to 7.74, and the difference can be attributed to rounding error.

Now armed with a price-adjusted personal consumption expenditures time series, we are in a position to assess just how tough times were in 1959. In constant-value dollar terms, personal consumption has increased a little over four times, from about $1.5 trillion to $6.0 trillion over the forty-year period. Remember, at the same time population rose too, from 178 million to 273 million persons. On a per capita basis, real personal consumption expenditures, therefore, have grown from $8,300 to $21,900—over 2.6 times. A doubling of the goods and services available on average to every man, woman, and child represents a great achievement and improvement in the human condition. Although past performance does not insure continued performance—as the investment brochures say—it does promise an even better future.

## PERSONAL CONSUMPTION EXPENDITURES

Armed with price and quantity indexes, we now can disaggregate expenditures for goods and services into their two components. The ability to hold constant—at least, conceptually—one of the two factors determining expenditures level reveals to us much more about economic activity than when they are combined.

### Patterns Among Durable, Nondurable, and Service Expenditures

Exhibit 5.4 contains information about the major product components of personal consumption expenditures (PCE) that deserves comment. For personal consumption expenditures in current dollars, *Services* experienced the fastest average annual overall rate of growth, 8.8 percent over the forty-year period. Slowest growth occurred in expenditures for *Nondurable goods*, 6.5 percent. In between fell *Durable goods* at 7.5 percent.

Disaggregating those expenditures expressed in current-value dollars into their price and quantity components reveals different patterns. The *PCE Price Index* for *Services* rose most rapidly, averaging 4.8 percent compounded annually. Inflation is lowest for *Durable goods*. Inflation for *Nondurable goods* occupies the intermediate position. *Price-Adjusted PCE* constitutes our surrogate for a measure of quantity. At 5.4 percent per year, the strongest growth occurs for *Durable goods*; *Services* come in second; and *Nondurable goods*, third.

Alert readers will notice that the sum of the price-adjusted expenditures for durable and nondurable goods and for services does not agree with the amount shown for the aggregate. According to the Bureau of Economic Analysis, "because the relative prices used as weights for any period other than the base period differ from those used for the base period, the chained-dollar values for the detail" do not sum to the aggregate.[7] The discrepancy represents one of the shortcomings of chain-weighted index construction. Fixed-weighted indexes avoid that problem. Fortunately, it does not handicap our purposes of showing relative change but does present a problem if one attempts to determine each component's contribution to the aggregate.

In the case of durable goods, high growth in purchases of output accompanied slow growth in price inflation. That outcome corresponds with the expectation that people will buy more of an item the lower its price. The relationship does not hold for nondurable goods and services, however. Despite higher inflation rates associated with services, growth of services purchased exceeded that of nondurable goods.

Components of personal consumption expenditures differ not only in rates at which their quantities grow but also exhibit different growth patterns over time. Exhibit 5.5 shows annual rates of change in price-adjusted expenditures for each of them. Greatest volatility occurs in expenditures for real *Durables*. On five different occasions growth rates spiked downward into negative territory. On the other hand, when expenditures for durables were brisk, they were very, very

**Exhibit 5.5**
**Rates of Change in Real Personal Consumption Expenditures by Product Categories, 1959 to 1999**

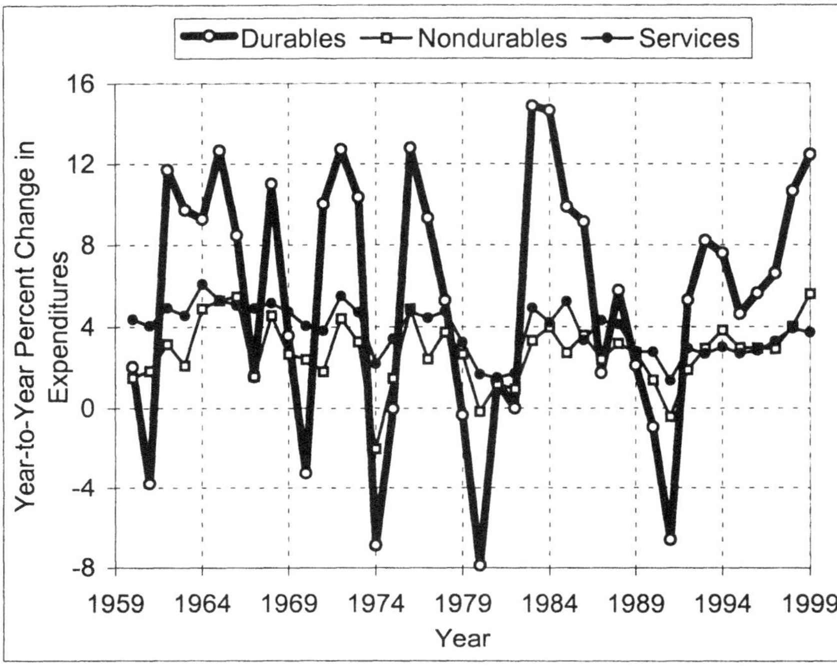


*Source* : United States. Department of Commerce. Bureau of Economic Analysis. "Underlying detail estimates for PCE, historical file." *State of the Nation Library* . 8 Sep. 2000: Table 207U. 8 Oct. 2000 <http://www.stat-usa.gov/online.nsf/NIPANav?OpenNavigator>.

brisk indeed. For eleven of the years, growth rates exceeded 10 percent. The prosperous years more than offset the lean ones and generate for durable goods the highest growth in *Price-Adjusted PCE* of the three product categories for the entire forty-year period. Rates of change in expenditures for real *Nondurables* and *Services* fall within a narrower band between no growth and 5 percent. Unlike food, shelter, clothing, and medical care, purchases of durable goods can be deferred when economic conditions appear bleak for consumers. Not everyone has to respond, of course, to make an impact on economic aggregates. Postponing expenditures for durable goods by just, say, one family in twenty will impact economic aggregates significantly. Although food and clothing are everyday necessities, expenditures for services demonstrate greater stability than those for nondurables. You can adjust purchases of food every time you go to the grocery store, and clothing—while not considered a durable good—does not wear out immediately. *Services* include among its subcomponents imputed housing services plus expenditures for utilities and medical care. They account for its consistent growth rate. The capital stock of residential structures generating housing services is relatively stable, and need for medical care arises independently of economic conditions.

## AN OVERVIEW OF PERSONAL CONSUMPTION ITEMS

When we see changes in the amount of personal consumption expenditure, two factors are at work. One is the change in the amount of goods and services people are buying. The other is change in the price level. Increases in expenditures do not necessarily mean increases in the quantities purchased. Price inflation may produce the result. Clearly, we are able to obtain greater insight into what is going on in the economy or a particular sector when we are able to disaggregate expenditures into the price and quantity parts.

However, examining expenditures expressed in current-value dollars over time is not a completely worthless exercise. An increase or decrease in a product's share of consumers' consumption expenditure dollar is not without significance. We just have to be wary of drawing conclusions about what is happening to the price or quantity of an item in the absence of additional information.

Armed with that cautionary note, we are prepared to inspect Exhibit 5.6. It provides a comparison of the product components of personal consumption expenditures in current-value dollar terms for 1959 and 1999. Note the three major categories: *Durable goods*, *Nondurable goods*, and *Services*. For 1999 we observe that *Services* account for 58 percent, the largest portion of the total. That was not the case in 1959. Then, the largest share of personal consumption expenditures went for *Nondurable goods*, 47 percent. In the intervening forty years, both the shares of *Durable* and *Nondurable goods* have shrunk as services increased.

Average annual growth rates in expenditures among the subcategories for *Durable* and *Nondurable goods* and *Services* exhibited in Exhibit 5.6 differ from that of the category to which they belong. For example, *Nondurable goods* expenditures grew at 7 percent. Among its subcategories, *Food,* its largest category, grew only at 6 percent; *Drug preparations and sundries* grew at 10 percent. With increasing levels of detail we see increased variation.

### Durable Goods

Exhibit 5.6 shows that the average growth rates among *Durable goods* subcategories varied from 7 percent to 9 percent. *Motor vehicles and parts* and *Furniture and household equipment* grew at a 7 percent annual rate and, because of their relative importance both in 1959 and 1999, determine the 7 percent growth rate for durable goods.

Four subcategories comprise *Motor vehicles and parts*: new automobiles, net purchases of used automobiles, other motor vehicles, and tires, tubes, accessories and parts. In 1959 sales of new automobiles accounted for 70 percent of the *Motor vehicle and parts* category; in 1999, just 30 percent. A foreigner who stopped reading at this point might jump to the conclusion that Americans have

**Exhibit 5.6**
**Personal Consumption Expenditures by Type of Product, 1959 and 1999**

| | | 1959 Amounts in $ Billions |
|---|---|---|
| **Durable goods** | | **$ 42.7** |
| Motor vehicles and parts | 18.9 | |
| Furniture & household equipment | 18.1 | |
| Ophthalmic & orthopedic appliances | 0.6 | |
| Recreational equipment | 2.0 | |
| Jewelry and watches | 2.0 | |
| Books and maps | 1.1 | |
| **Nondurable goods** | | **148.5** |
| Food | 80.7 | |
| Clothing and shoes | 26.4 | |
| Gasoline, fuel oil, and other energy goods | 15.3 | |
| Tobacco products | 6.6 | |
| Toilet articles and preparations | 2.7 | |
| Semidurable house furnishings | 2.7 | |
| Household supplies | 3.5 | |
| Drug preparations and sundries | 3.5 | |
| Nondurable toys & sport supplies | 2.4 | |
| Stationery and writing supplies | 1.1 | |
| Net foreign remittances | 1.0 | |
| Periodicals and sheet music | 2.1 | |
| Flowers, seeds, & potted plants | 0.6 | |
| **Services** | | **127.0** |
| Housing | 45.0 | |
| Household operation | 18.7 | |
| Transportation | 10.5 | |
| Medical care | 16.4 | |
| Recreation | 6.4 | |
| Personal care | 6.2 | |
| Personal business | 13.6 | |
| Education and research | 4.0 | |
| Religious and welfare activities | 5.0 | |
| Net foreign travel | 1.1 | |
| **TOTAL PERSONAL CONSUMPTION** | | **$ 318.1** |

*Source* : U.S. Department of Commerce. Bureau of Economic Analysis. "Selected NIPA Tables." <http://www.bea.doc.gov/bea/dn1.htm>.

**Exhibit 5.6 (continued)**
**Personal Consumption Expenditures by Type of Product, 1959 and 1999**

| Percent of Total | 1999 Amounts in $ Billions | Percent of Total | Annual Percent Change |
|---|---|---|---|
| **13** | **$ 761.3** | **12** | **7** |
| 6 | 320.7 | 5 | 7 |
| 6 | 288.5 | 5 | 7 |
| 0 | 22.1 | 0 | 9 |
| 1 | 51.3 | 1 | 8 |
| 1 | 48.8 | 1 | 8 |
| 0 | 29.8 | 0 | 9 |
| **47** | **1,845.5** | **29** | **7** |
| 25 | 897.8 | 14 | 6 |
| 8 | 307.0 | 5 | 6 |
| 5 | 142.7 | 2 | 6 |
| 2 | 66.0 | 1 | 6 |
| 1 | 57.5 | 1 | 8 |
| 1 | 38.3 | 1 | 7 |
| 1 | 57.1 | 1 | 7 |
| 1 | 136.8 | 2 | 10 |
| 1 | 63.1 | 1 | 9 |
| 0 | 23.1 | 0 | 8 |
| 0 | 1.6 | 0 | 1 |
| 1 | 37.0 | 1 | 7 |
| 0 | 17.5 | 0 | 9 |
| **40** | **3,661.9** | **58** | **9** |
| 14 | 906.2 | 14 | 8 |
| 6 | 360.2 | 6 | 8 |
| 3 | 256.5 | 4 | 8 |
| 5 | 943.6 | 15 | 11 |
| 2 | 237.1 | 4 | 9 |
| 2 | 70.1 | 1 | 6 |
| 4 | 586.2 | 9 | 10 |
| 1 | 148.9 | 2 | 9 |
| 2 | 170.2 | 3 | 9 |
| 0 | (17.0) | (0) | |
| **100** | **$ 6,268.7** | **100** | **8** |

*National Accounts Data*. 8 Aug. 2000: Table 2.2. 9 Sep. 2000.

lost their enchantment with the automobile. Our experience with traffic congestion keeps us from even considering that as a possibility no matter how brief our scan of this table.

Other motor vehicles make up the difference. In 1959 they accounted for just 3 percent of *Motor vehicles and parts*; in 1999, 37 percent. The numbers reflect what we see with our own eyes on the highways and byways. Pick-up trucks, vans, and recreational vehicles are everywhere! People have lost their enchantment with automobiles but are just as keen on owner-operated motorized vehicles of another kind.

Hidden within new automobiles is the share of the automobile market captured by foreign automobile makers. In 1959 new foreign automobiles accounted for 9 percent of the U.S. market. During the next decade foreign carmakers' share first declined and then increased; by 1969 they accounted for 10 percent. The decade of the 1970s, however, presented a different story. By 1974, 20 percent of the new automobiles sold in the United States were foreign made; by 1979, 29 percent. In 1987 the figure peaked at nearly 42 percent. By 1996 it had retreated to 30 percent. A rapid recovery has ensued. At the end of the period, it stands at 39 percent. Given the benefit of such information, an average annual growth rate for the forty-year period of 4 percent for domestic automobile producers and 9 percent for foreign should not be surprising. In this particular situation expenditure expressed in current values tells us what happened to quantities as well. The price indexes for domestic and foreign automobiles are very similar, rising at an average annual rate of 2.4 percent. Surprise! Surprise!

Even foreign automobiles did not keep pace with other motor vehicles. Expenditures for trucks for personal use grew annually at 14 percent; for recreational vehicles, at 13 percent. Prices, however, have risen more rapidly than for automobiles: 2.7 percent for trucks and 3.4 percent for recreational vehicles. People pay a premium for barreling down the highway in their home away from home and blocking the view ahead for those behind them.

Like *Motor vehicles and parts*, *Furniture and household equipment* lost market share for consumers' consumption dollar from 1959 to 1999. All items included in that category exhibited a similar pattern save one: video, audio, computer, and musical equipment. Technology accounts for the strength in this sector. At the beginning of the period, neither video equipment—other than television—nor computers were included in the series. Earlier technological marvels led the way. From 1959 to 1979 records, tapes, and discs enjoyed double-digit annual growth rates; from 1964 to 1979, audio equipment. The Department of Commerce began picking up other video equipment and computers in 1977. In 1999, at $13.6 billion and $31.9 billion, respectively, the rapid growth of other video equipment and computers has enabled them to account for about 46 percent of expenditures for video, audio, computer, and musical equipment. Audio equipment, records, tapes, and disks account for 29 percent.

Changes in prices and quantities for video, audio, computing equipment, and musical instruments are so spectacular that they deserve detailed inspection.

**Exhibit 5.7**
**Relationship Between Nominal and Real Expenditures and Price Index for Video, Audio, Computing, and Musical Equipment, 1959 to 1999**

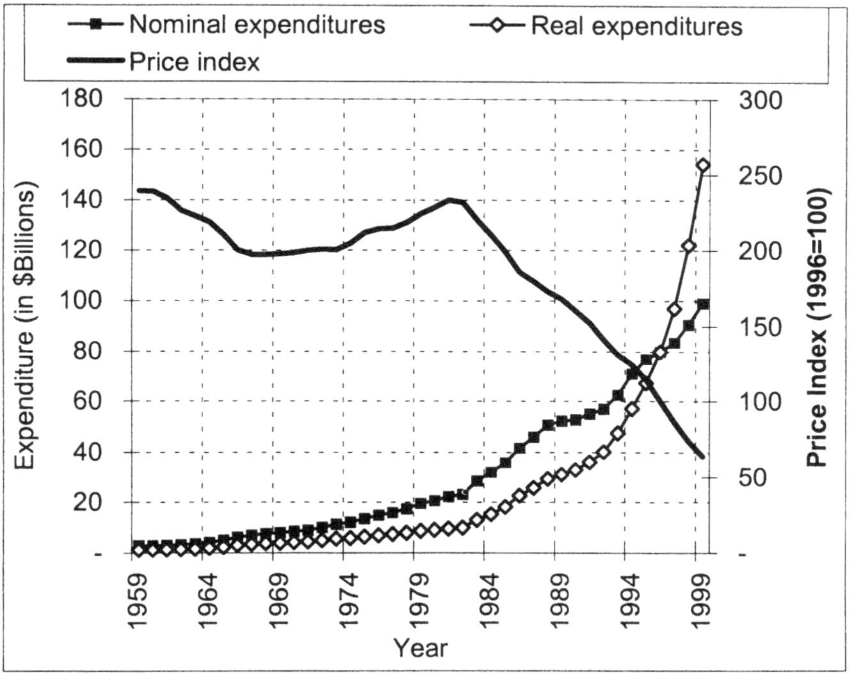


*Source*: United States. Department of Commerce. Bureau of Economic Analysis. "Underlying detail estimates for PCE, historical file." *State of the Nation Library*. 8 Sep. 2000: Tables 206U, 207U, and 705U. 8 Oct. 2000 <http://www.stat-usa.gov/online.nsf/NIPANav?OpenNavigator>.

Exhibit 5.7 provides that closer look. Here we have *Nominal* and *Real expenditures* expressed in billions of current- and constant-value dollars and the *Price Index* for each of the years from 1959 to 1999. The chart is a little tricky. It has two vertical axes, one on the left and one on the right. The one on the left measures expenditures in billions of dollars. The right axis measures the price index. The line descending from the top left corner of the graph to below the middle of the right-hand side relates to the right-hand axis. That's the *Price Index*! Prices for those electronic gadgets went down! Prices for the group are less than one-third of what they were forty years earlier. (The decline would be even greater if I had excluded musical instruments that went up about 2.2 percent a year.) Prices for computers, peripherals, and software in 1999 are 1 percent of their 1959 levels.

The falling price phenomenon creates an unusual relationship between *Nominal* and *Real expenditures*. Both lines representing them relate to the left axis. Ordinarily, we would expect to see on the graph price-adjusted expenditures start higher, intersect current-dollar expenditures at the base year from above, and end the period lower. For video, audio, computing equipment, and musical instruments, the relationship is reversed. The price-adjusted series, *Real expenditures*, rose from $1.3 billion in 1959 to $154.3 billion in 1999, 118 times greater—an average annual growth rate in price-adjusted expenditures of nearly 13 percent. Growth in output more than offset falling prices, causing *Nominal expenditures* to rise from $3.1 billion to $99.1 billion, thirty-two times. Consequently, the share of video, audio, computing equipment, and musical instruments increases from 17 to 34 percent of *Furniture and household equipment*. Here we see most vividly the promise of advances in technology: lower prices for better products.

### Nondurable Goods

Over the past forty years, *Nondurable goods*—the things we buy almost daily to keep body and soul together—as a share of personal consumption expenditures declined from 47 percent to 29 percent. With an average annual growth rate of 6 percent, the share of *Food*, the largest single nondurable, fell from 25 percent to 14 percent of total consumption expenditures. That outcome should not be surprising. People can only eat so much. Other things being equal—like food prices relative to other prices—expenditures for food can be expected to increase with population growth. Personal income has increased more rapidly than population. With rising income people may increase food quality, but percentage increases in expenditures for food tend to be less than percentage increases in income. In other words, food is inelastic with respect to income.

A look at the components of the food category shows that the pattern of expenditure for meals and beverages purchased at restaurants and other dining establishments differed from the other food purchases. While the others decreased, purchased meals and beverages increased its share of consumer dollars from 1959 to 1999, suggesting that people were more interested in how and where they ate than in what they ate. Although close, however, the percentage increase in purchased meals and beverages was less than the overall percentage increase in *Personal Consumption Expenditures*. Throughout the period the growth rate of food raised and consumed on farms has been negative, a consequence of a declining farm population and commercial specialization of agriculture.

For similar reasons, expenditures for *Clothing and shoes* are inelastic with respect to personal income. People can only wear so much, and fashion trends appear to point to wearing as little as possible.

The market share of *Gasoline, fuel oil, and other energy goods* slips from 5 percent to 2 percent. However, the information hides the turbulent history of that particular product during the past forty years. Exhibit 5.8 enables us to look between the end points and review what happened in terms of economic data.

**Exhibit 5.8**
**Expenditures, Relative Prices, and Quantity of Gasoline and Other Motor Fuels, 1959 to 1999**

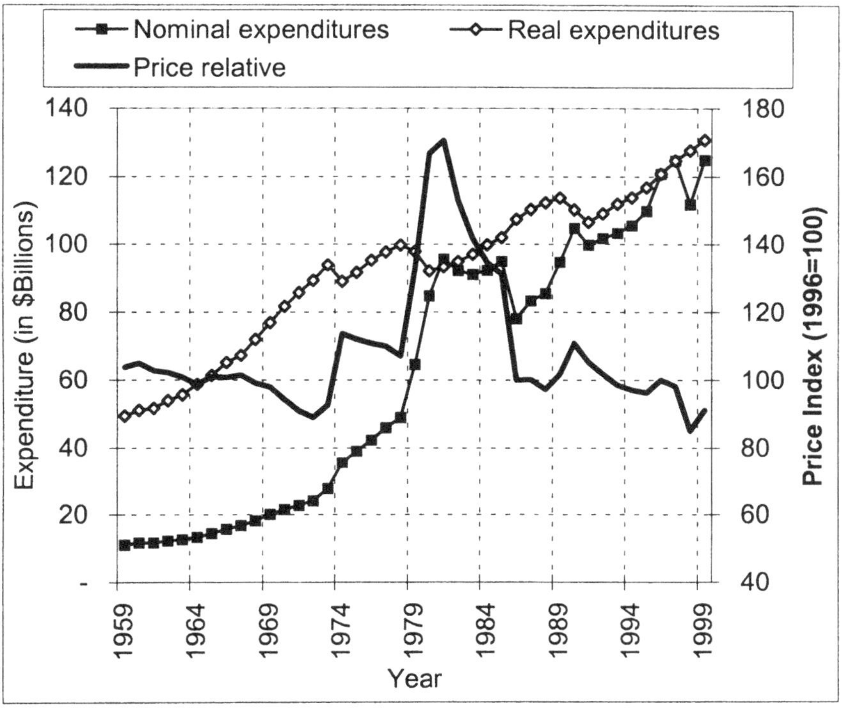


*Source*: United States. Department of Commerce. Bureau of Economic Analysis. "Underlying detail estimates for PCE, historical file." *State of the Nation Library*. 8 Sep. 2000: Tables 206U, 207U, and 705U. 8 Oct. 2000 <http://www.stat-usa.gov/online.nsf/NIPANav?OpenNavigator>.

As with Exhibit 5.7, the left and right vertical axes measure expenditure and the price index, respectively.

During the seventeen years from 1964 to 1981, the growth rate of *Nominal expenditures* for *Gasoline and Other Motor Fuels* exceeded that for total personal consumption expenditures. In subsequent periods its growth rate has fallen behind the total. *Nominal expenditures* for gasoline and other motor fuels in 1959 amounted to $11.1 billion; in 1999, $124.9—an eleven-fold increase in forty years. In Exhibit 5.8 *Nominal expenditures* are measured against the left axis and appear as a line emanating from the lower left corner and proceeding to the upper right-hand corner. *Nominal expenditures* progressed smoothly until 1973. Then, after a jump upward, they resumed a smooth rise until 1979. In 1979 expenditures began a rapid ascent for three years. For the next four years until 1985, they flattened out. In 1986 they dropped precipitously. Recovery followed until 1990. After a drop in 1991, smoother growth returned.

*Real expenditures* moved in the general direction of *Nominal expenditures* but at a slower and interrupted pace. On several occasions they headed south. Those changes in direction relate to jumps in the *Price Index*.

Moves up and down in expenditures compared to moves in the *Price Index* appear like ripples in a pond compared to waves in the ocean. To eliminate the effect of general price inflation, I divided the price index for gasoline and motor fuel by the price index for all personal consumption expenditures. Relative to other prices, gasoline prices tended downward from 1959 to 1972. The supply of oil exceeded demand, pushing prices lower. With gasoline becoming relatively cheaper, Detroit responded with gas-guzzling cars. Consumption increased at an average rate of 4.6 percent annually. The first price increase occurring in 1973 did not change consumption; the second, sharper increase in 1974 brought the relative price of gasoline to well above its 1959 level and caused a decided drop in consumption. After that spike world markets again became awash in oil; consumption increases resumed until 1979. A huge price increase in 1980 prompted a three-year decline in *Real expenditures*. After 1981 tendencies for downward pressure on prices again manifested themselves, but rising consumption offset their effect on *Nominal expenditures* until 1986, the year of the oil bust. A run up in prices preceding the Gulf Conflict in 1990 has since been followed by a decline with rising consumption helping to maintain and even increase nominal expenditures. The year 1999 harbingers a change with a rise in the *Price relative* for gasoline and other motor fuels. Even with that increase, the prices of gasoline and other motor fuels—stuff some said we would be running out of—are lower relative to other prices than in 1959. Exhibit 5.8 demonstrates that the market mechanism is alive and well. Increases in prices effectively reduce amounts demanded and ration scarce supplies—even something as essential as gasoline and other motor fuels.

The forty-year period opened with an assault by Iraq on Kuwait; thirty years later we witnessed a second attempt. The British easily quashed the first attempt; the second required a multinational force. In between occurred nationalization of oil company assets in the Middle Eastern countries; the rise and fall and, in the late 1990s, rise again in the Organization of Petroleum Exporting Countries (OPEC) as a determinant of the market price of oil; transformation of the world oil market from one managed by dominant multilateral producing and refining companies to one subject to worldwide supply and demand forces; a reduction in federal government regulation of domestic prices of petroleum products; a so-called Oil Embargo in the 1970s; energy conservation; the search for alternative fuels; little automobiles; a domestic oil boom and bust as prices rose and fell; an oil glut followed by consumer purchases of larger vehicles in the form of vans, pickup trucks, and four-wheel drive conveyances. Now in prospect is reversal of nationalization of oil resources by Saudi Arabia, Iraq, Libya, and Iran. Their recent invitations to Western oil companies to participate in equity shares for further development of their petroleum resources promises ample supplies for the near future. Only political instability in that oil-rich region remains unchanged.[8]

Within the *Gasoline, fuel oil, and other energy goods* category, fuel oil and other energy sources like coal exhibit decidedly declining shares of consumers' expenditures. Nominal expenditures for fuel oil and coal peaked in 1981. They have since declined in absolute as well as relative terms. Declining prices and a shift to gas and electricity for home heating have pushed growth in expenditures for those two products into negative territory. The replacements offer cleaner heat and greater convenience to householders.

Exhibit 5.6 shows that the market share of only one nondurable goods category has increased: *Drug preparations and sundries*. Its 10 percent average annual rate of increase from 1959 to 1999—related to the rising cost of medical care—pushes its share from 1 percent to 2 percent.

*Tobacco products* expenditures start out the period larger than those for all other nondurables except *Food, Clothing and shoes*, and *Gasoline, fuel oil, and other energy goods*. By 1999 those categories are surpassed by *Drug preparations and sundries*. The market-share decline in tobacco expenditures from 2 percent to 1 percent obscures a significant change in consumption. Those opposed to smoking can rejoice over the fact that in constant-value dollar terms, consumption in 1999 was less than in 1959. Hefty price increases (averaging 6.5 percent annually as compared to 4.0 percent for all personal consumption expenditures) have softened the revenue blow to tobacco company revenues.

### Services

Among the services subcategories, *Housing services* and *Household operation services* hold their own at 14 and 6 percent of market share, respectively. Within *Housing services*, growth of imputed rent for owner-occupied nonfarm dwellings outpaces the rate of increase in personal consumption expenditures. Rent from tenant-occupied nonfarm dwellings and other housing in the form of the rental value of farm dwellings, housing furnished by employers, and transient housing such as hotels and motels grew less rapidly.

*Household operation* includes expenditures for electricity, gas, water and sewage, refuse collection, telephone and telegraph, domestic services, and lots of other things like moving and storage, household insurance, and postage. As a group their expenditures keep pace with personal consumption expenditures, but among them growth rates differ.

Despite conversion of many households to gas as a form of energy, natural gas rose only at a 4.9 percent average annual rate over the period. Falling prices rather than a decline in use account for the low and close to no growth rates in nominal expenditures in the past decade. Water and other sanitation services increased their share of personal consumption expenditures. Annual average price increases in excess of 6 percent—as compared to the overall price index for personal consumption expenditures of 4.0 percent—accounts for much of the nominal expenditure increase. Getting rid of waste in a manner that complies with mounting regulation has become an expensive proposition.

Telephone and telegraph expenditures have grown at nearly 9 percent a year. Increases in level of service rather than price increases account for their growth in nominal expenditures. Over the forty-year period, the price rise of telephone and telegraph services averaged only 1.6 percent per year. Domestic service grew at an average annual rate of only 4 percent.

Market share for *Transportation* expenditures increases from 3 percent to 4 percent of personal consumption expenditure. User-operated transportation and purchased intercity transportation account for most of the transportation dollar, and they increased their shares. Purchased local transportation has declined substantially relative to other expenditures for consumer services. Mass transit systems, taxicabs, railway, bus, and other forms of local transportation—despite subsidies for many of them—fail to meet the market test.

*Medical care* has tripled its share of personal consumption expenditures from 5 to 15 percent, a reflection of an 11 percent annual growth rate. For hospitals and nursing homes, the share has more than tripled. Expenditures for nursing homes increased at an average annual rate approaching 15 percent.

Unlike the Internal Revenue Service, which does not treat employer-paid group medical care insurance premiums as income—at least not as taxable income—the Department of Commerce makes no such distinction when constructing the national income and product accounts. Those premium payments are treated as a source of personal income. An offsetting entry, health insurance expenditure, is recorded under *Medical care*.

The relationship between nominal and real expenditures and prices for *Medical care* contrasts with those for *Video, audio, computer, and musical equipment* and for *Gasoline and other motor fuels*. In the case of electronic equipment, price declines were accompanied by rapid advances in quantity sold resulting in an overall increase in nominal expenditures. In the case of *Gasoline and oil*, increases in its price relative to other products reduced quantity consumed and relative price decreases increased consumption. Exhibit 5.9 presents the relationship for *Medical care*. Here everything increases: *Price Index*, *Real expenditures*, and, of course, their product, *Nominal expenditures*. Note in particular the *Price Index*. It shows that the price of medical care relative to other goods and services rises and rises substantially. The 1959 index stands at 49; by 1999 it is 102—more than double. It shows that the cost of medical care was increasing at twice the rate of prices for all personal consumption items. Prices in 1999 are roughly five times those in 1959; medical costs are ten times greater. Despite the rise, *Real Expenditures* move upward. Under third-party payer arrangements, those receiving services do not pay for them, and usual market restraints break down. Here we see the perils of a breakdown in the market mechanism.

Returning to Exhibit 5.6, we see that market share changes in the remaining categories of expenditures for services are less dramatic. *Personal business* services show a substantial increase in share that can be attributed to financial services furnished without payment: imputed expenditures for service charges of financial intermediaries and services furnished without payment by domestic

**Exhibit 5.9**
**Nominal and Real Expenditures and Relative Prices for Medical Care, 1959 to 1999**

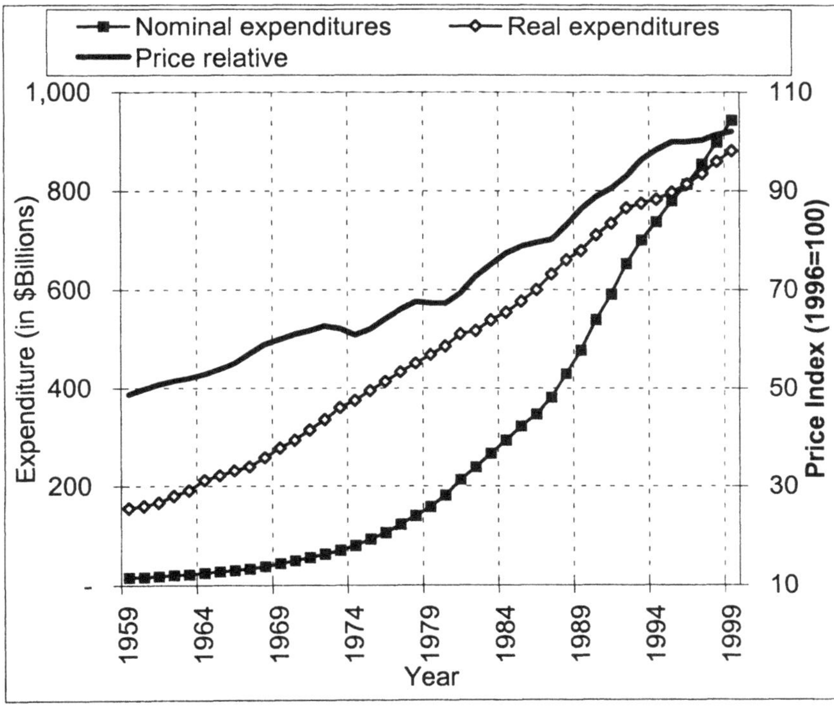


*Source*: United States. Department of Commerce. Bureau of Economic Analysis. "Underlying detail estimates for PCE, historical file." *State of the Nation Library*. 8 Sep. 2000: Tables 206U, 207U, and 705U. 8 Oct. 2000 <http://www.stat-usa.gov/online.nsf/NIPANav?OpenNavigator>.

securities dealers. Their growth averaged 11 percent annually. The expense of handling life insurance and other *Personal business* services, with growth averaging 9 percent a year, likewise increased their share of consumers' expenditure dollar. The remaining items under *Services* account for 10 percent of personal consumption expenditures in 1999 and, with the exception of *Personal care*, either maintained or increased their market share over the forty-year period.

## Concluding Observations

During the forty years from 1959 to 1999, personal consumption expenditures increased in proportion with personal income. However, growth among the components of personal consumption expenditures has been uneven, with durable and nondurable goods increasing less than in proportion and with the most rapid rise occurring in expenditures for services. Medical care was responsible for a major portion of the growing share of personal consumption expenditures for services, but expenditures for other services such as personal business services, recreational services, education and research, and religious and welfare activities show long-term gains.

Three factors account for shifts in consumer outlays for goods and services: changes in preferences, technology advances resulting in new goods and services, and changes in prices. Advertising attempts to modify preferences through the power of suggestion, but other, more pervasive forces are at work. Changes in the overall level of income as well as its distribution can influence preferences or at least their manifestations in the marketplace. Home buying and furnishing occupy a high place in priorities of young families. Paying for higher education expenditures rise in importance as children reach college age. Retirement brings expenditures for recreation and travel. A growing elderly population tends to push up expenditures for medical care. Preference changes occur, but determining how to measure those changes independently of their effect on consumer outlays poses an insurmountable problem.

In a market-based economy, consumers are supreme. Growth and profits accrue to producers and service providers who meet consumers' wants and needs in a cost-efficient manner and at an appropriate quality and price level. So great is the stimulus under this system that businesses are led to develop new products and services unheard of a short time ago but commonplace now. Innovations in electronics come readily to mind: cellular telephones, facsimile machines, beepers, and compact disc players. But advances are not limited to that field. In pharmaceuticals, for example, new prescription drugs such as Viagra are enabling many older American men to rise up when an occasion demands. Once again, however, although we know technological changes are occurring and we know them when we see them, like pornography, it's difficult to describe and measure.

Unlike the others, the remaining factor, prices, is capable of being measured. Prices result from social interaction between consumers and producers and between producers and suppliers of factor inputs in the context of a market economy. They serve as guides to consumers who want to optimize their satisfaction from goods and services with the limited purchasing power available to them. They signal producers on cost minimizing combinations of factor inputs to attain a given level of output quality and quantity. No one consumer or producer sets a price. A price unilaterally set that is not in accordance with the general milieu will not survive long. Prices are a collective phenomenon that enables individuals to exploit their comparative advantage in strength, intelligence, and skill and producers to use division of labor to find the most efficient means of production.

## PERSONAL SAVING

In 1959 households and nonprofit organizations saved almost 7 percent of personal income. In 1999 they saved less than 2 percent. Earlier in this chapter we observed that per capita real personal consumption expenditures had doubled over the past forty years. On average people have two-and-one-half times as many goods and services—enhanced in quality as well as quantity—by the end of the period than at the beginning. One might suppose that saving out of a larger real income would be easier than out of a smaller one and that as time passed the percentage of income set aside for saving would increase. But our figures suggest that less rather than more is being saved out of each income dollar in recent times.

### Pattern of Saving Rates through Time

Apparent reduced frugality of individuals and households should not be ascribed to moral decadence. Saving competes for consumer preferences along with all other goods and services. Even though incomes have increased, people do not choose to increase their consumption of all goods and services. People's expenditures in real terms for fresh fruits has increased only 45 percent during the forty-year period, while expenditures for fats and oils has nearly doubled. Some self-appointed critics are led to conclude that not only are people saving less but also they are not eating healthy foods. Reduction in tobacco product consumption, on the other hand, signals a healthy trend, at least according to critics of the weed. Use of mass transit systems, taxicabs, and intercity railways is down. Shoe repair and barber shops do less business in 1999 than in 1959 despite there being more people with more income wearing shoes and growing hair on their heads—most of them anyway. And so it goes. Other "inferior" goods and services—products that people consume less of as their incomes and standards of living rise and as new products become available—include motion picture theaters, dry cleaning, bowling, and billiards.

A story can be told about why consumer preferences have shifted away from each one of those goods and services. So also, reasons for a decline in the rate of saving can be sought and discovered.

We begin our quest with a return to Exhibit 5.1 and an examination of changes in percent of personal income devoted to saving for each of the years during the period. There we see that for much of the period, the rate of saving ranged between 6 percent and 8 percent. On a few occasions—most notably in the 1970s and early 1980s—the saving rate exceeded 8 percent. Not until after 1985 did the savings rate leave those precincts and begin—with a pause from 1988 to 1992—a decidedly downward trend. Not only has personal saving declined relative to personal income but also it has declined in dollar amount. It peaked in 1992 at $413.7 billion. For every year since then, the amount saved fell reaching $147.6 billion in 1999, a level closely approximating that of 1978, when personal income was one-fourth of 1999 personal income. Something must have happened on or around 1985 to change people's preference for saving. What could it be?

### Stock Market Performance

The stock market appears to be one good place to look. Recent performance in that arena seems to be associated with the saving as a percent of personal income. Many ways of gauging stock market performance exist. We'll use the familiar Dow-Jones Industrial Average Index. It may not be broadly representative of the whole market, but as the most widely cited indicator, it influences people's perceptions—and perceptions count when determining behavior.

From 1959 to 1982 the Dow-Jones Industrial Average fluctuated in a rather narrow range. Within that interval 1972 marked the high point at 1,020. The low point occurred in 1960. By 1982, standing at 1,046, the index was 54 percent higher than 1959's index of 679. Over those twenty-three years it had grown at an average annual rate of a little less than 1.9 percent. Being in the stock market during that period could not have been comforting to the fainthearted. For nine of the twenty-three years, the Dow-Jones declined. Some of those drops were deep, the most notable being 1974's 28 percent fall that was preceded by 1973's nearly 17 percent decline.

In 1982 the Dow-Jones average reached 1,000. Conditions did not augur well, since the index fell by 9 percent in 1981, and the two preceding breaks in stock market prices had consisted of a pair of bad years—bad at least from the perspective of owners and sellers. However, 1982's performance of an attention-getting nearly 20 percent gain pushed the index into four-digit territory. Another 20 percent increase followed in 1983. A modest decline in 1984, however, kept euphoria from developing.

Then came 1985 and five good years despite the sharp drop in October 1987. From each preceding year the index went up. By 1989 the index stood at 2,753, more than double the 1984 figure of 1,212. Compounded, the index appreciated at an 18 percent annual rate in a five-year period. Whoopee! Why save out of income if you can double your money in the stock market? The saving rate declined from 9.4 percent in 1984 to 6.6 percent in 1989.

A reality check came in October 1987. Confidence was rattled and the saving rate bounced back up to 6.8 percent of personal income in 1988 from 1987's 6.4 percent. Even for 1987, however, the year concluded with the index up by a modest 2.3 percent. After that now-considered "minor" incident, the index took off again. During the following ten years from 1989, the index has increased over four times to 11,497 for 1999. Double-digit appreciation of the market value of portfolios quickly became a norm. At no time from 1959 to 1984 had the Dow-Jones index increased in more than three consecutive years. Uncertainties in the late 1980s—recent memories of the October 1987 collapse, the Iraqi invasion of Kuwait, threat of future energy shortages, and a downturn in economic activity—kept the saving rate in the 6 percent to 7 percent range.

By 1993 those dark clouds on people's mental horizon had dissipated. Saving as a percentage of personal income resumed its downward spiral, from 6.3 percent in 1993 to 5.4 percent in 1994, and so on, until it reached 1999's 1.9 percent.

The price performance of corporate equities in the organized stock exchanges may not be the only reason for a decline in the percent of personal income that is saved. It may not even be a reason. However, the association between the two phenomena suggests a strong connection.

### Wealth Effects

The national income and product accounts (NIPA) contribute next to nothing in describing the effect of stock market prices on consumer behavior. They deal with outputs of goods and services and inputs of factors of production. Exchanging financial instruments in organized market exchanges does not count. The NIPA do not address capital gains and losses. The stock market is all about capital gains and losses. The NIPA deal with flows; wealth is a stock.

What the Department of Commerce leaves out with its NIPA the Board of Governors of the Federal Reserve System picks up with the flow-of-funds accounts. In particular, our interest concerns the Federal Reserve's time series of balance sheets for households and nonprofit organizations.

In chapter 3 we observed that saving occurring during a year produces an equal change in wealth for that year. Changes in wealth are accompanied by changes in financial and tangible assets and in liabilities such that

$$\Delta FA + \Delta TA = \Delta L + \Delta W$$

where

$\Delta FA$ stands for change in financial assets,

$\Delta TA$ change in tangible assets,

$\Delta L$ change in liabilities, and

$\Delta W$ change in wealth.

Changes in assets, both financial and tangible, are valued in the prices prevailing in that year.

Perceived wealth of consumers is conceptually equivalent to net worth that appears in the balance sheets constructed by the Federal Reserve for households and nonprofit organizations. However, year-to-year changes in this net worth are not equal to savings—usually. The reason they are not equal is because *all* assets—prior accumulations as well as current year changes—are valued at prevailing prices. Tangible assets, net of depreciation, are valued at their replacement value; equities and other marketable securities are valued at their market value. Given secular trends of rising prices during the past forty years, changes in the net worth of household and nonprofit organizations balance sheets exceed accumulated savings by a considerable margin.

Exhibit 5.10 shows the extent of the difference. The chart displays the rather tenuous relationship between *Personal Saving* and year-to-year changes in *Net Worth*. The left vertical axis measures changes in saving in billions of dollars; the right axis measures changes in net worth in trillions of dollars. Their parting of company becomes particularly apparent from 1992 to 1999. While saving tends downward, changes in net worth streak upward. As a result from

**Exhibit 5.10**
**Amount Change in Saving and Personal Net Worth, 1959 to 1999**

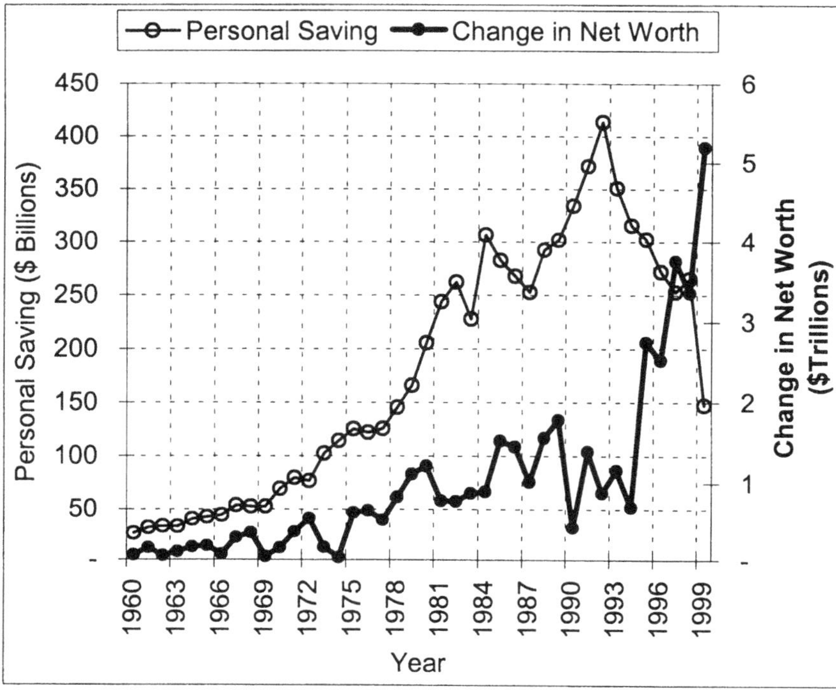


*Sources* : U.S. Department of Commerce. Bureau of Economic Analysis. "Selected NIPA Tables." *National Accounts Data* . 8 Aug. 2000: Table 2.1. 9 Sep. 2000. <http://www.bea.doc.gov/bea/dn1.htm>. Board of Governors, Federal Reserve System. *Flow of Funds Accounts of the United States* . 15 Sep. 2000: "Z.1 Historical data." 18 Sep. 2000. <http://www.bog.frb.us/releases/z1/current/data.htm/>.

1989 to 1999, net worth (wealth) more than doubled, from \$20.2 trillion to \$42.3 trillion. During the same period the sum of personal saving over those ten years equaled \$3.0 trillion. The difference reflects price appreciation of existing assets. Quite a disconnect!

No wonder people feel like spending more and saving less out of current income. They may not have access to those numbers, but they just feel wealthier with each monthly statement from their broker.

The most recent decade was not the only one to witness rapid rises in net worth. From 1977 to 1987 it more than doubled from \$6.4 trillion to \$16.9 trillion. From 1967, as well, we see net worth more than doubling. Thus, disparities between the saving and changes in net worth occur even in earlier years when the stock market was more quiescent, or at least less directed upward. Other factors were at work as well. They can be detected (dimly perhaps) by

**Exhibit 5.11**

**Major Components of Household and Nonproft Organization Assets as Percents of Total Assets, 1959 to 1999**

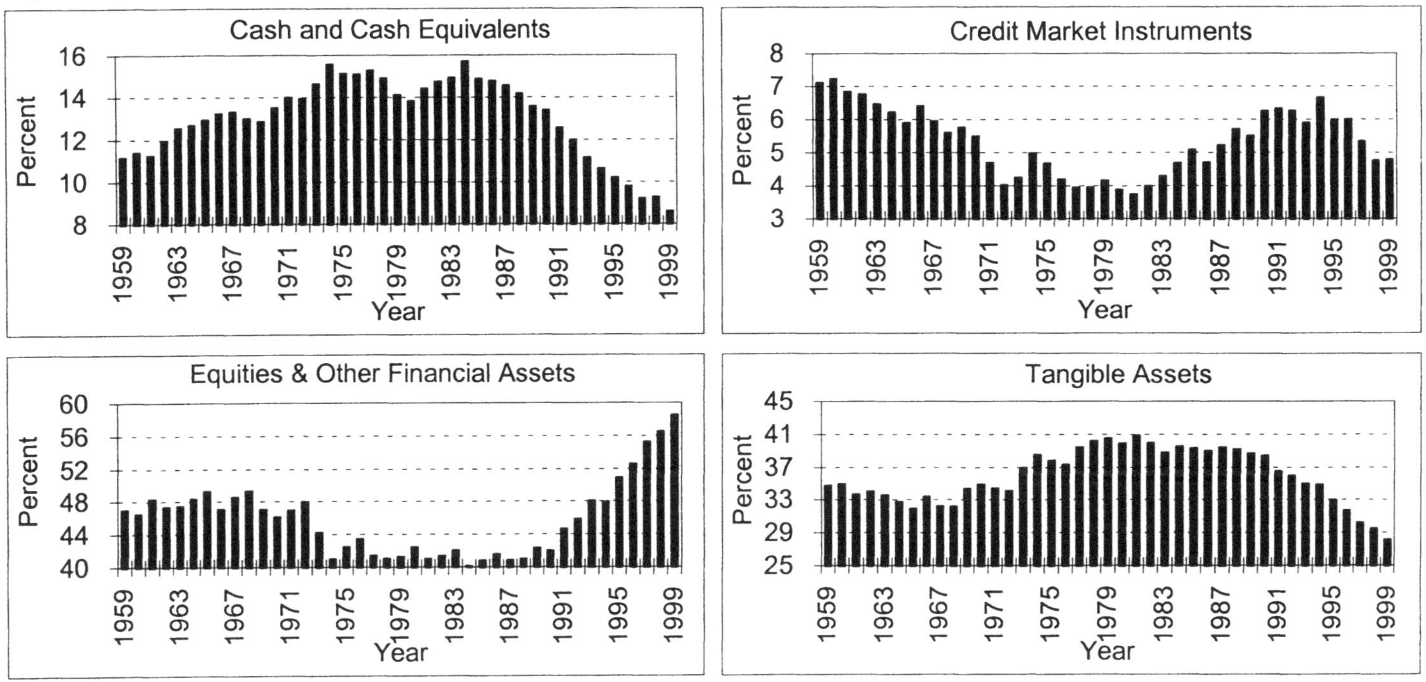


*Sources* : U.S. Department of Commerce. Bureau of Economic Analysis. "'Annual Only' NIPA Tables." *National Accounts Data* . 30 Aug 2000: Table 3.4. 5 Sep. 2000. <http://www.bea.doc.gov/bea/dn1.htm>.

examining the composition of total assets held by households and nonprofit organizations.

### Asset Composition

In Exhibit 3.5 we saw that total assets held by households and nonprofit organizations can be grouped into four major categories:

- Cash and cash equivalents,
- Credit market instruments,
- Equities and other financial assets, and
- Tangible assets.

The first three are financial assets and collectively constitute a little over two-thirds of total assets in 1999.

Those four categories are expressed as percentages of total assets for each of the years from 1959 to 1999 in Exhibit 5.11. For the first thirteen years, until 1972, *Equities and Other Financial Assets* ranged between 45 percent and 50 percent of total assets. They nosed downward to between forty percent and 45 percent after 1972 and the 21 percent two-year drop in the Dow-Jones in 1973 and 1974. While *Equities and Other Financial Assets* languished, *Tangible Assets* flourished. They consist mainly of household real estate. During the 1973 to 1992 period, they accounted for 35 percent to 40 percent of total assets, up from the 30 percent to 35 percent range they occupied from 1959 to 1972.

Those were the years when homeowners found their residences to be a sound investment. In addition to providing shelter, houses tended to appreciate faster than cost-of-living hikes. Mortgage financing often leveraged houses' appreciation. Real estate investment provided the impetus for net worth growth for much of the forty-year period. With the financial crisis confronting savings and loan associations in the 1980s and early 1990s, however, the efficacy of that investment vehicle began to fade. After 1993 we see *Tangible Assets* sliding below 35 percent of total assets and declining to 28 percent by 1999.

Investing in corporate equities came into fashion. *Equities and Other Financial Assets* broke above 45 percent of total assets in 1992. In the next seven years, they climbed to 58 percent of total assets, well above preceding year highs. Their growth relative to other assets manifests their enormous contribution to the growth in the perceived net worth of households and nonprofit organizations over the last decade. And with the perception came a reduction in the rate of saving.

But is the value attributed to net worth under those circumstances real? Will it last? Perhaps we should check with some former presidents of savings and loan associations.

## NOTES

1. Barber B. Conable, *Congress and the Income Tax,* with A. L. Singleton (Norman: University of Oklahoma Press, 1989) 8.

2. Donald W. Kiefer, *Tax Cuts and Rebates for Economic Stimulus: the Historical Record*, 2 Jan. 1992: 1, *Major Studies and Issue Briefs of the Congressional Research Service* (Washington, DC: Congressional Research Service, Library of Congress, 1992): microfilm 92-20 S, reel 1, fr. 00661.

3. Conable 80.

4. Irving Fisher, *The Making of Index Numbers, A Study of Their Varieties, Tests, and Reliability*, 3rd ed., Revised (1927; New York: August M. Kelley, 1967).

5. Peter A. Johnson, *The Government of Money, Monetarism in Germany and the United States* (Ithaca and London: Cornell University Press, 1998) 176–82.

6. John Maynard Keynes, *The General Theory of Employment, Interest, and Money* (New York: Harcourt, Brace and Company, 1936) 383–84.

7. U.S. Department of Commerce, Bureau of Economic Analysis, *National Income and Product Accounts of the United States, 1929–94*, vol. 1 (Washington, DC: U.S. Government Printing Office, April 1998) M11.

8. David Ignatius, "The Oil Game Turns Cutthroat," *Houston Chronicle* 14 Feb. 1999: 1C and 4C.

# 6

# The Sector We Love to Hate—Part I

In a capitalistic, market-oriented economy, consumers show what they want and need through their purchases of goods and services. By manifesting individual preferences in their spending patterns, they collectively determine what is produced at what prices. In a democracy people govern themselves. In a democracy operating under a representative form of government, they govern themselves through their elected representatives. In the economy they vote with their dollars; in the political arena they vote with their ballots. As with a market-oriented economy where people determine what goods and services are produced, people ultimately are in charge of their government.

As with the economy, just because we are ultimately in charge does not mean we have to accept or must be satisfied with the outcome. Some who mistrust the marketplace have made a good living taking producers to task for unsafe products, price manipulation, and misleading advertising. So also, we do not have to be happy with the taxes we pay, sloppy and inadequate services provided by government agencies, or excessive regulation. Both economic and political institutions are imperfect. Our preferences and judgments may be perfectly sound, but the reality they evoke is not.

## ECONOMIC ROLE OF GOVERNMENT

The spectacular economic development and progress witnessed over the past forty years can be attributed in large measure to a proper balance between the public and private sectors of the society. Four factors account for that happy situation:

- A legal system that insures individual rights and treats all citizens equally regardless of status,
- Political stability,
- Private property, and
- A market-oriented economy.

The four factors coexist and are interdependent. The first three—often taken for granted in the United States—are necessary for the fourth to operate. The fourth demonstrates the advantages of the other three.

The first three factors fall within the purview of government. They are brought about as government carries out its four functions of

- Enacting and enforcing legislation,
- Maintaining law and order,
- Correcting market imperfections, and
- Providing public goods and services.

Private markets operate efficiently when:

- Individuals can be excluded from consuming goods if they do not pay for them,
- There are no external effects, and
- The market is perfectly competitive.[1]

Under conditions of perfect competition in both markets for goods and services and for inputs to the production process and with rational behavior and complete knowledge on the part of consumers, economic analysis demonstrates that a market-oriented economy results in an optimum allocation of resources and outputs. By optimum we mean that no other combination of inputs and outputs can result in an overall improvement in satisfaction or well-being of consumers.

In practice the assumptions required for optimum performance of the market system are not attained. Markets for goods and services and for factor inputs are not perfectly competitive. Consumers do not act with complete knowledge. Monopolies exist. Collusion among producers occurs, sometimes explicitly, more often tacitly. (How do you suppose prices of four gasoline filling stations at the same intersection happen to be the same?) A producer may not incur all of the costs associated with producing a product—a situation referred to as externalities.

While not perfect, historical experience shows that the performance of private sector market economies in producing marketable goods and services is unsurpassed. However, a group of essential goods and services is not marketable. Those products are called public goods and services. All people in a community benefit when public goods and services are provided, regardless of whether they pay or not. Under such circumstances no one is inclined to pay for them, thus convincingly discouraging businesses from engaging in producing those types of goods and services. No definition serves to clarify the concept as well as some examples. At the national level national defense serves as a prime example; at the state level, highways and roads; and at the local level, police and fire protection. For a nation, a state, and a community, all those goods and services are important, but no one individual would be willing to pay for them unless assured that everyone else was compelled to pay as well. Misery loves company.

Some goods, like a stick of chewing gum, are clearly private. Others, like national defense, are clearly public. Many goods and services possess both public and private aspects, however. Education—or at least opportunity for education—benefits an individual. Population statistics show that incomes tend to rise as years of education increase. A society also benefits from having an educated citizenry. Education exemplifies that group of products called mixed public-private goods and services. Both government and the private sector often provide such goods and services. Government provides much public education without charge for the primary and second grades and with subsidized tuition for postsecondary education. Private institutions also provide similar opportunities, however, and some individuals prefer the latter.

Some services can be provided efficiently only as natural monopolies. One electric power grid and one water and sewerage distribution system are sufficient per city, neighborhood, and household. Some municipalities operate their own utilities; others choose to regulate private companies to provide such services. Trash collection similarly is a mixed good. It can and sometimes is provided privately; however, a single collector for a given area usually offers greater efficiency. Communities offering that service either provide it directly or contract with a private firm.

Production of goods and services, whether they are public or private, require inputs of real resources. Public goods and services pose a special challenge since users can consume them without paying. We will next examine how government in the United States has met that challenge by examining sources of government revenue.

## FEDERAL STRUCTURE

Government in the United States does not exist as a single entity. The U.S. Constitution establishes a federal system of government in which state governments surrender certain governmental functions to the national government. The Constitution empowers the national government to provide "for the common defense" and for the "general welfare," to regulate interstate commerce, to coin money, and to collect taxes. Under the Constitution states cannot make treaties, maintain armies and navies, engage in war, coin money, tax imports or exports, or deny citizens their rights. With those exceptions all other functions of government are reserved to the states.

Under such an arrangement states and their subdivisions traditionally have provided those services directly affecting the day-to-day lives of people. Education, public health, police and fire protection, care for the indigent, chartering of corporations, enacting and enforcing criminal and civil law, licensing of professional service providers, street and highway maintenance, recording of real estate titles and other property transactions, and providing for public recreational areas make up some of the many functions of state and local government. The national government has moved into some of those areas through generous interpretations of the interstate commerce and general welfare clauses as well as through a Constitutional clause that allows Congress to pass any laws "necessary and proper" to execute governmental functions.

Despite occasional aberrations, the federal model serves to put the unit of government closest to a policy issue or public need in charge of its resolution. A new ballpark in a small town on the Middle Western plains may seem of small consequence in Washington, DC. But it is appropriately a major concern for the local town board. Similarly, a Mongol invasion of Alaska may seem remote to the citizens of Crawfish Sluice in southern Louisiana, but the matter will receive the full attention of the national government.

One of the consequences of our form of government is that we have not one but two sets of data dealing with government revenue: one for the national government and the other for state and local government. We could deal immediately with the two parts combined, but such an arrangement would obscure important differences between the two levels of government. In accordance with our practice of starting with the more familiar and proceeding to the less, we will begin with state and local government receipts and expenditures. In the next chapter we will then examine those of the national government. That chapter will conclude with a summary bringing together state and local receipts and expenditures with those of the national government to form the source-of-funds and use-of-funds sides of the account for the government sector of the national income and product accounts (NIPA).

## STATE AND LOCAL GOVERNMENT RECEIPTS

State and local governments appear to be more popular (or less unpopular) than the national government in our federal system. A 1994 survey conducted by the Advisory Commission on Intergovernmental Relations asked respondents, "From which level of government do you feel you get the least for your money?"[2] Twice as many responses indicated that the federal government delivered the least service for their tax dollars. Between state and local governments, local government was viewed slightly more favorably. The returns indicate that if you are a man, a head of a household, aged thirty-five to forty-four, a college graduate, a white collar, sales, or clerical employee living in the North and large central cities, you are likely to agree with those findings.

Since income cannot be obtained from sale of public goods and services, governments must assess and collect taxes in order to secure revenue to produce them. Mixed goods and services provide an alternative source of government revenue. For some of them charges are possible. Not everyone needs or wants a hunting or fishing license. Those who feel an obligation to help manage the wildlife population (and/or enjoy killing animals) can be charged a fee for a license entitling them to undertake that pursuit. Charges, usually at subsidized rates, can be levied on those entering state and national recreational areas. College tuition, also at subsidized rates, is charged to those attending public post-secondary educational institutions. Examples abound.

### Personal Taxes and Nontaxes

Exhibit 6.1 shows the major categories of receipts for state and local governments. In 1999 those receipts totaled to over $1.1 trillion. *Personal taxes and nontaxes* we already have seen in our treatment of outlays of personal income. In this exhibit it heads the list. In 1999 it amounted to $249.7 billion and accounted for 22 percent. Within the category *Personal income taxes* predominated, amounting to $194.8 billion, 17 percent of the total. Despite its performance as a revenue producer, seven states (14 percent) showed little or no revenue from personal income taxes in 1991–92.[3]

*Nontaxes* and *Other* produced another 5 percent of state and local government receipts. In 1999 *Nontaxes* generated $35.1 billion for state and local government coffers. They consist largely of donations and unclaimed bank deposits. Who gives money to a state or local government? Examples of such philanthropic individuals include alumni of state colleges and universities and grateful patients (or their heirs) who have been treated at the medical facilities of state medical schools. In cases of unsuccessful outcomes, the size of an estate may influence the heirs' gratitude.

*Other* produced $19.8 billion. Include are drivers' licenses and hunting, fishing, and other personal licenses.

### Corporate Profits Tax

Next comes something we did not see in our examination of personal income and the household sector: *Corporate profits tax.* Businesses organized as corporations produce most of the national output of goods and services. The corporate form of business organization offers advantages over partnerships and sole proprietorships for large enterprises. As legal entities corporations enjoy perpetual life unless their charter specifies a termination date. With limited liability for shareholders and liquidity to owners of marketable shares of stock, they offer attractive investments and can amass large amounts of funds for capital formation. In addition, their separate status as a financial unit enables them to grow through retained earnings.

They also can be taxed, and that fact offsets to some extent their inherent advantages. Not all states look to corporations as a source of income tax revenue, however. Four states—New Hampshire, Texas, Washington, and Wyoming—garnered no corporation profits tax revenue in 1991–92.[4] For all state governments taken together, corporation profit taxes make up a relatively small portion of total receipts. As shown in Exhibit 6.1, the take amounted to $36.6

**Exhibit 6.1**

**State and Local Government Receipts, 1959 and 1999**

| | 1959 Amounts in $ Billions | Percent of Total | 1999 Amounts in $ Billions | Percent of Total | Annual Percent Change |
|---|---|---|---|---|---|
| **Personal taxes and nontaxes** | **$ 4.2** | **11** | **$ 249.7** | **22** | **11** |
| Personal income taxes | 2.2 | 6 | 194.8 | 17 | 12 |
| Nontaxes | 0.4 | 1 | 35.1 | 3 | 12 |
| Other | 1.6 | 4 | 19.8 | 2 | 6 |
| **Corporate profits tax** | **1.2** | **3** | **36.6** | **3** | **9** |
| **Indirect taxes and nontaxes** | **29.3** | **75** | **617.5** | **54** | **8** |
| Sales taxes | 11.1 | 29 | 307.1 | 27 | 9 |
| Property taxes | 14.8 | 38 | 238.5 | 21 | 7 |
| Other | 3.3 | 8 | 71.9 | 6 | 8 |
| **Social insurance contributions** | **0.4** | **1** | **9.6** | **1** | **8** |
| **Federal grants-in-aid** | **3.8** | **10** | **229.3** | **20** | **11** |
| **TOTAL RECEIPTS** | **$ 38.9** | **100** | **$ 1,142.7** | **100** | **9** |

*Source*: U.S. Department of Commerce. Bureau of Economic Analysis. "Selected NIPA Tables." *National Accounts Data*. 8 Aug. 2000: Table 3.3. 9 Sep. 2000. <http://www.bea.doc.gov/bea/dn1.htm>.

billion in 1999, only 3 percent of total receipts. Competition among states for existing and new industry tends to act as a deterrent to exploitation of corporate profits as a revenue source. Besides, from solicitation of campaign funds, many politicians know the heads of those businesses.

### Indirect Taxes and Nontax Receipts

Receipts from *Indirect taxes and nontaxes* provided the largest single source of revenue, $617.5 billion, 54 percent in 1999. Taxes can be grouped into two categories: direct taxes and indirect taxes. Direct taxes are those that persons—be they individuals, households, estates, trusts, foundations, or corporate entities—pay directly on their income or for services they receive. Although no longer recorded as such in the NIPA, estate and gift taxes fall into the direct tax category. A marriage license fee belongs in the direct nontax payment category. Indirect taxes are taxes on things.

In 1999 *Sales taxes* constituted the most important single source of state and local government receipts, $307.1 billion, 27 percent. General retail sales taxes alone generated $215.2 billion. Confronted with falling tax receipts during the Great Depression, retail sales taxes became popular with state governments during the 1930s. When applied to a broad base of goods and services, they provide a relatively stable source of revenue to governmental units. However, since both rich and poor pay the same tax rate on much the same essentials of life, the tax has been criticized for its greater relative burden on low-income taxpayers. Despite that limitation, most states and some cities now use general retail sales taxes both to raise revenue and provide relief for payers of property taxes. In only four states can general retail sales taxes be avoided—Delaware, Montana, New Hampshire, and Oregon.[5]

Although general retail sales taxes constituted the major source of the $307.1 billion in 1999 sales tax receipts, $91.9 billion is still left unaccounted for. Application of separate sales taxes to other products often is intended to accomplish various policy objectives in addition to raising revenue. All fifty states tax motor fuel, alcoholic beverages, tobacco products, and public utilities.[6] Motor fuel taxes lead the pack of specific sales taxes in receipt generation, producing $29.6 billion in 1999. The revenue they generate may be dedicated for highway and road construction and maintenance. Levies on alcoholic beverages and tobacco serve as a "sin" tax and attempt to discourage consumption. For 1999 taxes on puffing the weed produced twice as much in the way of state receipts as taxes on gulping the sauce, $8.4 billion as compared with $4.0 billion. For those accustomed to the pleasures of smoking and drinking, quantities consumed tend to be inelastic with respect to price increases induced by high tax rates and, in the short run at least, to health warnings. If health warnings are correct and ignored by smokers, demand for tobacco products can be expected to "die off." Imbibers' prospects may be more favorable.[7] Butts are down, but bottoms are up. Inelasticity with respect to price and ease of collection make public utilities and insurance receipts tempting targets for sales taxes. Peoples' addiction to electricity and other public utilities cost them $18.0 billion in taxes in 1999, more than they paid in alcohol and tobacco taxes.

*Property taxes* constitute the second most important source of receipts for state and local governments in 1999. The property tax has been around a long time and offers special advantages to local government. Most property tax receipts are raised on real estate. Sales taxes and income taxes both on individuals and corporations may induce people and businesses to move elsewhere. Land, however, is fixed both in amount and location. Moreover, in spite of stories about the poor elderly widow unable to pay her property tax and losing her home, a case can be made that the property tax is a relatively progressive component in the arsenal of state and local taxing instruments.

Property taxes moreover provide a relatively stable source of revenue in times of both high and low economic activity. Their administration, in concept at least, is fairly straightforward. Property values are assessed. A governmental unit—for example, a school district, city, or county—estimates its revenue needs for the year. Those needs are divided by total assessed valuation to determine a tax rate. In practice assessing values on property is a judgment call in the absence of comparable market transactions. The process is tedious, not popular with the electorate, and its results are subject to challenge. Despite such impediments, property taxes continue as an important part of state and local tax receipts.

A variety of taxes and nontaxes accounted for the $71.6 billion of *Other* remaining under *Indirect taxes and nontaxes*. The category consists of both taxes and nontaxes. It includes receipts from motor vehicle licenses, severance taxes, business licenses, stamp taxes, rents and royalties, special assessments, fines, donations, and beginning with 1997, settlements with tobacco companies.

For motorists in many states, the effort required to obtain motor vehicle licenses looms larger than its $5.2 billion relatively small contribution to total state and local government receipts suggests. The process can entail waiting in long lines. Even in states adopting more convenient collection arrangements, the process imposes on taxpayers at a minimum not only paying the tax but also affixing a tag somewhere on their automobiles. Severance taxes, charges on extraction of minerals, also produce modest receipts, $3.1 billion. Sixteen states impose no severance taxes. Neither does the District of Columbia, where the main extraction industry is extracting tax revenue from everywhere else. Business licenses and documentary and stamp taxes are more lucrative, generating $31.6 billion for state and local coffers.

Indirect nontaxes—rents and royalties, special assessment, fines, and other sources—produced $31.9 billion for state and local governments.

### Social Insurance Contributions

*Social insurance contributions* constitute the smallest amount of state and local government receipts shown separately in Exhibit 6.1. They amounted to a modest $9.6 billion. In 1999 employers "contributed" $7.7 billion for workers' compensation. Personal contributions for temporary disability insurance added $1.9 billion.

### Federal Grants-in-Aid

Last but not least *Federal grants-in-aid* appear in Exhibit 6.1 as source of receipts for state and local governments. At $229.3 billion they loom large as a source of state and local receipts. One dollar in five that state and local governments collect comes from the federal government. Only sales taxes and property taxes exceed grants-in-aid.

Why does the national government give money to state and local governments? Undoubtedly, politics and the eagerness of most representatives of the people to continue in office play a role. Bringing back home some funds from Washington appears popular even when the government first has to take away everything that it gives. Economists have managed to distill from reality four rationalizations attributing useful purposes to grants-in-aid:

- To offset externalities between regions of certain public goods;
- To enforce grantor preferences for merit goods;
- To correct for fiscal imbalances; and
- To equalize economic conditions among regions.[8]

A region interested in improving its welfare programs for low-income families may hesitate to undertake such an action because of concerns that poor people from other nearby regions will invade it. Regulations and penalties on local industries for air and water pollution may be deferred because much of the benefit will accrue to regions downstream or downwind. Such externalities tend to limit local and regional government action.

An educated population generally is considered desirable and indeed necessary for a democracy. Left to their own devices and pressed with private wants and needs, individuals might tend to underinvest in human capital. Communities and states, as well, with many public needs to address and limited resources may fail to make sufficient provision for education. Economists call education and like items "merit" goods.[9] From the perspective of a national government, the need for greater spending for merit goods can be realized through grants-in-aid—money with strings attached. The extent of benefit to a society of such grants depends, of course, on the impeccably good judgment of the central government in distinguishing between those goods that are meritorious and those that are not and how much of a good thing is really needed.

Tornadoes, floods, hurricanes, earthquakes! State and local governments may be unable to cope financially with such emergency situations. A disaster is declared. Federal funds flow. Such occurrences provide examples of the third purpose for grants-in-aid.

Those who feel qualified to judge consider some sections of the country to be too prosperous and others to be too poor. Equalization grants are intended to rectify imbalances and bring the resulting distribution more in line with what they feel is suitable. In a free trade area such as the United States where people's movement from poor to more prosperous regions is limited only by their inclination, the necessity for such grants seems limited.

In part, the growth of grants-in-aid also reflects advantages the federal government has over state and local governments in its taxing power. The fixed costs of setting up a collection system can be spread over the entire nation, thus, in concept at least, reducing costs of administration per dollar gathered for government coffers. In addition, a nationwide tax avoids dislocations that occur when adjacent states have differing tax levels and structures. For example, a state with a sales tax higher than its neighbors will find that some of its citizens, especially those living near its borders, may travel into other states to make their purchases.

The Morrill Act of 1862 represents the first major instance of aid to states from the national government. It established land grant colleges and instituted standards for states that received the grants. It served as a model for subsequent federal programs in agriculture, highways, vocational education and rehabilitation, forestry, and public health. The Great Depression of the 1930s brought a further extension of such programs into income security and other welfare needs. Following World War II federal grants to state and local governments became a significant factor in the national government's expenditures.[10]

Agriculture, education, energy, environment, health, training, and transportation are among the other areas for which state and local governments receive federal largess. These grants-in-aid come in two flavors: mandatory and discretionary. In the case of mandatory grants, the criteria on which funds are determined and distributed are defined in the authorizing legislation. Consequently, the funding those programs receive is not determined in the annual appropriation process and can be changed only by amending or repealing (fat chance) the legislation that established those entitlements. Examples include Medicaid, Temporary Assistance to Needy Families, and Food Stamp programs.

Discretionary grants receive annual scrutiny through the appropriation process in Congress. Programs falling into that category include highways, Head Start and other education programs for the disadvantaged, and other family services programs.

Medicaid is the largest grant program. Another, much smaller, health-related program is the Children's Health Insurance Program. It extends health insurance coverage to uninsured children.[11] The list of other programs goes on and on: some familiar, others obscure and known only to the grantspersons assigned to insure that their governmental unit receives its maximum amount from the national trough. Some of them challenge economists' rationalizations for grants-in-aid. In the energy field we have a couple of programs spawned by the energy crisis of the 1970s. The Weatherization Assistance Program provides support to weatherize low-income homes, and the State Energy Program helps states fund innovative energy conservation projects and improve energy efficiency of state and municipal buildings. Externalities appear negligible. Saving energy seems meritorious, and husbandry of resources generally is a good thing. Why not special treatment for saving (dare they be mentioned?) paper clips, rubber bands, and pieces of string? Fiscal imbalance may be hard to prove. The fourth rationalization for grants-in aid, equalizing economic conditions among regions, is not likely to happen. People in North Dakota are going to be cooler in winter than people in Florida.

### Comparisons of Sources of Receipts over Time

Exhibit 6.1 presents a somewhat different picture of the pattern of sources of state and local government receipts in 1959. The total was considerably smaller of course, just $38.9 billion—a figure that is approximated in 1999 by receipts from the *Corporate profits tax* alone. Growth from $38.9 billion to $1,142.7 billion represents an annual rate of growth averaging 9 percent. Not all parts of the total maintained such a robust growth rate, but others exceeded it.

The outcomes of more and less rapid growth among the components of government receipts are reflected in Exhibit 6.1 in their percentages of total receipts for 1959 and 1999. A glance shows that *Personal taxes and nontaxes* and *Federal grants-in-aid* increased their shares over the forty-year period. The *Corporate profits tax* and *Social insurance contributions* held their own at 3 percent and 1 percent, respectively. *Indirect taxes and nontaxes* experienced a relative decline.

In 1959 *Personal taxes and nontaxes* accounted for 11 percent of total receipts; in 1999, 22 percent. Their importance doubled in relative terms. *Personal income taxes and nontaxes* grew at a brisk 11 percent average annual rate. *Personal income taxes* increased their contribution to total receipts from 6 percent in 1959 to 17 percent in 1999. Growth in *Other*, on the other hand, ambled along at a mere 6 percent and dropped in importance from 4 percent to 2 percent of the total. Part of the explanation for the rising importance of the personal income tax as a source of revenue is that more and more states have adopted it. *Federal grants-in-aid* also doubled in importance, from 10 to 20 percent. Much of the rapidity of its growth can be attributed to the introduction and expansion of Medicaid.

What happened to *Indirect taxes and nontaxes*? In 1959, 75 percent of state and local receipts came from that source. While over half continues to come from those sources, their importance has eroded substantially. Sales taxes and property taxes clearly dominate the scene. In 1959 property taxes alone accounted for 38 percent of all state and local receipts. In the subsequent forty years, with cries for property tax relief in the background, their growth averaged 7 percent a year, so their rank in importance as a source of receipts has fallen from first to third place. Despite property taxes' decline and predictions of their demise, state and/or local governments in all fifty states collect them and are likely to do so for a long time to come. From 1959 to 1999 the relative share of *Sales taxes* decreased slightly, from 29 percent to 27 percent. *Other* indirect taxes and nontaxes offset the increase by declines from 8 percent to 6 percent.

### Summary

For state and local governments, we have identified three sources of receipts totaling over $1.1 trillion in 1999. Taken in order of importance they are: (1) taxes, both direct and indirect; (2) federal grants-in-aid; and (3) nontaxes. What about contributions for social insurance? Those "contributions" are taxes by another name. Try not making your "contribution." Nontax payments are relatively inconsequential as a source of revenue, around 6 percent of the total. Federal grants-in-aid account for a fifth. All the rest, nearly three-fourths, comes from taxes.

## STATE AND LOCAL GOVERNMENT USES OF CURRENT FUNDS

Exhibit 6.2 presents state and local government uses of current funds. *Consumption expenditures* head the list. Like personal consumption expenditures, they constituted the largest share taking up $855.0 billion, 75 percent of total outlays in 1999. *Transfer payments to persons* made up the second largest expenditure block accounting for $252.0 billion, 22 percent of the total. *Net saving* at $50.0 billion mades up 4 percent of the uses of state and local funds.

That those three items are important is hard to dispute. For 1999 their three percentages add up to 101 percent of total uses of current funds. For 1959 they also add up to 101 percent. They seem to be overachievers and lead to curiosity about the other smaller expenditure categories.

### The Smaller Expenditure Categories

For 1999 two items in Exhibit 6.2, *Net interest paid* and *Dividends received*, are negative! Then come *Subsidies*, a small addition to expenditure, followed by *Government enterprise surpluses*, another deduction from expenditures. Taken together the foursome nets to a reduction in 1999 expenditures of $14.3 billion. Surpluses of government enterprises account for the largest reduction.

*Interest paid* consists of monetary interest paid on public debt and other financial obligations. *Interest received* consists of monetary and imputed interest received on loans and investments, including the balances of state and local *Social insurance funds.*[12] As we saw in Exhibit 2.7, it also includes imputed interest received. Defined on that basis, state and local governments receive more interest than they pay, and the net is shown as a negative number. Two factors account for the phenomenon. Unlike the national government, whose ability to issue currency and coin enables it to run chronic deficits, state and local governments must balance expenditures with receipts. Indeed, some state constitutions require that the government not incur a current deficit. Consequently, in attempting to assure positive balances, they tend to run a surplus and invest it in

**Exhibit 6.2**

**State and Local Government Uses of Current Funds, 1959 and 1999**

| | 1959 Amounts in $ Billions | Percent of Total | 1999 Amounts in $ Billions | Percent of Total | Annual Percent Change |
|---|---|---|---|---|---|
| **Consumption expenditures** | **$ 31.1** | **80** | **$ 855.0** | **75** | **9** |
| **Transfer payments to persons** | **4.3** | **11** | **252.0** | **22** | **11** |
| **Net interest paid** | **0.7** | **2** | **(3.0)** | **(0)** | |
| Interest paid | 1.8 | 5 | 75.1 | 7 | 10 |
| Interest received | (1.0) | (3) | (78.1) | (7) | 12 |
| **Dividends received** | **-** | | **(0.4)** | **(0)** | |
| **Subsidies** | **-** | | **0.5** | **0** | |
| **Government enterprises surplus** | **(1.1)** | **(3)** | **(11.4)** | **(1)** | **6** |
| **Net saving** | **3.8** | **10** | **50.0** | **4** | **7** |
| Social insurance funds | - | | (0.4) | (0) | |
| Other | 3.7 | 10 | 50.4 | 4 | 7 |
| **TOTAL EXPENDITURES** | **$ 38.9** | **100** | **$ 1,142.7** | **100** | **9** |

*Source* : U.S. Department of Commerce. Bureau of Economic Analysis. "Selected NIPA Tables." *National Accounts Data* . 8 Aug. 2000: Table 3.3. 9 Sep. 2000. <http://www.bea.doc.gov/bea/dn1.htm>.

low-risk interest-bearing securities like bonds and notes issued by the U.S. government. State and local governments can issue their own bonds usually to finance capital projects. Interest earned by holders of those bonds usually is exempt from federal income taxes and, therefore, is lower than taxable interest rates.

In addition to interest, state and local governments receive dividends from investments in corporate stocks. Those holdings commonly reflect investments of trust funds and endowments. For example, endowments of state colleges or universities and pension funds for state employees customarily contain a substantial portion of corporate common stocks that earn dividends as well as generate a possibility for capital gains.

State and local governments subsidize certain activities and support income-generating enterprises that produce goods and services for sale to the public. Subsidies supposedly enable goods or services to be sold at prices below their cost of production. (They also hide inefficiencies.) If subsidized goods and services are in fact sold at lower prices, presumably more of them will be consumed. Given limited resources, more consumption of subsidized items means less of others will be available. Why the altered distribution is a good thing is a judgment call. Some authority substitutes its judgment for private market discipline. As indicated by Exhibit 6.2, state and local government subsidies constitute less than one-half of 1 percent of total expenditures.

State and local government enterprises operate very much like many private businesses. Their products usually contain aspects of both public and private goods. Since they can be sold to the public, government enterprises usually can cover a substantial portion of their operating costs. Within the NIPA, government enterprises are treated as noncorporate enterprises. According to the Bureau of Economic Analysis, "This classification determines how their income is recorded. . . . For a government enterprise, this means that the saving is consolidated with that of its owner, general government"[13] However, like *Net interest paid* and *Dividends received*, it is shown in the NIPA as a deduction from costs rather than an addition to income.

The goods and services produced by government enterprises are recorded at their cost of production—the sum of employee compensation and consumption of fixed capital—rather than the amount at which they are sold. A government enterprise "may follow a policy of setting prices at a level at which the proceeds will not cover the full cost of current production."[14] The recording practice adopted makes the value assigned to outputs of government enterprises independent of their policy decisions.

Many of the enterprises in which state and local governments engage have their counterparts in the private sector. Water companies, sewerage disposal plants, liquor stores, and gas and electric utilities on balance generate surpluses. All have their counterparts in the private sector where returns are earned for investors. Particularly profitable government enterprises include such things as lotteries, off-track betting, and local parking. In those areas as well, private service providers exist. State governments developed a new source of revenue during the forty-year period: lotteries. Before 1963 they were banned in every state.[15] New Hampshire broke the prohibition in 1964. As of fiscal year 1991–92, thirty-four state and local government lotteries were in operation.

Toll facilities, airline terminals, and port facilities commonly are public entities, although exceptions can be found. They, too, produce positive returns. The two public enterprises showing losses are housing renewal and public transit.[16] Unlike public authorities, private real estate developers undertake housing and urban renewal projects to make a living. The largest deficits belong to public transit, which competes unsuccessfully with private transportation, user-operated vehicles, and common carriers. The likelihood of its ever breaking even with greater volume appears remote.

For the nation as a whole, however, the positive margin on state and local government enterprises as a group is an illusion. State and local subsidies amount to a paltry $500 million, but, as we shall see, the national government has been less constrained in the subsidy arena than have state and local governments.

### Components of Government Uses of Current Funds over Time

In 1959 consumption expenditures accounted for an even larger share of state and local government expenditures than in 1999. Exhibit 6.2 shows that 80 percent, four out of every five dollars, of state and local government expenditure was used for consumption of goods and services in 1959. Transfer payments to persons were less important, 11 percent as opposed to 22 percent in 1999. Saving by state and local governments was significantly more important. One dollar out of every ten was set aside for saving purposes in 1959. Once again, those three components add up to 101 percent of total expenditures.

In 1959 state and local governments paid more in interest than they received, and the positive difference made up 2 percent of total expenditures. Surpluses of government enterprises contributed a larger offset, 3 percent in 1959, than the 1 percent offset in 1999. Forty years later the other items had a negligible effect on total expenditure.

### Consumption Expenditures

Accounting as it does for 75 percent of total state and local government expenditures, consumption expenditures merit a closer look. Exhibit 6.3 provides that closer look. Like personal consumption expenditures, state and local government consumption expenditures can be categorized by type of product purchased: durable goods, nondurable goods, and services. Of the three, government purchases of *Services* constitute by far the largest portion of total consumption expenditures. In turn, a major portion of consumption expenditures for services consists of government *Employee compensation*.[17] In our examination of personal income, we noted that a very small portion of personal consumption

**Exhibit 6.3**
**State and Local Government Consumption Expenditures, 1999**

| | 1999 Amounts in $ Billions | | Percent of Total | |
|---|---|---|---|---|
| **Durable goods** | | **$ 15.9** | | **2** |
| Gross expenditures | 17.2 | | 2 | |
| Sales | (1.3) | | (0) | |
| **Nondurable goods** | | **91.3** | | **11** |
| Gross expenditures | 104.6 | | 12 | |
| Sales | (13.3) | | (2) | |
| **Services** | | **747.7** | | **87** |
| Gross consumption expenditures | 940.4 | | 110 | |
| Tuition and related educational charges | (40.7) | | (5) | |
| Health and hospital charges | (101.2) | | (12) | |
| Other sales | (50.7) | | (6) | |
| Employee compensation | | 624.1 | | 73 |
| Consumption of fixed capital | | 83.0 | | 10 |
| Other services | | 40.6 | | 5 |
| **TOTAL CONSUMPTION EXPENDITURES** | | **$ 855.0** | | **100** |

*Source* : U.S. Department of Commerce. Bureau of Economic Analysis. "Selected NIPA Tables." *National Accounts Data* . 8 Aug. 2000: Table 3.7. 9 Sep. 2000. <http://www.bea.doc.gov/bea/dn1.htm>. and "'Annual Only' NIPA Tables." *National Accounts Data* . 30 Aug 2000: Table 3.9. 5 Sep. 2000. <http://www.bea.doc.gov/bea/dn1.htm>.

expenditures consists of compensation paid by individuals and households for domestic services. In the case of government consumption expenditures, *Employee compensation* accounts for a much larger portion—at 73 percent, almost three-fourths.

Labor is a service; therefore, the $624.1 billion spent in 1999 as compensation for government employees appears under services. Although large, *Employee compensation* entered under *Services* does not constitute the total payroll for state and local government employees. Employee compensation also is recorded as part of the capital costs of government investments. The compensation of government architects, engineers, and construction supervisors is charged to capital projects rather than to current fund expenditures. Such services could be—and often are—obtained on contract. In both cases the costs are capitalized as investments rather than current expenses.

Purchases of police cars and other government vehicles and of office furniture and equipment fall into the *Durable goods* category. The category excludes items classified as investments—for example, buildings, highways, dams—except for goods transferred to foreign countries by the national government.

We will encounter those compensation amounts contained within capital costs as we proceed.

In addition to purchases of labor services shown as *Employee compensation*, *Services* include *Consumption of fixed capital.* Office buildings, highways, bridges, roads, and other publicly provided infrastructure wear out in the process of yielding up their services. An estimate of that wear and tear accounts for 10 percent of government consumption of goods and services. After accounting for *Employee compensation* and *Consumption of fixed capital*, what is left over, *Other services*, amounts to only 5 percent of total consumption—less than state and local government purchases of *Nondurable goods*.

State and local governments produce as well as consume goods and services. Receipts for those outputs are treated as general government sales and deducted from government purchases of goods and services when they are (1) for products similar to those sold by private business and (2) incidental to the primary function of government units.[18] Sales of such *Durable* and *Nondurable goods* are relatively insignificant. For *Services*, however, they are substantial. *Tuition and related educational charges* of public colleges and universities and charges for *Health and hospital charges* comprise the largest amount of goods and services produced by state and local governments.

### Transfer Payments to Persons

In Exhibit 6.2 state and local government *Transfer payments to persons* show a dramatic increase in relative share, rising from 11 percent of total expenditures in 1959 to 22 percent 1999. In 1999 they amounted to $252.0 billion. Taken together, *Consumption expenditures* and *Transfer payments to persons* accounted for 97 percent of total expenditure in 1999. Such spectacular growth and significant size deserve a closer look. *Transfer payments to persons* can be broken down into four components shown in Exhibit 6.4.

Of the four, *Medical Care* is by far the largest, accounting for $189.0 billion of the $252.0 billion. All but $5.0 billion of that figure consists of Medicaid, conjured up and in part funded by the federal government but administered by the states. *Medical Care* is classed as a public assistance program. It shares that berth with *Other Public Assistance* programs, a collection of welfare programs substantially less significant in fiscal terms. Those programs include:

- Family assistance,
- Supplemental security income,
- General assistance,
- Energy assistance, and
- Other programs.

Expenditures for food under the supplemental program for women, infants, and children, foster care, adoption assistance, and payments to nonprofit welfare

**Exhibit 6.4**

**State and Local Government Transfer Payments to Persons as Percents of Total Transfers, 1959 to 1999**

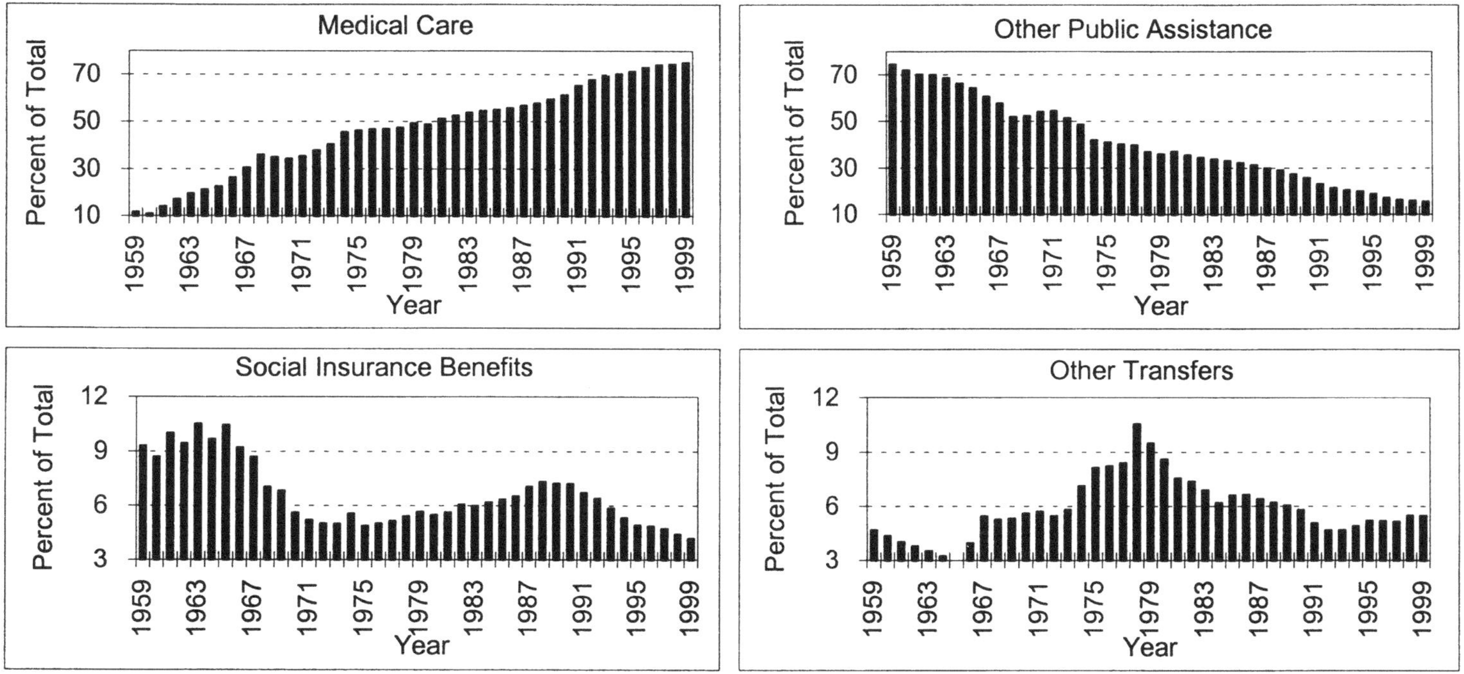


*Source* : U.S. Department of Commerce. Bureau of Economic Analysis. "'Annual Only' NIPA Tables." *National Accounts Data* . 30 Aug 2000: Tables 3.12. 5 Sep. 2000. <http://www.bea.doc.gov/bea/dn1.htm>.

institutions are found in the last catchall category. Funding in 1999 for other public assistance programs amounted to $38.7 billion.

*Social Insurance Benefits* consist of payments for temporary disability insurance and workers' compensation. In 1999 they total to $10.5 billion. Into *Other Transfers* fall programs for education, employment and training, veterans' benefits, crime-victim payments, and Alaska dividends—a reward the state of Alaska presents to its residents for living there. Those items total to $13.8 billion.

Exhibit 6.4 shows graphically the four major components as percents of *Total transfers* for each of the years from 1959 to 1999. Vertical axes measure percents of total transfers. For both graphs in the top row, the percentages range from 10 percent to 80 percent. As *Medical Care* has increased its relative share, *Other Public Assistance* has declined. In 1959 *Medical Care* transfers made up 12 percent of total transfers, and *Other Public Assistance* made up 74 percent. By the end of the forty-year period, their relative importance is reversed. *Medical Care* accounts for 75 percent, and *Other Public Assistance*, for 15 percent. Together they account for from 80 percent to 90 percent of total transfer payments to persons. Future growth of medical care's share appears likely.

Graphs for *Social Insurance Benefits* and *Other Transfers* occupy the lower half of Exhibit 6.4. The vertical scale in those cases ranges from 3 percent to 12 percent. For *Social Insurance Benefits* the decade of the 1960s marked the years when its share of total transfers payments approximated 9 percent. A rapid decline then followed, reaching a low point in 1975 at 5 percent. Gradually, its percentage rose and by 1990 stood at 7 percent. Since then its relative share has declined, reaching a forty-year low of 4 percent in 1999.

*Other Transfers* reached its high point of over 10 percent in 1978 when employment and training programs received enthusiastic support and funding. When those programs failed to correct all of the world's problems, support and funding faded. Consequently, *Other Transfers* ends the period with its share of total transfer payments very close to the beginning, around 5 percent.

## SAVING AND INVESTMENT OF STATE & LOCAL GOVERNMENT

In the aggregate receipts of state and local governments exceed their consumption expenditures, transfer payments, and other expenditure items. Consequently, the balancing entry—appearing as an expenditure item—is a surplus. If their expenditures exceeded their receipts, the entry would be negative, indicating that they were resorting to a fourth source of government revenue, borrowing.

As shown in Exhibit 6.2, *Net saving* has two parts: *Social insurance funds* and *Other*. As we have seen already, *Social insurance funds* include temporary disability insurance and workers' compensation insurance programs. When employer and personal contributions to the programs and interest received on fund balances exceed transfer payments and costs of administering the programs, they

**Exhibit 6.5**
**State and Local Government Net Savings, 1959 to 1999**

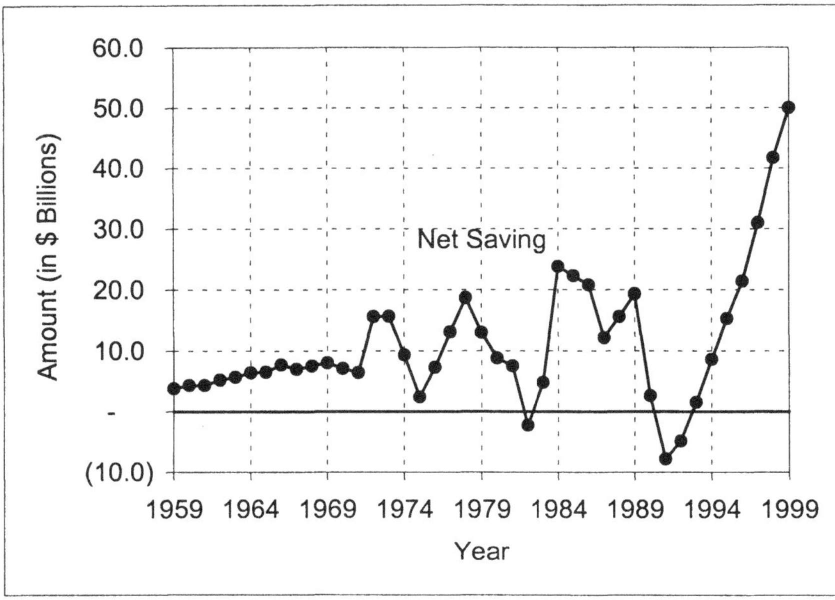


*Source* : U.S. Department of Commerce. Bureau of Economic Analysis. "Selected NIPA Tables." *National Accounts Data* . 8 Aug. 2000: Table 3.3. 9 Sep. 2000. <http://www.bea.doc.gov/bea/dn1.htm>.

generate a surplus. When disbursements exceed receipts they generate a deficit, which was the case for 1999.

*Other* sources of state and local surpluses include funds tucked away in state college and university endowment funds, trust funds for certain state agencies, and in the general fund. Receipts collected as part of general tax revenues and not designated for a particular purpose may exceed general expenditures. In 1999 those sources produced a surplus of $50.4 billion. After allowance for the deficit in the social insurance funds, *Net savings* amounted to $50.0 billion.

Exhibit 6.5 shows the pattern of net savings of state and local governments during the forty-year period from 1959 to 1999. Generally, net savings is positive. On two occasions, however, in 1982 and in 1991–92, it wandered into negative territory. Those deficits occurred during times of sharp recession in business activity. Other ups and downs as well reflect fluctuations in the business cycle. When business turns down, government receipts decline, but government disbursements remain relatively constant and may even increase. Since the deficits of 1991–92, net saving has increased rapidly, corresponding closely with the continuous economic expansion that has occurred during that same period. The $50.0 billion surplus for 1999 represents a forty-year high. The prevalence of surpluses over deficits for most years results in an accumulation of

**Exhibit 6.6**
**State and Local Government Saving and Investment, 1999**

| | **1999 Amounts in $ Billions** | | | **Percent of Total** | | |
|---|---|---|---|---|---|---|
| **STATE & LOCAL GOV'T SURPLUS** | | | **$ 50.0** | | | **26** |
| Change in liabilities | | | 81.4 | | | 43 |
| Discrepancy | | | 60.1 | | | 31 |
| **CHANGE IN LIAB & NET WORTH** | | | **191.6** | | | **100** |
| Change in financial assets | | | 87.5 | | | 46 |
| Change in tangible assets (Net investment) | | | 104.1 | | | 54 |
| Capital expenditures (Gross invst) | | $210.9 | | | 110 | |
| Structures | $ 157.5 | | | 82 | | |
| *Employee comp* | *8.4* | | | *4* | | |
| *Other expenditure* | *149.1* | | | *78* | | |
| Equipment | 53.4 | | | 28 | | |
| Consumption of fixed capital | | (106.8) | | | (56) | |
| **CHANGE IN TOTAL ASSETS** | | | **$ 191.6** | | | **100** |

*Source*: U.S. Department of Commerce. Bureau of Economic Analysis. "Selected NIPA Tables." *National Accounts Data*. 8 Aug. 2000: Table 3.7. 9 Sep. 2000. <http://www.bea.doc.gov/bea/dn1.htm>. and Board of Govemors, Federal Reserve System. "Z.1 Historical data." 15 Sep. 2000 *Flow of Funds Accounts of the United States*: F.105. 18 Sep. 2000. <http://www.bog.frb.us/releases/z1/current/data.htm>.

financial assets that explains in part why state and local governments pay less interest than they receive.

What do state and local governments do with their savings? Like households and nonprofit organizations, their savings are reflected in changes in holdings of assets and liabilities. Exhibit 6.6 shows that *Change in total assets* of state of local governments increased $191.6 billion. Since *State and local government surplus* (Net Saving) amounted to only $50.0 billion, liabilities had to increase as well, by $81.4 billion. An allowance for a *Discrepancy* of $60.1 billion bludgeons the *Change in total assets* into alignment with the *Change in liabilities and net worth.*

Increases in holdings of credit market instruments of $43.4 billion account for almost half of the $87.5 billion *Change in financial assets*. The largest portion of those credit market instruments consists of U.S. government securities. Increases in cash and cash equivalents of $19.8 billion, and of equities, taxes receivable, and other financial assets account for the rest.

The *Change in tangible assets (Net investment)* of $104.1 billion is calculated as the difference between *Capital expenditures (Gross investment)* of $210.9 billion and *Consumption of fixed capital* of $106.8 billion. Gross investment takes two forms: *Structures*, amounting to $157.5 billion, and *Equipment*, amounting to $53.4 billion. Part of that $157.5 billion in expenditures for structures takes the form of $8.4 billion in government *Employee compensation* for those engaged in construction projects. As *Other expenditures* indicate, most public construction is performed by contract with the private sector. However, government-employed civil engineers, architects, and others plan projects, set specifications, and inspect on-site work in progress to assure quality. Their compensation becomes part of governments' capital cost.

Much of the capital expenditures are financed through issues of municipal securities. They increased $52.7 billion, constituting most of the $81.4 billion *Change in liabilities* of state and local governments.

## FUNCTIONS OF STATE AND LOCAL GOVERNMENT

A look at the kinds of services state and local governments perform appears to be a good way to conclude this chapter. In 1999 state and local governments took in $1,142.7 billion in receipts. They spent $1,092.7 billion and saved the rest. Why? What kinds of products and services did state and local governments provide with those expenditures? What are the functions of state and local governments?

Thanks to the national accounting wizards, we can determine not only what state and local governments spent the money for—durable goods, nondurable goods, and services—but also the functions those purchases were intended to perform. Accounting classifications among state and local governments vary, but with the help of appropriate definitions those expenditures can be grouped into a set of common functions. They indicate what services state and local governments furnish and provide quantitative evidence of what state and local governments do.

Exhibit 6.7 displays government expenditures in a bar graph by function as percentages of total expenditures. Two sets of percentages are provided for each function, one for 1959 and the other for 1999 so we can assess the extent to which the relative importance of government functions has shifted from the beginning to the end of the forty-year period.

Based on the eight functions and the percentages shown for each in Exhibit 6.7, the main business of state and local governments is *Education*: primary, secondary, and postsecondary. It accounted for 40 percent of all expenditures in 1959 and for 38 percent in 1999. Portions of those expenditures are funded through intergovernmental transfers, such as "federal grants-in-aid to schools as provided under the various 'title' programs; state 'foundation' aid; federal aid channeled through state government to local schools; and interlocal payments for education services."[19] Although the list of such programs is long, and the noise from Washington, DC, concerning what needs to be done about the nation's

**Exhibit 6.7**
**State and Local Government Expenditure by Function as Percents of Total Expenditure, 1959 and 1999**

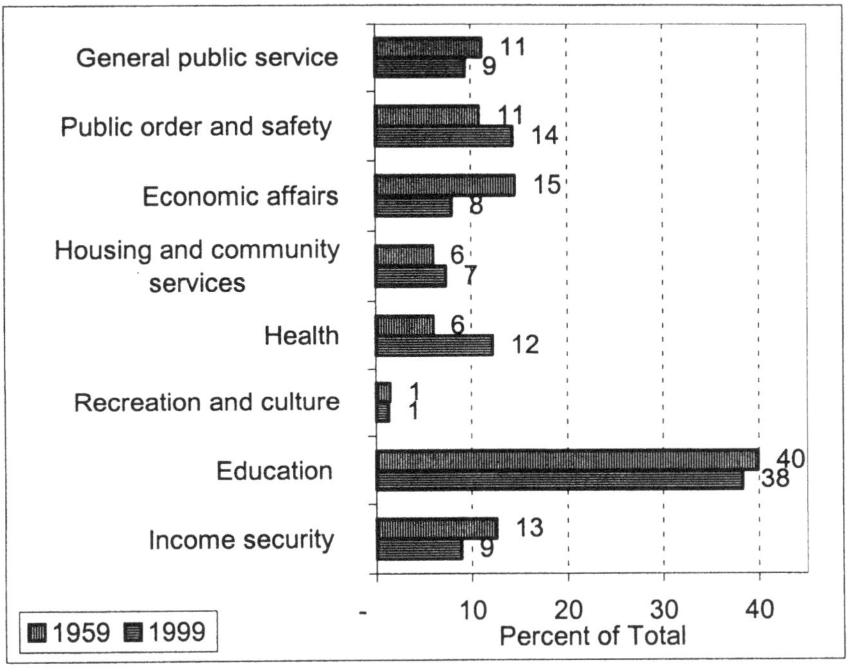


*Source*: U.S. Department of Commerce. Bureau of Economic Analysis. "'Annual Only' NIPA Tables." *National Accounts Data*. 11 Oct. 2000: Table 3.16. 30 Oct. 2000. <http://www.bea.doc.gov/bea/dn1.htm>.

schools is loud, state and local governments rather than the federal government bear most of the cost of education. In 1999 state and local consumption expenditures for education amounted to $418.4 billion compared to federal grants-in-aid for education of $19.7 billion. Some candidates for and holders of national office have found pontificating on educational issues to be good politics. For the price of the buttons they want to design the coat. Or, more apropos, for the price of a school bell, they want to design the school.

In terms of expenditures by function, *Public order and safety* currently constitutes the second most important function of state and local government. It includes expenditures for police, fire protection, law courts, and prisons. From 1959 to 1999 its share has risen from 11 to 14 percent of the total. Local government payments constitute the most important portion of those expenditures.[20] An increase in the state and local prison population is one of the causes and effects of that rapid expenditure increase. In 1960 the number of prisoners totaled 190,000. In 1997 it exceeded one million.[21]

Close after *Public order and safety* comes *Health*. Its 11 percent growth per year over the past forty years has outstripped all other functions and accounts for the rise in its share of total expenditures from 6 to 12 percent. Once again Medicaid has its impact. *Housing and community services* achieves a modest gain in share of total expenditure, changing from 6 percent in 1959 to 7 percent in 1999. In that function we find water, sewerage, sanitation, and related services.

Not all functions can increase their share during the same period, of course. *Economic affairs* shows a substantial drop from 15 percent in 1959 to 8 percent in 1999. Activities related to agriculture, energy, natural resource development, and transportation as well as general economic development and planning and labor affairs fall under that function. *Income security*, a function dealing with disability, welfare, and social services, also takes a hit declining from 13 percent to 9 percent over the forty-year period. A less dramatic decline from 11 percent to 9 percent is registered by *General public service*, an area that tends to housekeeping functions such as executive and legislative branch support, tax collection and financial management, and payment of net interest. *Recreation and culture*, which had only 1 percent in 1959, has managed to hold on to its meager share.

## NOTES

1. James Simon and Christopher Nobes, *The Economics of Taxation*, 4th ed. (New York: Prentice Hall, 1992) 6.
2. Advisory Commission on Intergovernmental Relations, "Public Attitudes on Government and Taxes," *Intergovernmental Perspectives* 20.3 (Summer/Fall 1994): 29–30.
3. U.S. Department of Commerce, Bureau of the Census, *1992 Census of Governments, Government Finances, Compendium of Government Finances*, Vol. 4, No.5 (Washington, DC: U.S. Government Printing Office, Feb. 1997) 28–29.
4. *1992 Census of Governments* 28–29.
5. *1992 Census of Governments* 28–29.
6. *1992 Census of Governments* 28–29.
7. Ralph L. Sacco, Mitchell Elkind, Bernadette Boden-Albada, I-Feng Lin, Douglas E. Kergman, W. Allen Hauser, Steven Shea, and Myunghee C. Palk, "The Protective Effect of Moderate Alcohol Consumption on Ischemic Stroke," *The Journal of the American Medical Association*, 281.1 (6 Jan. 1999): 53–60, 22 Dec. 2000 <http://jama.ama-assn.org/issues/v281n1/toc.html>.
8. Raghbendra Jah, *Modern Public Economics*, (London and New York: Routledge, 1998) 484–89.
9. Stephen J. Bailey, *Business Sector Economics: Theory, Policy, and Practice*, (Houndmills, Basngstroke, England: MacMillan, 1995) 6.
10. U.S. Executive Office of the President, *Analytical Perspectives, Budget of the United States Government, Fiscal Year 2000*, (Washington, DC: U.S. Government Printing Office, 1999) 235, 22 Dec. 2000 <http:w3.access.gpo.gov/usbudget/fy2000/maindown.html>.
11. *Analytical Perspectives* 234.
12. U.S. Department of Commerce, Bureau of Economic Analysis, *Government*

*Transactions*, Methodology Paper Series MP-5 (Washington, DC: U.S. Government Printing Office, November 1988) 10.

13. *Government Transactions* 6.

14. *Government Transactions* 6.

15. Charles T. Clotfelter and Phillip T. Cook, *Selling Hope, State Lotteries in America,* (Cambridge, MA: Harvard University Press, 1963) 9.

16. U.S. Department of Commerce, Bureau of Economic Analysis, "'Annual Only' NIPA Tables," *National Accounts Data*, 30 Aug 2000: Table 3.13, 5 Sep. 2000 <http://www.bea.doc.gov/bea/dn1.htm>.

17. U.S. Department of Commerce, Bureau of Economic Analysis, *National Income and Product Accounts of the United States, 1929–1994*. vol. 1 (Washington, DC: U.S. Government Printing Office, 1998) M-6.

18. *Government Transactions* 5.

19. *1992 Census of Governments* xiii.

20. *1992 Census of Governments* xiv.

21. U.S. Department of Commerce, Bureau of the Census, *Statistical Abstract of the United States, 1982–83* and *1999* (Washington, DC: U.S. Government Printing Office, 1982 and 1998) 191 and 231.

# 7

# The Sector We Love to Hate—Part II

Fifty states, 3,043 counties, 19,279 municipal governments, 16,656 township governments, 14,422 school district governments, and 31,555 special district governments comprise state and local government. The task of collecting data from all those units falls to the Bureau of the Census of the U.S. Department of Commerce that conducts a census of governments at five-year intervals on years ending in 2 and 7. The results of its labors are published in *Government Finances*.[1] There is only one national government, and most of the national income and product account data are drawn from its budget.

## RECEIPTS OF THE NATIONAL GOVERNMENT

With the exception of grants-in-aid, sources of receipts for the federal government are the same as those for state and local governments. Exhibit 7.1 displays federal government receipts for 1999 and provides a basis for comparison with those shown in Exhibit 6.1 for state and local governments. Over the past forty years, state and local government receipts have risen more rapidly than those for the federal government—an average annual rate of 9 percent compared with 8 percent.

### Personal Tax and Nontax Receipts

In 1999 the federal government garnered almost $1.9 trillion in receipts. Receipts from *Personal taxes and nontaxes* amounting to $902.2 billion constitute the most important source of federal government receipts, 48 percent. Federal personal income taxes make up the major source of personal tax and nontax receipts and have the distinction of being considered the least fair of all taxes levied by any level of government in the United States.[2] Although personal tax

Exhibit 7.1

**Federal Government Receipts, 1959 and 1999**

| | 1959 Amounts in $ Billions | Percent of Total | 1999 Amounts in $ Billions | Percent of Total | Annual Percent Change |
|---|---|---|---|---|---|
| **Personal taxes and nontaxes** | **$ 38.5** | **44** | **$ 902.2** | **48** | **8** |
| Income taxes | $38.5 | 44 | $892.7 | 48 | 8 |
| Nontaxes | - | | 9.5 | 1 | |
| **Corporate profits tax** | **22.5** | **26** | **219.3** | **12** | **6** |
| Federal Reserve banks | $ 0.9 | 1 | $ 25.4 | 1 | 9 |
| Other | 21.6 | 25 | 193.9 | 10 | 6 |
| **Indirect busn taxes & nontaxes** | **12.6** | **14** | **100.5** | **5** | **5** |
| Excise taxes | $11.2 | 13 | $ 65.6 | 3 | 5 |
| Customs duties | 1.0 | 1 | 19.2 | 1 | 8 |
| Nontaxes | 0.4 | 0 | 15.8 | 1 | 10 |
| **Social insurance contributions** | **13.4** | **15** | **652.5** | **35** | **10** |
| Employer contributions | $ 7.5 | 9 | $315.9 | 17 | 10 |
| Personal contributions | 5.9 | 7 | 336.6 | 18 | 11 |
| **TOTAL RECEIPTS** | **$ 87.0** | **100** | **$ 1,874.6** | **100** | **8** |

*Source* : U.S. Department of Commerce. Bureau of Economic Analysis. "Selected NIPA Tables." *National Accounts Data* . 8 Aug. 2000: Table 3.2. 9 Sep. 2000. <http://www.bea.doc.gov/bea/dn1.htm>. and "'Annual Only' NIPA Tables." *National Accounts Data.* 30 Aug 2000: Table 3.6. 5 Sep. 2000. <http://www.bea.doc.gov/bea/dn1.htm>.

and nontax receipts constitute a rapidly growing segment of state and local government revenues, they accounted for only a little over a fifth of their total in 1999. We already have had a chance to examine personal taxes and nontaxes from a payer's side when we looked at outlays of personal income so additional coverage is not necessary here.

### Corporate Profits Taxes

In 1909 the federal government enacted a new tax, the corporate profits tax. Until World War II it constituted a major source of revenue.[3] The *Corporate profits tax* continues to be much more important as a revenue source for the federal government than for state and local governments. Only 3 percent of state and local government revenue comes from corporate profits tax as compared to 12 percent for the federal government.

Despite nine decades of use, the corporate profit tax remains controversial. Who bears the burden of the tax remains a mystery. Do stockholders in the form of reduced dividends? Do owners of capital assets in lowered returns on their investments? Are consumers saddled with higher prices and reduced availability of goods and services? Do wage earners through smaller paychecks and reduced benefits? Empirical evidence found in the professional literature remains inconclusive.[4]

In Exhibit 7.1 two categories for *Corporate-profits-tax* collections are shown: one for *Federal Reserve banks* and one for *Other*. Acting under instructions of the Board of Governors of the Federal Reserve System, the twelve Federal Reserve banks—among other assignments—control the money supply. Carrying out that function turns out to be enormously profitable. They require commercial banks that are members of the Federal Reserve System to maintain reserves with them equal to a specified proportion of customers' deposits. On those reserves the Federal Reserve banks pay no interest to the commercial banks. With the reserves the Federal Reserve banks buy bonds and notes issued by the U.S. government, and for those securities they receive interest income. With no interest expense and with only interest income, a profit results even after paying the expenses for all the other services the Federal Reserve banks perform. During the forty-year period from 1959 to 1999, corporate profits taxes paid by the Federal Reserve banks have increased almost twenty-eight times, more than keeping pace with the overall increase in federal government receipts.

Despite the participation of the Federal Reserve banks, most corporate taxes fall within the *Other* category. Of the $219.3 billion in corporate income taxes collected by the federal government, $193.9 billion consist of collections from private business firms.

**Indirect Business Taxes and Nontaxes**

For the federal government *Indirect business taxes and nontaxes* provided $100.5 billion, making up 5 percent of total collections in 1999. For state and local governments, they constitute the largest share, 54 percent.

Three major components of the federal government's *Indirect business taxes and nontaxes* are shown in Exhibit 7.1: *Excise taxes*, *Customs duties*, and *Nontaxes*. *Excise taxes* constitute by far the largest share of indirect business taxes and nontaxes—65 percent of the $100.5 billion in 1999. *Excise taxes* are really sales taxes by another name; however, the federal government has left revenue generation through general retail sales taxes to state and local governments, but there are exceptions.

A close look at an airline ticket will show at least one tax. You will see another tax on your telephone bill. The U.S. government levies both of them. Economists Richard and Peggy Musgrave observe, "Federal sales taxes are imposed largely at the manufacturer level, the major exceptions being telephone services and air transportation, which are, in effect, charged at retail. Most federal sales taxes (including those on alcohol, tobacco, gasoline, and tires) are levied on a unit basis, while others (including telephone taxes) are of the *ad valorem* type."[5]

Like state and local governments, the "sinful" products of alcohol and tobacco are singled out. The federal government levies *Excise taxes* on them. In 1999 those levies generated $12.8 billion, 20 percent of the $65.6 billion in federal receipts from excise tax revenue. In 1959 receipts from excises on those two products generated 44 percent of all revenue from *Excise taxes*. Their dwindling share, however, does not demonstrate that virtue is prevailing or that the taxpaying public has discovered alternative sinful pursuits. A low rate of growth in excises on products enjoyed by guzzlers and puffers has been coupled with vigorous government pursuit of other more lucrative sources of tax revenue.

Over their long history, federal excise taxes on alcoholic beverages have produced violence as well as revenue for the federal government. The nation's first excise taxes, as recommended by Alexander Hamilton and enacted by Congress in 1791 and 1792, applied to distilled spirits.[6] Author W. Bluott Browlee asserts, "There were two things wrong with Hamilton's tax. First, it was the hated excise—a tax which ranked first among the grievances that drove immigrants to America. . . . the second thing wrong with the tax was that money was almost nonexistent among the farmers on the frontier. Farmers used whiskey as money for trade."[7] Their liquid assets were not in a form suitable to pay the tax, and the Whiskey Rebellion ensued. With the aid of 15,000 troops under George Washington's leadership, the rebellion was put down, and the federal government turned to import duties as a source of revenue.

The Civil War brought the United States of America's reliance on excise taxes as well as high tariffs to finance the campaign against the Confederate States of America. After the war the whiskey tax continued as the only excise tax generating revenue for the federal government. Its continuance produced a second whiskey rebellion. This conflict between federal tax agents and southern moonshiners, not as short-lived as the first, helped spawn the Ku Klux Klan and the Internal Revenue Bureau, forerunner of the Internal Revenue Service.[8]

The low growth rate in excise revenue from alcoholic beverages and tobacco products has enabled gasoline excises to become the dominant source of total indirect business tax and nontax receipts. Introduced in the late 1950s as a legacy of the Eisenhower administration and the interstate highway system, gasoline excises generated $23.9 billion in 1999, accounting for 36 percent of $65.6 billion in excise taxes.

Diesel fuel and air transportation became objects of fortune for federal excise collectors in the mid 1970s. In 1999 they generated $8.3 billion and $10.1 billion respectively for federal coffers. Actually flying high generates more excise revenue than virtual high flying with either alcohol or tobacco. Could it be that altitude is addictive? Interminable terminal waits and cancelled and delayed flights might suggest that airlines are trying hard to break travelers of the habit.

Other excises include taxes on such products as telephone services, tires, coal, nuclear fuel, and trucks. All those excises produced $10.4 billion in revenue in 1999. Is the nuisance worth the return? Excise taxes tend to be enduring. However, one excise tax has come and gone: the crude oil windfall profits tax. It generated federal government revenue from 1980 to 1986. In its 1981 heyday 58 percent of federal excise taxes came from that source. Introduced with the OPEC-induced price hikes in 1980, it disappeared with the collapse of world crude oil prices in 1986. Gone but not forgotten, it may be back as a resurgent OPEC is once again decisively influencing oil prices.

The Constitution of the United States empowers Congress to levy customs duties on imports. At one time they comprised a major source of revenue for the federal government. Now generating $19.2 billion, *Customs duties*' importance has declined to a mere 1 percent of total federal government receipts. Other taxes have far outstripped customs duties' revenue generating power, but among their peers in the *Indirect business taxes and nontaxes* category, they appear to be staging a comeback. From 1959 to 1999 customs duties' share of total federal *Indirect business taxes and nontaxes* increased from 8 to 19 percent.

Last and least among the items in the *Indirect business taxes and nontaxes* category is *Nontaxes*. At $15.8 billion they account for less than 1 percent of total receipts in 1999. Nontaxes consist of Outer Continental shelf royalties, deposit insurance premiums, other royalties, fines, and fees. Introduced in the early 1960s, royalties from the Outer Continental shelf are a product of new technologies enabling undersea drilling for oil. Their contribution to the $15.8 billion in *Nontaxes* amounts to $3.4 billion. From their inception in 1961, they have grown rapidly, about 10 percent a year. In years past Outer Continental shelf royalties have been larger. The year 1997 records a high point, $4.7 billion. The amount of offshore drilling fluctuates in response to world oil markets, so growth in Outer Continental shelf royalties has not been a continuous one.

### Social Insurance Contributions

*Social insurance contributions* provide the federal government with its second largest source of receipts. Of the $1.9 trillion in 1999 federal government receipts, social insurance contributions accounted for $652.5 billion, 35 percent. For state and local governments, on the other hand, social insurance contributions account for only 1 percent of total receipts. The federal government clearly is into the social insurance business in a big way.

Of the $652.5 billion, employers contributed $315.9 billion; personal contributions amounted to $336.6 billion. Personal contributions exceed employer contributions. For Old Age, Survivors, Disability, and Hospital Insurance (OASDHI), employer-employee shares are about equal. However, self-employed persons pay both the employer and employee shares. Supplementary medical insurance premiums paid by persons further increase the personal contributions. Those two factors more than offset instances in which employers pay more than employees.

### Comparisons of Sources of Receipts, 1959 and 1999

In 1959 federal government receipts amounted to $87.0 billion, quite a contrast to 1999's $1,874.6 billion figure. When receipts exceeded $100 billion in 1962, people thought it worthy of comment. Since 1995 federal government receipts have increased by more than $100 billion each year. Comparing dollar amounts then and now often startles but rarely is instructive. Useful relative comparisons, however, can be made.

*Personal taxes and nontaxes* provide the predominant source of federal government revenue in 1999. In 1959 they also constituted the most important source of funds. As Exhibit 7.1 shows, the share of receipts from *Personal taxes and nontaxes* has grown from 44 percent to 48 percent. Nontaxes contribute very little. None are recorded for 1959. In 1999 the $9.5 billion produced from that source are less than 1 percent of the $1.9 trillion in total receipts. Despite ostensible cuts in personal tax rates, personal taxes do tend to increase more rapidly than overall economic growth because of their progressive feature. As household incomes increase the marginal tax rate increases.

Receipts from the *Corporate profits tax* and from *Indirect business taxes and nontaxes* show relative declines. In 1959 approximately one dollar in four of federal receipts came from the *Corporate profits tax*. By 1999 around one dollar in eight came from that source. Even more drastic has been relative decline of *Indirect business taxes and nontaxes*: from 14 percent in 1959 to 5 percent in 1999. Since many of the excise taxes, the most important source of *Indirect business taxes and nontaxes*, are based on number of units rather than value, a decline in share of total receipts in a forty-year period characterized by price inflation is not surprising.

Contributions for social insurance make up for most of the relative declines in the corporate profits tax and indirect business taxes and nontaxes. In 1959

**Exhibit 7.2**
**Federal Government Social Insurance Program Contributions as Percents of Total Contributions, 1959 and 1999**

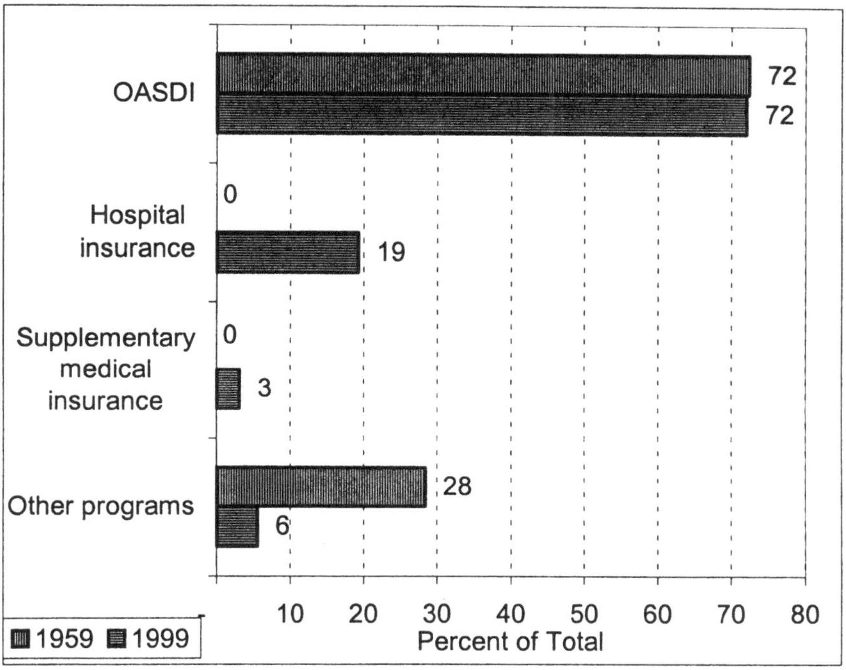


*Source*: U.S. Department of Commerce. Bureau of Economic Analysis. "'Annual Only' NIPA Tables." *National Accounts Data*. 30 Aug 2000: Table 3.6. 5 Sep. 2000. <http://www.bea.doc.gov/bea/dn1.htm>.

about one dollar in seven came from that source. In 1999 *Social insurance contributions* generated more than one dollar in three of federal receipts. Its share has more than doubled. *Personal taxes and nontaxes* increased their share with an average annual growth rate of 8 percent. Social insurance contributions have grown at a 10 percent average annual rate over the past forty years.

What accounts for the burgeoning growth in social insurance programs? We had a chance to inspect personal contributions to social insurance programs in chapters 2 and 4, and that inspection gives us a clue. In Exhibit 7.2 personal and employer contributions are combined and grouped into four categories. Contributions for *OASDI* dominate total contributions in relative size. They have maintained their share at 72 percent. Like total contributions they have increased at an average annual rate of 10 percent.

In 1959 the remaining 28 percent was made up of *Other programs*. They include unemployment insurance, railroad retirement, pension benefit guarantee, veterans life insurance, workers' compensation, and military medical insurance. As a group they have not kept up. With a growth rate of 6 percent a year, their share has declined from 28 percent of all contributions in 1959 to 6 percent in 1999.

*Hospital insurance* (Medicare) and *Supplementary medical insurance* make up the difference. As we already have noted, both programs were initiated in 1966. Contributions for Medicare are not voluntary. Employers and employees each pay into the program based on salaries and wages paid. Contributions to supplementary medical insurance, on the other hand, are voluntary. All persons eligible for Medicare and U.S. residents age sixty-five and older are eligible to enroll. In fiscal year 1999 36.9 million persons were enrolled in the program, generating $20.3 billion in contributions. Benefit outlays for fiscal year 1999 amounted to $79.2 billion.[9]

Involuntary contributions beat voluntary by a wide margin. Contributions for *Hospital insurance* account for 19 percent of all contributions for social insurance programs in 1999. *Supplementary medical insurance* contributions amount to 3 percent. Together those two programs generated 22 percent of the total. Each of the two programs has grown at a 13 percent annual rate over the thirty-four years of their existence. Nothing grows like that forever. Over the past ten years, their growth has fallen to 7 percent annually for *Hospital insurance* and 5 percent for *Supplementary medical insurance.*

## NATIONAL GOVERNMENT CURRENT EXPENDITURE

Like state and local governments, the federal government consumes goods and services, makes transfer payments, pays interest, offers subsidies, operates government enterprises, and has a surplus or deficit. Although the format is similar, the amounts and relative magnitudes involved are very different.

In Exhibit 7.3 we see that in 1999 *Consumption expenditures* amounted to $470.8 billion or 25 percent of total uses of funds of $1.9 trillion. By contrast, state and local governments used 75 percent of their funds for consumption expenditures.

Transferring money represents a major preoccupation of the federal government. With an outlay of $746.1 billion in 1999, *Transfer payments* rank first in size among federal uses of funds, accounting for 40 percent of the total. Most of those transfers go to persons, $734.5 billion, 98 percent of the $746.1 billion. The remaining 2 percent goes to the rest of the world. Transfer payments do not stop with *Transfer payments. Grants-in-aid,* $229.3 billon, 12 percent of all outlays, represent another form of transfers. Some might consider *Net interest paid* of $264.7 billion a transfer payment. A product of past federal government borrowing, lenders include the rest of the world as well as persons and businesses. The federal government receives as well as pays interest, a modest $17.1 billion. It consists of monetary interest received on loans to persons, businesses, and the rest of the world and interest from invested trust fund balances. It also includes imputed interest estimated by the Bureau of Economic Analysis. Only $1.4 billion of the $17.1 billion take the form of imputed interest.

Exhibit 7.3

Federal Government Uses of Funds, 1959 and 1999

| | 1959 Amounts in $ Billions | Percent of Total | 1999 Amounts in $ Billions | Percent of Total | Annual Percent Change |
|---|---|---|---|---|---|
| **Consumption expenditures** | **$ 52.0** | **60** | **$ 470.8** | **25** | **6** |
| **Transfer payments (net)** | **20.4** | **23** | **746.1** | **40** | **9** |
| To persons | $18.6 | 21 | $734.5 | 39 | 10 |
| To the rest of the world (net) | 1.8 | 2 | 11.6 | 1 | 5 |
| **Grants-in-aid** | **3.8** | **4** | **229.3** | **12** | **11** |
| **Net interest paid** | **6.4** | **7** | **264.7** | **14** | **10** |
| Interest paid | n/a | | 281.8 | 15 | |
| To persons and business | n/a | | $186.7 | 10 | |
| To the rest of the world | 0.3 | 0 | 95.1 | 5 | 15 |
| Interest received | n/a | | (17.1) | (1) | |
| **Subsidies** | **1.1** | **1** | **43.5** | **2** | **10** |
| **Government enterprises surpluses** | **0.1** | **0** | **(4.2)** | **(0)** | |
| **Net saving** | **3.2** | **4** | **124.4** | **7** | **10** |
| Social insurance funds | $ (0.7) | (1) | $ 90.7 | 5 | |
| Other | 3.9 | 4 | 33.7 | 2 | 6 |
| **TOTAL USES OF FUNDS** | **$ 87.0** | **100** | **$ 1,874.6** | **100** | **8** |

*Note* : n/a, not available

*Source* : U.S. Department of Commerce. Bureau of Economic Analysis. "Selected NIPA Tables." *National Accounts Data* . 8 Aug. 2000: Table 3.2. 9 Sep. 2000. <http://www.bea.doc.gov/bea/dn1.htm>.

*Subsidies* represent a form of transfers with yet another name. With an outlay of \$43.5 billion in 1999, they accounted for 2 percent of total outlays. The agriculture and housing sectors of the economy are beneficiaries of federal subsidies. In 1999 agriculture received \$20.6 billion; housing, \$21.9 billion. Another \$1 billion was dribbled out largely to railroads and mass transit systems.

Collectively, all those transfers—transfer payments, grants-in-aid, net interest paid, and subsidies—make up a little more than two-thirds of the federal government's total outlays in 1999. Uncle Sam's inclination to take from some and give to others has become a consuming obsession. State and local governments are not so possessed. As shown in Exhibit 6.1, in 1999 they took in more interest than they paid; *Transfer payments* amounted to 22 percent of *Total uses of funds*, and subsidies constituted a vanishing small portion of total outlays. Uncle Sam is often behind the scenes promoting and funding (partially) transfer payments. Under such circumstances give-away habits appear difficult to resist.

Government enterprises generated a small margin of return for the federal government, \$4.2 billion, and a negligible amount relative to total uses of funds. Of course, some of the government enterprises generating a margin also are recipients of subsidies. Generators of a surplus include the Federal Housing Administration and the Tennessee Valley Authority. Losers include the Postal Service, the Bonneville Power Administration, other electric power agencies, and insurance agencies other than those insuring deposits in financial institutions.

*Net saving* appears last on the list in Exhibit 7.3. In 1999 it amounted to \$124.4 billion, 7 percent of total uses of funds. *Social insurance funds* provided most of the saving, \$90.7 billion. Long-term actuarial projections indicate that, without corrective (and unpleasant) action, those savings are expected to disappear as the Medicare and OASDI programs march toward bankruptcy. For the near term, however, they are in the black. So too are general government operations, designated *Other*. Surpluses from general government operations in 1998 and 1999 represent phenomena that have not occurred in twenty-eight years. Before then the last time the federal government recorded a surplus in its general operations occurred in 1969.

## Comparison of Uses of Current Funds over Time

*Consumption expenditures* did not always account for 25 percent of total uses of funds. *Transfer payments* did not always account for 40 percent of the total. Exhibit 7.3 provides comparisons of federal government uses of funds in 1999 with 1959.

In 1959 at 60 percent of total uses of \$87.0 billion of available funds, *Consumption expenditures* were preeminent. Consumption expenditures for national defense alone accounted for 48 percent of all uses of funds. In 1999 national defense consumption expenditures make up 17 percent. Its relative decline accounts for a large measure of consumption expenditures' fall from 60 to 25 percent of the total. However, other consumption expenditures have declined in relative importance as well.

**Exhibit 7.4**
**Federal Government Consumption Expenditures, 1999**

| | | 1999 Amounts in $ Billions | | Percent of Total |
|---|---|---|---|---|
| **Durable goods** | | **$ 23.7** | | **5** |
| **Nondurable goods** | | **17.5** | | **4** |
| **Services** | | **429.6** | | **91** |
| Employee compensation | $220.4 | | 47 | |
| Consumption of fixed capital | 87.3 | | 19 | |
| Other services | 121.9 | | 26 | |
| **CONSUMPTION EXPENDITURES** | | **$ 470.8** | | **100** |

*Source* : U.S. Department of Commerce. Bureau of Economic Analysis. "Selected NIPA Tables." *National Accounts Data* . 8 Aug. 2000: Table 3.7. 9 Sep. 2000. <http://www.bea.doc.gov/bea/dn1.htm>.

All the transfer payments show significant gains. *Transfer payments* grew from 23 percent to 40 percent of total uses, reflecting their 9 percent average annual growth rate. *Grants-in-aid* tripled their relative importance, from 4 to 12 percent, thanks to an 11 percent annual growth rate. *Net interest paid* and *Subsidies* doubled their relative importance reflecting their 10 percent growth rates.

Federal government enterprises in 1959 generated a negligible deficit, thus contributing to uses of funds. Forty years later they are generating a negligible surplus and offsetting uses of funds. Improvement is a gradual thing.

*Net saving* showed considerably more vigor. The 7 percent net saving figure in 1999 surpassed 1959's 4 percent by a significant margin. Absent a decision in the 1980s to accumulate surpluses for the social insurance programs, however, the gain would have been much smaller.

### Consumption Expenditures

Despite the diminished stature of federal government's *Consumption expenditures* shown in Exhibit 7.3, it amounted to $470.8 billion in 1999 and deserves a closer look. In Exhibit 7.4 we see that $429.6 billion of consumption expenditures took the form of purchases of *Services*. In that regard the federal government's pattern of consumption expenditures resembles that of state and local governments. For the federal government, the predominance of *Services* is even more pronounced: 91 percent of the total as compared to state and local government's 87 percent in 1999. For all products consumed, sales constitute an insignificant deduction from all categories of consumption expenditures and are not shown separately in Exhibit 7.4.

Among *Services*, compensation of general government employees is the largest category accounting for over half of all services consumed and 47 percent of total consumption expenditures in 1999. Not all the federal government payroll is included in that figure. Compensation of government employees engaged in construction and related capital formation activities is not counted here. It is counted as a part of the capital expenditures for those structures. *Consumption of fixed capital* represents the wear, tear, and obsolescence of the government's prior investment in its fixed assets. In 1999 it amounted to $87.3 billion, 19 percent of consumption.

*Other services* represent purchases of services. At $121.9 billion and 26 percent of total consumption, it exceeded by a substantial margin expenditures for *Durable* and *Nondurable goods*.

### Transfer Payments

As *Consumption expenditure*'s growth rate of 6 percent per year led to its decline in relative importance, *Transfer payments'* 9 percent growth rate brought about its ascendancy to the largest share of total uses of current funds. As shown in Exhibit 7.3, the percentage of *Transfer payments* rose from 23 percent in 1959 to 40 percent in 1999. Not only have transfer payments altered the distribution of total uses of funds for the federal government but also their internal composition has changed.

Exhibit 7.5 provides a basis for examining more closely the internal composition of the federal government's *Transfer Payments to Persons*. It displays bar charts for six components of transfer payments for each of the years from 1959 to 1999. The vertical axis of the charts shows component expenditures as percents of total transfers. The vertical axes have been adjusted to the range of each of the components. Social security—Old age, Survivors, and Disability Insurance (*OASDI*)—begins and ends the period accounting for over half of all transfer payments to persons, 55 percent at the beginning and 52 percent at the end. In between it rises to a little over 66 percent in 1965 and 1966. Only in 1975 does it dip slightly below 50 percent. Responsibility for its declining share lies mainly with Hospital Insurance (Medicare) and Supplementary Medical Insurance. From zero from 1959 to 1965, their percentage has risen to nearly 30 percent in 1997. They closed the period at 28 percent.

*Other Social Insurance* programs accounted for 24 percent in 1959. Their share peaked at 28 percent in 1961. Since that high point the share has generally declined, closing the period at a little less than 5 percent. Included in the category are unemployment insurance, railroad retirement benefits, pension benefit guarantees, veterans life insurance, workers compensation, and military medical insurance.

Insertion of the federal government into *Public Assistance Programs* was spawned in 1960s. It represents a new area of endeavor for the federal government. Such welfare activities were left to the state and local governments until initiation of food stamp benefits, supplemental security income, direct relief, earned income tax credit, and black lung benefits. The food stamp program, designed to provide persons with little or no income with access to a nutrition-

**Exhibit 7.5**

**Federal Government Transfer Payments to Persons as Percents of Total Transfers, 1959 to 1999**

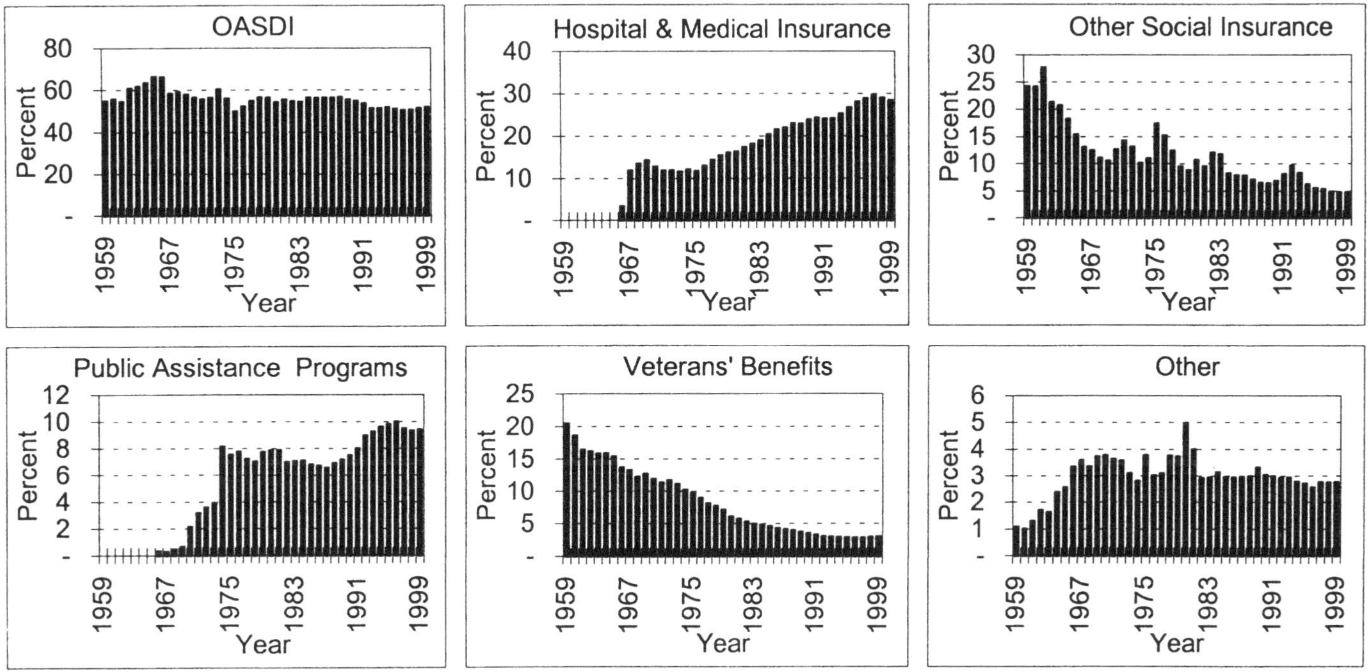


*Source*: U.S. Department of Commerce. Bureau of Economic Analysis. "'Annual Only' NIPA Tables." *National Accounts Data*. 30 Aug 2000: Table 3.12. 5 Sep. 2000. <http://www.bea.doc.gov/bea/dn1.htm>.

ally adequate diet, began on a trial basis with the Food Stamp Act of 1964. The Food and Consumer Service of the Department of Agriculture administers the program and uses local welfare offices and national food marketing and banking systems to operate it.[10] The supplemental security income program was established in 1972 to provide income support to persons sixty-five or older, blind or disabled adults, and blind or disabled children. In 1969 legislation enacted by Congress enabled black lung benefits to be paid to coal miners totally disabled as a result of pneumoconiosis and to their widows and dependents.

From zero in 1959 through 1965, *Public Assistance*'s growth in share of total transfers has not been continuous. It reached 8 percent in 1974, but that high point was not exceeded until 1991. The year 1996 marked a forty-year high point. *Public Assistance Programs* closes the period at a little over 9.4 percent.

*Veterans' Benefits* begins the period with a strong 20 percent share of total transfers. Since then its share generally has declined, reaching lows of around 3 percent from 1992 to 1999.

*Other* transfer programs include payments to nonprofit institutions, aid to students, and payments for medical services of retired military personnel and their dependents at nonmilitary facilities. From a modest beginning around 1 percent, they rose as a group to close to 4 percent by the late 1960s. A peak approximating 5 percent occurred in 1980 followed by a rapid fall back to the 3 percent range for the remainder of the period.

All those changes took place in an environment of rapid increases in transfer payments. During the forty-year period, transfer payments to persons increased from $18.6 billion to $734.5 billion. In such a context truly spectacular rates of increase are required to increase total share.

### Federal Grants-in-Aid to State and Local Governments

Like *Net interest paid*, *Subsidies*, and *Net savings*, *Grants-in-aid to state and local governments* have enjoyed a double-digit average annual growth rate over the forty years from 1959 to 1999. Indeed, their collective average annual growth rate of 11 percent tops the others. As a result and as shown in Exhibit 7.3, their share of federal government expenditures has risen from 4 percent to 12 percent. Not all grants-in-aid programs have fared equally in the expansion, however.

*Grants-in-aid to state and local governments* can be categorized by function. Exhibit 7.6 groups grants-in-aid into six functional categories for each of the years from 1959 to 1999. For each function outlays appear as percents of total grants-in-aid.

Step back from Exhibit 7.6. Look at all six graphs together. In the big picture it becomes clear that only one function has increased appreciably its share of total grants-in-aid. That function pertains to *Health*, largely consisting of Medicaid. Its lowest share occurs at the beginning of the period, a little over 5 percent. Its largest share occurs at the end, almost 54 percent. All the other grants-

**Exhibit 7.6**

**Federal Grants-in-Aid to State and Local Government by Major Function as Percents of Total Grants-in-Aid, 1959 to 1999**

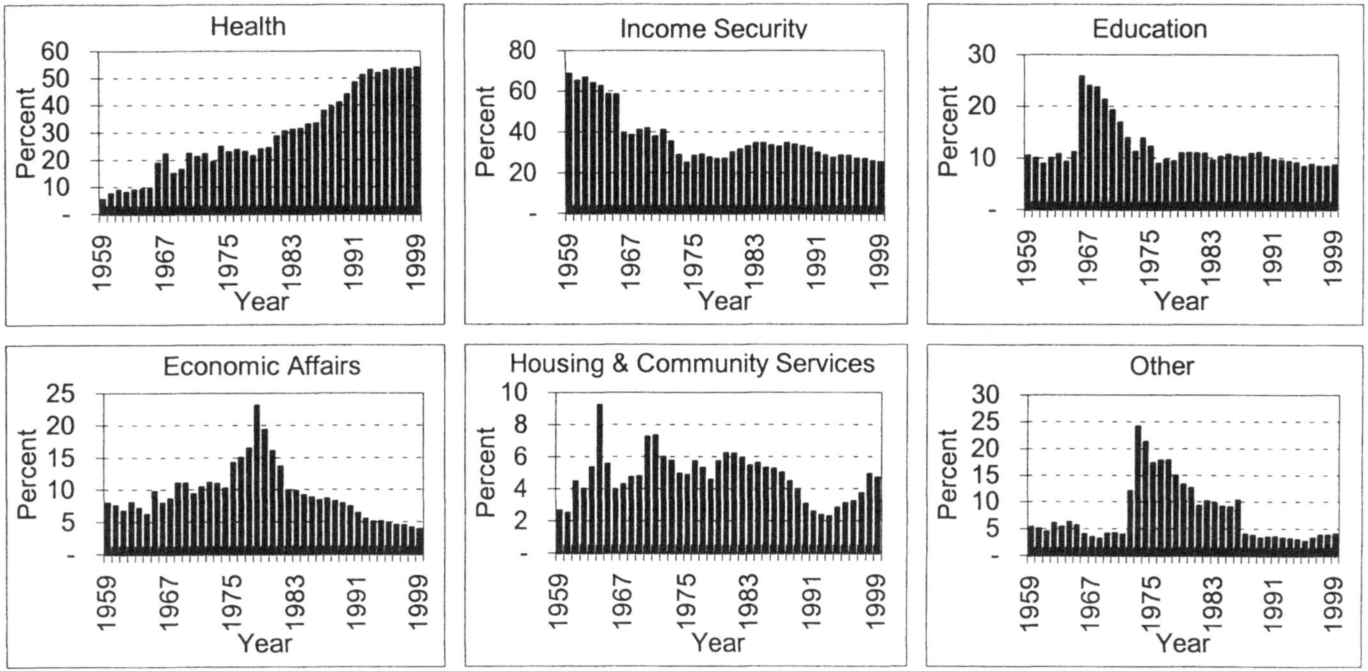


*Source*: U.S. Department of Commerce. Bureau of Economic Analysis. "'Annual Only' NIPA Tables." *National Accounts Data*. 11 Oct. 2000: Table 3.17. 30 Oct. 2000. <http://www.bea.doc.gov/bea/dn1.htm>.

in-aid functions—with perturbations in between—end the forty-year period generally either close to or below their share at the beginning.

Exhibit 7.6 indicates that *Income Security* has been a big loser. In 1959 *Income Security* dominated federal grants in aid to state and local government. Its share then was 68 percent of the total, and it included welfare and social services, unemployment, and other programs. Despite picking up disability programs in 1970, by 1999 its share of total grants-in-aid had dropped to 25 percent, its smallest share for the entire period.

*Education* enjoyed a spike in its share of total grants-in-aid in 1966 along with *Health*. From 1959 to 1966 its share jumped from 11 percent to 26 percent. Unlike *Health*, however, which proceeded, somewhat unevenly, on to ever-greater shares, 1966 proved to be *Education*'s high watermark. Its share declined over the next ten years, eventually reaching a plateau in the 8 to 11 percent range. It concludes the period with a share at close to 9 percent—less than its beginning share of between 10 and 11 percent.

*Economic Affairs*, *Housing and Community Services*, and *Other* account for more modest shares of total grants-in-aid. They end the period with shares of 4 percent, 5 percent, and 4 percent, respectively. Each one, however, enjoyed brief moments of bounty. *Economic Affairs* includes programs in agriculture, energy, natural resources, transportation, and general economic and labor affairs. It also included programs in space, but that effort came in 1979 and went in 1982. *Economic Affairs* attains its largest share of grants-in-aid funding in 1978, a point preceded by rising shares and followed by declining shares reflecting largely the pattern of funding for general economic and labor affairs programs. Despite the momentary glory, it ends the period with a 4 percent share, about half its 1959 share of 8 percent.

Support for *Housing and Community Services* shows a very different pattern. Support has waxed and waned several times during the forty-year period. In 1959 its share of total grants-in-aid stood at less than 3 percent. In 1964 its share peaked at 9 percent. Other high points occurred in 1970–71, 1976, and 1980–81. In 1991 its share again slipped to less than 3 percent. Since that time it has enjoyed an increasing share, and in 1999 stood at 5 percent.

Programs in general public service, national defense, public order and safety, and recreation and culture comprise *Other*. It begins the period with a 5 percent share and ends with 5 percent of total grants-in-aid. In between, particularly 1972 to 1986, it was favored with funding ranging as high as 24 percent. Funding for programs in general public service, public order and safety, and recreation and culture received infusions of funds. However, the largess was not to continue. In 1999 the programs as a group were funded at a lower percentage than that received decades earlier.

Not all federal assistance rendered to state and local governments appears in the national income and product accounts (NIPA). Certain concessions are made in the federal tax codes that enhance the tax capability of state and local governments. The exclusion of interest income earned on securities issued by state and local governments from federal personal and corporation income taxes enables those governments to issue financial instruments at interest rates below those of taxable bonds. The deductibility of personal income and property taxes from gross income for federal tax purposes tends to increase the amount of taxes state and local governments can generate from those tax sources. For 1999 those two "tax expenditures" benefits for state and local governments are estimated to total over $81.7 billion.[11] The NIPA do not reflect those instances of federal government largess, however.

Capital fund transfers represent another set of transactions ignored by the NIPA. The federal government extends investment grants to state and local governments from capital funds. In 1999 capital fund grants totaled $31.9 billion. Grants for highways received the largest measure of support, $23.4 billion. In 1959 highways received $3.0 billion out of $3.1 billion in capital transfers. Since then their relative fortunes have waned. In 1959 only air transportation contended for funding. Since then highways and air transportation have been joined with programs for transit and railroads, housing, and community service. Moreover, the interstate highway system has moved from construction to maintenance, and growth in highway mileage has slowed. From 1960 to 1975 highway mileage increased about 10 percent; since then it has stabilized even though the number of automobiles on them has not.[12]

### Net Interest Paid

Like state and local governments, federal government expenditures include provision for *Net interest paid.* In this case, however, net interest is not negative; it is positive and very positive indeed. At over a quarter of a trillion dollars in 1999, as seen in Exhibit 7.3, it accounts for 14 percent of total expenditures, up from 7 percent forty years prior and exceeding grants-in-aid to state and local governments. The interest is paid to holders of U.S. Government debt that amounted to $5.7 trillion outstanding as of September 30, 1999. The public does not hold all of that debt. The Federal Reserve banks and government accounts, including social insurance trust funds, held at that time an amount equal to $2.5 trillion. Of the private sector's holdings of $3.2 trillion, the foreign and international investors held 1.3 trillion.[13] The federal government's outstanding debt is not something we just owe to ourselves. Over one-third of the interest payments are made to the rest of the world. That U.S. government bonds and notes are an attractive investment to foreigners can be taken as a compliment, but the obligation and debt service also represent a stream of claims on future output of the economy. Moreover, should those obligations appear less attractive, foreigners are free to redeem or sell them, an event that could occur when not convenient for the nation's economic stability.

The federal government does receive a relatively small amount of interest income, amounting only to 1 percent of total expenditures in 1999. According to the Bureau of Economic Analysis, "Interest received consists largely of interest on direct loans made by a large number of Federal agencies, such as the Department of Agriculture, Agency for International Development, and the Department of Housing and Urban Development."[14]

### Subsidies

Growth in *Subsidies* has more than kept pace with the overall increase in government expenditures. Averaging 10 percent a year, subsidies in 1999 accounted for 2 percent of *Total uses of funds*—a doubling in relative importance since 1959. As already noted, the federal government exhibits a greater propensity for subsidization than state and local governments. However, their subsidies were a negligible portion of their total expenditures.

### Government Enterprises

Exhibit 7.3 shows that in 1959 government enterprises generated a deficit rather than a surplus. In 1999 the current surplus of government enterprises has switched from positive (meaning that costs exceeded revenues) to negative (meaning that on balance government enterprises earned a surplus)—but not by much.

### Surplus or Deficit

The sum of *Consumption expenditures*, *Transfer payments*, *Grants-in-aid* to state and local governments, *Net interest paid*, and *Subsidies* less *Government enterprises surpluses* equals federal government expenditures of current funds. As shown in Exhibit 7.3, in 1959 a surplus equal to 4 percent of total uses of funds was realized. With *Total uses of funds* of $87.0 billion, *Net saving* figures to $3.2 billion. In 1999 with *Total uses of funds* at $1.9 trillion and *Net saving* amounting to 7 percent of the total, a surplus of $124.4 billion was realized. In between the story is very different.

From 1970 to 1997 current expenditures of the federal government consistently exceeded current receipts—for twenty-seven years. To the surprise of those older than twenty-eight years, despite year-after-year deficit spending, the world as we knew it did not come to an end. Then in 1998 to everyone's surprise the federal government realized a surplus of $49.0 billion thanks to a surplus of receipts over disbursements in the social insurance funds. Not until 1999 did general government receipts exceed the government's cost of operations.

Exhibit 7.7 shows federal government surpluses and deficits for each year from 1959 and 1999. It displays three sets of surplus-deficit time series: *Social Insurance Funds*, *Other*, and *Total*—the sum of the preceding two. The year 1959 was one of eleven years in forty registering an overall surplus; the other twenty-nine years show deficits. The last year in which federal government receipts exceeded expenditures before a long string of deficits was 1969.

The social insurance programs of the federal government have had deficit years as well as surplus ones. The Old Age, Survivors, Disability, and Hospital

**Exhibit 7.7**
**Federal Government Surplus (Deficit), 1959 to 1999**

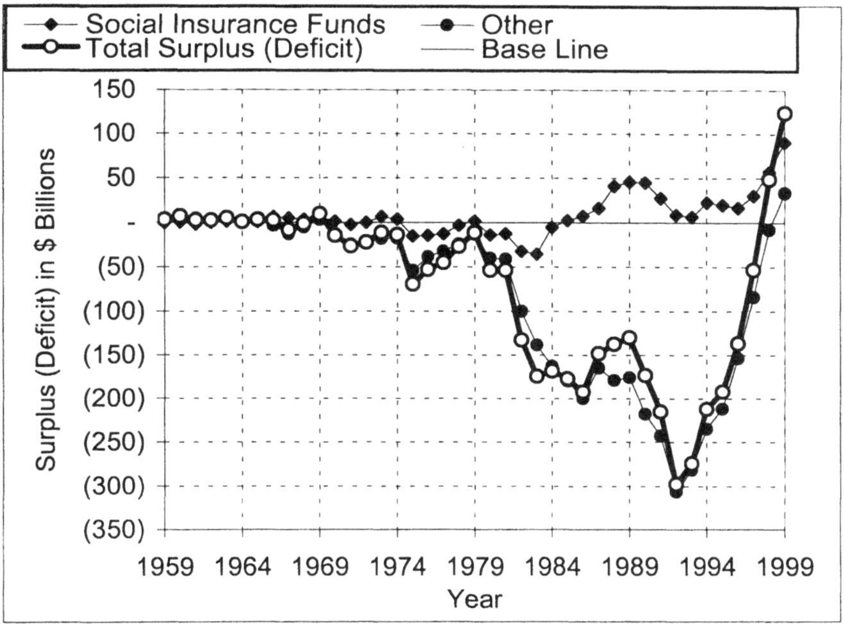


*Source* : U.S. Department of Commerce. Bureau of Economic Analysis. "Selected NIPA Tables." *National Accounts Data* . 8 Aug. 2000: Table 3.2. 9 Sep. 2000. <http://www.bea.doc.gov/bea/dn1.htm>.

Insurance Program was designed to operate like a gigantic pyramid scheme. Current contributions are used to meet only current obligations. Congress became aware of the long-term consequences of such an approach in the early 1980s and increased contributions in an attempt to accumulate funds to meet future withdrawals. As a consequence the social insurance fund has contributed substantially to reducing the federal government overall deficit in the last fifteen years of the period.

Surpluses and deficits for *Other* federal government receipts and expenditures show greater fluctuations. Before the long string of deficits, the last surplus occurred in 1969 and amounted to $3.4 billion. Since then to 1998 only deficits were recorded. The greatest deficit, $307 billion, took place in 1992. Subsequently, with continuous economic growth, the annual deficit has become smaller, shrinking to "only" $7.9 billion in 1998. The 1998 deficit was more than offset by a $56.9 billion surplus of the social insurance funds. With 1999 even *Other* government operations showed a surplus, $33.7 billion. Coupled with a $90.7 billion social insurance fund surplus, it produced total federal government saving of $124.4 billion.

**Exhibit 7.8**
**Federal Government Saving and Investment, 1999**

| | | | 1999 Amounts in $ Billions |
|---|---|---|---|
| **SURPLUS (Saving)** | | | **$ 124.5** |
| Change in liabilities | | | (34.3) |
| Discrepancy and Adjustments | | | (7.9) |
| **CHANGE IN LIABILITIES AND NET WORTH** | | | **$ 82.3** |
| Change in financial assets | | | 77.3 |
| Change in tangible assets (Net investment) | | | 5.0 |
| Capital expenditures (Gross investment) | | $97.8 | |
| Structures | $ 16.3 | | |
| *Employee compensation* | *1.8* | | |
| *Other expenditures for structures* | *14.5* | | |
| Equipment | 81.5 | | |
| Consumption of fixed capital | | (92.8) | |
| **CHANGE IN TOTAL ASSETS** | | | **82.3** |

*Sources*: Board of Governors, Federal Reserve System. "Z.1 Historical data." 15 Sep. 2000. *Flow of Funds Accounts of the United States.* 18 Sep. 2000: Table F106. <http://www.bog.frb.us/releases/z1/current/data.htm> and U.S. Department of Commerce. Bureau of Economic Analysis. "Selected NIPA Tables." *National Accounts Data*. 8 Aug. 2000: Table 3.7. 9 Sep. 2000. <http://www.bea.doc.gov/bea/dn1.htm>.

## SAVING AND INVESTMENT OF THE NATIONAL GOVERNMENT

For households and nonprofit organizations and for state and local governments, we have examined the effect of saving on assets, liabilities, and net worth. Saving affects an entity's balance sheet. For most of the forty-year period, the federal government provided an opportunity to examine the balance sheet effects of *dis*saving—spending more than is earned. In 1998 and 1999 the question has once again become not how the federal government financed its deficit but rather what it did with the money it saved from current receipts.

Exhibit 7.8 provides an answer. Federal government *Surplus (Saving)* appears as $124.5 billion. (With the change in data sources from the Department of Commerce to the Board of Governors of the Federal Reserve System, it seems to have picked up $100 million.) From the standpoint of a balance sheet, it represents a gain in net worth. Decreasing liabilities constitutes one response to spending less than current receipts. The negative figure for *Change in liabilities* reflects that response. Liabilities indeed do fall, not by $124.5 billion but by less than a third of that amount, $34.3 billion. A decrease of $71.2 billion in U.S. Treasury issues of bills, notes, and bonds outstanding is partially offset by a $42.5 billion increase in reserves for the civil service retirement and disability fund, the judicial retirement fund, the military retirement fund, and the foreign-service retirement and disability fund. Those two changes, with minor adjustments in other liabilities, bring the net reduction in liabilities to $34.3 billion.

A $7.9 negative entry for *Discrepancy and adjustments* further offsets the surplus. A discrepancy of $5.8 billion accounts for most of the $7.9 billion and results from differences in data sources for assets and liabilities. Differences in treatment between the NIPA and the flow of funds produce the adjustments. A deduction of $3.8 billion is made for the Railroad Retirement Board and federal government life insurance reserves that the Federal Reserve attributes to the federal government and that the BEA attributes to persons. A $1.7 billion addition adjusts for Federal Reserve recognition of federal government sales of access rights that are ignored in the NIPA.

Increasing assets provides another response to saving. Financial assets rise by $77.3 billion while tangible assets increase by $5.0 billion. A $66.2 billion increase in checkable deposits and currency accounts for most of the growth in financial assets.

Capital expenditures of $16.3 billion for *Structures* and $81.5 billion for *Equipment* are partially offset by *Consumption of fixed capital* of $92.8 billion. The net positive *Change in tangible assets* in 1999 signals a modest increase in the federal government's investment in infrastructure. And none too soon. Have you driven on an interstate highway recently? Most of them no longer are new, and their state of repair shows it. Less visible is deterioration of the bridge you count on to cross the next river. Much has figured in the news of the antiquated computer equipment used by air traffic controllers. Rather than being an exception, the outdated equipment manifests a sign of the times. Deterioration comes on gradually, and our ever-adaptable species adjusts accordingly. The inconvenience, discomfort, inefficiency, and potential danger can be chalked up to a lack of investment. As more federal money goes to regulation and reallocation, less goes to keeping the economy running.

## MAJOR ACTIVITIES OF THE NATIONAL GOVERNMENT

What does the federal government do? In 1999 it spent $1,750.2 billion. So great was the imperative assigned to its activities that it spent billions more than it received in current income from 1970 to 1997. But 1998 broke the pattern of consecutive years of deficits. Over the entire twenty-eight-year period, those deficits accumulate to $3.2 trillion. What crises did such expenditure prevent or overcome? How has the nation's survival been assured by the abandonment of a more constrained fiscal behavior that balances expenditure with income?

Elected representatives evidently felt that the federal government's programs offered greater benefits than the people who voted them into office realized. If the public had enjoyed the same insights and enhanced judgment, they would have accepted the higher taxes those programs required. But, since the people lacked the vision, information, and wisdom that come to holders of elected position, the elected felt imposing such budget-balancing taxes would be unwise for the continuance of their elected status.

We have examined in some detail how the federal government disposed of $1.7 trillion in 1999. What was the government trying to accomplish? The answer may seem more complex than it really is. It becomes somewhat less complicated if we ask what are the major expenditures of the federal government by function. Exhibit 7.9 identifies six functions and displays their expenditure amounts as percentages of total expenditures from 1959 to 1999.

Two of those functions stand out with respect to imperatives. One is *National Defense*, a function assigned to the federal government by the Constitution of the United States. The Constitution of the United States charges the federal government to provide for the "common defense" (as well as for a postal service). As the distribution of current expenditures by function indicates, the government takes its assignment of national defense seriously. About 18 percent of its expenditures were dedicated to that activity in 1999. Exhibit 7.9 shows that in 1959 *National Defense* accounted for an even larger share, 50 percent!

Those who conclude from the beginning and ending points that the reduction results from a peace dividend following the end of the Cold War, the dissolution of the USSR, and the rusting away of the Iron Curtain would reach an erroneous conclusion. In terms of total expenditure, the relative importance of national defense as a federal government function was almost halved about a decade before the "Evil Empire" ceased to pose a credible threat. From 1959 to 1969 the share of expenditure for national defense ranged from 45 percent to 50 percent of total expenditure. By 1979 that percentage had fallen to 26 percent. From then until 1989 it fluctuated between 26 percent and 28 percent. During the last decade it has dropped from 26 percent to 18 percent. Not one but two "peace" dividends have been declared: one from 1969 to 1979, the other from 1989 to 1999.

Within each of those decades, the slide of *National Defense* from more than half to less than 20 percent has not been continuous. The proportion of government expenditures devoted to *National Defense* has waxed and waned in response to world conditions and the predilections of political leaders in the White House and Congress. Within the time interval, the high point of *National Defense* expenditures as a percent comes in 1959. Hostilities toward Cuba that led to the Bay of Pigs invasion in 1961 did not offset a declining trend. From its high of 54 percent, national defense's portion began tending downward despite the USSR erection of the Berlin Wall in August 1961 and the Cuban Missile Crisis in October 1962. The trend continued until 1965 when it reached 45 percent of total consumption expenditures and gross investment.

**Exhibit 7.9**

**Federal Government Current Expenditures by Function as Percents of Total Expenditures, 1959 to 1999**

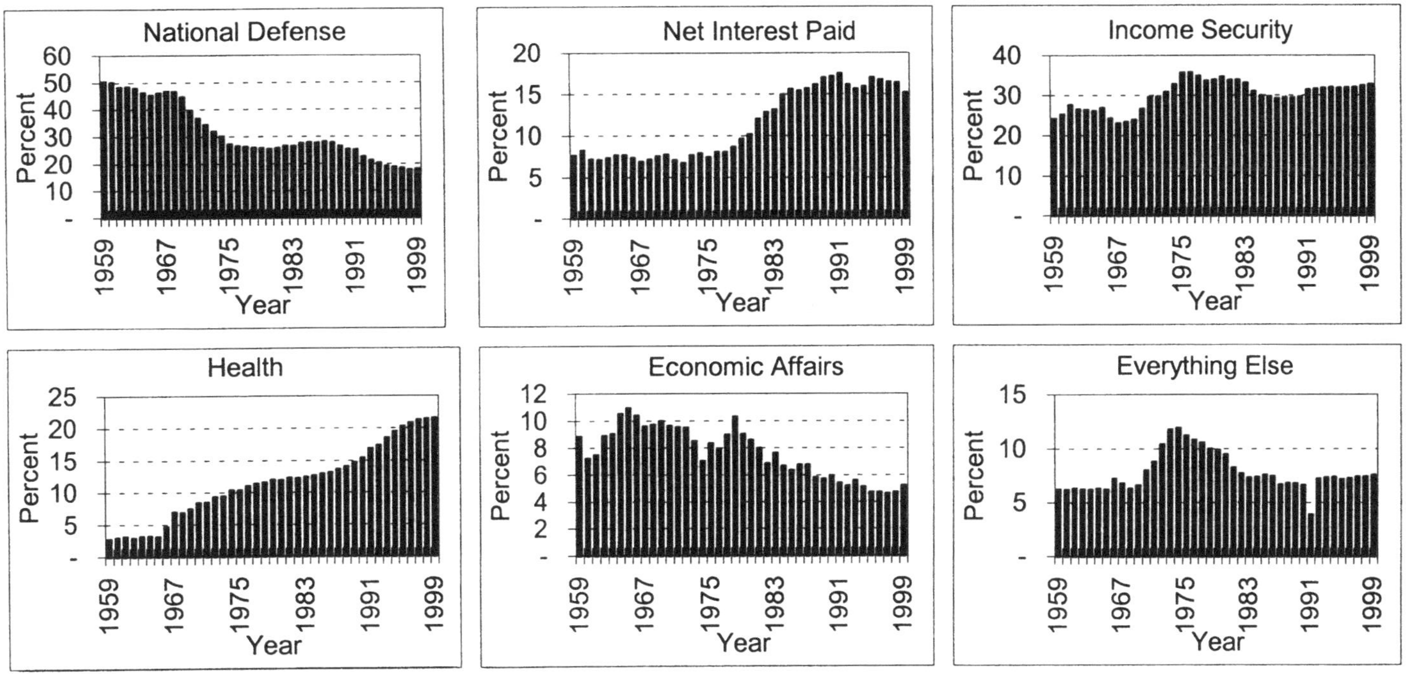


*Source*: U.S. Department of Commerce. Bureau of Economic Analysis. "'Annual Only' NIPA Tables." *National Accounts Data*. 11 Oct. 2000: Table 3.16. 30 Oct. 2000. <http://www.bea.doc.gov/bea/dn1.htm>.

With the United States engaging ground troops in the war between North and South Vietnam and its bombing of North Vietnam, the share of national defense began rising again, reaching a high of 47 percent in 1968. Thereafter, for the next twelve years, its share began a slide that brought it to approximately 25 percent in 1980. Under President Ronald Reagan's campaign against the "Evil Empire," the federal government's share of expenditures devoted to *National Defense* again rose, reaching 28 percent in 1987. With the signing of an arms agreement between the United States and the USSR, tearing down of the Berlin Wall in 1989, and the dissolution of the Soviet Union in 1991, conditions became suitable for another decline in relative national defense spending to begin. While of continuing importance, expenditure for national defense has shrunk relative to other government functions.

Another constitutional imperative concerns *Net Interest Paid*. Interest and principal on the debt of the U.S. Government—a product of past wars (clearly extraordinary conditions when survival was at stake)—and more recent extravagance require payment. Private citizens own much of the debt. Private property rights constitute one of the foundations upon which a market economy is based and merit protection by the government formed to protect them. Unlike *National Defense*, whose general trend as a share of total expenditures has been downward, the share of *Net Interest Paid* trended upward—a product of many years of deficit funding. With recent annual declines in the deficit and the emergence of surpluses, *Net Interest Paid* has declined, having peaked in 1991 at 18 percent. By 1999 its share stood at 15 percent.

At the beginning of the period, *National Defense* and *Net Interest Paid* accounted for 58 percent of total government expenditure. By the end they accounted for 33 percent. What took up the slack? The functions of *Income Security* and *Health* rose to the occasion. In 1959 27 percent of government expenditure was allocated to *Income Security* and *Health*; by 1999, 54 percent. Medicare, Medicaid, increases in other social insurance benefits, and entry of the federal government into public assistance programs make the growth in their shares no surprise.

The federal government's passion for transfer payments appears to be warming rather than cooling. The shares of both *Income security* and *Health* have continued to increase since 1995—with health accounting for the lion's share.

Those four functions—*National Defense*, *Net Interest Paid*, *Income Security*, and *Health*—made up 87 percent of total expenditures in 1999. Just 13 percent is left over for the other two categories, *Economic Affairs* and *Everything Else*. Moreover, the leftover has declined slightly in the past forty years. In 1959 the four larger functions accounted for 85 percent of the total.

Of the two remaining functions, *Economic Affairs* tend downward as a share of total expenditures. Consisting of programs dealing with general economic development, labor affairs, agriculture, energy, natural resources, transportation, the postal service, and space exploration, they began the period at 9 percent of total expenditures and ended at 5 percent. Hefty funding for the space program drove expenditure to high points of 10 and 11 percent of the total in 1964, 1965, and 1966. After the moon landings interest and funding retreated, and funding for the space program did not regain its 1965 level until 1979. Another high point topping 10 percent for *Economic Affairs* was reached in 1978. This time general economic and labor affairs received favored treatment. Thereafter, with modest interruptions, *Economic Affairs*' share has slid downward.

*Everything Else* includes executive and legislative operations, tax collection and financial management, revenue sharing grants, public order and safety, housing and community services, recreation and culture, and education. With a starting percentage of total expenditure of 6 percent and an ending one of 8 percent, *Everything Else* registers a slight gain. But the forty-year period was more interesting than the beginning and ending points suggest. In 1974 it reached a peak of nearly 12 percent. That high point was preceded by two years of rapid increase and followed by a more gradual decline.

The rise and fall of *Everything Else* can be attributed largely to a program that has come and gone: revenue sharing. It was an interesting experiment. Its origins and demise are instructive. And it may be back someday.

According to author Bernard Herber, "In 1964, a special economic task force suggested to President Johnson that an elaborate extension of the federal revenue-sharing system should be made so as to include the *unconditional revenue-sharing* technique."[15] Eight years later the recommendation came to fruition under the New Federalism program of the Nixon administration. Because of considerable controversy surrounding the approach, revenue sharing was considered an experiment, and initially the Congress limited the term of the enabling legislation to five years, beginning retroactively to January 1, 1972, and terminating December 31, 1976. Funds from personal income tax revenues were set aside in a special trust fund and amounted to $30.2 billion for the period. Few constraints were put on the funds. Initially one-third went to state governments, and two-thirds went to local governments that included county, municipal, township or other general-purpose governmental units.

Supporters contended, among other things, that unconditional revenue sharing resulted in neither expansion nor contraction of the public sector relative to the private (conservatives liked the idea of no expansion; liberals liked no contraction of the public sector), reduced reliance on conditional grant programs that were complex and cumbersome to administer (which appealed to states), and enabled inequality among regions with respect to tax burden and capacity for public services to be addressed. Moreover, state and local governments seemed likely to meet public needs more effectively at their level than a central authority in Washington, DC. Detractors feared that state and local governments would lose their independence as they increasingly relied on the grants, would replace their own receipts with federal funds, and cited instances of state and local government corruption, and failure to anticipate future needs.[16]

In the end detractors won. Congress preferred to dole out public funds to state and local governments on terms that it dictated, and private interest groups with national agendas unable to "win support for nationally operated programs" settled on conditional grants-in-aid as their next best option.[17] Legislation enabling unconditional revenue sharing was renewed several times with diminishing funding. With federal deficits mounting in the 1980s, it was terminated in 1986.

For the time, being the federal government's experiment with unconditional revenue sharing is over. Thus, we see that grants-in-aid can be classified not only on the basis of their funding arrangement (mandatory, discretionary) but also on the terms with which assistance is provided to lower government levels (conditional or categorical, and unconditional). Now they all are conditional and enable the "federal government to tailor its assistance to those activities that have the largest spill-over effects. It can set minimum standards and require matching funds to assure state or local government support and participation."[18] Inside the beltway confidence in the trustworthiness of officials elected to state and local governments to serve their constituents well does not seem strong. Only election by the same constituency to national office confers on politicians a special wisdom on how taxpayer dollars should be used.

## GOVERNMENT RECEIPTS AND EXPENDITURES

In this section we bring together receipts and expenditures of state and local governments with those of the federal government. While dealing with them separately provides insights into their respective sources of income and functions, consolidation becomes necessary to tie them into the NIPA. First, we will look at sources of current income, then expenditures, and finally at saving and investment.

### Government Receipts

Exhibit 7.10 brings together data on government receipts extracted mainly from Exhibit 6.1 for state and local governments and from Exhibit 7.1 for the federal government. In Exhibit 6.1, state and local government receipts for 1999 totaled $1,142.7 billion; in Exhibit 7.1, federal government receipts, $1,874.6 billion. In Exhibit 7.10, combined receipts, *Current Receipts*, total $2,788.0 billion. Something does not add up! The sum of the whole is $229.3 billion short of the sum of the parts. Federal grants-in-aid cancel in the consolidation process. Within the government family, just as with households, giving an allowance to the little ones does not increase the family's ability to purchase real goods and services. Just the distribution changes.

The display lends itself to ready comparisons between the federal government and state and local governments. For 1999 the federal government's receipts of *Personal taxes and nontaxes* and *Corporate profits taxes* exceed those of state and local governments. More *Indirect business taxes and nontaxes* receipts go to state and local governments than to the federal government. *Social insurance contributions* that go mainly to the federal government come about equally from employer and personal contributions.

Changes in the relative importance of the four sources of *Current Receipts* appear in Exhibit 7.10. Examination of government receipts thus aggregated

**Exhibit 7.10**

**Government Sources of Funds, 1959 and 1999**

| | 1959 Amounts in $ Billions | | Percent of Total | | 1999 Amounts in $ Billions | | Percent of Total | | Annual Percent Change | |
|---|---|---|---|---|---|---|---|---|---|---|
| **Personal taxes and nontaxes** | | **$ 42.8** | | **35** | | **$ 1,152.0** | | **41** | | **9** |
| State and local | $ 4.2 | | 3 | | $249.7 | | 9 | | 11 | |
| Federal | 38.5 | | 32 | | 902.2 | | 32 | | 8 | |
| **Corporate profits tax** | | **23.6** | | **19** | | **255.9** | | **9** | | **6** |
| State and local | $ 1.2 | | 1 | | $ 36.6 | | 1 | | 9 | |
| Federal | 22.5 | | 18 | | 219.3 | | 8 | | 6 | |
| **Indirect busn taxes & nontaxes** | | **41.9** | | **34** | | **718.1** | | **26** | | **7** |
| State and local | $29.3 | | 24 | | $617.5 | | 22 | | 8 | |
| Federal | 12.6 | | 10 | | 100.5 | | 4 | | 5 | |
| **Social insurance contributions** | | **13.8** | | **11** | | **662.1** | | **24** | | **10** |
| Employer contributions | $ 7.9 | | 6 | | $323.6 | | 12 | | 10 | |
| Personal contributions | 6.0 | | 5 | | 338.5 | | 12 | | 11 | |
| **CURRENT RECEIPTS** | | **$ 122.1** | | **100** | | **$ 2,788.0** | | **100** | | **8** |

*Source* : U.S. Department of Commerce. Bureau of Economic Analysis. "Selected NIPA Tables." *National Accounts Data* . 8 Aug. 2000: Tables 3.1, 3.2, and 3.3. 9 Sep. 2000. <http://www.bea.doc.gov/bea/dn1.htm>.and "'Annual Only' NIPA Tables." *National Accounts Data* . 30 Aug 2000: Table 3.6. 5 Sep. 2000. <http://www.bea.doc.gov/bea/dn1.htm>.

suggests that *Personal taxes and nontaxes* constitute a major source of government receipts throughout the period that has grown in relative importance. *Social insurance contributions* have more than doubled their relative importance, increasing from 11 percent of total receipts in 1959 to 24 percent in 1999. Those increases in relative support have come at the expense of *Corporate profits taxes* and *Indirect business taxes and nontaxes*. They shrink relative to *Social insurance contributions* and *Personal taxes and nontaxes*. In 1959 the two of them account for 53 percent of total receipts; in 1999, 35 percent. The drop in the relative importance of *Corporate profits taxes* has been especially drastic. It has been more than halved during the forty-year period.

Although the business sector ostensibly pays directly about half of the contributions to social insurance, it can be argued that the real burden of such taxes fall directly on employed individuals. Businesses quite reasonably view levies associated with social insurance as part of employees' total compensation package. Over the past forty years, the share of the burden on households and individuals for support of government activities appears to have increased.

### Government Uses of Current Funds

A consolidated view of how the national, state, and local levels of government dispose of their receipts of current funds in 1999 appears in Exhibit 7.11. Exhibit 6.2 displaying state and local government uses of funds and Exhibit 7.3 for federal government uses of funds provide most of the basis for constructing Exhibit 7.11.

*Consumption expenditures* have been reconstituted using data appearing in Exhibits 6.3 and 7.4. *Employee compensation* accounted for most of government sector consumption. Close to one-fourth of consumption expenditures consisted of *Other consumption expenditures*: *Durable goods*, *Nondurable goods*, and *Other services*. Estimates of *Consumption of fixed capital* made up the rest.

Next on the list and next in relative importance come *Transfer payments*. They accounted for nearly $1.0 trillion and 36 percent of total uses of current funds. Most of the governments' transfer activities concern moving resources around among its citizens. The rest of the world received $11.6 billion in 1999, an immaterial amount relative to total uses of funds approximating $2.8 trillion.

*Net interest paid* of $261.7 billion made up 9 percent of total uses of current funds. In this case, the amount paid to the rest of the world is significant. Interest and principal on U.S. debt held by foreigners amounted to $95.1 billion, 3 percent of the total. U.S. persons and businesses received $261.8 billion, 9 percent of the total. Interest received by government offsets those payments by $95.2 billion. Reference to Exhibit 6.2 shows that state and local governments interest receipts of $78.1 billion accounted for most of that $95.2 billion.

*Subsidies* of $43.9 billion reflect mainly federal government programs and made up 2 percent of total uses of current funds. Both the federal and state and local governments contributed to *Net saving* of $174.4 billion. For 1999 the federal government made the larger contribution, $124.4 billion.

**Exhibit 7.11**

**Government Uses of Funds, 1959 and 1999**

| | 1959 Amounts in $ Billions | | Percent of Total | | 1999 Amounts in $ Billions | | Percent of Total | | Annual Percent Change | |
|---|---|---|---|---|---|---|---|---|---|---|
| **Consumption expenditures** | | **$ 83.2** | | **68** | | **$ 1,325.7** | | **48** | | **7** |
| Employee compensation | $44.2 | | 36 | | $844.5 | | 30 | | 8 | |
| Consumption of fixed capital | 13.6 | | 11 | | 170.3 | | 6 | | 7 | |
| Other consumption expenditures | 25.4 | | 21 | | 310.9 | | 11 | | 6 | |
| **Transfer payments** | | **24.7** | | **20** | | **998.1** | | **36** | | **10** |
| To persons | $22.9 | | 19 | | $986.5 | | 35 | | 10 | |
| To the rest of the world (net) | 1.8 | | 1 | | 11.6 | | 0 | | 5 | |
| **Net interest paid** | | **7.1** | | **6** | | **261.7** | | **9** | | **9** |
| Paid to persons & business | - | | | | $261.8 | | 9 | | | |
| Paid to rest of world | 0.3 | | 0 | | 95.1 | | 3 | | 15 | |
| Interest received | - | | | | (95.2) | | (3) | | | |
| **Dividends received** | | **-** | | | | **(0.4)** | | **(0)** | | |
| **Subsidies** | | **1.1** | | **1** | | **43.9** | | **2** | | **10** |
| **Government enterprises' surplus** | | **(1.0)** | | **(1)** | | **(15.6)** | | **(1)** | | **7** |
| **Net saving** | | **7.0** | | **6** | | **174.4** | | **6** | | **8** |
| Social insurance funds | $ (0.7) | | (1) | | $ 90.3 | | 3 | | | |
| Other | 7.7 | | 6 | | 84.1 | | 3 | | 6 | |
| **USES OF CURRENT FUNDS** | | **$ 122.1** | | **100** | | **$ 2,788.0** | | **100** | | **8** |

*Sources*: U.S. Department of Commerce. Bureau of Economic Analysis. "Selected NIPA Tables." *National Accounts Data*. 8 Aug. 2000: Tables 3.1 and 3.7. 9 Sep. 2000. <http://www.bea.doc.gov/bea/dn1.htm>. and "'Annual Only' NIPA Tables." *National Accounts Data*. 30 Aug 2000: Table 8.20. 5 Sep. 2000. <http://www.bea.doc.gov/bea/dn1.htm>.

Exhibit 7.11 also shows relative changes in government sector expenditure for 1959 and 1999. In 1959 *Consumption expenditures* accounted for 68 percent of total expenditures; by 1999 its share had dropped to 48 percent. For purposes of this comparison, *Transfer payments* include *Subsidies* less *Government enterprises' surpluses*. So defined, the relative share of *Transfer payments* nearly doubled from 20 percent to 37 percent during the same period. Because the federal government financed its chronic deficits with bond issues, *Net interest paid* increased from 6 percent to 9 percent. In a sense, interest payments are *Transfer payments* as well, although in the main they are distributed to people in very different income brackets than those receiving food stamps and earned income tax credits. Granting that latitude, shares of total expenditures for consumption of goods and services and for transfers of income among citizens have become roughly equal. Government by design or accident has become less engaged in providing public services and more engaged in income redistribution over the forty-year period from 1959 to 1999.

### Government Saving and Investment

A consolidation of the data appearing in Exhibits 6.6 and 7.8 produces Exhibit 7.12, saving and investment for the government sector. Thanks to federal as well as to state and local government frugality and investment in structures and equipment, changes to the government sector's balance sheet appear respectable for 1999. Taken together, national, state, and local governments show a *Surplus (Saving)* of current funds of $174.5 billion, and *Change in tangible assets (Net investment)*—public infrastructure and equipment net of depreciation—increases by $109.1 billion. Government *Change in financial assets* of $164.8 billion exceeds *Net investment*, however. Despite a reduction in federal government liabilities, liabilities increase by $47.2 billion, indicating that state and local government financed their acquisition of assets through borrowing. A *Discrepancy* of $54.3 billion shows that financial assets and liabilities do not match perfectly in the Federal Reserve flow-of-funds accounts. Two additional adjustments are required: a $1.7 billion addition and a $3.8 billion reduction to recognize differences in accounting practice between the flow-of-funds accounts and NIPA. NIPA does not recognize sales of federal access rights, but the flow-of-funds accounting system does. NIPA attributes growth in government employee insurance and pension funds to persons; the flow of funds accounts, to the government. The two adjustments reconcile the data to NIPA.

With the *Discrepancy* and adjustments, the *Change in liabilities and net worth* totals $273.9 billion. Total assets change by a like amount. The *Change in financial assets* of $164.8 billion was accompanied by a *Change in tangible assets* (*Net investment*) of $109.1 billion. Achieving that augmentation of public sector infrastructure, facilities, and equipment required *Capital expenditures* (*Gross investment*) of $308.7 to offset $199.6 billion of *Consumption of fixed capital*.

**Exhibit 7.12**
**Government Saving and Investment, 1999**

| | | | 1999 Amounts in $ Billions |
|---|---|---|---|
| **SURPLUS (Saving)** | | | **$ 174.5** |
| Change in liabilities | | | 47.2 |
| Discrepancy | | | 54.3 |
| Federal access rights adjustment | | | 1.7 |
| Gov't insur & pension fund adjustment | | | (3.8) |
| **CHANGE IN LIABILITIES & NET WORTH** | | | **$ 273.9** |
| Change in financial assets | | | 164.8 |
| Change in tangible assets (Net investment) | | | 109.1 |
| Capital expenditures (Gross investment) | | $308.7 | |
| Structures | $ 173.8 | | |
| *Employee compensation* | *10.2* | | |
| *Other expenditures for structures* | *163.6* | | |
| Equipment | 134.9 | | |
| Consumption of fixed capital | | (199.6) | |
| **CHANGE IN TOTAL ASSETS** | | | **$ 273.9** |

*Source*: Board of Governors, Federal Reserve System. "Z.1 Historical data." *Flow of Funds Accounts of the United States.* 15 Sep. 2000: Tables F.105 and F.106. 18 Sep. 2000. <http://www.bog.frb.us/releases/z1/current/data.htm> and U.S. Department of Commerce. Bureauof Economic Analysis. "Selected NIPA Tables." *National Accounts Data*. 8 Aug. 2000: Table 3.7. 9 Sep. 2000. <http://www.bea.doc.gov/bea/dn1.htm>.

### Government Output

Production of public goods and services (as well as some mixed public goods and services) provides a reason for the existence of government. How much of those outputs do the U.S. governments—national, state, and local—produce? In a national accounting system, one would expect to find an answer to such a question.

Public goods and services pose a special measurement problem. They are not marketable. The market provides a mechanism for determining prices of private goods and services. Their quantities, too, are discernible. The product of prices and quantities provides an estimate of the value of output of private goods and services. Since a measure of the value of the output of public goods

**Exhibit 7.13**

**Government Output of Goods and Services, 1959 and 1999**

| | 1959 Amounts in $ Billions | Percent of Total | 1999 Amounts in $ Billions | Percent of Total | Annual Percent Change |
|---|---|---|---|---|---|
| **State & local government output** | **$ 27.5** | **47** | **$ 726.5** | **73** | **9** |
| Employee compensation | $23.1 | 40 | $632.5 | 63 | 9 |
| Consumption of fixed capital | 3.3 | 6 | 83.0 | 8 | 8 |
| Gov't enterprise surplus net subsidy | 1.1 | 2 | 11.0 | 1 | 6 |
| **Federal government output** | **30.8** | **53** | **270.2** | **27** | **6** |
| Employee compensation | $21.7 | 37 | $222.2 | 22 | 6 |
| Consumption of fixed capital | 10.3 | 18 | 87.3 | 9 | 5 |
| Gov't enterprise surplus net subsidy | (1.2) | (2) | (39.3) | (4) | 9 |
| **TOTAL GOVERNMENT OUTPUT** | **$ 58.4** | **100** | **$ 996.6** | **100** | **7** |

*Source*: U.S. Department of Commerce. Bureau of Economic Analysis. "Selected NIPA Tables." *National Accounts Data*. 8 Aug. 2000: Tables 3.1, 3.2, 3.3 and 3.7. 9 Sep. 2000. <http://www.bea.doc.gov/bea/dn1.htm>.

and services is not available, we have to settle for the next best thing: an approximation based on the value of the inputs used to produce those outputs.

Not all government expenditures count in determining the value of public goods and services. Only expenditures for inputs of factors of production that could have been used to produce private goods and services are included. Purchases of goods and services produced by the private sector—that is, expenditures for durable goods, nondurable goods, and services—are not included. They are private sector outputs. Transfer payments and interest payments are excluded. They just transfer resources from one group to another and contribute nothing to overall output. Just compensation of government employees and allowances for depreciation in the form of consumption of fixed capital plus whatever surplus government enterprises earn on their outputs are counted in establishing a value for government produced goods and services.

The results of that tabulation are presented in Exhibit 7.13. In 1999 the value of *Total Government Output* of goods and services amounts to $996.6 billion. Separate estimates are provided for state and local governments and the federal government. In 1999 *State and local government output* accounts for $726.5 billion, 73 percent of the total; *Federal government output* accounts for $270.2 billion, 27 percent. In 1959 the federal government produced 53 percent of total government output, leaving 47 percent to state and local government. While state and local governments increased output at a rate averaging 9 percent per year, the federal government's output averaged only a 6 percent growth rate.

A similar change has occurred in the value of components of government output as well. In 1959 compensation of federal government employees were nip and tuck with that of state and local government employees—$21.7 billion versus $23.1 billion. In 1999 compensation of state and local government employees exceeded that of the federal government by a margin of nearly three to one. In 1959 federal government *Consumption of fixed capital* was three times that of state and local governments. By 1999 the $83.0 billion in *Consumption of fixed capital* by state and local governments had come within $4.3 billion of matching *Consumption of fixed capital* by the federal government.

Those figures, combined with earlier findings, tell us much about the changing roles of the levels of government in the U.S. economy. In 1959 state and local government uses of funds totaled $38.9 billion. The $27.5 billion in state and local government output accounted for 71 percent of the total. In 1999, with $726.5 billion in output and $1,142.7 billion in uses of current funds, that percent is 64 percent. State and local governments have continued to devote a major portion of their resources to delivery of public goods and services.

For the federal government a different picture emerges. Output as a percentage of uses of current funds amounted to 44 percent in 1959. In 1999 it had fallen to 14 percent. Per tax dollar the federal government is less engaged in meeting citizens' needs for public goods and services than state and local governments, and in the past forty years that disengagement has become more evident. Instead, it has moved toward redistribution of income from young to old, from working to idle, from healthy to ill. Good politics, mediocre economics.

## NOTES

1. U.S. Department of Commerce, Bureau of the Census, *1992 Census of Governments, Government Finances, Compendium of Government Finances*, Vol. 4, No. 5 (Washington, DC: U.S. Government Printing Office, Feb. 1997) vii.

2. Advisory Commission on Intergovernmental Relations, "Public Attitudes on Government and Taxes," *Intergovernmental Perspectives* 20.3 (Summer/Fall 1994).

3. Joseph A. Pechman, *Federal Tax Policy*, 5th ed. (Washington, DC: The Brookings Institution, 1987) 135.

4. Pechman 145.

5. Richard A. Musgrave and Peggy B. Musgrave, *Public Finance in Theory and Practice*, 5th ed (New York: McGraw-Hill Company, 1989) 395.

6. W. Elliott Brownlee, *Federal Taxation in America: A Short History*, (Washington, DC: Woodrow Wilson Center Press, 1996) 17.

7. Charles Adams, *Those Dirty Rotten Taxes: The Tax Revolts that Built America* (New York: Free Press, 1998) 66.

8. Brownlee 117–19.

9. U.S. Department of Health and Human Services, Office of the Assistant Secretary for Planning and Evaluation, "93.774: Medicare: Supplementary Medical Insurance," *Catalog of Federal Domestic Assistance*, 8 Nov. 2000 <http://aspe.os.dhhs.gov/cfda/P93774.htm>.

10. U.S. Social Security Administration, *The Social Security Bulletin Annual Statistical Supplement, 1997* (Washington, DC: U.S. Government Printing Office, 1988) 124.

11. United States, Executive Office of the President, Office of Management and Budget, *Analytical Perspectives, Budget of the United States Government, Fiscal Year 2001*, (Washington, DC: U.S. Government Printing Office, 1999) 111, 9 Nov. 2000 <http://frwebgate.access.gpo.gov/cigbin/waisgate.cgi?WAISdocID=9398117137+0+0+0&WAISaction=retrieve>.

12. U.S. Department of Commerce, Bureau of the Census, *Statistical Abstract of the United States*, (Washington, DC: U.S. Government Printing Office, 1982) 609. And (1999) 649.

13. U.S. President, *Economic Report of the President, 2000* (Washington, DC: U.S. Government Printing Office, 2000) 408, 9 Nov. 2000 <http://frwebgate.access.gpo.gov/cig-bin/waisgate.cgi?WAISdocID=97641 7228+17+0+0&WAISaction=retrieve>.

14. U.S. Department of Commerce, Bureau of Economic Analysis, *Government Transactions* Methodology Paper Series MP-5 (Washington, DC: U.S. Government Printing Office, November 1988) 48.

15. Bernard P. Herber, *Modern Public Finance, The Study of Public Sector Economics* (Homewood, IL: Richard D. Irwin, Inc., 1975) 445.

16. Herber 446–47.

17. Pechman 290.

18. Pechman 289.

# 8

# Us and Them

Exchanges of goods and services across state boundaries occur in response to differences in products and differences in prices. Climate and natural resources account for some of the differences. Corn and wheat can be grown more efficiently in Kansas than in Wyoming. Coal, oil, iron, and copper can only be obtained where such deposits exist, and some locations offer more economical access than others. Historical accident may cause productive efficiency to vary even among regions with similar resource endowments. Increasing returns to scale often characterize industries with large fixed investments. As their output grows unit cost falls. Market dominance in such an industry precludes starting up similar enterprises in other regions. Growth of supporting industries, concentration of expertise, and trained labor further reinforce a pioneer's advantage. Association of Detroit with automobile manufacturing and of Silicon Valley with computer manufacturing comes to mind as examples.

The framers of the Constitution of the United States get credit for establishing this country as one of the largest open markets in the world. Article I, Section 8 (3) gives Congress the power "to regulate commerce with foreign nations, and among the several states, and with the Indian tribes." Further, Section 10 (2) provides:

> No state shall, without the consent of the Congress, lay any imposts or duties on imports or exports, except what may be absolutely necessary for executing its inspection laws: and the net produce of all duties and imposts, laid by any state on imports or exports, shall be for the use of the treasury of the United States, and all such laws shall be subject to the revision and control of the Congress.

In addition, the Constitution empowers Congress to coin money and prohibits states from engaging in that activity. Consequently, the same currency passes for legal tender from sea to shining sea. The Supreme Court has determined that commerce includes any commercial activity involving more than one state and has generously defined regulation to include activities of the national government that encourage, protect, promote, preserve, or restrain interstate commerce.

Within the United States, movement of goods and services across the country is constrained by transportation costs, time involved in shipment, the knowledge of producers of potential demand, and knowledge of buyers of supply sources. The former seek out areas where their goods and services will command the highest price; the latter, suppliers providing goods and services at the lowest cost.

When goods and services cross national borders, however, transactions become considerably more complicated. As a sovereign state the United States has the power to regulate transactions with parties outside the country. The same Constitution that granted Congress the power to regulate interstate commerce and establish its currency also granted it the power to levy and collect import duties. Other sovereign states have the same powers, so international transactions involve customs duties and dealing in other currencies.

## INTERNATIONAL TRADE

In a free trade area such as the United States, domestic trade seems to take place naturally. With international trade, however, involvement of governments contributes little to and is liable to detract from the benefits gained from exchange of goods and services across nations' boundaries. We already have seen that import duties contribute relatively little to the federal government's receipts—just 1 percent in 1999. Nevertheless, that 1 percent is just enough for the Department of Census to require that importers tabulate goods and services coming into the United States. Import duties raise the cost of an imported product to domestic consumers. So, also, does the cost of the additional effort needed to record such transactions. At least collection of data of imports and exports provides the international trade statistics that we are about to examine.

Governments also can impose import quotas on goods and services and require inspections for public health and safety and for environmental reasons. Shifts in the value of currencies among countries add to the uncertainties (and thus the cost of international transactions). Import quotas limit the quantity of goods and services that can be brought into a country. In that sense they perform the same function as import duties. However, at least import duties have the saving grace of generating government revenue. Import quotas merely confer extra profits to those businesses fortunate enough to obtain import licenses by increasing the differential between import costs and the selling prices. They shelter domestic firms unable to compete with low-cost foreign competitors.

International transactions involve not one but two markets. Say, after careful consideration of the automobile market, you decide to purchase the same automobile as your neighbor, an Itchietoo from Japan. Chances are that you will not buy it directly from its manufacturer but rather from a dealer who in turn acquired it from an importer. Whatever the sequence of transactions involved in your eventual acquisition, someone in the United States must pay someone in Japan for the automobile. The person in Japan will expect to be paid in Japanese yen, but the purchaser in the United States has dollars to spend. Consequently, not one but two markets are involved in international transactions: a market for the product and a market for currencies.

In the latter market currencies are priced in terms of one another. The price is called an exchange rate. Exchange rates fluctuate in response to changes in supply and demand, introducing an additional uncertainty as to price of a product. Since importers buy goods and services denominated in the currency of a source country, exchange rates, as well as product prices, determine their costs.

## ACCOUNTING FOR U.S. INTERNATIONAL TRANSACTIONS

Despite those and other impediments, international trade happens! Those transactions are recorded in the balance of payments accounts of the United States compiled by the Bureau of Economic Analysis (BEA) of the Department of Commerce. On a monthly basis the Bureau of the Census tabulates administrative documents that importers and exporters must file with the United States Customs Service. From those tabulations the BEA prepares annual and quarterly estimates of merchandise exports and imports, freight and port expenditures, and unit value indexes used to compute constant-dollar-value estimates of exports and imports.

In addition, the BEA surveys private organizations—primarily businesses—engaging in transactions with foreigners either on their own behalf or for others. Data collected include receipts and payments of income on investments, other services receipts and payments, and private remittances

For the Department of the Treasury, the Federal Reserve Bank of New York operates the international capital reporting system, which covers purchases and sales of securities and outstanding claims and liabilities reported by banks and nonbank businesses. From those data the Federal Reserve produces monthly and quarterly reports on holdings of and transactions in stocks, bonds, and other claims and liabilities. The BEA uses that information along with representative estimates of yields on such financial instruments to calculate receipts and payments of income on private investments and payments to foreign holders of U.S. Government securities.[1]

Conjuring up a general picture of goods and services flowing into and out of a country is relatively easy, but when measuring such transactions definitions must be more precise. National boundaries must be defined. The international transactions account includes U.S. territories, Puerto Rico, and the Mariana Islands as part of the United States; however, the NIPA excludes them. Data used in this chapter conform to the NIPA definition.

Distinguishing between foreigners and U.S. residents also cannot be taken for granted. According to the Bureau of Economic Analysis, "individuals, governments, business enterprises, trusts, associations, and similar institutions that are physically located in the United States and that have resided, or expect to reside, in this country for 1 year or more" are considered to be U.S. residents.[2] U.S. citizens residing in another country may be U.S. residents if they are employees of the U.S. Government or military personnel posted abroad or if they are assigned by a U.S. business abroad for less than a year. U.S. affiliates of foreign companies are treated as U.S. residents.

Most foreigners consist of people who live outside the United States. Employees of international institutions located in the United States, foreign nationals employed by their home governments in the United States, and foreign affiliates of U.S. companies constitute exceptions.

## EXPORTS AND IMPORTS OF GOODS AND SERVICES

Goods and services we sell to foreigners constitute exports. Exhibit 8.1 shows that in 1999 the United States exported $990.2 billion in goods and services. *Goods* accounted for more than 70 percent of the total. Exports of goods do not include military transactions. Deliveries of goods and services by U.S. military agencies under foreign military sales program contracts, sales of excess property of military installations abroad, sales of petroleum products and other goods and services to foreign naval vessels and aircraft, and logistical support provided to U.S. allies and U.N. emergency forces are recorded as exports of services.[3]

The United States is not primarily a seller but rather a buyer. U.S. purchases from the rest of the world amounted to over $1.2 trillion in 1999—$254.0 billion more than our exports that year. The negative number indicates that the United States purchased more than it sold in 1999. Hence, we owed foreigners more than they owed us. Learning how we paid for that deficit must await examination of international flow-of-funds transactions. Before launching into that territory of discovery, we should take a closer look at the composition of exports and imports of goods and services.

### Goods

In 1999 exported manufactured goods—capital goods, automobiles, and most consumer goods—accounted for nearly half of the $990.2 billion total of U.S. goods and services exports. Those figures seem to accord with our notion that the United State is a highly developed industrial nation. However, about 20 percent of exports consist of *Industrial supplies and materials* and *Foods, feeds, and beverages*—raw and semi-finished goods, a manifestation of the country's relative abundance of natural resources.

Like exports of goods, imports can be broken down by product. From a product perspective, Exhibit 8.1 shows that imports of *Capital goods, except automotive* constitute the largest category, $297.1 billion or 24 percent of the $1,244,2 billion total of imported goods and services. When other manufactured goods imports in the form of automobiles and consumer goods are considered,

**Exhibit 8.1**
**U.S. Exports and Imports of Goods and Services by Product, 1999**

| | 1999 Exports in $Billions | 1999 Imports in $Billions | Net Exports |
|---|---|---|---|
| **Goods** | **$ 699.2** | **$ 1,048.6** | **$ (349.4)** |
| Foods, feeds, and beverages | 45.5 | 43.6 | 1.9 |
| Industrial supplies and materials | 141.8 | 148.6 | (6.8) |
| Durable goods | 53.8 | 78.9 | *(25.1)* |
| Nondurable goods | 87.9 | 137.5 | *(49.6)* |
| Capital goods, except automotive | 311.8 | 297.1 | 14.7 |
| Civilian aircraft, engines, and parts | 52.9 | 23.8 | *29.1* |
| Computers, peripherals, and parts | 46.7 | 81.5 | *(34.8)* |
| Other | 212.1 | 191.9 | *20.2* |
| Automotive vehicles, engines, & parts | 75.8 | 179.4 | (103.6) |
| Consumer goods, except automotive | 80.8 | 239.6 | (158.8) |
| Durable goods | 41.4 | 123.8 | *(82.4)* |
| Nondurable goods | 39.4 | 115.8 | *(76.4)* |
| Other | 43.6 | 72.5 | (28.9) |
| **Services** | **$ 291.0** | **$ 195.6** | **$ 95.4** |
| U.S. military & defense-related services | 15.4 | 13.7 | 1.7 |
| Travel | 74.9 | 59.4 | 15.5 |
| Passenger fares | 19.8 | 21.4 | (1.6) |
| Other transportation | 27.0 | 34.1 | (7.1) |
| Royalties and license fees | 36.5 | 13.3 | 23.2 |
| Other private services | 96.5 | 46.7 | 49.8 |
| Other | 21.0 | 7.2 | 13.8 |
| **TOTAL EXPORTS AND IMPORTS** | **$ 990.2** | **$ 1,244.2** | **$ (254.0)** |

*Source*: U.S. Department of Commerce. Bureau of Economic Analysis. "Selected NIPA Tables." *National Accounts Data*. 8 Aug. 2000: Table 4.3. 9 Sep. 2000. <http://www.bea.doc.gov/bea/dn1.htm>.

the percentage rises to almost 58 percent—a larger share of total imports than a similar set of exported manufactured goods is to total U.S. exports of goods and services.

Not surprisingly, given the percentages of exports and imports of manufactured goods, imports of *Industrial supplies and materials* and *Foods, feeds, and beverages* as a percent of total imports are relatively less than exports of those products, 15 percent versus 19 percent.

Within those broad categories striking differences in the composition of products occur. In 1999 the United States exported about $45.5 billion and imported \$43.6 billion of *Foods, feeds, and beverages*. Within that major category exports of agricultural products exceeded imports, but the reverse was true for nonagricultural products. Grains—wheat, corn, and soybeans—account for about one-third of U.S. agricultural exports—all produced using large amounts of land, highly mechanized, and using relatively little labor. On the other hand, about 54 percent of our agricultural imports consists of coffee, cocoa, sugar, vegetables, fruits, nuts, wine, and related products—products associated with intensive land use and substantial amounts of labor. With respect to nonagricultural products, we import three times more fish and shellfish than we export; in addition, over 20 percent of our nonagricultural imports of *Foods, feeds, and beverages* consists of whiskey and other distilled spirits. (Hic!)

Our \$148.6 billion in imports of *Industrial supplies and materials* exceeds exports of \$141.8 billion by \$6.8 billion. Detail for exports and imports under that major category shows that petroleum and petroleum products contributed a net export deficit of \$67.8 billion to that category in 1999. That petroleum imports account for the difference should come as no surprise. A large excess of imports of iron and steel products and nonferrous metals over exports adds to the deficit. The U.S. chemical industry comes through with a surplus.

U.S. exports of *Capital goods except automotive* in 1999 amounted to \$311.8 billion, \$14.7 billion more than imports. The greatest contributor to that excess was *Civilian aircraft, engines, and parts*. Net exports of that item of \$52.9 billion surpass imports by \$29.1 billion. Net exports get another boost from *Other*, \$20.2 billion. That category includes oil drilling, mining, and construction machinery, industrial engines, pumps, and compressors, machine tools and metal-working machinery, measuring, testing, and control instruments, and other industrial, agricultural, and service industry machinery. *Computers, peripherals, and parts* imports exceed exports by \$34.1 billion and offset positive net exports in the other two subcategories.

For the remaining major categories—*Automotive vehicles, engines and parts*, *Consumer goods, except automotive*, and *Other*—imports exceed exports by wide margins. U.S. imports of automobiles and accessories are more than twice our exports; for *Consumer goods*, nearly three times.

At the top of the net export column, we see a negative \$349.4 billion. That difference is called the Balance on Goods, and its sign indicates that overall our payments for imports of goods exceeded our receipts from exports. *Consumer goods, except automotive* constitute the largest single category of excesses of imports over exports, \$158.8 billion, although in terms of imported goods trade volume they rank after *Capital goods, except automobiles*. Another consumer-related item, automobiles, makes the second largest contribution, a negative \$103.6 billion, to net exports. *Industrial supplies and materials*—petroleum products, in particular—account for another negative \$6.8 billion. We have to have \$67.8 billion in foreign fuel for all those foreign cars.

**Services**

Unlike net exports of goods, net exports of *Services* for 1999 is a positive $95.4 billion. U.S. exports of services of $291.0 billion were exceeded only by one goods category: *Capital goods, except automobiles*.

*Travel*—foreign travelers' expenditures for lodging, food, transportation, entertainment, personal purchases, gifts, and other outlays while visiting the United States—generates $74.9 billion in private sector service exports in 1999. The amount is similar in value to $75.8 billion in 1999 exports of *Automotive vehicles, engines, and parts* and the $80.8 billion of exports of *Consumer goods, except automotive*. We're a tourist attraction! *Passenger fares* from airplanes and ships owned by U.S. residents and carrying foreign residents to or from the United States or between other countries produce $19.8 billion in service exports. *Other transportation*, amounting to about $27 billion, includes freight revenues for international transport of U.S. exports and foreign freight, receipts for charter of U.S. vessels, freight cars, and containers by foreign operators, and expenditures of foreign-operated carriers while in U.S. ports. Collectively, those three transportation-related services generate $121.7 billion in receipts.

Exceeding either passenger fares or receipts for other transportation services are *Royalties and license fees*, $36.5 billion in 1999. Patents, trademarks, copyrights, manufacturing rights, and techniques owned by U.S. residents and leased or sold to foreigners yield those fees. U.S. affiliates account for most of the receipts. Other unaffiliated fees consisting of copyrights, trademarks, franchises, rights to broadcast live events, and other intangible property rights make up the remainder.

*Other private services* account for the largest portion of private exports of services, $96.5 billion in 1999, somewhat more than either U.S. exports of *Automotive vehicles, engines, and parts* or *Consumer goods, except automotive*. Like royalties and license fees, *Other private services* are divided into two broad classes: services rendered to foreign affiliates of U.S. resident firms and unaffiliated services. Fees for management, professional, and technical services, rental of tangible property (including motion picture films and television tapes), payments for operating leases of one year or less, net rent on uncapitalized operating leases of more than one year, research and development assessments, and overhead expenses apportioned among the foreign affiliates of U.S. enterprises comprise sources of affiliated services.

Unaffiliated *Other private services* are rendered to foreigners both within the United States and abroad. They include foreign-service operations of U.S. construction, engineering, consulting, and other technical service companies, international cable, radio, telephone, and satellite services, international reinsurance transactions of U.S. companies, and expenditures in the United States by foreign embassies, consulates, foreign government agents, and international organizations.

Exports of *U.S. military and defense-related services* are relatively small—$15.4 billion in 1999. Under military sales contracts, the Department of Defense sells and transfers military goods and services to a foreign purchaser on a cash or credit basis. Purchases by foreigners directly from commercial suppliers are not included. Imports of *U.S. military and defense-related services* amount to $13.7 billion and consist of direct defense expenditures. Direct defense expenditures include

- Personal expenditures abroad by U.S. military and civilian personnel employed by military agencies;
- U.S. Department of Defense payments to foreign residents for military equipment, petroleum, and goods purchased for resale to U.S. personnel in overseas post exchanges and commissaries;
- Compensation to foreign personnel, including retirement and other fringe benefits;
- Expenditures overseas by U.S. and foreign contracts engaged to construct, operate, and maintain U.S. military installations based in other countries;
- Expenditures for construction projects managed by U.S. military agencies for foreign governments; and
- Contributions related to U.S. participation in international military organizations.

Imports and exports of *U.S. military and defense-related services* contribute $1.7 billion to the $95.4 billon in total net exports of services.

*Travel* exports and imports make a $15.5 billion contribution to net exports. U.S. residents don't seem to relish visiting other places as much as foreigners like to visit the United States. U.S. payments to foreign air and ocean carriers for *Passenger fares* to haul around U.S. tourists and business persons are a little more than payments by other countries to U.S. carriers to transport their residents—$19.8 billion in exports over $21.4 billion in imports.

*Other transportation*, amounting to $34.1 billion and consisting of U.S. freight payments to foreign-operated ocean, air, and other carriers for international movement of U.S. goods, breaks the pattern. Our payments exceed our receipts by $7.1 billion—a significant margin of difference. The world's gross tonnage of oceangoing ships of 1,000 gross tons and above amounts to about 490,000 tons. The tonnage of ships registered under the U.S. flag amounts to around 12,500 tons, between 2 and 3 percent of the total. In terms of tonnage, the U.S. fleet ranks behind Japan, China, Norway, Singapore, Cyprus, Bahamas, Malta, Greece, Liberia, and Panama.[4] Liberia and Panama—two "flags of convenience" countries—alone account for over 30 percent of the world's tonnage. They "place minimal restrictions on the nationalities of owners, crew, ship construction, and ship repair." On the other hand, "the United States requires that U.S. flagships that transport cargo from one U.S. port to another (cabotage) must be owned, at least 75 percent, by U.S. citizens, must be crewed exclusively by U.S. citizens, must meet U.S. Coast Guard safety requirements, and must have been constructed in the United States from U.S. components."[5] Clearly the agendas of people other than U.S. ship owners and operators were at work when U.S. flagship requirements were set.

*Royalties and license fees* paid to affiliated and unaffiliated foreigners reflect payments made by U.S. residents for the use or sale of intangible property or rights after deductions for such items as U.S. taxes. In 1999 they amounted to $13.3 billion, significantly less than the $36.5 billion U.S. residents received for use of their intangible property or rights. Payments and receipts for *Other private services* exhibit a similar excess of receipts over payments, $49.9 billion in payments versus $96.5 billion in receipts. That pattern holds true for both affiliated and unaffiliated services. Among unaffiliated services, however, U.S. payments for insurance and telecommunication services exceed receipts, but the difference is not sufficient to reverse the total for the group.

## INTERNATIONAL RECEIPTS AND PAYMENTS

The preceding examination of exports and imports of goods and services shows that the United States purchased $254.0 billion more from the rest of the world than the rest of the world purchased from us. But exchanges of goods and services do not constitute the entire universe of international transactions. U.S. residents employed by rest-of-the-world entities and U.S. investors who hold claims on foreign assets receive income. In a similar manner, foreign residents receive payments from the United States. In addition, the United States, on balance, transfers funds to the rest of the world.

Exhibit 8.2 displays a summary of the complete set of international payments and receipts. It includes data for 1959 as well as for 1999. We will begin by concentrating on 1999.

### U.S. Receipts from the Rest of the World

In Exhibit 8.2, *Exports of goods and services* are reduced to three categories: *Durable goods*, *Nondurable goods*, and *Services*. When examining purchases of goods and services by the household and government sectors, we saw that services constitute the largest category of expenditure and durable goods the least. Not so for rest-of-the-world purchases. *Durable goods*, at $504.2 billion, account for over half the $990.2 billion in exports of goods and services. *Services* come in second largest with $291.0 billion. Last come *Nondurable goods* with $194.7 billion.

In 1999 *Income receipts* amounted to $305.9 billion. Of its three components, *Employee compensation receipts*, *Interest receipts*, and *Corporate profits receipts*, *Corporate profits receipts*, at $169.3 billion, constitute over half. If you buy shares of a foreign corporation, the dividends that you hope you earn on that investment will appear in this category. *Interest receipts* provide the second most important source with $134.4 billion. That figure includes interest received by U.S. owners of bonds, loans, deposits, and other claims on foreigners, as reported by U.S. banks. U.S. banks also report the fee income they earn on their international transactions. *Employee compensation receipts* result from employment of U.S. residents by foreign firms or governments and by international agencies and amount to only $2.2 billion. Collecting information on all compensation paid by foreigners to U.S. residents working abroad presents reporting

**Exhibit 8.2**
**U.S. Receipts from and Payments to the Rest of the World, 1959 and 1999**

| | | **1959 Amounts in $ Billions** |
|---|---|---|
| **U.S. RECEIPTS FROM REST OF WORLD** | | **$ 25.0** |
| Exports of goods and services | | 20.6 |
| Durable goods | 8.9 | |
| Nondurable goods | 7.5 | |
| Services | 4.2 | |
| Income receipts | | 4.3 |
| Employee compensation receipts | 0.2 | |
| Interest receipts | 0.8 | |
| Corporate profits receipts | 3.4 | |
| **U.S. PAYMENTS TO REST OF WORLD** | | **$ 26.2** |
| Imports of goods and services | | 22.3 |
| Durable goods | 6.6 | |
| Nondurable goods | 8.7 | |
| Services | 7.0 | |
| Income payments | | 1.5 |
| Employee compensation payments | 0.2 | |
| Interest payments | 0.6 | |
| Corporate profits payments | 0.7 | |
| Transfer payments (net) | | 2.4 |
| From persons (net) | 0.5 | |
| From government (net) | 1.8 | |
| From business | 0.1 | |
| **U.S. NET FOREIGN INVESTMENT** | | **(1.2)** |

*Source*: U.S. Department of Commerce. Bureau of Economic Analysis. "Selected NIPA Tables." *National Accounts Data*. 8 Aug. 2000: Table 4.1. 9 Sep. 2000. <http://www.bea.doc.gov/bea/dn1.htm> and "'Annual Only' NIPA Tables." *National*

difficulties, and the estimates consist only of payments to employees of foreign affiliates of U.S. businesses and to employees in other capacities in Germany, Canada, and the United Kingdom.[6]

### U.S. Imports and Payments to the Rest of the World

At $1,244.2 billion, *Imports of goods and services* comprise 77 percent of the $1,609.2 billion in *U.S. Payments to the Rest of the World.* As in the case of foreigners' purchases of U.S. goods and services, our imports of $1,244.2

| Percent of Total | | 1999 Amounts in $ Billions | | Percent of Total | |
|---|---|---|---|---|---|
| | **95** | | **$ 1,296.1** | | **81** |
| | 79 | | 990.2 | | 62 |
| 34 | | 504.5 | | 31 | |
| 29 | | 194.7 | | 12 | |
| 16 | | 291.0 | | 18 | |
| | 16 | | 305.9 | | 19 |
| 1 | | 2.2 | | 0 | |
| 3 | | 134.4 | | 8 | |
| 13 | | 169.3 | | 11 | |
| | **100** | | **$ 1,609.2** | | **100** |
| | 85 | | 1,244.2 | | 77 |
| 25 | | 715.4 | | 44 | |
| 33 | | 333.2 | | 21 | |
| 27 | | 195.6 | | 12 | |
| | 6 | | 316.9 | | 20 |
| 1 | | 7.6 | | 0 | |
| 2 | | 251.4 | | 16 | |
| 3 | | 57.9 | | 4 | |
| | 9 | | 48.1 | | 3 |
| 2 | | 26.6 | | 2 | |
| 7 | | 11.6 | | 1 | |
| 0 | | 9.9 | | 1 | |
| | **(5)** | | **(313.2)** | | **(19)** |

*Accounts Data.* 30 Aug 2000: Tables 6.2B, 6.15B and 6.17B. 5 Sep. 2000. <http://www.bea.doc.gov/bea/dn1.htm>.

billion consist mainly of *Durable goods*. Compared with exports, *Nondurable goods* and *Services* trade places. In the case of imports, *Nondurable goods* at $333.2 billion rank second in importance and *Services* at $195.6 billion come in with the smallest figure.

*Income payments* amount to $316.9 billion, one-fifth of all U.S. payments to the rest of the world. As a group *Income payments* surpass U.S. payments to foreigners for services. The pattern of income payments varies from that of *Income receipts*. For the United States, *Corporate profits receipts* constitute the most important source of income. The $251.4 billion in *Interest payments* make up 79 percent of its $316.9 billion in *Income payments*. The rest of the world has found U.S. Treasury securities and corporate bonds attractive investments with funds made available by chronic U.S. deficits in balance of payments. U.S. *Corporate profits payments* to foreigners at $57.9 billion are just a little over one-third of U.S. *Corporate profits receipts*.

In addition to importing more goods and services than we export and paying more for factors of production than we receive, we give money away. *Transfer payments (net)* amount to $48.1 billion in 1999. Transfer payments from Uncle Sam amount to $11.6 billion. The figure includes U.S. Government grants, pension payments, and other transfers and is net of grants received from foreigners. Grants transfer real resources and financial assets to foreigners under foreign assistance programs for which repayment either is not expected or is indeterminate. Grant payments take the form of goods, services, and disbursements of cash delivered by the U.S. Government. U.S. Government pensions and other transfers consist of

- Social Security payments, government employee retirement, and disability payments to annuitants living abroad;
- Educational and cultural exchange programs by the U.S. Department of State;
- Research grants;
- Damage claims paid by U.S. armed services;
- Cash payments of claims settled by international agreements; and
- Payments to certain international organizations for membership assessments and special assessments other than those for foreign assistance.

*Transfer payments (net) from business* report in with a smaller amount, $9.9 billion. *Transfer payments from persons (net)*, at $26.6 percent, account for 55 percent of all transfers. Shown net of similar transfers received by U.S. residents from foreign individuals, nonprofit institutions, and governments, they take the form of goods, services, cash, and other financial claims. Pensions, gifts, and grants from individuals and nonprofit institutions, inheritances, and emigrants' and immigrants' transfers are included in the total; not included are pension payments to foreign residents by U.S. businesses.

Forty years before the situation was somewhat different. High growth rates—results of a combination of expansion of international trade and price inflation—create huge differences between the 1959- and 1999-dollar amounts. For both years *U.S. Payments to Rest of World* furnish the largest number. Paying more than we receive is not new, but the magnitudes of changed.

In 1959, as in 1999, imports exceeded *Exports of goods and services*. However, examination of the details shows that *Durable goods* exports exceeded *Durable goods* imports in 1959! In *Nondurable goods* and *Services*, imports exceeded exports and tipped the sum of goods and services to one of net imports. In 1999 imports of both *Durable* and *Nondurable goods* exceed exports, but U.S. exports of *Services* exceed imports. The growth of service exports reflects in part the maturing status of the United States, and New York City in particular, as the world's financial center.

In 1999 *Income payments* exceeded *Income receipts*. In contrast, *Income receipts* of 1959 were nearly three times larger than *Income payments* and more than compensated for the excess of imports over exports of goods and services. However, *Transfer payments* of $2.4 billion resulted in a net of foreign investment in the United States of $1.2 billion. In 1959 *Transfer payments* constituted a much more significant part of U.S. international transactions than they did in 1999. In 1959 *Transfer payments* accounted for 9 percent of *U.S. Payments to the Rest of the World*; in 1999 for 3 percent. Then *Transfer payments from government (net)* of $1.8 billion accounted for most of the transfers; in 1999 *Transfer payments from persons (net)*, at $26.6 billion, predominated.

From 1959 to 1999 we saw that personal income and government receipts rose at an average annual rate of 8 percent. In Exhibit 8.2 we see that growth in U.S. receipts from and U.S. payments to the rest of the world averaged 10 percent and 11 percent per year, respectively. International transactions have become an increasingly significant consideration for the U.S. economy.

### U.S. Net Foreign Investment

*U.S. Payments to Rest of World* stood at $1,609.2 billion in 1999. It exceeded *U.S. Receipts from Rest of World* of $1,296.1 billion by $313.2 billion. Data for 1959 indicate show that payments exceeded receipts then as well but by a much smaller amount. In that year receipts were 95 percent of payments. In 1999 they were 81 percent. The gap has widened by 14 percentage points. The difference between receipts and payments is labeled *U.S. Net Foreign Investment* and appears in Exhibit 8.2 as negative $1.2 billion for 1959 and negative $313.2 billion for 1999.

*Imports of goods and services*, *Income payments*, and *Transfer payments (net)* constitute sources of funds for foreigners. With those funds they can buy U.S. goods and services and pay for factors of production that U.S. residents provide to the rest of the world. Although those two uses are significant, they are not sufficient to absorb all the payments the U.S. government and its citizens are obligated to make.

## NET FOREIGN SAVING AND INVESTMENT IN THE UNITED STATES

Foreigners have dollars. What are they going to do with them? In addition to buying U.S. exports of goods and services and paying for factor income that U.S. residents provide to the rest of the world, they can purchase assets in the United States. The flow-of-funds accounts produced by the Board of Governors of the Federal Reserve System provide information on what the rest of the world bought. Data presented in Exhibit 8.3 summarize what assets foreigners acquired as well as what additional liabilities they incurred.

**Exhibit 8.3**
**Rest-of-World Saving and Investment in the United States, 1999**

| | | 1999 Amounts in $ Billions |
|---|---|---|
| **NET FOREIGN SAVING IN THE UNITED STATES** | | **$ 313.1** |
| **Net Change in Rest-of-World Liabilities owed to U.S.** | | **394.1** |
| U.S. official foreign exchange & net IMF position | (8.6) | |
| Other U.S. Government assets | (2.8) | |
| Private deposits | 86.5 | |
| Credit market instruments | 30.0 | |
| Foreign corporate equities | 114.4 | |
| Direct investment abroad | 150.9 | |
| Other claims on foreign assets | 23.7 | |
| **Discrepancy** | | **6.8** |
| **CHANGE IN LIABILITIES AND NET WORTH** | | **714.0** |
| Foreign official assets in the U.S. | 32.5 | |
| Cash and cash equivalents | 61.9 | |
| U.S. government securities | 53.3 | |
| U. S. corporate bonds | 160.6 | |
| Other credit market instruments | (35.8) | |
| U. S. corporate equities | 98.1 | |
| Foreign direct investments in U.S. | 275.5 | |
| Other claims on U.S. assets | 67.9 | |
| **CHANGE IN REST OF WORLD ASSETS IN U.S.** | | **$ 714.0** |

*Sources* : Board of Governors, Federal Reserve System. "Z.1 Historical data." 15 Sep. 2000.
*Flow of Funds Accounts of the United States* : Table F.107. 18 Sep. 2000
<http://www.bog.frb.us/releases/z1/current/data.htm>

The bottom line of Exhibit 8.3 shows that foreigners' 1999 net acquisition of financial assets increased by $714.0 billion. Since their 1999 receipts from the United States exceed their payments to the United States by only $313.1 billion, their liabilities owed to the United States increased by $394.1 billion, which with a *Discrepancy* adjustment of $6.8 billion matches their net investment.

In 1999 *Foreign direct investment in U.S.* of $275.5 billion accounted for 39 percent of rest-of-the-world acquisitions of the $714.0 billion in U.S. financial assets. Direct investment is defined as ownership of at least 10 percent of the voting stock or equivalent interest in an affiliate located in another country. *U.S. corporate bonds* constituted another major acquisition at $160.6 billion.

*U.S. corporate equities* came in third in attractiveness with $98.1 billion. *Cash and cash equivalents*—currency, checking accounts, time deposits, and other assets readily convertible to cash—increased by $61.9 billion. Foreign residents increased their holdings of U.S. government securities by $53.3 billion. Their governments acquired $32.5 billion in U.S. government securities to add to their *Foreign official assets in the U.S.* Only foreign holdings of *Other credit market instruments* consisting of open market paper and loans to U.S. corporate business showed a decline. With so many opportunities for shopping for assets in the United States, foreigners have found a wide variety of attractive options.

Of the $394.1 billion increase in rest-of-the-world liabilities in 1999, two items accounted for almost 73 percent: $150.9 billion in U.S. *Direct investment abroad* and $114.4 billion in U.S. holdings of *Foreign corporate equities*. U.S. residents purchased $114.4 billion in foreign corporate stocks; foreigners purchased $98.1 billion in U.S. corporate stocks. Could it be that a stock always looks like a better buy on the other side of the ocean?

## U.S. INTERNATIONAL FINANCIAL CONDITION

Exhibit 8.2 shows that U.S. international payments exceeded their receipts both in 1959 and 1999. Exhibit 8.4 shows what has happened throughout the forty-year period. For each of the years, surpluses appear as positive numbers; deficits, as negative. On the graph the horizontal axis measures years. The left vertical axis measures the amount of annual deficits and surpluses.

For the first twenty-three years of the forty-year period, the United States usually generated a surplus in its balance of payments. Exceptions occurred in 1959, 1972, 1977, and 1978. On balance the United States was a net investor in the rest of the world. Beginning in 1982 a turnaround began. In that and the following eighteen years—with the exception of 1991—the U.S. balance of payments shows deficits. Not only are they deficits, but also they are large deficits.

As a result of those deficits, the rest of the world has been acquiring claims on assets in the United States. At the same time the United States has been acquiring claims on foreign assets. The BEA summarizes the results of those acquisitions—the international financial position of the United States—at the end of each calendar year. That summary is replicated in Exhibit 8.5. It displays a more detailed version of the items presented in Exhibit 8.3. In this case the amounts shown represent a stock of assets or liabilities at a particular moment of time rather than a flow over a period of time.

### United States Assets Abroad

The table is divided into two parts: *U.S. Assets Abroad* and *Foreign Assets in the United States* (our liabilities, what we owe to the rest of the world). The *U.S. Year-end International Position* is defined as U.S. assets abroad less

**Exhibit 8.4**
**United States Net Foreign Investment, 1959 to 1999**

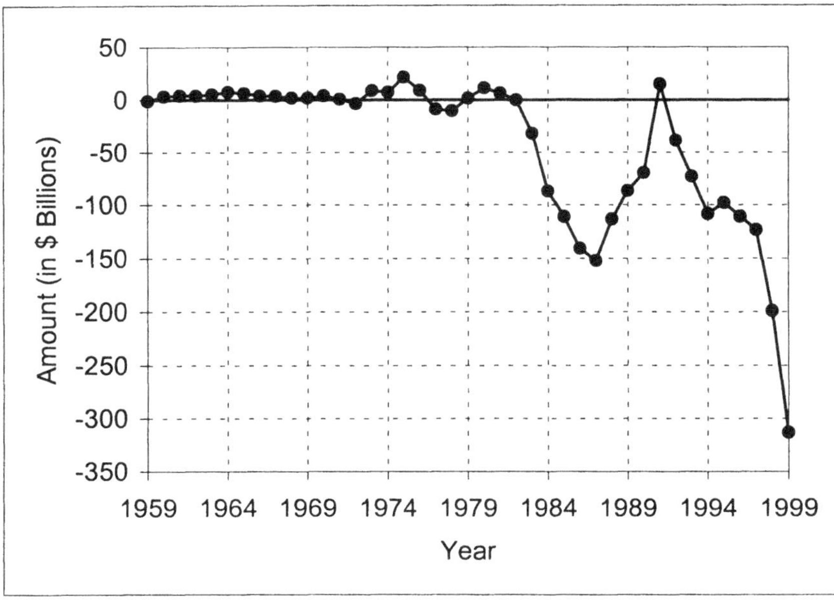


*Source*: U.S. Department of Commerce. Bureau of Economic Analysis. "Selected NIPA Tables." *National Accounts Data*. 8 Aug. 2000: Table 4.1. 9 Sep. 2000. <http://www.bea.doc.gov/bea/dn1.htm>.

foreign assets in the United States, which, as the table shows, turns out to be almost $1.1 trillion dollars in net debt to foreigners.

*U.S. Government Official Reserve Assets*. You need a cash balance to compensate for the lack of synchronization between receipts and disbursements. So do nations. For international transactions, the cash balances of the United States are called official assets and consist of:

- Gold,
- Special drawing rights,
- Reserve position in the International Monetary Fund, and
- Foreign currencies.

Use of *Gold* in payment of foreign exchange transactions dates back to antiquity. *Special drawing rights* and the *International Monetary Fund reserve position* are not so ancient and represent creations since World War II.

As World War II began to draw to a close, government planners—primarily from the United Kingdom and the United States—started to envision a new world order. Normal international trade relations had been disrupted by the war effort. The decade preceding World War II had been characterized by a worldwide depression, a reduction of international trade, rising trade barriers, unstable exchange rates, and a shortage of internationally acceptable reserve assets. An attempt in the 1920s to resurrect the international gold standard, which had prevailed from the late nineteenth century until World War I, had been fraught with difficulties.

In 1944 the United Nations convened the Monetary and Financial Conference in Bretton Woods, New Hampshire. Subsequently better known as the Bretton Woods Conference, that meeting resulted in the formation of two international organizations: the International Monetary Fund and the International Bank for Reconstruction, more familiarly known now as the World Bank.[7] Policy makers realized that long-term financing would be required to assist European countries recover from the devastation of their cities, production facilities, and infrastructure wrought by World War II. The World Bank was set up to meet that need. It still exists today but now addresses the long-term capital financing needs of underdeveloped countries.

Participants in the Bretton Woods Conference created the International Monetary Fund to help establish an international monetary system that would facilitate rather than hamper international trade among nations. They judged a return to the gold standard of the 1880s and 1890s to be unfeasible. However, fond memories remained of a system of fixed exchange rates among national currencies and use of gold as a universally accepted means of discharging national debts.

In order to participate in gold standard arrangements, governments had to be willing to allow international transactions to influence the level of domestic economic activity. An increase in imports over exports tended to result in a lowered level of domestic economic activity, falling prices, unemployment, and reduced demand for all goods, including imports. The fall in prices made domestic goods appear cheaper to foreigners and tended to increase exports. Thus international trade balances were restored, albeit sometimes at considerable cost to the economic welfare of the citizenry.

As a consequence of the Great Depression, responsibility for domestic full employment and high levels of economic activity at home devolved to national governments. Electorates expected their governments to take corrective action. Now that the political fortunes of those in office depended on maintaining national prosperity, national governments were no longer willing to abide by the gold standard rules of the game.

The International Monetary Fund was designed to capture the benefits of the gold standard while recognizing the realities of the post-World War II political landscape by establishing a system of pegged but adjustable exchange rates and permitting temporary trade imbalances by making short-term loans of three to five years to deficit countries. To peg rates, the United States—which held most of the world's monetary gold—pegged the dollar at $35 per ounce of gold. Other countries then defined the price of their currencies in terms of the dollar. Fluctuations in the agreed upon price were allowed up to plus or minus 1 percent from the stated price. If the price of a country's currency on the world currency

**Exhibit 8.5**
**International Investment Position of the United States at Year-End, 1999**

| | | 1999 Amounts In $ Billions |
|---|---|---|
| **U.S. Assets Abroad** | | **$ 5,889.0** |
| U.S. official reserve assets | | $ 136.4 |
| Gold | $ 76.0 | |
| Special drawing rights | 10.3 | |
| International Monetary Fund reserve position | 18.0 | |
| Foreign currencies | 32.2 | |
| U.S. Government assets, other than official assets | | 84.2 |
| U.S. credits and other long-term assets | $ 81.7 | |
| U.S. foreign currency & short-term assets | 2.6 | |
| U.S. private assets | | 5,668.4 |
| Direct investment abroad | $1,331.2 | |
| Foreign bonds | 556.7 | |
| Foreign corporate stocks | 2,026.6 | |
| U.S. claims on unaffiliated foreigners | 643.7 | |
| U.S. claims reported by U.S. banks | 1,110.1 | |
| **Foreign Assets in the United States** | | **$ 6,971.5** |
| Foreign official assets in the United States | | $ 869.3 |
| U.S. Treasury securities | $ 578.2 | |
| Other U.S. Government securities | 50.7 | |
| Other U.S. Government liabilities | 14.7 | |
| U.S. liabilities reported by U.S. banks | 138.6 | |
| Other foreign official assets | 87.1 | |
| Other foreign assets in the United States | | 6,102.2 |
| Direct investment in the United States | $1,125.2 | |
| U.S. Treasury securities | 660.7 | |
| U.S. currency | 250.7 | |
| U.S. corporate and other bonds | 1,063.7 | |
| U.S. corporate stocks | 1,445.6 | |
| U.S. liabilities to foreigners | 473.8 | |
| U.S. liabilities reported by U.S. banks | 1,082.5 | |
| **U. S. YEAR-END INTERNATIONAL POSITION** | | **$ (1,082.5)** |

*Source*: Scholl, Russell B. "The International Position of the United States at Yearend 1999." *Survey of Current Business* Jul. 2000: 56.

exchange market approached one or the other of those limits, the country was expected to take corrective action. For example, if the price of its currency approached the upper limit, the country was expected to sell its currency in the market, increasing its supply and lowering its price. If pressure in one direction or the other became chronic, a country was permitted to revalue the price of its currency in terms of the dollar upward or downward.

To make loans to countries with what were judged to be short-term balance of payments deficits, the International Monetary Fund assessed its member countries a quota (membership fee) determined by a formula based upon a country's national income and the amount of its foreign trade. A country with a deficit could borrow up to 125 percent of its quota in five installments called tranches. The first tranche was automatic. Beyond the first tranche the International Monetary Fund attached increasingly stringent conditions: requirements like reducing the government's deficit spending, increasing taxes, decreasing the money supply, increasing interest rates—advice not always (rarely?) welcome.

For about twenty years that arrangement worked well. The soundness of the U.S. dollar was judged to be as good as gold, and it became the international currency. Central banks used it instead of, or as well as, gold to settle their international trade accounts. In such a stable environment, international trade increased rapidly. By the mid 1960s, however, stresses began to appear. The demand for international liquidity was increasing more rapidly than the supply of monetary gold. U.S. dollars filled the gap, but the supply of dollars in international hands both as official reserves and private holdings began to exceed the value of U.S. gold reserves.

The United States stood ready to trade dollars for gold at $35 an ounce. Hungry speculators began to smell meat cooking, and their gold purchases put further pressure on U.S. gold reserves. A pending shortage of a generally accepted international medium of exchange, erosion of confidence, and speculative pressures led to an evolution of new arrangements in the late 1960s and early 1970s. The first break was devaluation of the British pound sterling—the second most important international currency—from $2.80 to $2.40 in 1967. In 1968 central banks collectively agreed that they no longer would buy and sell gold to private individuals although they would continue trading it among themselves. That action separated the official gold prices from world free-market prices and froze the quantity of monetary gold. With market price of gold at $300 and $400 per ounce, private individuals would not be selling it to their central banks at $35 per ounce.

To provide an alternative source of generally accepted international liquidity, the International Monetary Fund in 1970, with agreement of its members, created special drawing rights (SDRs). Initially SDRs were defined in terms of the U.S. dollar; now they are defined as the weighted average of major world currencies. Each country received an amount of credit in proportion to its quota. Countries can use their SDRs like gold or dollars to discharge balance of payments of deficits. If a country holds less than its quota, however, it pays interest; if it holds more, it receives interest income.

In 1971, in response to continued U.S. deficits, rising domestic price inflation, and low economic growth, President Richard M. Nixon announced to the world that the United States would no longer buy and sell gold with foreign central banks at $35 an ounce. Later that year, a meeting in Washington, DC, resulted in the Smithsonian Agreement that included exchange rate adjustments upward for the German mark and the Japanese yen and downward for the dollar. The price of gold in terms of the dollar was set at $38 an ounce. In addition, fluctuations of 2-1/4 percent above or below the established exchange rates were permitted. Continued pressure on the dollar prompted a further devaluation in 1973 to $42.22 an ounce of gold, its official current value.

Additional changes took place in 1976 with the Jamaica Accords. Under the new amendments each nation was free to choose its own exchange rate agreement. It could let its exchange rate float or fix its rate to a particular currency or group of currencies. The role of gold was diminished; the International Monetary Fund abandoned the notion of defining a currency in terms of an official price of gold. Arrangements were made for an enhanced role for special drawing rights. The amendments also recognized the monitoring and advisory role of the International Monetary Fund, helping nations maintain a stable environment for international trade relations.

The U.S. Treasury and the Federal Reserve System hold the foreign currencies that make up the U.S. official reserve assets. Changes in holdings result from transactions associated with U.S. exchange market intervention through the Federal Reserve System and the Exchange Stabilization Fund, with foreign monetary authorities under reciprocal currency arrangements, with the International Monetary Fund, and from U.S. Treasury Department borrowing of foreign currencies in foreign capital markets.[8]

The Exchange Stabilization Fund was established under the Gold Reserve Act of January 30, 1934, with a $2 billion appropriation derived from devaluation of the U.S. dollar in terms of gold. The fund

> engages in monetary transactions in which one asset is exchanged for another, such as foreign currencies for dollars or dollars for special drawing rights. It is under the control of the Secretary of the Treasury, subject to approval of the President. The fund provides flexibility to respond quickly to unexpected stresses in international financial markets.[9]

Since its initial appropriation the Exchange Stabilization Fund has required no additional infusion. Interest on investments and loans and net gains from foreign exchange market transactions produce income and resources for its activities. When founded and until 1973, it managed the dollar exchange rate. As a result of growth in its portfolio, it provided a source of funds for the U.S. contribution to the International Monetary Fund at its inception in 1945. In 1976 and 1977 its purpose changed from maintaining a fixed dollar exchange rate to "being consistent with U.S. obligations in the IMF regarding orderly exchange arrangements and a stable system of exchange rates."[10] Only occasionally does the Exchange Stabilization Fund get mentioned in the news as when it was called upon to make a $20 billion loan to Mexico during its financial crises in the mid 1990s.

*Other U.S. Government Assets.* Exhibit 8.5 shows $84.2 billion in *U.S. Government assets, other than official assets.* Those assets consist of U.S. Government credits extended to foreign residents, capital subscriptions in, or contributions to, international financial institutions, repayments of credits by foreign residents, and net changes in other U.S. Government assets. *U.S. credits and other long-term assets* amounted to $81.7 billion and reflect transfers of resources to foreign residents under foreign assistance programs enacted by the U.S. Congress that require repayment over a period of years, usually with interest. Among the assets recorded here are capital subscriptions in, or contributions to, international financial institutions that provide long-term economic assistance to foreign countries.[11]

*U.S. foreign currency and short-term assets*—just $2.6 billion—include financing of U.S. farm product exports by acceptance of foreign currencies under the Agricultural Trade Development and Assistance Act, foreign currencies collected as interest, principal, reverse grants, or other assistance programs, foreign currency holdings of U.S. Government disbursing officers, accounts receivable of U.S. Government agencies that report their current transactions on an accrual rather than cash basis, and advances of the Exchange Stabilization Fund not treated as reserve assets.

*U.S. Private Assets. U.S. private assets*, at $5,668.4 billion, constituted 96 percent of the total $5,889.0 billion in *U.S. Assets Abroad. Direct investment abroad*, holdings of *Foreign corporate stocks*, and *U.S. claims reported by U.S. banks* make up the major components of private assets. The magnitude of private assets far surpasses U.S. Government assets. *Direct investment* usually is considered to be a long-term commitment of resources in the ownership, control, and management of a business enterprise located in another country. The amount invested as of 1999, $1,331.2 billion, represents prior acquisitions of equity interest, reinvested earnings, and intercompany debt flows of U.S. direct investors to their incorporated and unincorporated foreign affiliates.[12]

*Foreign bonds* of $556.7 billion reflect net purchases by U.S. residents of financial instruments issued by foreign central governments and their political subdivisions, by corporations or their equivalents, and of international and regional organizations whether located in the United States or abroad. *U.S. claims on unaffiliated foreigners* are reported from two sources: reports from nonbanking concerns and from U.S. banks. The former arises from a business's investment activities, from sales of goods and services in normal business operations, and from disposal of assets used by the business. The claims take such forms as demand and time deposits and certificates of deposit held with banks abroad, loans to unaffiliated foreigners, other debt instruments, and accounts receivable.

In addition to banks, other depository institutions, bank holdings companies, and brokers report claims on foreigners and dealers. Their reports also appear in this category. Two categories of claims are identified: a financial institution's own claims and claims it holds on behalf of domestic customers. The claims may be payable in either dollars or foreign currencies. In the case of the latter, the outstanding amount is converted to dollars based on exchange rates prevailing on the report date. Bank claims consist of such assets as loans, advances, overdrafts granted to foreigners, acceptances payable by foreigners, items in process of collection, and demand and time deposits with unaffiliated foreign banks.

**Foreign Assets in the United States**

Just as we have claims on foreigners and hold assets abroad, they have claims on us and hold assets here. Despite the U.S. deficits in its balance of payments, we have acquired $5,889.0 billion of assets in other countries. Covering our excess of imports over exports and acquisition of claims against other countries requires that foreign assets in the United States exceed that $5,889.0 billion. And sure enough, they do! *Foreign Assets in the United States* amount to $6,971.5 billion.

*Foreign Assets in the United States* consist of two components: *Foreign official assets in the United States* and *Other foreign assets in the United States*. *Foreign official assets in the United States*, which are held by foreign central banks or their governments, amount to $869.3 billion—small compared to total *Foreign Assets in the United States* but over six times *U.S. official reserve assets*. The diminutive holdings of *U.S. official reserve assets* and *Foreign official assets in the United States* suit their role. They constitute the ultimate terms of settlement among countries.

*Foreign Official Assets in the United States.* Foreign official agencies are defined as the treasuries, ministries of finance or corresponding departments, central banks, stabilization funds, governmental exchange control authorities, diplomatic and consular establishments, and other agencies of national governments. Most *Foreign official assets in the United States* took the form of $578.2 billion in holdings of *U.S. Treasury securities*. *Other U.S. Government securities*, at $50.7 billion, constituted another major part of foreign exchange reserves denominated in U.S. dollars of foreign monetary authorities.

*Other U.S. Government liabilities* of $14.7 billion arise from U.S. military agency sales contracts and other U.S. Government transactions arranged with or through foreign official agencies. *U.S. liabilities reported by U.S. banks*, $138.6 billion, for foreign official agencies include such claims as negotiable certificates of deposit issued by U.S. banks, commercial paper issued by U.S. financial and nonfinancial businesses, and short-term obligations of U.S. Government corporations and agencies and of state and local governments. *Other foreign official assets*, $87.1 billion, consist of foreign government investments in U.S. corporate stocks and in debt securities of private corporations and state and local governments.

*Other Foreign Assets in the United States. Other foreign assets in the United States* in 1999 amounted to $6,102.2 billion. They constituted 88 percent of the $6,971.5 billion in *Foreign Assets in the United States*. At 96 percent, private claims of U.S. citizens make up a larger share of total U.S. claims on foreigners than foreign private—or at least "other than official"—claims make up of total foreign claims on the United States.

Foreign *Direct investment in the United States* corresponds in nature and form to U.S. direct investment abroad. It is more than $200 billion less than U.S. *Direct investment abroad*. *U.S. Treasury securities* amounting to $660.7 billion consist of bills, certificates, and marketable bonds and notes issued by the Treasury Department or one of its agencies, the Federal Financing Bank, and purchased by foreign residents. Along with their governments, citizens of the rest of the world held $1.2 trillion in U.S. Treasury debt in 1999. Holding U.S. Treasury securities confers the benefit of interest income. However, some foreigners were content to hold $250.7 billion in U.S. government currency, evidences of debt that bear no interest. Federal Reserve studies indicate that foreigners hold over half of U.S. dollar notes in circulation mainly in the form of $100 bills.[13] In some countries with unstable currencies, it operates as the preferred medium of exchange and way of preserving purchasing power.

Financial claims other than U.S. securities popular with foreigners include issues of stocks and bonds of U.S. corporations and securities of state and local governments and of U.S. Government corporations and federally sponsored agencies. *U.S. corporate stocks* at $1.4 trillion constitute the largest single asset held by foreigners.

*U.S. liabilities to foreigners* and *U.S. liabilities reported by U.S. banks* amounted to $473.8 and $1,082.5 billion, respectively, in 1999. Like U.S. claims on foreigners, they are reported by both nonbanking concerns and by financial institutions and have their counterparts in U.S. claims reported by those entities.

For the United States, *Direct investment abroad*, holdings of *Foreign corporate stocks*, and *U.S. claims reported by U.S. banks* make up the major components of private assets. Foreign *Direct investment in the United States* of $1,125.2 billion is somewhat less than U.S. direct investment abroad, as are foreign claims on U.S. liabilities to counterpart U.S. claims on foreigners. Their $1,445.6 billion holdings of *U.S. corporate stocks* is substantially less. Foreign holdings of *U.S. Treasury securities* of $660.7 billion, *U.S. currency* of $250.7 billion, and *U.S. corporate and other bonds* of $1,445.6 billion more than compensate for those shortfalls.

Despite the overall $1.1 trillion net indebtedness of the United States, U.S. *Direct investment abroad*, $1.3 trillion—considered to be a long-term commitment—outstripped foreign *Direct investment in the United States*, $1.1 trillion. Claims reported by banks, holdings of U.S. Treasury securities, and holdings of corporate and other securities are liquid assets that can be redeemed on short notice. Foreign holdings of U.S. commitments, therefore, tend to be shorter term than U.S. holdings of foreign assets. Like commercial banks, U.S. short-term liabilities exceeded its short-term assets. The data suggest that the United States has become banker to the world.

## THE INTERNATIONAL VALUE OF THE DOLLAR

In Exhibit 8.1 we saw that in 1999 U.S. imports of goods from the rest of the world exceeded our exports by $349.4 billion. Our deficit in exports was not confined to a few products. Only in agricultural products and in capital goods excluding automobiles did U.S. sales of goods exceed purchases. Exhibit 8.2 revealed that U.S. payments owed to the rest of the world in 1999 were matched by only 81 cents in receipts from the rest of the world. Exhibit 8.4 showed us that the U.S. balance of payments has been in chronic deficit since 1991. In 1999 the deficit reached an all-time high (or low) of 313.2 billion. Exhibit 8.5 showed that at the end of 1999 the United States owed the rest of the world $1.1 billion in debt.

What has been the effect of the large deficits in the U.S. balance of payments on exchange rates? Comparisons of exchange rates among countries do not always tell the same story. During any interval of time, some currencies appreciate with respect to the dollar; others depreciate. As Michael Leahy of the Federal Reserve System observes, "in general, an index of the foreign exchange value of a currency is intended to distill into a single number key information from often divergent movements in bilateral exchange rates."[14] In the early 1970s the G-10 index was developed shortly after the breakdown of the fixed exchange rate system developed under the Bretton Woods Agreement. It measured the foreign exchange value of the dollar based on trade-weighted shares of the bilateral exchange rates of the ten major foreign countries participating in the Smithsonian Accord of December 1971.

More recently six new indexes have been developed. According to Leahy,

> Like the G-10 index, the new indexes are designed principally to measure competitiveness in world markets. However, the new indexes are created with a different weighting scheme that focuses more directly on the competitiveness of U.S. goods in the U.S. and foreign markets. In addition, the new indexes summarize and characterize the dollar's movements in foreign exchange markets against a broader set of currencies and are designed to take account of the changing structure of trade patterns and exchange rates.[15]

There is a broad index, a major currency index, and an "other important trading partner" (OITP) index. Initially, the broad index included the currencies of thirty-five countries. On January 1, 1999, the euro replaced ten of those currencies, and the index currently is based on twenty-five currencies. The other two indexes are subsets of the broad index. The major currency index includes the euro and the currencies of Australia, Canada, Japan, Sweden, Switzerland, and the United Kingdom. The OITP includes currencies of major U.S. trading partners.

We shall use the broad index to examine the effect of U.S. balance of trade deficits on the international value of the dollar. Each of the new indexes appears in two forms: nominal and price-adjusted or real. The nominal and real broad indexes tell rather different stories, because some of the countries have experienced high internal rates of price inflation and persistent devaluations of their

**Exhibit 8.6**
**Indexes of the Foreign Exchange Value of the U.S. Dollar, 1971 to 1999**

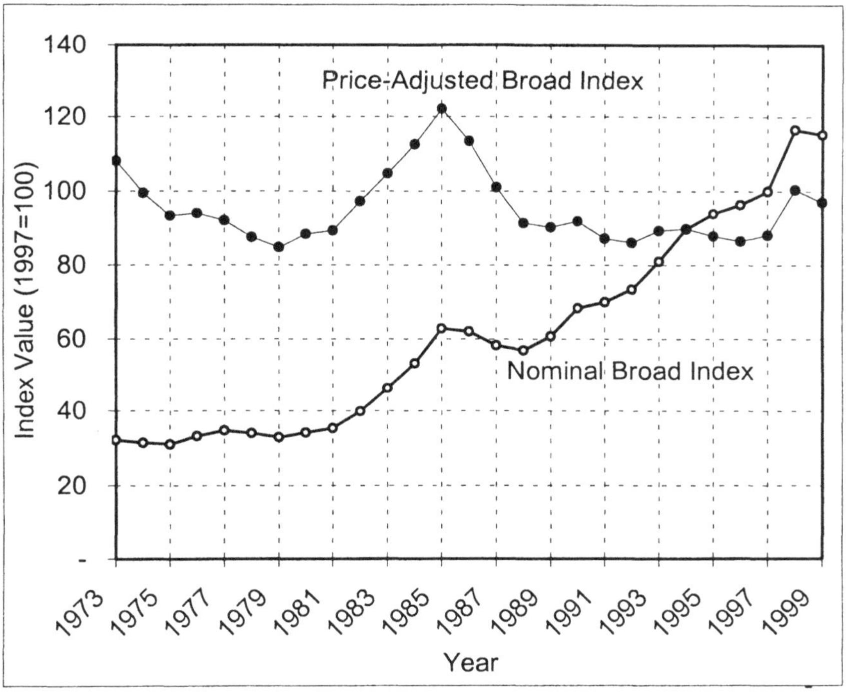


*Source* : Board of Governors of the Federal Reserve System. *Summary Measures of the Foreign Exchange Value of the Dollar*. 6 Nov. 2000. 13 Nov. 2000. <http://www.federalreserve.gov/releases/h10/Summary/>.

currencies. Leahy asserts that "the inclusion of such countries restricts the usefulness of the nominal versions of these indexes to analysis of shorter-term developments in foreign exchange markets because, over the longer term, large nominal depreciations of a few currencies swamp information on the value of the dollar against other currencies."[16]

To illustrate the point, the nominal and price-adjusted broad indexes for the foreign exchange value of the U.S. dollars appear in Exhibit 8.6. The horizontal axis measures years from 1973—the earliest date for the indexes—to 1999. Based on the nominal index, the value of the U.S. dollar appears to have appreciated substantially. In 1973 the index value was 32.1. With few interruptions, the index value has risen. In 1999 it stands at 115.2, 15 percent higher than the 1997 base value of 100.0. Conclusion? The U.S. dollar buys more foreign currency units today than twenty-six years ago despite its long run of balance of trade deficits. But much of that phenomenal performance can be attributed to runaway inflation occurring in some of our trading partners.

The *Price-Adjusted Broad Index* presents a different picture. It begins the period in 1973 with an index value of 108.1. A downward trend ensues, reaching a nadir of 84.8 in 1979. That decline occurs despite—as we saw in Exhibit 8.4—U.S. international payments and receipts being generally in balance. However, the U.S. economy was going through a rough time during the decade of the 1970s: high inflation, wide swings in employment, interest rates, and economic activity. The decline shows the perils of unstable domestic economic conditions.

In the 1980s the situation changed. Columnist and author David DeRosa asserts, "President Ronald Reagan's tax cuts and Federal Reserve Chairman Paul Volcker's anti-inflation tight monetary policy pushed up the dollar."[17] The U.S. internal rate of price inflation declined, and the U.S. dollar began appreciating. In 1985 it reached its highest index value, 122.2. In that year finance ministers of France, Germany, the United Kingdom, Japan, and the United States launched "the first large-scale coordinated central bank attack on the foreign exchange market since exchange rates were allowed to float against the dollar in 1973."[18] The attack produced the desired dollar depreciation that continued until 1989. Since 1988 the index generally fluctuated in a fairly narrow range around 90. For 1999 it registered a value of 97.0.

Given the sizable deficits, why has the value of the U.S. dollar not plummeted on world currency exchange markets? Because the rest of the world wishes to hold dollars and claims on U.S. dollars. U.S. balance of payments deficits enable foreigners to save by holding U.S. assets:

Negative *U.S. net foreign investment* ≡ Positive *net foreign saving in the United States*

U.S. citizens will not sell real estate, bonds, corporate stocks, and other financial instruments to Japanese investors who just have a yen for them. U.S. citizens want U.S. dollars for those assets. Japanese investors obtain those dollars by selling more goods and services to the U.S. than we sell to them.

Moreover, the U.S. dollar serves as the principal medium of exchange on the international foreign exchange market. As DeRosa observes, "it is a wholesale market where an estimated one trillion dollars per day moves around the world. Most of the trading, some 90 percent, involves transactions for which the U.S. dollar is one side."[19] The U.S. balance-of-payments deficits provide liquidity for the world's international trade. Are our deficits a peril or a promise?

## SUMMARY

A massive inflow of foreign capital into the United States has taken place since 1984. Such evidence makes lamentations about investments of U.S. multinational firms abroad and exporting of jobs ring hollow. In 1996, for example, John Sweeney observed, "The [workers] think government should make some new rules that encourage companies to invest in America instead of shipping jobs overseas and that guarantee fair trade, where countries that sell products here also open their markets to us and agree to basic human rights and worker protections."[20] If foreign governments heard his message and heeded it, the inflow of foreign capital into the United States would not exceed the outflow.

Those foreign investments facilitate capital formation in this country, create employment, and feed growth in incomes and prosperity that—with few interruptions—has characterized the past decade. However, the United States already is an industrialized nation. Many places in the world are not. Why do not such massive capital infusions occur there?

A deficit in the U.S. balance of payments for goods does not require foreigners to invest in the United States. It merely makes such investment possible. Foreigners invest in the United States not because they have to but because they want to. They want to because an investment here promises a combined greater return and lower risk than anywhere else. The spirit of entrepreneurship, advanced management and production techniques, the social, legal, constitutional, and political environment interact here to offer the world not only a safe haven for capital but also a profitable one.

What recourse do foreigners have when U.S. imports exceed exports? They could insist that they be paid in terms of their own currencies. They could sell their holdings of U.S. Government securities and their holdings of stocks and bonds issued by U.S. corporations. They could withdraw their balances in U.S. commercial banks. As a consequence, the value of the U.S. dollar on international currency exchange markets would drop, U.S. stock market indexes would plummet, interest rates would rise, domestic employment would decline, and national output would fall. Those events would dampen U.S. residents' demand for foreign-made goods and "correct" the U.S. balance-of-payments deficit. But is that a problem we want to correct?

## NOTES

1. U.S. Department of Commerce, Bureau of Economic Analysis, *Foreign Transactions*, Methodology Paper No. 3 Series MP-3 (Washington, DC: U.S. Government Printing Office, May 1987) 13.
2. *Foreign Transactions* 10.
3. *Foreign Transactions* 19.
4. U.S. Department of Transportation, Maritime Administration, *Merchant Fleets of the World: Oceangoing Steam and Motor Ships of 1,000 Tons and Over as of October 1, 1998* (Washington, DC: U.S. Department of Transportation, Oct. 1998).
5. Lawrence J. White, *International Trade in Ocean Shipping Services: the United States and the World*, (Cambridge, MA: Ballinger, 1988) 5.
6. *Foreign Transactions* 18.
7. Dennis R. Appleyard and Alfred J. Field, Jr., *International Economics: Payments, Exchange Rates, and Macro Policy* (Chicago, IL: Richard D. Irwin, 1993) 235–53.
8. U.S. Department of Commerce, Bureau of Economic Analysis, *The Balance of Payments of the United States: Concepts, Data Sources, and Estimating Procedures* (Washington, DC: U.S. Government Printing Office, May 1990) 79.
9. Arlene Wilson, *The Exchange Stabilization Fund* (Washington, DC: Congressional Research Service, Library of Congress, 1995) 2, *Major studies and issue briefs of the Congressional Research Service, Supplement: 1995* (Arlington, VA: University Pub-

lications of America, 1996) reel 9, fr. 00475.

10. White: 4.

11. *The Balance of Payments of the United States* 81.

12. *The Balance of Payments of the United States* 90.

13. Kurt Schuler, "Basics of Dollarization," Testimony before U.S. Joint Economic Committee, January 1999.

14. Michael P. Leahy, "New Summary Measures of the Foreign Exchange Value of the Dollar," *Federal Reserve Bulletin* (Oct. 1998): 811.

15. Leahy 811.

16. Leahy 182.

17. David F. DeRosa, *In Defense of Free Capital Markets: The Case Against a New International Financial Architecture* (Princeton, NJ: Bloomberg Press, 2001) 37.

18. DeRosa 8.

19. DeRosa 4.

20. John J. Sweeney, "The Gap between the Rich and Everyone Else: Honest Labor and the Standard of Living," The City Club, Forum Foundation, Cleveland, Ohio, 7 Jun. 1996, *Vital Speeches of the Day* 62.18 (1 Jul. 1996): 549–51.

# 9

# Getting Down to Business

So far we have examined three sectors of the economy: the household sector, the government sector, and the rest of the world. Individuals, households, and non-profit institutions serving primarily persons populate the household sector. The national government, fifty state governments, and thousands of local government units comprise the government sector. The rest of the world is populated with, well, everyone else—people and institutions that do not claim or are not entitled to claim the United States as their place of residence.

From whence do the goods and services that we consume, that governments use, and that the rest of the world buys come? The answer to that question leads us to the fourth sector of the economy, the business sector. Among his few but noteworthy remarks, Calvin Coolidge observed that "the chief business of the American people is business."[1] It is to that major preoccupation—and occupation—of the American people to which we now turn.

## COMPOSITION OF THE BUSINESS SECTOR

For purposes of the national income and product accounts (NIPA), the Bureau of Economic Analysis (BEA) of the Department of Commerce defines business firms as "all entities that produce goods and services at a price intended at least to approximate the cost of production, corporate and noncorporate private entities organized for profit." They also include such entities as mutual financial institutions, private noninsured pension funds, cooperatives, nonprofit organizations serving primarily business, Federal Reserve banks, federally sponsored credit agencies, and government enterprises.[2] As we observed in chapter 2, services generated by dwellings occupied by their owners and by buildings and equipment owned by nonprofit institutions serving primarily individuals are treated as business sector outputs.

**Exhibit 9.1**

**Number of Federal Income Tax Returns and Business Receipts by Type of Firm, 1996**

| Industry | Sole Propietorships | | Parternships | | Corporations | | Total | |
|---|---|---|---|---|---|---|---|---|
| | Number of Returns | Business Receipts | Number of Returns | Business Receipts | Number of Returns | Business Receipts | Number of Returns | Business Receipts |
| **Amounts** | | | | | | | | |
| Agricultural services, forestry, fishing | 552 | $ 20 | 131 | $ 15 | 159 | $ 112 | 842 | $ 147 |
| Mining | 108 | 6 | 25 | 24 | 36 | 128 | 169 | 157 |
| Construction | 2,097 | 127 | 74 | 45 | 471 | 700 | 2,642 | 872 |
| Manufacturing | 507 | 32 | 34 | 150 | 326 | 4,567 | 867 | 4,749 |
| Transportation and public utilities | 825 | 42 | 30 | 101 | 206 | 1,184 | 1,060 | 1,327 |
| Wholesale and retail trade | 3,151 | 261 | 168 | 212 | 1,142 | 4,383 | 4,462 | 4,856 |
| Finance, insurance, and real estate | 1,271 | 65 | 892 | 120 | 724 | 1,176 | 2,887 | 1,361 |
| Services | 8,234 | 287 | 297 | 249 | 1,557 | 1,409 | 10,088 | 1,945 |
| Nature of business not allocable | 210 | 2 | 4 | 0 | 10 | 1 | 224 | 4 |
| **All industries** | **16,955** | **$ 843** | **1,654** | **$ 916** | **4,631** | **$ 13,659** | **23,241** | **$ 15,419** |

*Note* : Number of returns in thousands; dollar amounts in $ billions.

**Exhibit 9.1 (continued)**

**Number of Federal Income Tax Returns and Business Receipts by Type of Firm, 1996**

| Industry | Sole Propietorships | | Parternships | | Corporations | | Total | |
|---|---|---|---|---|---|---|---|---|
| | Percent of Returns | Percent of Business Receipts | Percent of Returns | Percent of Business Receipts | Percent of Returns | Percent of Business Receipts | Percent of Returns | Percent of Business Receipts |
| **Percents of all industries total** | | | | | | | | |
| Agricultural services, forestry, fishing | 2% | 0% | 1% | 0% | 1% | 1% | 4% | 1% |
| Mining | 0 | 0 | 0 | 0 | 0 | 1 | 1 | 1 |
| Construction | 9 | 1 | 0 | 0 | 2 | 5 | 11 | 6 |
| Manufacturing | 2 | 0 | 0 | 1 | 1 | 30 | 4 | 31 |
| Transportation and public utilities | 4 | 0 | 0 | 1 | 1 | 8 | 5 | 9 |
| Wholesale and retail trade | 14 | 2 | 1 | 1 | 5 | 28 | 19 | 31 |
| Finance, insurance, and real estate | 5 | 0 | 4 | 1 | 3 | 8 | 12 | 9 |
| Services | 35 | 2 | 1 | 2 | 7 | 9 | 43 | 13 |
| Nature of business not allocable | 1 | 0 | 0 | 0 | 0 | 0 | 1 | 0 |
| **All industries** | **73%** | **5%** | **7%** | **6%** | **20%** | **89%** | **100%** | **100%** |

*Source*: U.S. Department of the Treasury. Internal Revenue Service. "1996, Sole Proprietorship Returns. A Collection of Text, Figures, and Tables." *SOI Bulletin*, Summer 1998: Table 1. 17 Nov. 2000 <http://www.irs.ustreas.gov/plain/tax_stats/soi/sole_non.html>. "Partnership Returns, 1996. An Article Containing PDF Text, Figures, and Tables. *SOI Bulletin*, Fall 1998: Table 1. 17 Nov. 2000 <http://www.irs.treas.gov/plain/tax_stats/soi/part_his.html>. *1996 Corporation Income Tax Returns. A Collection of 25 Tables, the Explanation of Terms, and the Sampling/Data Limitations Description*. IRS Publication 16 (Revised 9-99): Table 1. 17 Nov. 2000 <http://www.irs.ustreas.gov/plain/tax_stats/soi/corp-complete.html>.

Business firms are grouped into four categories based on their legal form of organization: sole proprietorships, partnerships, corporations, and government enterprises. For private sector entities, the tax form they file determines their category. An individual operating a business or practicing a profession for income or for profit on a continuous or regular basis reports the earnings and expenses of the enterprise on Schedule C (Profits or Loss from Business). Rentals of real estate and royalty income and expenses are reported on Schedule E (Supplemental Income and Loss). Individuals operating farms report—as the letter and title of the form implies—on Schedule F (Farm Income and Expenses).[3] Enterprises filing those schedules fall within the sole proprietorship category and accompany federal individual income tax returns, IRS Form 1040.

When two or more persons wish to form a relationship to jointly carry on a trade or business, they can establish a partnership. Each partner contributes money, property, labor, or skill to the effort and expects to share in profits or losses generated by the enterprise. Partnerships for tax purposes include limited partnerships, syndicates, groups, pools, joint ventures, and other unincorporated enterprises through which or by which any business, financial operation, and venture is carried on. They dissolve when operations cease or when more than 50 percent of the share of the capital or profits is sold or exchanged with another party in a twelve-month period. Partnerships file IRS Form 1065.[4]

Corporate business entities file federal corporate tax returns (IRS Form 1120 Series). That requirement encompasses "mutual financial institutions and cooperatives subject to Federal income tax, private noninsured pension funds, nonprofit institutions, nonprofit institutions that primarily serve business, Federal Reserve banks, and Federally sponsored credit agencies."[5]

Government enterprises consist of government agencies like the U.S. Postal Service and the Tennessee Valley Authority that maintain their own separate accounts, sell goods and services to the public, and manage to cover most of their operating costs. Some of their transactions are included in the business sector, and some are included in the government sector. Sales to final users are recorded as sales by private noncorporate businesses, their purchases of materials and business services are treated as intermediate goods and services, and employee compensation and consumption of fixed capital are deducted to calculate their income. The other transactions are included in the government sector.

## Number of Firms and Business Receipts by Industry and Firm Type

Given that federal income tax returns provide the principal basis for pigeonholing business firms, information on tax returns and business receipts reported by the Internal Revenue Service (IRS) provides a basis for assessing the population of the business sector. Exhibit 9.1 summarizes that information for nine industrial divisions for the most recent year available, 1996, and three business categories—sole proprietorships, partnerships, and corporations. In the top half of the table, number of returns is shown in thousands; dollar amounts for business receipts, in billions. The bottom half shows number and dollar amounts as percentages of total number of returns and business receipts across all business categories.

The two total columns on the right-hand side of the table indicate that firms across all business categories and industrial divisions filed a total of over 23.2 million federal income tax returns for 1996. A look at the detail making up that total shows that businesses engaged in providing *Services* account for almost 10.1 million—43 percent. Firms engaged in *Wholesale and retail trade* come next in terms of number of returns filed, 4.5 million, 19 percent of the total.

As percentages in the lower portion of Exhibit 9.1 show, 73 percent of total returns are filed by *Sole Proprietorships*. *Sole Proprietorships* in the *Services* sector alone account for 35 percent of all returns. Add in *Wholesale and retail trade* and *Construction* outfits and you have captured 58 percent of all business firms. *Corporations* figure next in terms of the number of returns, 20 percent. Once again, among corporations, *Service* enterprise returns are most numerous followed by *Wholesale and retail trade*. *Partnerships* come in last with 7 percent of all returns. Among partnerships, *Finance, insurance, and real estate* entities predominate.

In the case of *Business receipts*, totaling about $15.4 trillion for 1996, we get a very different pattern. *Wholesale and retail trade* firms generate business receipts of $4.8 trillion, 31 percent of the total. Next come firms in the *Manufacturing* sector, $4.7 trillion, another 31 percent. After accounting for service sector firms with business receipts of $1.9 trillion, 13 percent of the total, not much is left for the other six sectors—just 25 percent of the total. But one-fourth of $15.4 trillion still is a very big number.

The lower portion of Exhibit 9.1 shows that *Corporations* generate 89 percent of all business receipts. That does not leave much for the numerous *Sole Proprietorships* and scarce *Partnerships* to apportion among them—just 5 percent for the former and 6 percent for the latter. Division of business receipts by number of returns produces average business receipts for sole proprietorships of a little under $50,000. For partnerships, they average $554,000—over eleven times greater than sole proprietorships.

For corporations business receipts average almost $2.9 million—serious business relative to sole proprietorships and partnerships. Among *Corporations* most business receipts are generated by firms engaged in *Manufacturing* and in *Wholesale and retail trade*. Together, corporations engaged in those two activities account for 58 percent of the total of all business receipts reported.

## Profits, the Driving Force of Business

In our examination of the household sector, we assumed that individuals seek to earn income and spend it in such a manner that their satisfaction or sense of well-being is maximized. Economists assume that expectations of profits motivate entrepreneurs, people who establish and manage business firms. Around that assumption they have constructed and continue to construct elaborate and ever more sophisticated models of rational behavior. While attributing a profit motive to the behavior of businesspersons may seem reasonable, evidence from tax returns suggests that success in such an endeavor is not easily attained.

Businesses are required to file income tax returns regardless of their profitability. The Internal Revenue Service publishes data on not only all returns but also on those returns with net income. Exhibit 9.2 summarizes that information for 1996, the latest data available. The table shows the number of total returns and returns with net income by major industry divisions for each type of business organization. The third column for each business type expresses the number of returns with net income as a percent of total returns.

Of the total 23.2 million returns filed, 16.1 million—69 percent—of them produced net income for the managers and owners. When we look at the types of business organizations, we see that 74 percent of the returns for *Sole Proprietorships* earned net income, and 61 percent of *Partnerships* earned net income. For *Corporations* the percentage was only 56 percent. *Sole Proprietorships* engaged in *Construction* generated the highest percentage of returns with net income, 87 percent, a high percentage reflecting high levels of economic activity. A downturn in economic activity is liable to impact that good performance in construction adversely. *Wholesale and retail trade* proprietorships and partnerships fare less well and show that only 55 percent and 54 percent of returns filed produced net income for their owners.

For returns with the lowest percentage of positive returns, look to the corporate sector. Only 13 percent of *Corporations* whose *Nature of business* was *not allocable* turned in returns with net income. Being unique and difficult to categorize does not seem to provide an advantage. Compared to sole proprietorships and partnerships, the corporate form of business organization appears not to confer profitability advantages to firms in *Agriculture, forestry, and fishing; Mining; Construction; Transportation and public utilities; Finance, insurance, and real estate*; and *Services*. Only in *Manufacturing* and *Wholesale and retail trade* do the percentages of returns with net income of corporations surpass those of sole proprietorships and partnerships.

Entrepreneurship occurs at the frontier where discovery is made about consumer wants and needs for goods and services. What will consumers pay? What level of quality and at what price will they buy? What is the cost of making available those products? How can costs be cut? The service improved? Such discoveries are hard won. In the process entrepreneurs put their financial security at risk. Rewards may be great, but the struggle is continuous. Today's successes may prove to be tomorrow's failures, outmoded by changes in taste and outdistanced by more alert rivals. Clearly, the game is not for everyone. Promises of great rewards entail perils of risk and financial loss.

A safe haven exists for those inclined to large-scale business affairs but not inclined to the risks of rough-and-tumble entrepreneurship. It appears to be the large corporation.

**Exhibit 9.2**

**Number of Business Firms: Total and with Net Income, 1996**

| | Number of Returns (in thousands) | | | | | | | | | | | |
|---|---|---|---|---|---|---|---|---|---|---|---|---|
| | Sole Proprietorships | | | Partnerships | | | Corporations | | | All Businesses | | |
| Major Industry Division | Total | With net income | Percent of Total | Total | With net income | Percent of Total | Total | With net income | Percent of Total | Total | With net income | Percent of Total |
| Agricultre, forstry, fishing | 552 | 399 | 72% | 131 | 80 | 61% | 159 | 90 | 57% | 842 | 568 | 68% |
| Mining | 108 | 65 | 61 | 25 | 16 | 63 | 36 | 18 | 51 | 169 | 99 | 59 |
| Construction | 2,097 | 1,817 | 87 | 74 | 51 | 69 | 471 | 301 | 64 | 2,642 | 2,169 | 82 |
| Manufacturing | 507 | 328 | 65 | 34 | 19 | 57 | 326 | 191 | 59 | 867 | 539 | 62 |
| Transport & publ utilities | 825 | 609 | 74 | 30 | 16 | 55 | 206 | 112 | 54 | 1,060 | 737 | 69 |
| Wholesale & retail trade | 3,151 | 1,724 | 55 | 168 | 91 | 54 | 1,142 | 653 | 57 | 4,462 | 2,468 | 55 |
| Finance, insur, real estate | 1,271 | 969 | 76 | 892 | 548 | 61 | 724 | 341 | 47 | 2,887 | 1,858 | 64 |
| Services | 8,234 | 6,443 | 78 | 297 | 187 | 63 | 1,557 | 881 | 57 | 10,088 | 7,512 | 74 |
| Business not allocable | 210 | 170 | 81 | 4 | 2 | 46 | 10 | 1 | 13 | 224 | 173 | 77 |
| Total returns | 16,955 | 12,524 | 74% | 1,654 | 1,010 | 61% | 4,631 | 2,588 | 56% | 23,241 | 16,122 | 69% |

*Source*: U.S. Department of the Treasury. Internal Revenue Service. "1996, Sole Proprietorship Returns. A Collection of Text, Figures, and Tables." *SOI Bulletin*, Summer 1998: Table 1. 17 Nov. 2000 <http://www.irs.ustreas.gov/plain/tax_stats/soi/sole_non.html>. "Partnership Returns, 1996. An Article Containing PDF Text, Figures, and Tables. *SOI Bulletin*, Fall 1998: Table 2. 17 Nov. 2000 <http://www.irs.treas.gov/plain/tax_stats/soi/part_his.html>. *1996 Corporation Income Tax Returns. A Collection of 25 Tables, the Explanation of Terms, and the Sampling/Data Limitations Description*. IRS Publication 16 (Revised 9-99): Table 1. 17 Nov. 2000 <http://www.irs.ustreas.gov/plain/tax_stats/soi/corp-complete.html>.

### Income and Expenses of the Corporate Sector

Since corporations obviously account for such a large portion of total business receipts, they deserve a closer look. Statistical data published by the Internal Revenue Service on federal corporate income tax returns are based on a stratified sample of less than 100,000 of the 4.6 million returns filed. From 1916 through 1950 all returns were tabulated. Stratified sampling was introduced in 1951 and, according to the IRS, "Since then, the size of the samples has generally decreased while the population has increased."[6] One hundred percent of all returns of corporations with total assets of $50 million or over are included. The sampling rate diminishes as total asset size becomes smaller. For corporations with total assets under $50,000, the sample rate is less than one-half of one percent. As we shall see, in the aggregate, slighting the sampling size of small corporations is likely to have small effects on the results since they account for a relatively small portion of total business activity.

### Profitability and Corporate Size

Internal Revenue Service statistics stratify federal corporation income tax returns not only by industry and by net income but also by size of total assets. Twelve total asset categories currently are in use. The size categories range from corporations reporting no assets at all to those with total assets of over $250 million.

Exhibit 9.3 displays two sets of columns. The first set pertains to all corporations with and without net income; the second, to corporations only with net income. The first three columns in each set contain the *Number of returns*, *Total receipts*, and *Total receipts less total deductions* for all industries by size of total assets.

For the set of columns for *All Returns*, we see that *Net receipts*—total receipts less total deductions—*as Percent of total receipts* equals 5 percent. But that percentage varies when firms are grouped by size. Firms with zero assets show the lowest percentage. They generate $252 billion in receipts, but only $2 billion remains after deductions. Net receipts amount to just 1 percent of total receipts. Assets appear to confer profit-making advantages, and the more the merrier. For firms with assets of less than $50 million, net receipts are no more than 2 percent of total receipts. Net receipts as a percent of total receipts for corporations with assets ranging from $50 million to $100 million rise to 4 percent. For corporations with assets between $100 million and $250 million, it becomes 5 percent. Corporations with assets greater than $250 million enjoy net receipts amounting to 7 percent of total receipts. After total assets of $50 million, more assets bring higher percentages of net receipts.

When we cull out firms with losses and deal with those having a profit, a somewhat different pattern emerges. Results appear in the second set of columns, *Returns with Net Income*. *Net receipts as percent of total receipts*

**Exhibit 9.3**

**Federal Corporate Income Tax Returns with and without Net Income by Size of Total Assets, 1996**

| | All Returns | | | | Returns with Net Income | | | | | |
|---|---|---|---|---|---|---|---|---|---|---|
| Size of Total Assets | Number of returns | Total receipts | Total receipts less total deductions | Net receipts as % of total receipts | Number of returns | Total receipts | Total receipts less total deductions | Net receipts as % of total receipts | Number of returns as % of all returns | Total receipts as % of all returns |
| Zero assets | 280 | $ 252 | $ 2 | 1 | 95 | $ 167 | $ 15 | 9 | 34 | 66 |
| 1-$100,000 | 2,417 | 515 | 12 | 2 | 1,287 | 331 | 26 | 8 | 53 | 64 |
| $100,000-$250,000 | 747 | 418 | 7 | 2 | 444 | 289 | 17 | 6 | 59 | 69 |
| $250,000-$500,000 | 441 | 416 | 9 | 2 | 270 | 304 | 17 | 5 | 61 | 73 |
| $500,000-$1 million | 308 | 503 | 9 | 2 | 195 | 377 | 18 | 5 | 63 | 75 |
| $1 million-$5 million | 323 | 1,485 | 27 | 2 | 214 | 1,163 | 51 | 4 | 66 | 78 |
| $5 million-$10 million | 48 | 719 | 14 | 2 | 34 | 582 | 24 | 4 | 70 | 81 |
| $10 million-$25 million | 30 | 823 | 18 | 2 | 22 | 663 | 32 | 5 | 71 | 81 |
| $25 million-$50 million | 13 | 534 | 13 | 2 | 9 | 418 | 24 | 6 | 72 | 78 |
| $50 million-$100 million | 8 | 505 | 19 | 4 | 7 | 395 | 29 | 7 | 77 | 78 |
| $100 million-$250 million | 8 | 741 | 38 | 5 | 6 | 603 | 52 | 9 | 80 | 81 |
| $250 million or more | 8 | 8,614 | 630 | 7 | 7 | 7,662 | 664 | 9 | 83 | 89 |
| **Total** | **4,631** | **$ 15,526** | **$ 798** | **5** | **2,588** | **$ 12,955** | **$ 968** | **7** | **56** | **83** |

*Note* : Number of returns in thousands. Amounts in $ billions.

*Source* : U. S. Department of the Treasury. Internal Revenue Service. *1996 Corporation Income Tax Returns* . IRS Publication 16 (Revised 9-99): Table 4. 17 Nov. 2000 <http://www.irs.ustreas.gov/plain/tax_stats/soi/corp-complete.html>.

naturally becomes larger. For all profitable corporations, net receipts amount to 7 percent of total receipts. Analysis of firms by size shows that firms with the least and most total assets earn highest net receipts as percentages of total receipts. For firms with no assets and for firms with total assets of $100 million or more, net receipts amount to 9 percent of total receipts. Between those two extremes percentages decline, reaching their lowest point at 4 percent for corporations with total assets between $1 million and $10 million.

In Exhibit 9.2 we observed than 56 percent of returns of corporations report positive net income. That percentage appears again at the bottom of the column second from the right in Exhibit 9.3. As we proceed up that column, we find that the larger a corporation is in terms of total assets the more likely it is to be profitable. Eighty-three percent of corporations with total assets of more than $250 million report positive net income. That percentage declines with decreasing asset size reaching 34 percent for corporations with no assets. Given that for all corporations the number of returns with net income averages only 56 percent, a large corporation would appear an attractive sanctuary for the risk averse.

Although corporations with *Net Income* account for only 56 percent of all returns, their *Total receipts* account for 83 percent of all corporation total receipts. Stated differently, 44 percent of corporations with no *Net Income* account for only 17 percent of *Business receipts*. From that observation can be drawn a startling conclusion. To make a profit it helps to produce products that people buy. *Total receipts* for profitable corporations with no assets only comprise 66 percent of business receipts for that asset category, but that appears to be a pretty good showing considering that they make up only 34 percent of the returns. With few exceptions, *Total receipts* of corporations with net income make up an increasing percentage of *Total receipts* of all corporations as their total assets rise.

Inspection of Exhibit 9.3 reveals that profitable corporations with total assets over $250 billion account for almost $7.7 trillion—59 percent—of the $12.9 trillion of Total *receipts* of corporations blessed with *Net Income.* They generate nearly 69 percent of *Total receipts less total deductions*—$664 billion out of $968 billion.

## Concentration in the Corporate Sector

As we already know from Exhibit 9.3, the number of corporate returns totals 4.6 million. Total assets held by the corporations in each size category totals to over $28.6 trillion. Tabular data developed by the Internal Revenue Service shows that over half the corporations reporting for 1996 had total assets ranging from $100,000 to $250,000—2.4 million out of 4.6 million.[7] Their total assets amount to $121 billion, 4 percent of the $28.6 trillion total. Only about 8,200 corporations—less than 0.2 percent of the 4.6 million returns filed—reported total assets of over $250,000,000. Their total assets amount to $24.3 trillion—85 percent of the $28.6 trillion in corporate assets. 85 percent!

**Exhibit 9.4**
**Distribution of Total Assets among Active Corporations, 1996**

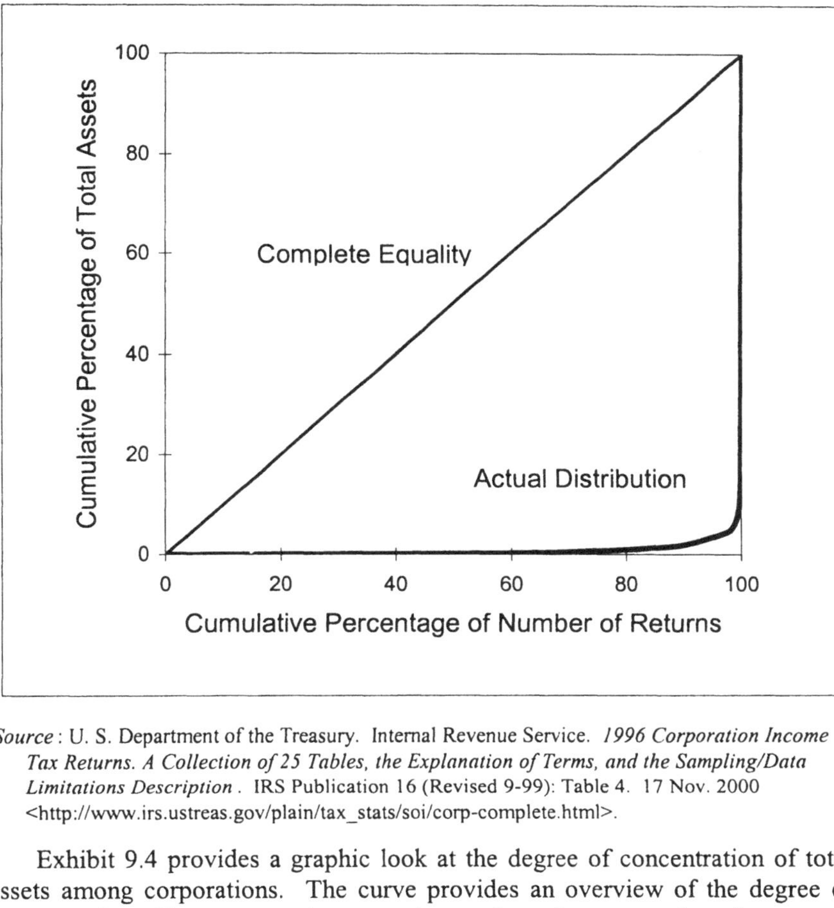


*Source*: U. S. Department of the Treasury. Internal Revenue Service. *1996 Corporation Income Tax Returns. A Collection of 25 Tables, the Explanation of Terms, and the Sampling/Data Limitations Description*. IRS Publication 16 (Revised 9-99): Table 4. 17 Nov. 2000 <http://www.irs.ustreas.gov/plain/tax_stats/soi/corp-complete.html>.

Exhibit 9.4 provides a graphic look at the degree of concentration of total assets among corporations. The curve provides an overview of the degree of concentration. To construct the curve the number of returns and total assets are accumulated beginning with the zero-asset category and ending with total assets over $250 million. Accumulative returns and asset amounts then are expressed as percentages of their respective totals. Almost 91 percent of all corporations reporting in 1996 had total assets of less than $1 million; however, collectively, they accounted for only 2.0 percent of all assets held by corporations.

Exhibit 9.4 plots the cumulative percentage of the number of returns along the horizontal axis and the cumulative percentage of total assets along the vertical. The resulting curve follows the horizontal very closely and then climbs along the right border of the chart, revealing an extreme divergence from the line of complete equality represented by the diagonal line proceeding from the lower left-hand corner to the upper right-hand corner. The divergence in the distribution between number of returns and total assets for corporations contrasts markedly from that seen in Exhibit 4.8 for the distribution between the number of returns for personal income taxes and the adjusted gross income of persons. As with households and individuals, we can calculate a Gini coefficient for corporations providing an index of inequality. The Gini coefficient, based on number of federal personal income tax returns and adjusted gross income of households and individuals, equaled 0.57. For the number of federal corporate income tax returns and total assets, the coefficient is 0.98.

The distribution between federal corporate income tax returns and *Business receipts* provides an alternative basis for viewing the degree of concentration. In 1996 for all industries, the Gini coefficient based on receipts is less than that based on total assets—0.87 versus 0.98. Nevertheless, the index of inequality is high. Calculation of Gini coefficients for 1959 shows high inequality levels thirty-seven years earlier: 0.94 for total assets and 0.81 for business receipts. However, inequality is higher in 1996 than 1959. An increase from 0.94 to 0.98 may not seem like a marked increase. In part, that appearance may be a product of what the Gini coefficient measures—level of inequality. Focusing on equality—a more positive approach—gives a different impression. An index of equality would equal 0.06 in 1959 and 0.02 in 1996. The reduction in equality of asset distribution among corporations—albeit small—would be seen to have fallen to a third of its former level in 1996. The rise in the Gini coefficient for the distribution of business receipts from 0.81 to 0.87 implies a drop in the equality coefficient from 0.19 to 0.13—32 percent.

While espousing the freedom of action bestowed by a laissez-faire free-market economy, it is no wonder that businessmen attempt to eliminate competition through market domination. Larger firms enjoy greater likelihood of profitability. The larger a firm is, the higher its profit margins on sales. What accounts for those higher profit margins? Productivity gains from economies of scale, advanced management practices, use of the most advanced technologies? Or an economic rent exacted from consumers by limiting supply, raising prices, raising barriers to entry by competing firms, wringing special concessions from government at the local, state, and national levels? Gigantic enterprises usually offer the twin benefits of high profitability and security, whatever their causes.

Should the degree of concentration of economic activity, wealth, and income in the corporate sector be a source of concern? It has been a concern. The year 1990 marked the 100th anniversary of the Sherman Act, "the foundation of antitrust" in the United States.[8] But the results, effectiveness, and future of that policy remain uncertain.

One author on the subject of antitrust legislation and litigation in the United States, Donald Dewey, asserts:

> From the beginning, two seldom-voiced presumptions about antitrust enforcement have contended for favor in the courts and Congress. One says that all doubts should be resolved in favor of freedom of contract—provided that the cost is not too great. The other says that all doubts should be resolved in favor of decentralized decision-making—provided the cost is not too great.[9]

Abridging the rights of private property—entailed by antitrust enforcement—erodes one of the essential environmental conditions of a market economy. On the other hand, large corporations stand like feudal fortresses of centralized control over wealth, income, and power in fertile fields of decentralized decision-making. One cannot help but wonder in such centrally planned enclaves how much initiative is lost, ingenuity stifled, and progress denied. When too much becomes owned by too few in a democracy, support for the sanctity of private property is liable to wane.

### Volume of Transactions

Exhibit 9.1 presents information on the number of federal business income tax returns filed and their business receipts. The volume of business receipts is of particular interest. The overview of the NIPA in chapter 1 identified gross domestic product as the most general and encompassing of the measures of national output. In 1996 gross domestic product equaled $7.8 trillion, but Exhibit 9.1 shows that business receipts amount to $15.4 trillion. Clearly, something has been left out of gross domestic product.

## INPUT-OUTPUT ANALYSIS

Gross domestic product measures the output of final goods and services—products purchased within the United States by people and governmental units, and exports bought by the rest of the world. Much of the cost that firms incur consists of purchases of intermediate goods and services—products that are employed in producing other goods and services—that are not included in gross domestic product.

One of the purposes of the system of national accounts is to provide a description of the relationships among economic units—how business firms, people, governments, and the rest of the world interact to produce goods and services and to consume and invest them. By its focus on final output and goods and services, gross domestic product does not reveal much about how the business sector produces goods and services.

For a description of how the business sector operates, input-output analysis comes to the rescue. It is an integral part of the NIPA but is less widely advertised and used. In addition to showing the interdependence among producers and consumers in the economy, input-output analysis can be used to assess the economic impact of natural disasters, strikes and lockouts, or other interruptions to the normal flow of economic activity. It can be adapted to evaluate economic effects on employment, a region, or a particular industry of changes in such things as demand for particular products, supply shortages, price increases, and exchange rate fluctuations. The BEA of the Department of Commerce uses the results of input-output analysis as a benchmark in the construction of national income and product account statistics.[10] For just plain folks, an understanding and appreciation of input-output analysis contributes to a better understanding of the NIPA and recognition of its limitations.

### Development of Input-Output Analysis

Wassily Leontief pioneered the effort to develop input-output analysis. Born in the Soviet Union, he received his doctorate in economics in Germany in 1928 and came to the United States in 1931. After working briefly at the National Bureau for Economic Research, he joined the Harvard University faculty where he stayed for forty-five years. His early interest in technological change in the United States led to development of input-output analysis, "a method of analysis that takes advantage of the relatively stable pattern of the flow of goods and services among the elements of our economy to bring a much more detailed statistical picture of the system into the range of manipulation by economic theory."[11]

During World War II he worked for the Bureau of Labor Statistics constructing input-output accounts for the United States in anticipation of postwar demobilization. After World War II "interest in I-O accounts grew quickly in the United States and elsewhere, as their usefulness for policy making in both centrally planned and free-market economies was recognized. . . . As the I-O accounts were developed, their usefulness as an integrating tool for, and a check on the accuracy of, other economic accounts also become increasingly apparent."[12]

The significance of his contribution to input-output analysis and to the discipline of economics and national income accounting is evidenced by the award of the Nobel Prize in Economics to Wassily Leontief in 1973.

### Construction of the Input-Output Accounts

Despite the importance of input-output analysis and its advantages, availability of data serves to limit its popularity. Data for benchmark input-output accounts were first collected 1947. Then eleven years elapsed before a second set was put together. A third effort occurred in 1963. For 1967 and every five years thereafter, benchmark input-output accounts have been prepared. In addition to not being available on a current (annual, quarterly, or monthly) basis, a delay occurs between the times of data collection and of publication. At the time of this writing (January 2001), the most recently published input-output data available pertain to 1997. That information was published in December 2000, three years after the fact: "One of the most serious concerns of those who use input-output models in applied work is that the table of technical coefficients available to them for the economy they are studying may reflect data from a much earlier year."[13]

Data collection for the input-output accounts requires substantial effort. Economic censuses conducted every five years by the Bureau of the Census (who else?) of mining, of construction, of manufacturing, of transportation, communications and utilities, of financial, insurance, and real estate industries, of service industries, and of governments constitute a major source of data. Other government agencies contributing to the effort include the U.S. Department of Agriculture, the National Oceanic and Atmospheric Administration (for fisheries), U.S. Army Corps of Engineers and Department of Transportation, U.S. Department of Labor, U.S. Department of Education, and many others. Reliance also is placed on data gathered by various trade associations and industry groups.[14] Gathering the information—itself a major undertaking—must be followed by tabulation, data processing, and construction of the input-output accounts. That chore falls to the BEA.

The end product is a matrix showing "the production of commodities (goods and services) by each industry, the use of commodities by each industry, the commodity composition of gross domestic product (GDP), and the industry distribution of value added."[15] The matrix, in its full-blown detail, deals with 498 industries. For our purposes a matrix of nine major industry groups and nine major commodity categories will suffice.

### Summary of Input-Output Accounts for 1997

Exhibit 9.5 distills the Herculean effort of constructing the input-output accounts for the United States in 1997 by all those government agencies and private associations into a single page: "With these estimates, BEA has expanded its input-output information from a frequency of once every 5 years to once a year, while reducing the lag between the year measured and the estimate released from five years to three."[16] The input-output matrix consists of nine rows and nine columns. Although labels for the rows and columns are similar, row labels represent commodities; column labels, industries. Various conventions are required to classify transactions into the cells of the matrix to produce useful information. For example, most goods require transportation and pass through wholesale and retail traders on their way to intermediate and final users. However, "to show the relationship between the production of commodities and their purchase by intermediate and final users, commodities are shown as if they move directly to users."[17] Commodity transactions are shown in terms of producers' prices, and transportation costs and trade margins are shown separately. For example, in Exhibit 9.5 *Total Final Output* expenditures for agricultural products amount to $42 billion. That $42 billion figure is expressed in terms of producer prices. It does not include costs of transportation and services of wholesale food distributors and grocery stores. They appear in the $563 billion figure for transportation and in the $1,050 billion figure for trade.

Just because a firm is classified in a particular industry does not prevent it from engaging in other productive activities. For example, a manufacturing firm may employ a crew to maintain and repair its facilities. To account for those secondary activities and attempt to keep the inputs required for the main activity of firms within an industry as homogeneous as possible, secondary activities are

**Exhibit 9.5**

**Input-Out Analysis and Final Output, 1997 (In $ Billions)**

| Commodity \ Industry | Agriculture, forestry, and fisheries | Mining | Construction | Manufacturing | Transport, communi cation, and utilities | Trade | Finance | Services | Other | **Total Intermediate Products** | **Total Final Output** | **Total Commodity Output** |
|---|---|---|---|---|---|---|---|---|---|---|---|---|
| Agricultural products | $ 75 | $ 0 | $ 5 | $ 149 | $ 0 | $ 2 | $ 10 | $ 11 | $ 1 | $ 253 | $ 42 | $ 295 |
| Minerals | 0 | 33 | 7 | 115 | 62 | 0 | 0 | 0 | 3 | 219 | (56) | 164 |
| Construction | 3 | 5 | 1 | 27 | 44 | 12 | 71 | 27 | 25 | 216 | 729 | 944 |
| Manufactured items | 52 | 15 | 281 | 1,372 | 77 | 68 | 19 | 322 | 18 | 2,224 | 1,583 | 3,807 |
| Transportation | 13 | 13 | 23 | 177 | 190 | 66 | 50 | 116 | 21 | 669 | 563 | 1,231 |
| Trade | 15 | 4 | 75 | 234 | 18 | 31 | 5 | 64 | 3 | 449 | 1,050 | 1,499 |
| Finance | 22 | 29 | 15 | 68 | 37 | 101 | 384 | 223 | 7 | 886 | 1,423 | 2,310 |
| Services | 8 | 6 | 92 | 229 | 131 | 201 | 173 | 473 | 12 | 1,324 | 2,066 | 3,390 |
| Other | 0 | 2 | 1 | 34 | 26 | 18 | 32 | 29 | 4 | 145 | 918 | 1,061 |
| **Intermediate Inputs** | $188 | $105 | $500 | $2,407 | $ 585 | $ 499 | $ 744 | $1,265 | $ 93 | $6,386 | | |
| **Total Value Added** | 110 | 70 | 444 | 1,478 | 613 | 996 | 1,606 | 1,938 | 1,064 | | $8,318 | |
| **Total Industry Output** | $298 | $175 | $944 | $3,884 | $1,198 | $1,495 | $2,350 | $3,203 | $1,156 | | | $14,704 |

*Source*: U.S. Department of Commerce. Bureau of Economic Analysis. "Interindustry Relationships in the U.S. Economy: New Annual Input-Output Estimates for 1997." *BEA News Release*. 18 Dec. 2000. 8 Jan. 2001. <http://www.bea.doc.gov/bea/newsrel/io1200.htm>.

redefined. Construction activity performed by firms classified in other industries is redefined to the construction industry. Similarly, "manufacturing in trade and service establishments is redefined to the appropriate manufacturing industries."[18] Other redefinitions involve retail trade, sales of purchased goods, rental activities, and preparation of meals and beverages.

For most industries a firm's primary activity determines its classification. *Agriculture, forestry, and fisheries*, *Mining*, and *Construction* constitute exceptions. In those industries the product produced determines its classification. The products of a farm producing both milk and corn, for example, would be classified as dairy farm and grain products rather than being determined by the farm's classification. *Other* industries include not only government enterprises, general government industry, and households but also inventory valuation adjustment. In Exhibit 9.5 *Other* commodities include non-comparable imports in addition to the outputs of those industries.

The cells in the matrix can be interpreted as industry output or as commodity input depending on the perspective. From the perspective of a column or industry, a cell represents an input. For example, take the entry in the cell in the first column of the first row, $75 billion. In 1997 the *Agriculture, forestry, and fisheries* industrial group used $75 billion of *Agricultural products* to produce its output. For farm boys (and girls), that makes sense. To grow corn farmers have to plant corn. If raising swine is their specialty, they feed corn to the hogs. In addition to its own products, the agriculture industry used $3 billion of *Construction* (barns, chicken coops), $52 billion of *Manufactured items* (tractors, fertilizer), $13 billion in *Transportation, communication, and utilities* (getting the produce and animals to market, electricity for the milking machines), $15 billion in trade, $22 billion in *Finance* (borrowing from the bank), and $8 billion in *Services* (veterinarians). As the row just outside the matrix indicates, those purchases of intermediate goods and services used as inputs by farmers totaled to $188 billion.

In addition, under valued added, farmers spent $110 billion on employee compensation (including their own), indirect business taxes, and such expense items as rent, interest, and proprietor's income and/or corporate profits, depending on the form of business organization. Also included under value added are allowances for consumption of fixed capital (depreciation), business transfer payments, and government subsidies to business less current surplus of government enterprises. The total at the bottom of the column represents the value of the agriculture, forestry, and fisheries industry's total output for 1997, $298 billion.

How was agricultural output used? The answer to that question is addressed by examining each cell from the perspective of the first row, *Agricultural products*. As we already have observed, $75 billion was used by farmers themselves and others in the agriculture industry to produce the rest of the agricultural products. *Manufacturing* (butchers, bakers, candlestick makers) uses most of the *Agricultural products*, $149 billion. Food processing is classified as a manufacturing industry. Those corn flakes for breakfast did not grow in a box. Chickens do not hop up on grocery shelves, pluck off their feathers, and wrap themselves in cellophane before they die. Other users of *Agricultural products* include the *Construction* industry at $5 billion (e.g., lumber from forest products); *Trade*, $2 billion; *Finance*, $10 billion; the *Services* industry, $11 billion; and *Other*, $1 billion. The column just outside the matrix measures the total of intermediate farm products used by those industries, $253 billion.

Subtracting total intermediate agricultural products from total agriculture commodity output produces final agricultural product. That difference, amounting to $42 billion, represents the portion of *Total final output* consisting of *Agricultural products*. Those final products are consumed by the household and government sectors, exported (net of imports) to the rest of the world, and added to inventories.

A similar interpretation can be attached to the other rows and columns of the input-output matrix and the rows and columns outside the matrix. Note that the sum of *Total Intermediate Products*, $6,386 billion, equals *Intermediate Inputs*. One firm's sale to another firm is that firm's purchase. In addition, the rows representing *Total Final Output* sum to $8,318 billion and equal the column sums of *Total Value Added*. It is equivalent to Gross Domestic Product. Conceptually, *Total Industry Output* for each column should equal its respective total commodity output for each row. Although they aggregate to the same number, $14,704 billion, discrepancies between particular pairs of rows and columns occur as a result of classification and aggregation discrepancies. To return to our earlier example using agriculture, its *Total Industry Output* is $298 billion; its *Total Commodity Output* is $295 billion. Conceptually, the two numbers should be equal.

### Production Functions and Input-Output Analysis

The columns of the input-output matrix in Exhibit 9.5 represent mixes of inputs industries use to produce their goods and services. They differ from one another, and the differences are more easily seen in Exhibit 9.6. In Exhibit 9.6 entries in each column in Exhibit 9.5 are divided by total industry output for that column. For example, division of the $110 billion in *Total Value Added* used by *Agriculture, forestry and fisheries* by $298 billion in *Total Industry Output* for agriculture results in the quotient 0.37. In other words, 37 cents of each dollar of agriculture industry output consists of *Value Added*. *Intermediate Inputs* account for the other 63 cents per dollar of output and constitute the relatively most significant single input component of *Total Industry Output* for *Agriculture, forestry, and fisheries*. Among the intermediate product inputs, *Agriculture products* account for 25 cents of each dollar of total output in that industry group; *Construction*, for 1 cent; *Manufacturing*, for 17 cents; and so on.

The differing proportions shown in the column elements represent different recipes used by industry to produce various goods and services. Those recipes—production functions, in professional parlance—used by firms tend to change in response to changes in such things as technology and relative prices. The ques-

**Exhibit 9.6**

**Coefficients for Input Requirements by Industry, 1997**

| Commodity \ Industry | Agriculture, forestry, and fisheries | Mining | Construction | Manufacturing | Transportation, communication, and utilities | Trade | Finance | Services | Other |
|---|---|---|---|---|---|---|---|---|---|
| Agricultural products | 0.25 | 0.00 | 0.01 | 0.04 | 0.00 | 0.00 | 0.00 | 0.00 | 0.00 |
| Minerals | 0.00 | 0.19 | 0.01 | 0.03 | 0.05 | 0.00 | 0.00 | 0.00 | 0.00 |
| Construction | 0.01 | 0.03 | 0.00 | 0.01 | 0.04 | 0.01 | 0.03 | 0.01 | 0.02 |
| Manufacturing products | 0.17 | 0.09 | 0.30 | 0.35 | 0.06 | 0.05 | 0.01 | 0.10 | 0.02 |
| Transportation | 0.04 | 0.07 | 0.02 | 0.05 | 0.16 | 0.04 | 0.02 | 0.04 | 0.02 |
| Trade | 0.05 | 0.02 | 0.08 | 0.06 | 0.01 | 0.02 | 0.00 | 0.02 | 0.00 |
| Finance | 0.07 | 0.16 | 0.02 | 0.02 | 0.03 | 0.07 | 0.16 | 0.07 | 0.01 |
| Services | 0.03 | 0.03 | 0.10 | 0.06 | 0.11 | 0.13 | 0.07 | 0.15 | 0.01 |
| Other | 0.00 | 0.01 | 0.00 | 0.01 | 0.02 | 0.01 | 0.01 | 0.01 | 0.00 |
| **TOTAL INTERMEDIATE INPUTS** | 0.63 | 0.60 | 0.53 | 0.62 | 0.49 | 0.33 | 0.32 | 0.39 | 0.08 |
| **TOTAL VALUE ADDED** | 0.37 | 0.40 | 0.47 | 0.38 | 0.51 | 0.67 | 0.68 | 0.61 | 0.92 |
| **TOTAL INDUSTRY OUTPUT** | 1.00 | 1.00 | 1.00 | 1.00 | 1.00 | 1.00 | 1.00 | 1.00 | 1.00 |

tion becomes one of how rapidly do they change and how serious are those changes for analytical purposes. Given the lag between the year measured and data availability, using input-output analysis analytically requires investigators to assume that production functions are essentially constant or that changes are inconsequential.

### The Algebra of Input-Output Analysis

An economy's total output of a commodity is used in two ways: (1) as an intermediate product and (2) as a final product. For example, as shown in Exhibit 9.5, *Total Commodity Output* for *Manufactured items* in 1997 amounted to about \$3.8 trillion, of which \$2.2 trillion was used for intermediate products and \$1.6 trillion was used for final output. If we designate

$T_i$ As total commodity output for commodity *i*,

$F_i$ As total final output for commodity *i*,

$U_i$ As total intermediate products for commodity *i*,

then in mathematical terms the relationship can be expressed:

$$T_i = F_i + U_i .$$

Total intermediate products consist of the amounts of a commodity used as inputs by industries. In terms of Exhibit 9.5, $U_i$ appears as the number in *i*th row the column labeled *Total Intermediate Products* and represents the sum of the columns of the input-output matrix for the *i*th commodity. Reference to Exhibit 9.6 suggests that total intermediate products, $U_i$, can also be expressed as the sum of each of the coefficients in a row multiplied by its respective total industry output. If we designate

$T_j$ As total output of industry *j*, and

$c_{i,j}$ As the coefficient of commodity *i* and industry *j*, and

*n* As the number of commodities and industries,

then total output for commodity *i* can be expressed:

$$T_i = F_i + c_{i,1} \cdot T_1 + c_{i,2} \cdot T_2 + \ldots + c_{i,j} \cdot T_j + \ldots + c_{i,n-1} \cdot T_{n-1} + c_{i,n} \cdot T_n .$$

Totals of outputs for all commodities produce a set of equations of the form:

$$T_1 = F_1 + c_{1,1} \cdot T_1 + c_{1,2} \cdot T_2 + \ldots + c_{1,j} \cdot T_j + \ldots + c_{1,n-1} \cdot T_{n-1} + c_{1,n} \cdot T_n$$

$$T_2 = F_2 + c_{2,1} \cdot T_1 + c_{2,2} \cdot T_2 + \ldots + c_{2,j} \cdot T_j + \ldots + c_{2,n-1} \cdot T_{n-1} + c_{2,n} \cdot T_n$$

$$\vdots$$

$$T_i = F_i + c_{i,1} \cdot T_1 + c_{i,2} \cdot T_2 + \ldots + c_{i,j} \cdot T_j + \ldots + c_{i,n-1} \cdot T_{n-1} + c_{i,n} \cdot T_n$$

$$\vdots$$

$$T_{n-1} = F_{n-1} + c_{n-1,1} \cdot T_1 + c_{n-1,2} \cdot T_2 + \ldots + c_{n-1,j} \cdot T_j + \ldots + c_{n-1,n-1} \cdot T_{n-1} + c_{n-1,n} \cdot T_n$$

$$T_n = F_n + c_{n,1} \cdot T_1 + c_{n,2} \cdot T_2 + \ldots + c_{n,j} \cdot T_j + \ldots + c_{n,n-1} \cdot T_{n-1} + c_{n,n} \cdot T_n .$$

In terms of Exhibit 9.5, $T_1$ stands for *Total industry output* of agriculture, forestry, and fisheries, and in Exhibit 9.6 the coefficient $c_{1,1}$ equals 0.25, the proportion of agricultural products used to produce total output in that industry.

In the first equation $T_1$ appears twice: first on the left-hand side of the equation and then on the right-hand side multiplied by the first coefficient, $c_{1,1}$. Similarly, for the second equation $T_2$ appears both on the left-hand side and on the right as the multiplier of the second coefficient, $c_{2,2}$. And so on, for each of the equations. Eliminating the duplication and solving each equation for final output produces:

$$F_1 = (1-c_{1,1})\cdot T_1 - c_{1,2}\cdot T_2 - \ldots - c_{1,j}\cdot T_j - \ldots - c_{1,n-1}\cdot T_{n-1} - c_{1,n}\cdot T_n$$
$$F_2 = -c_{2,1}\cdot T_1 + (1-c_{2,2})\cdot T_2 - \ldots - c_{2,j}\cdot T_j - \ldots - c_{2,n-1}\cdot T_{n-1} - c_{2,n}\cdot T_n$$
$$\vdots$$
$$F_i = -c_{i,1}\cdot T_1 - c_{i,2}\cdot T_2 - \ldots + (1-c_{i,i})\cdot T_i - \ldots - c_{i,n-1}\cdot T_{n-1} - c_{i,n}\cdot T_n$$
$$\vdots$$
$$F_{n-1} = -c_{n-1,1}\cdot T_1 - c_{n-1,2}\cdot T_2 - \ldots - c_{n-1,j}\cdot T_j - \ldots + (1-c_{n-1,n-1})\cdot T_{n-1} - c_{n-1,n}\cdot T_n$$
$$F_n = -c_{n,1}\cdot T_1 - c_{n,2}\cdot T_2 - \ldots - c_{n,j}\cdot T_j - \ldots - c_{n,n-1}\cdot T_{n-1} + (1-c_{n,n})\cdot T_n .$$

What we now have is a set of $n$ simultaneous linear equations. They can be expressed more succinctly in matrix notation of the form:

$$\begin{bmatrix} F_1 \\ F_2 \\ \ldots \\ F_n \end{bmatrix} = \begin{bmatrix} (1-c_{1,1}) & -c_{1,2}\cdots & -c_{1,n-1} & -c_{1,n} \\ -c_{2,1} & (1-c_{2,2})\ldots & -c_{2,n-1} & -c_{2,n} \\ \ldots & \ldots & \ldots & \ldots \\ -c_{n,1} & -c_{n,2}\cdots & -c_{n,n-1} & (1-c_{n,n}) \end{bmatrix} \begin{bmatrix} T_1 \\ T_2 \\ \ldots \\ T_n \end{bmatrix}$$

The matrix notation can be reduced further to

$$[F_i] = [c_{i,j}]\cdot[T_i].$$

Typically, we know the final outputs, $F_i$, and want to investigate the effects of a change in final outputs on the economy. What we don't know is total commodity output, $T_i$, required to produce that final output. For example, an investigator might want to know what industries would be affected and by how much from an increase in demand for housing. Or an increase in imports of steel.

But the interrelationships among industries present a challenge. We cannot show total output for an industry until we know the total outputs for the other industries. And we cannot know the total outputs for the other industries until we know the total outputs of all of them. We have to determine a solution for all industries at once—simultaneously.

Happily, our simultaneous equations can perform that feat. However, not all simultaneous linear equations admit of solution. The number of equations has to be equal to the number of unknowns for a unique solution. Since the number of commodity categories equals the number of industry groups, we meet that condition. In addition, the coefficients in the $[c_{i,j}]$ matrix have to meet certain mathematical requirements. In order for the solution to make economic sense, "the sum of the coefficients of each column of its structural matrix should be less than or equal to 1 with at least one of the column sums strictly less than 1."[19] The upper portion of Exhibit 9.7 presents the values for the $[c_{i,j}]$ matrix. In all cases the columns sum to less than 1. Thus, our data satisfy that requirement.

High school students learn how to solve simultaneous linear equations in their algebra classes. Matrix algebra facilitates the process for a large number of equations, as in the case of our example. Solving our nine equations requires multiplying both sides of our condensed matrix equation by the inverse of the $[c_{i,j}]$ matrix. If we designate

$\left[c_{i,j}\right]^{-1}$ as the matrix inverse, the condensed version becomes

$$\left[T_i\right]=\left[c_{i,j}\right]^{-1}\left[F_i\right].$$

What happens to the $[c_{i,j}]$ matrix? Multiplying a matrix by its inverse produces an identity matrix, one with zeros in all cells except the diagonal running from the upper left to the lower right corners where ones appear. It is equivalent to one in scalar arithmetic. The lower portion of Exhibit 9.7 contains the cell values for $[c_{i,j}]^{-1}$.

With the values in the cells of the matrix inverse, we are in position to answer questions about the direct and indirect effects of an increase (or decrease) in final output of a particular commodity. For example, what is the impact of a $1,000,000 increase in the demand for U.S. agricultural products by the rest of the world? In order for final output to increase by $1,000,000, total agriculture industry output has to increase by $2,333,000. Part of the extra output of agricultural products, $1,367,000, is used as intermediate inputs by agriculture, forestry, and fisheries. Other parts are used as intermediate inputs by other industries whose output is indirectly stimulated by the additional final output of agricultural commodities. Completing the matrix multiplication shows that minerals output increases by $25,000; construction by $30,000; manufacturing by $420,000; transportation, communication and utilities by $109,000; trade by $102,000; finance by $154,000; services by $121,000; and other by $12,000. Other things being equal—like the input-output coefficients—total commodity output would increase by $2,333,000 to increase the final output of agricultural products by $1,000,000.

Of course, the effects would be different if the expansion of agricultural products involved grain or dairy products, or lumber or fish. To explore those effects requires use of far more industry detail than that provided by this aggregation to nine industry groups and nine commodities. The 1997 annual input-output tables for the U.S. economy dealing with ninety-seven industries offer

**Exhibit 9.7**

**Input-Output Coefficients Matrix and Its Inverse, 1997**

| Commodity \ Industry | Agriculture, forestry, & fisheries | Mining | Construction | Manufacturing | Transport, communctn, & utilities | Trade | Finance | Services | Other |
|---|---|---|---|---|---|---|---|---|---|
| Agricultural products | 0.75 | (0.00) | (0.01) | (0.04) | (0.00) | (0.00) | (0.00) | (0.00) | (0.00) |
| Minerals | (0.00) | 0.81 | (0.01) | (0.03) | (0.05) | (0.00) | (0.00) | (0.00) | (0.00) |
| Construction | (0.01) | (0.03) | 1.00 | (0.01) | (0.04) | (0.01) | (0.03) | (0.01) | (0.02) |
| Manufacturing products | (0.17) | (0.09) | (0.30) | 0.65 | (0.06) | (0.05) | (0.01) | (0.10) | (0.02) |
| Transportation, communication and utilities | (0.04) | (0.07) | (0.02) | (0.05) | 0.84 | (0.04) | (0.02) | (0.04) | (0.02) |
| Trade | (0.05) | (0.02) | (0.08) | (0.06) | (0.01) | 0.98 | (0.00) | (0.02) | (0.00) |
| Finance | (0.07) | (0.16) | (0.02) | (0.02) | (0.03) | (0.07) | 0.84 | (0.07) | (0.01) |
| Services | (0.03) | (0.03) | (0.10) | (0.06) | (0.11) | (0.13) | (0.07) | 0.85 | (0.01) |
| Other | (0.00) | (0.01) | (0.00) | (0.01) | (0.02) | (0.01) | (0.01) | (0.01) | 1.00 |
| **Inverse of Input-Out Coefficient Matrix** | | | | | | | | | |
| Agricultural products | 1.361 | 0.015 | 0.036 | 0.086 | 0.012 | 0.010 | 0.011 | 0.018 | 0.003 |
| Minerals | 0.025 | 1.247 | 0.033 | 0.067 | 0.086 | 0.010 | 0.005 | 0.013 | 0.007 |
| Construction | 0.030 | 0.050 | 1.014 | 0.024 | 0.055 | 0.017 | 0.041 | 0.019 | 0.024 |
| Manufacturing products | 0.420 | 0.234 | 0.527 | 1.635 | 0.196 | 0.124 | 0.063 | 0.216 | 0.044 |
| Transportation, communication and utilities | 0.109 | 0.138 | 0.080 | 0.115 | 1.222 | 0.075 | 0.043 | 0.072 | 0.027 |
| Trade | 0.102 | 0.052 | 0.123 | 0.114 | 0.042 | 1.037 | 0.014 | 0.042 | 0.008 |
| Finance | 0.154 | 0.271 | 0.069 | 0.082 | 0.088 | 0.109 | 1.212 | 0.117 | 0.014 |
| Services | 0.121 | 0.120 | 0.190 | 0.161 | 0.195 | 0.194 | 0.122 | 1.218 | 0.024 |
| Other | 0.012 | 0.023 | 0.012 | 0.022 | 0.033 | 0.018 | 0.019 | 0.017 | 1.005 |

more detail to deal with such questions. The benchmark input-output accounts also provide detailed estimates for 498 industries.

Effects of changes in final output on total output among industries are not the only issues that can be addressed through input-output analysis. The effects of changes in value added can be similarly addressed. For example, input-output analysis can be adapted to show how an increase in employee compensation in, say, the transportation industry impacts costs in other industries. To perform such calculations we essentially rotate Exhibit 9.5 about the main diagonal of the input-output matrix so that total commodity output appears as a row at the bottom of the table and total industry output appears as a column on the right-hand side. The calculations then proceed in a fashion analogous to examining the effects of changes in final output.

### Changes in the Composition of Final Output

The final output of industries does not change one industry at a time. In response to the demands of households, government, and the rest of the world, final outputs of all industries are changing simultaneously. An indication of the magnitude of those changes is revealed in Exhibit 9.8 that expresses the final output of major business sector industry divisions as a percent of gross domestic product for the years 1959 and 1999. Input-output analysis gives us an idea of the mind-boggling dance between the supply of and demand for primary factor inputs and intermediate goods and services required to accommodate those shifts. Note at the bottom of the table two deductions appear for 1999: one for a \$71.9 billion statistical discrepancy, the other for individuals and nonprofit institutions amounting to \$401.7 billon. Their output is included in the final output along with that of the business sector. The deduction reduces the source of funds to the amount available to the business sector.

From 1959 to 1999 large shifts in percentage point terms have occurred in *Manufacturing*; *Finance, insurance, and real estate*; and *Services*. In 1959 *Manufacturing* was the preeminent industry, accounting for 32 percent of the economy's final output. The next largest contender, *Finance, insurance, and real estate*, with a 15 percent share, was less than half the size. The *Services* division, at 11 percent, was tied with *Retail trade* for third place. By 1999 *Manufacturing* with a 19 percent share of total gross domestic product share had slipped to third place. Over the forty-year period, both durable and nondurable manufactured goods show low rates of growth, despite the fact that durable goods include computer manufacture. The social, economic, and philosophical impact of that innovation far outdistances its economic size relative to other industries. With 25 percent of total final output, *Services* had ascended to first place, its rise having been assisted by the rapid growth in health care services. *Finance, insurance and real estate* had maintained their second-place ranking but increased their share from 15 percent to 23 percent. Rapid growth in banking and other finance and insurance activities accounts for much of that gain.

**Exhibit 9.8**
**Business Sector Final Output by Industry, 1959 and 1999**

| | 1959 Amounts in $ Billions | Percent of Total | 1999 Amounts in $ Billions | Percent of Total |
|---|---|---|---|---|
| Agriculture, forestry,fishing | $ 20.3 | 5 | $ 125.4 | 2 |
| Mining | 12.6 | 3 | 111.8 | 1 |
| Construction | 23.6 | 5 | 416.4 | 5 |
| Manufacturing | 140.3 | 32 | 1,500.8 | 19 |
| Transportation, public utilities | 45.3 | 10 | 779.6 | 10 |
| Wholesale trade | 35.7 | 8 | 643.3 | 8 |
| Retail trade | 49.5 | 11 | 856.4 | 11 |
| Finance, insur., & real estate | 65.5 | 15 | 1,792.1 | 23 |
| Services | 48.4 | 11 | 1,986.9 | 25 |
| Government enterprises | 6.9 | 2 | 133.4 | 2 |
| Statistical discrepancy | 0.8 | 0 | (71.9) | (1) |
| Households & institutions | (12.4) | (3) | (401.7) | (5) |
| **FINAL OUTPUT** | **$ 436.6** | **100** | **$ 7,872.5** | **100** |

*Source* : U. S. Department of Commerce. Bureau of Economic Research. "Gross Product by Industry and the Components of Gross Domestic Income." *Gross Product by Industry Data* . 19 Dec. 2000: Table GPC. 20 Feb. 2001 <http://www.bea.doc.gov/bea/dn2/gpo.htm>. And "Selected NIPA Tables." *National Accounts Data* . 8 Aug. 2000: Table 1.7. 9 Sep. 2000. <http://www.bea.doc.gov/bea/dn1.htm>.

In the face of such shifts, only *Transportation and public utilities*, *Wholesale trade*, and *Government enterprises* maintained constant shares of total final output: 10 percent, 8 percent and 2 percent, respectively. Rapid growth in radio and television broadcasting and cable and other pay television services helped the former maintain its position. *Agricultural, forestry, and fishing*, *Mining*, *Construction*, and *Retail trade* all registered relative declines. Of the three, *Agriculture, forestry, and fishing* experienced the most precipitous decline, dropping from 5 percent in 1959 to 2 percent in 1998. *Mining*'s share, too, dwindled significantly from 3 percent to 1 percent.

## BUSINESS SECTOR SOURCES AND USES OF FUNDS

Input-output analysis breaks down the intermediate, final, and total outputs of all sectors of the economy into their commodity and industry components. The business sector consists of corporations, sole proprietorships, partnerships, other private business—mainly residential housing—and government enterprises and accounts for most of the output. However, households and nonprofit institutions, general government, and the rest of the world make more modest contributions to total commodity output. In this chapter we are focusing on the business sector.

Like each of the other economic sectors we have investigated in the national income and product account framework, the activities of the business sector can be grouped into those that generate funds and those that use funds. Product sales generate funds, and payments to the factors of production and other costs of doing business constitute uses of funds.

In 1999 the business sector—corporations, partnerships, sole proprietorships, other private business, and government enterprises—produced $7,872.5 billion in final outputs of goods and services.[20] What is true for the entire economy is also true for the business sector: sources and uses of funds are equal. Exhibit 9.9 presents components of business sector uses of funds. The bottom line—the business sector's *Total uses of funds*—equals the value of the goods and services it produced, $7,872.6 billion in 1999.

The cost of labor and property supplied by U.S. residents to produce goods and services appears by forms of business organization: corporations, proprietorships and partnerships, other private business, and government enterprises. *Corporate business* costs head the list, and, at $5.2 trillion account, for close to two-thirds of the business sector's uses of funds. Employee compensation—*Wages and salaries*, $3,082.1 billion, and *Supplements to wages and salaries*, $503.1—totals $3,585.2 and makes up 69 percent of corporations' cost of factors of production. It constitutes as well the largest use of funds for *Government enterprises*. For all four types of organizations, employment compensation amounts to $4,048.7 billion, 51 percent of all business sector uses of funds.

The cost of other factor inputs involves the use of property in the output of goods and services. They take the form of allowances for depreciation on plant and equipment and payments of interest, rents, and returns to owners.

Payments of interest appear for *Corporate business*, *Proprietorships and partnerships*, and *Other private business*. *Net interest paid* makes up over half of the total factor payments for *Other private business*, $341.5 billion out of $674.0 billion. It exceeds *Net interest paid* by each of the other two sectors although their costs of factor inputs exceed that of other private business by a wide margin.

*Consumption of fixed capital* is a factor input payment common to all forms of business organization. In the aggregate it totals to $990.8 billion. It "is a charge for the using up of private and government fixed capital located in the United States . . . based on studies of prices of used equipment and structures in resale markets."[21] Computer software is not used up, but it does become obsolete. The eleventh comprehensive revision of the NIPA released in October 1999 recognizes software as an investment and includes its loss of value from obsolescence in its estimates of consumption of fixed capital.[22] Those estimates, developed by the BEA, appear in Exhibit 9.9 as *Consumption of fixed capital*. The private sector has its own idea about how much its plant and equipment has

**Exhibit 9.9**
**Domestic Business Sector Uses of Funds, 1999**

| | | 1999 Amounts in $ Billions | Percent of Total | |
|---|---|---|---|---|
| **Corporate business** | | **$ 5,169.2** | | **66** |
| Wages and salaries | $3,082.1 | | 39 | |
| Supplements to wages and salaries | 503.1 | | 6 | |
| Net interest paid | 162.5 | | 2 | |
| Consumption of fixed capital | 676.9 | | 9 | |
| Capital consumption adjustment | 42.1 | | 1 | |
| Inventory valuation adjustment | (9.1) | | (0) | |
| Corporate profits before tax | 711.6 | | 9 | |
| **Proprietorships & partnerships** | | **1,244.1** | | **16** |
| Wages and salaries | $ 308.4 | | 4 | |
| Supplements to wages and salaries | 36.6 | | 0 | |
| Net interest paid | 120.2 | | 2 | |
| Consumption of fixed capital | 119.0 | | 2 | |
| Capital consumption adjustment | 45.0 | | 1 | |
| Inventory valuation adjustment | (1.4) | | (0) | |
| Proprietor income | 616.3 | | 8 | |
| **Other private business** | | **674.0** | | **9** |
| Wages and salaries | $ 17.8 | | 0 | |
| Supplements to wages and salaries | 2.2 | | 0 | |
| Net interest paid | 341.5 | | 4 | |
| Rent | 199.4 | | 3 | |
| Consumption of fixed capital | 165.6 | | 2 | |
| Capital consumption adjustment | (56.6) | | (1) | |
| Proprietor income with IVA | 4.1 | | 0 | |
| **Government enterprises** | | **127.8** | | **2** |
| Wages and salaries | $ 72.2 | | 1 | |
| Supplements to wages and salaries | 26.3 | | 0 | |
| Consumption of fixed capital | 29.3 | | 0 | |
| **Indirect business taxes & nontaxes** | | **718.1** | | **9** |
| **Business transfer payments** | | **39.7** | | **1** |
| **Subsidies net gov't enterprise surplus** | | **(28.4)** | | **(0)** |
| **Statistical discrepancy** | | **(71.9)** | | **(1)** |
| **TOTAL USES OF FUNDS** | | **$ 7,872.6** | | **100** |

*Source*: U.S. Department of Commerce. Bureau of Economic Analysis. "'Annual Only' NIPA Tables." *National Accounts Data*. 30 Aug 2000: Tables 1.15, 1.16, and 8.14. 5 Sep. 2000. <http://www.bea.doc.gov/bea/dn1.htm> and "Selected NIPA Tables." *National Accounts Data*: Table 1.9. 8 Aug. 2000. 9 Sep. 2000. <http://www.bea.doc.gov/bea/dn1.htm>.

depreciated, and the difference between the BEA's consumption of fixed capital and the private sector's estimate is shown as *Capital consumption adjustment.*

Buildings, machinery, equipment, and software either wear out as a result of being used to produce goods and services or become obsolete because of technological change and innovation. Unlike transactions involving the sale (and purchase) of goods and services where prices can be observed, depreciation represents an estimate by thousands of individuals and firms. Generally accepted accounting practice provides guidance on those estimates, but when filling out their income tax returns—the source of those estimates for the BEA—individuals and businesses may have something else in mind besides the effect of their estimates on the NIPA. Aware of possible biases and having government's usual predilections toward standardization, BEA's estimates of consumption of fixed capital attempt to use a consistent approach to measuring the extent to which the nation's stock of fixed capital loses value each year.

For *Corporate business*, for example, the BEA estimates *Consumption of fixed capital* as $676.9 billion. Corporations on their tax returns estimated their consumption of fixed capital to be $42.1 billion more. The difference appears as a *Capital consumption adjustment* in Exhibit 9.9. Businesses include $42.1 billion as depreciation expenses on the corporate income tax returns. The BEA shows *Capital consumption adjustment* in NIPA presentations as an adjustment increasing *Corporate profits before tax.*

In the case of *Proprietorships and partnerships*, BEA estimates *Consumption of fixed capital* as $119.0 billion. Proprietors and partners feel it is $45.0 billion more, as shown by the *Capital consumption adjustment.* In the case of *Other private business*, the *Capital consumption adjustment* is a negative $56.6 billion. Here, the BEA's estimate of consumption of fixed capital exceeds private estimates, suggesting that, based on its standard, the private sector underestimates the extent to which its fixed capital has depreciated and thus overestimates is rental income.

The *Inventory valuation adjustment* requires comment. The NIPA do not recognize capital gains and capital losses. A firm that records its withdrawals from inventory at the acquisition cost of those items may reflect implicit capital gains in its estimate of corporate profits. If replacement costs of the withdrawn items have increased, the cost of goods sold is understated, and profits are overstated. In national income accounting, that is a "no-no" since all inputs are to be valued at current prices. To avoid the distortion, costs of inventory withdrawals are calculated at their replacement cost, and differences between replacement and acquisition cost generate the inventory valuation adjustment. *Corporate profits before tax* and *Proprietor income* would be reduced. In the aggregate the *Inventory valuation adjustment* amounts to only a negative $10.5 billion—minus $9.1 billion for corporations and minus $1.4 billion for proprietorships and partnerships.

*Corporate profits before tax* extracted by the BEA from the federal corporate income tax returns of domestic corporations are altered to reflect NIPA standards. The corporate sector of the NIPA includes the Federal Reserve banks, Federal home loan banks, the Federal Home Loan Mortgage Corporation, and Federal land banks, but those entities do not file corporation returns. *Corporate profits before tax* for the banking industry includes the net earnings of the Federal Reserve banks based on the annual report of the Board of Governors of the Federal Reserve System. Net earnings on the financial statements prepared by the other agencies appear in the before tax profits of credit agencies other than banks.[23]

*Corporate profits before tax* reflect many other adjustments. Capital gains reported on the corporate returns among corporate receipts and capital losses reported as deductions on the returns are excluded from the NIPA. The national income accounts exclude allowances for depletion. In addition, actual bad debt losses replace allowances for bad debt on the deduction side for national income accounting purposes.

In addition to payments for the inputs used to produce goods and services, the business sector incurs other costs of doing business. They appear in Exhibit 9.9 as *Indirect business taxes and nontaxes* and *Business transfer payments*. Both of those concepts are familiar. Chapters 6 and 7 dealt with *Indirect business taxes and nontaxes* as sources of funds for the federal, state, and local governments. Chapter 2 dealt with personal income and covered business transfer payments to persons. In Exhibit 9.9 the $39.7 billion for *Business transfer payments* also includes $9.9 billion for transfer payments to the rest of the world consisting of income taxes paid to foreign governments on income earned abroad.

*Subsidies net of government enterprise surplus* amounting to negative $28.6 billion and a *Statistical discrepancy* of negative $71.9 billion bring total uses of funds into alignment with total sources. Subsidies represent a source of funds to the business sector and therefore appropriately are shown as negative figures in a presentation designed to show uses of funds. Surpluses of government enterprises, on the other hand, would be equivalent to corporate profits and proprietor income as uses of funds and appear as a positive number. That the figure is negative suggests that subsidies are greater than government enterprises surpluses, if any. Its negative sign suggests as well that subsidizing certain commodities at the expense of others has reduced the business sector's output of goods and services. Deflated output results from inflated egos substituting what they think consumers should have for what consumers really want.

As the year 2000 presidential election results demonstrate, measurement of reality—even something as discrete as a ballot vote—is subject to error and debate. For the NIPA that margin of error is reflected in the *Statistical discrepancy*. Estimates of uses and sources of funds do not come from the same sources, and something somewhere gets left out or added in erroneously. Just plain mistakes may explain some of the difference, too.

**Exhibit 9.10**
**Domestic Private Business Saving and Investment, 1999**

| | | 1999 Amounts in $ Billions | | | Percent of Total | |
|---|---|---|---|---|---|---|
| Corporate profits before tax | | | $ 822.9 | | | 22 |
| Domestic corporations | | $ 711.6 | | | 19 | |
| Foreign subsidiaries (net) | | 111.4 | | | 3 | |
| Profits tax liability | | | (255.9) | | | (7) |
| Profits after tax | | | $ 567.0 | | | 15 |
| Dividends (net) | | | (370.7) | | | (10) |
| Undistributed profits | | | $ 196.3 | | | 5 |
| Domestic corporations | | $ 126.7 | | | 3 | |
| Foreign subsidiaries | | 69.6 | | | 2 | |
| Inventory valuation adjustment | | | (9.1) | | | (0) |
| Capital consumption adjustment | | | 42.1 | | | 1 |
| **CORPORATE NET SAVING** | | | **$ 229.3** | | | **6** |
| Change in liabilities | | | 3,406.3 | | | 92 |
| Flow-of-funds discrepancy | | | 87.2 | | | 2 |
| Federal access rights adjustment | | | (1.7) | | | (0) |
| **CHANGE IN LIAB & NET WORTH** | | | **$ 3,721.2** | | | **100** |
| Change in financial assets | | | 3,294.8 | | | 89 |
| Change in tangible assets (Net inv.) | | | 426.4 | | | 11 |
| Capital expenditures (Gross inv.) | | $1,242.1 | | | 33 | |
| Nonresidential | $ 1,144.4 | | | 31 | | |
| Residential | 54.4 | | | 1 | | |
| Busn. inventories | 43.3 | | | 1 | | |
| Consumption of fixed capital | | (815.7) | | | (22) | |
| **CHANGE IN TOTAL ASSETS** | | | **$ 3,721.2** | | | **100** |

*Source*: Board of Governors, Federal Reserve System. "Z.1 Historical data." 15 Sep. 2000. *Flow of Funds Accounts of the United States*. 18 Sep. 2000. <http://www.bog.frb.us/releases/z1/current/data.htm>

## Saving and Investment

Sales of the final output of the private business sector constitute a source of funds. The figures appearing in Exhibit 9.9 for business sector value added show how the funds are used. For the other three sectors that we have examined, tables for use of funds show saving (or dissaving) by the sector. No such figure can be found in Exhibit 9.9. Where has it gone?

In accordance with the conventions of the NIPA, *Proprietor income* is attributed to persons in the household and nonprofit institutions sector. Only *Corporate profits before tax* remains as a likely candidate for a source of saving, but taxes and dividends have not yet been deducted. For those adjustments we turn to Exhibit 9.10.

*Corporate profits before tax* for 1999 of $711.6 billion in Exhibit 9.9 represents only the profits of domestic corporations. Some U.S. domestic corporations have foreign subsidiaries. Corporate profits receipts from them amounted to $169.3 billion in 1999. Foreign corporations have subsidiaries in the United States, and those firms' profits result in a deduction of $57.9 billion to produce a *Foreign subsidiaries (net)* figure of $111.4 billion. Profits of *Domestic corporations* and *Foreign subsidiaries (net)* sum to $822.9 billion, *Corporate profits before tax* for 1999.

Deduction of a *Profits tax liability* of $255.9 billion nets to $567.0 billion, *Profits after tax* in 1999. The profits tax liability amounts to 31 percent of *Profits before tax.* Data for 1959 show that in that year the profits tax liability amounted to 44 percent of profits before tax. The effective tax rate has dropped! Artificial legal persons, namely, corporations, have fared better at tax collectors' hands than real persons. Our earlier examination revealed in Exhibit 5.1 that personal taxes and nontaxes as a percentage of personal income reached a forty-year high in 1999. Perhaps the differing trends in tax burdens reflect emergence of sound tax policy. Or perhaps they result from the fact that real people vote with ballots while artificial persons—or their masters—vote with campaign contributions.

Corporations can do two things with profits after tax: they can declare dividends or they can retain the earnings. The latter course of action represents net saving. In 1999 *Dividends (net)* amounted to $370.7 billion, about 65 percent of *Profits after tax.* In 1959 dividends accounted for 43 percent of after-tax profits. What the tax collector relieves, stockholders receive.

Of the $196.3 billion in *Undistributed profits*, a.k.a., retained earnings, *Domestic corporations* held $126.7 billion, and *Foreign subsidiaries* held $69.6 billion. That domestic retained earnings exceed foreign retained earnings is not surprising. However, relatively a far greater share of subsidiaries' profits before tax is retained than those of domestic corporations. The $126.7 billion in domestic corporation retained earnings is 18 percent of its $711.6 billion *Corporate profits before tax.* For subsidiaries the percentage is 62 percent. In 1959, on the other hand, retained earnings of both domestic corporations and foreign subsidiaries were 32 percent of their respective profits before tax. Sometimes getting offshore profits on shore is not a sure thing.

The BEA would not consider *Undistributed profits* to be equivalent to corporate net saving because it does not recognize adjustments for inventory valuation and capital consumption. Adding those two figures, a negative $9.1 billion for *Inventory valuation adjustment* and $42.1 billion for the *Capital consumption adjustment*, to undistributed profits produces *Corporate Net Saving*.

*Corporate Net Saving* of $229.3 billion represents the NIPA-defined change in net worth of the business sector. *Change in Liabilities and Net Worth* amounts to $3,721.2 billion. That increase results from an accompanying *Change in liabilities* of $3,406.3 billion plus a corrective *Flow-of-funds discrepancy* adjustment of $87.2 billion for statistical error occurring in the construction of flow of funds data and a reduction of $1.7 billion for *Federal access rights adjustment*. Federal access rights are not recognized by the NIPA but are included in the flow of funds accounts.

The *Change in financial assets* of $3,294.8 billion and the *Change in tangible assets (Net investment)* of $426.4 billion equate to the total *Change in Liabilities and Net Worth*. The *Change in financial assets* accounts for a much larger share of the *Change in Total Assets* in 1999 than in 1959. In 1959 it accounted for 72 percent; in 1999, 91 percent. The portfolio of corporate assets appears to be shifting away from capital items.

*Capital expenditures (Gross investment)* of $1,242.1 billion are offset by $815.7 billion for *Consumption of fixed capital* of corporations, proprietorships, and partnerships, and the portion of other private business that does not relate to investments of households and nonprofit institutions. The deductions result in a net change in tangible assets of $426.4 billion, an addition to the stock of productive capital. We shall see later that the stock of capital used in production makes a difference in the amount of goods and services produced.

## SUMMARY

In 1996, the business sector consisted of 23.2 million businesses. Most of them were sole proprietorships. Just 7 percent were partnerships. Corporations made up 20 percent of the total.

Maximizing profits motivates business behavior. The evidence presented here indicates that profit making constitutes a challenging goal. Only 69 percent of businesses reported positive net income. Corporations fared poorest in the profit-making arena with just 56 percent reporting positive net income. Despite being outnumbered and outperformed in percent making a profit, corporations account for 89 percent of all business receipts.

Corporations differ greatly among themselves with respect to size. Most of them—90 percent—have total assets of less than $1 million. The largest, those with total assets of over $250 million—0.2 percent of the number of corporations—hold 85 percent of the assets and account for 56 percent of business receipts. With greater size come apparent promises of improved performance and larger profit margins. Competition among equals imperils achieving that profit objective but is essential in a free-enterprise system.

Input-output analysis provides insights into the relationships among industries. One firm's output often serves as other firms' input in the march toward producing final goods and services for consumers, government, and the rest of the world. Input-output analysis provides a structure for viewing those interrelationships and can be used to estimate the total economic effects of changes in final output, factor price changes, and other exogenous influences.

From 1959 to 1998 growth in the output of service industries surpassed that of the others and now exceeds the output of any one of the other major industry groups. Those industries dealing with raw material products—agriculture, forestry, fishing, and mining—have shown the slowest growth rates, and their share of total output of goods and services has dropped markedly. Manufacturing was the largest industry group in 1959, accounting for 28 percent of total output. By the end of the thirty-nine-year period, its share declined to 16 percent, having been surpassed in size not only by services but also by finance, insurance, and real estate.

Only undistributed profits of corporations comprise the net savings of the business sector. Net income of sole proprietorships and partnerships are attributed to households and nonprofit institutions. Undistributed profits together with a net increase in liabilities over financial assets provided the funding for business sector net investment in 1999. The resulting capital formation contributes to worker productivity.

We now have completed our examination of the four major economic sectors. Assembling those four sectors into the national accounting aggregates now can begin.

## NOTES

1. Calvin Coolidge, Speech to the American Society of Newspaper Editors, 17 Jan. 1925, John Bartlett, *Bartlett's Familiar Quotations*, 125th ed. (Boston, Toronto: Little, Brown and Company, 1991) 736.
2. U.S. Department of Commerce, Bureau of Economic Analysis, *National Income and Product Accounts of the United States, 1929–94*, Vol. 1 (Washington, DC: U.S. Government Printing Office, April 1998) M-15.
3. U.S. Department of the Treasury, Internal Revenue Service, *1995 Instructions for Form 1040 and Schedules A, B, C, D, E, EIC, and SE.* (Washington, DC: U.S. Government Printing Office, 1994).
4. U.S. Department of the Treasury, Internal Revenue Service, *1995 Instructions for Form 1065* (Washington, DC: U.S. Government Printing Office, 1994).
5. *National Income and Product Accounts of the United States, 1929–94* M-15.
6. U.S. Department of the Treasury, Internal Revenue Service, *Statistics of Income—1994: Corporation Income Tax Returns* (Washington, DC: U.S. Government Printing Office, 1997) 7.
7. U.S. Department of the Treasury, Internal Revenue Service, *Statistics of Income—1996: Corporation Income Tax Returns*, IRS Publication 16 (Revised 9-99): Table 4, 17 Nov. 2000 <http://www.irs.ustreas.gov/plain/ tax_stats/soi/corp-complete.html>.
8. Donald Dewey, *The Antitrust Experiment in America* (New York: Columbia University Press, 1990) 6.
9. Dewey 43.
10. U.S. Department of Commerce, Bureau of Economic Analysis, "Benchmark Input-Output Accounts for the U.S. Economy, 1992," *Survey of Current Business* (Nov.

1997): M-13.

11. Wassily Leontief, *Input-Output Economics,* 2nd ed. (New York, Oxford: Oxford University Press, 1986) 4.

12. U.S. Department of Commerce, Bureau of Economic Analysis, "Wassily Leontief and His Contributions to Economic Accounting," *Survey of Current Business* (Mar. 1999): 9.

13. Ronald E. Miller and Peter D. Blair, *Input-Output Analysis: Foundations and Extensions* (Englewood Cliffs, NJ: Prentice Hall, Inc., 1985) 266.

14. "Benchmark Input-Output Accounts for the U.S. Economy, 1992," *Survey of Current Business*: M-8.

15. "Benchmark Input-Output Accounts for the U.S. Economy, 1992," *Survey of Current Business*: M-2.

16. U.S. Department of Commerce, Bureau of Economc Analysis, "Interindustry Relatioships in the U.S. Economy: New Annual Input-Output Estimates for 1997," *BEA News Release* (18 Dec. 2000), 8 Jan. 2001 <http://www.bea.doc.gov/bea/newsrel/io1200.htm>.

17. "Benchmark Input-Output Accounts for the U.S. Economy, 1992," *Survey of Current Business*: M-23.

18. "Benchmark Input-Output Accounts for the U.S. Economy, 1992," *Survey of Current Business*: M-14.

19. Leontief, 26.

20. U.S. Department of Commerce, Bureau of Economic Analysis, "Selected NIPA Tables," *National Accounts Data*, 8 Aug. 2000: Table 1.7, 9 Sep. 2000 <http://www.bea.doc.gov/bea/dn1.htm>.

21. *National Income and Product Accounts of the United States, 1929–94* M-8.

22. Eugene P. Seskin, "Improved Estimates of the National Income and Product Accounts for 1959-98: Results of the Comprehensive Revision," *Survey of Current Business* (December 1999): 23.

23. U.S. Department of Commerce, Bureau of Economic Analysis, *Corporate Profits: Profits Before Tax, Profits Tax Liability, and Dividends* Methodology Paper No. 2 (Washington, DC: U.S. Government Printing Office, 1985) 18.

# 10

# Bringing the Sectors Together

The national income and product statistics available for each of the major economic sectors together with flow-of-funds data, balance-of-payments accounts, and input-output analysis tell us much about the output of goods and services, their uses, and flows of income and expenditures. However, dealing individually with each sector does not present a comprehensive and complete picture of the economy. Data for households and nonprofit institutions serving primarily people, for government, for the rest of the world, and for business are interrelated.

For an overview of the entire economy, we need an aggregate that brings sector information together in a meaningful manner. The national income and product statistic accomplishing that objective is known as Gross Domestic Product (GDP). It is the most familiar and widely used economic aggregate not only in the United States but also throughout the world. GDP has become the generally accepted accounting standard for estimating a country's output of goods and services produced by the factors of production located within its borders. It serves as an indicator for measuring short-term economic performance and for comparing U.S. economic productivity with other countries.

Estimates of annual GDP represent the prices and quantities of final outputs—goods and services for consumption and investment—produced by labor and other inputs located in the United States.[1] It includes such things as refrigerators, lettuce, haircuts, houses, garbage hauling, gasoline, police protection, and computers. It's called gross because no allowance is made for depreciation or capital consumption—the disappearance of machinery, equipment, and structures used up in producing other goods, services, machinery, and equipment. The grossness of GDP results in an estimate that provides a gauge of all the output produced by an economy over a specified period of time. Although ignoring depreciation may seem to result in an overstatement, the absolute accuracy of any output at a point in time is not as important as consistency and comparability over time. Moreover, neglecting to recognize consumption of fixed capital is not the only failure to recognize resources used up in the production process. Production of goods and services frequently involves depletion of nonrenewable energy sources and mineral deposits and fouling fresh water, clean air, and other things people value. We even use up ourselves. No allowances are made for those losses. If an attempt were made, who could set a generally accepted value on them?

As already observed, GDP represents the market value of the *final* goods and services produced in the United States during a given period. Those goods and services have a measurable market value because they are bought and sold. Note the emphasis on *final* goods and services produced by the economy. The accounting convention of measuring only *final* goods and services relates in a very fundamental way to the purpose of all economic activity. The purpose of all those people dutifully going off to work every weekday morning—and often on weekends as well—is consumption—using up goods and services to satisfy human wants and needs.

Typically people do not consume everything they produce, however, either as individuals or as a society. Something is set aside. From the standpoint of an individual, prospects of such things as buying Christmas toys, a vacation trip, a college education, and retirement provide incentives for putting something aside for personal saving. For businesses, governments, and the economy as a whole, some saved resources are used to produce capital goods, investments that assist in producing future goods and services—such things as buildings, machinery, highways, and airports. Thus it is that GDP profoundly reflects the purpose of all economic activity, providing for the welfare and enjoyment of the population, and the question of economic choice, addressing how much to consume today and how much to invest today for tomorrow.

Note also that in order to be counted in GDP, goods and services have to be produced by labor and capital located in the United States. GDP measures goods and services produced by factors of production *located in* the United States. Under that definition the output of an automobile plant owned by a Japanese firm but located in Kentucky gets counted. Similarly, the market value of grapes picked by a farm worker in California who is a resident of Guatemala is recorded as part of GDP. On the other hand, some U.S. residents own factors of production located in the rest of the world. Output from those facilities is not included in U.S. GDP.

GDP can be constructed from information we have accumulated about the four economic sectors. Consequently, GDP contains no new information but summarizes it in a manner that shows the relationship between final goods and services produced and the costs involved in their production. However, GDP is not formed by simply combining (adding up) the four sectors. Constructing GDP from the accounts for the four economic sectors involves consolidation—selecting some transactions and omitting others and is not entirely straightforward. Showing the relationship between the four sectors and GDP constitutes a major function of this chapter.

## GROSS DOMESTIC PRODUCT

Like accounts for each of the economic sectors, GDP is recorded with two sets of entries, one recording the market value of the goods and services produced and sold for consumption and investment and the other recording the costs involved in producing those goods and services. The definition of GDP determines the relevant transactions in the sector accounts. First, for the output (or source-of-funds) side of GDP, we wish to identify all transactions involving marketable goods and services. Those exchanges include:

- purchases and sales of goods and services for consumption,
- purchases and sales of structures and equipment for investment, and
- exports and imports of goods and services.

For the value-added (or uses-of-funds) side of GDP, we need to identify those transactions involved in the cost of producing goods and services. They include:

- payments to/receipts from factors of production:
    - employee compensation
    - rent
    - interest
    - profit;
- business transfer payments;
- indirect business taxes;
- government subsidies net of government enterprise current surpluses;
- consumption of fixed capital; and
- receipts from/payments to factor income from/to rest of the world.

Like each of the individual sectors, double-entry accounting requires that GDP uses of funds equals its sources of funds.

Exhibit 10.1 displays the results of bringing together information from each of the four sectors and displaying them in the GDP format for the year 1999. Sure enough, GDP uses of funds equals its sources of funds. The balancing number is $9,299.2 billion—almost, but not quite, $9.3 trillion.

Cost of producing goods and services—the valued-added or income or uses-of-funds side of GDP—appears on the left side of Exhibit 10.1. It measures amounts paid by producers to employees for labor compensation and to owners of property in the form of rent, interest, and profits. It also includes allowances for the consumption of productive capital, other costs associated with production processes, and certain adjustments. Those other costs include taxes and business transfer payments. Adjustments include recognition of government subsidies net of surpluses of government enterprises, net factor payments to the rest of the world, and a statistical discrepancy.

Final goods and services produced—the product or output or sources-of-funds side of GDP—appears on the right in the table and can be presented in

**Exhibit 10.1**
**Gross Domestic Product Uses and Sources of Funds, 1999**

| Exhibit References | | | 1999 Amounts in $ Billions |
|---|---|---|---|
| | **Compensation of employees** | | **$ 5,299.8** |
| 2.2 | Wage and salary accruals | | 4,475.1 |
| 2.2 | Private sector | $3,750.7 | |
| 2.2 | Government | 724.4 | |
| | Supplements to wages and salaries | | 824.6 |
| 7.10 | Employer social insur contributions | $ 323.6 | |
| 2.3 | Other labor income | 501.0 | |
| 2.4 | **Proprietors' income with IVA & CCAdj** | | **663.5** |
| 2.5 | **Rental income of persons with CCAdj** | | **143.4** |
| | **Corporate profits with IVA & CCAdj** | | **856.0** |
| | Corporate profits with IVA | | 813.9 |
| 9.10 | Profits before tax | $ 823.0 | |
| 9.10 | Inventory valuation adjustment | (9.1) | |
| 9.10 | Capital consumption adjustment | | 42.1 |
| | **Net interest** | | **507.1** |
| 2.7 | Paid by domestic business | $ 624.2 | |
| 2.7 | Paid by rest of the world | (117.0) | |
| | **NATIONAL INCOME** | | **7,469.7** |
| 9.9 | **Business transfer payments** | | **39.7** |
| 2.8 | Payments to persons | $ 29.7 | |
| | Payments to the rest of the world | 9.9 | |
| 7.10 | **Indirect business tax and nontax accruals** | | **718.1** |
| | **Subsidies less government enterprise surplus** | | **(28.4)** |
| 7.11 | Government subsidies | $ (43.9) | |
| 7.11 | Surplus of government enterprises | 15.6 | |
| | **Consumption of fixed capital** | | **1,161.0** |
| 9.9 | Private | | 961.4 |
| 7.12 | Government | | 199.6 |
| | **GROSS NATIONAL INCOME** | | **9,360.1** |
| 8.2 | Income from the rest of the world | | (305.9) |
| 8.2 | Income paid to the rest of the world | | 316.9 |
| | **GROSS DOMESTIC INCOME** | | **(9,371.1)** |
| 9.9 | Statistical discrepancy | | (71.9) |
| | **GROSS DOMESTIC PRODUCT** | | **$ 9,299.2** |

*Sources* : U.S. Department of Commerce. Bureau of Economic Analysis. "Selected NIPA Tables." *National Accounts Data* . 8 Aug. 2000: Tables 1.9, 1.14, & 3.1. 9 Sep. 2000. <http://www.bea.doc.gov/bea/dn1.htm>.and "'Annual Only' NIPA Tables." *National Accounts Data* . 30 Aug. 2000: Tables 6.15B & 8.16. 5 Sep. 2000. <http://www.bea.doc.gov/bea/dn1.htm>.

**Exhibit 10.1 (continued)**
**Gross Domestic Product Uses and Sources of Funds, 1999**

| Exhibit References | | | 1999 Amounts in $ Billions | |
|---|---|---|---|---|
| | **Personal consumption expenditures** | | | **$ 6,268.7** |
| 3.3 | Durable goods | | $ 761.3 | |
| 3.3 | Nondurable goods | | 1,845.5 | |
| 3.3 | Services | | 3,661.9 | |
| | **Gross private domestic investment** | | | **1,650.1** |
| | Fixed investment | | | 1,606.8 |
| | Structures & producers' durable equipment | | $1,203.1 | |
| 3.4 | Nonprofit institutions | 58.7 | | |
| 9.10 | Business sector | 1,144.4 | | |
| | Residential | | 403.8 | |
| 3.4 | Households | $ 349.4 | | |
| 9.10 | Business sector | 54.4 | | |
| 9.10 | Change in business inventories | | | 43.3 |
| | **Net exports of goods and services** | | | **(254.0)** |
| | Exports | | | 990.2 |
| 8.2 | Durable goods | | $ 504.5 | |
| 8.2 | Nondurable goods | | 194.7 | |
| 8.2 | Services | | 291.0 | |
| | Imports | | | (1,244.2) |
| 8.2 | Durable goods | | $ (715.4) | |
| 8.2 | Nondurable goods | | (333.2) | |
| 8.2 | Services | | (195.6) | |
| | **Government consumption & investment** | | | **1,634.4** |
| 7.11 | Consumption expenditures | | | 1,325.8 |
| 7.12 | Gross investment | | | 308.7 |
| | **GROSS DOMESTIC PRODUCT** | | | **$ 9,299.2** |

*Note*: IVA, inventory valuation adjustment; CCAdj, capital consumption adjustment.

*Sources*: U.S. Department of Commerce. Bureau of Economic Analysis. "Selected NIPA Tables." *National Accounts Data*. 8 Aug. 2000: 1.1, 1.6, 3.7, 4.1. 9 Sep. 2000. <http://www.bea.doc.gov/bea/dn1.htm>. and Board of Governors, Federal Reserve System. "Z.1 Historical data." *Flow of Funds Accounts of the United States*. 15 Sep. 2000: Table F.6. 18 Sep. 2000. <http://www.bog.frb.us/releases/z1/current/data.htm>.

various forms: by type of product, by purchaser, by use, by area of the country, and by state. Here sources of funds are shown by purchaser and use.

All the basic numbers have been seen before, but anyone who, having read this material once, remembers exactly where should get a life. For those of us whose recall is not so perfect, the first column of Exhibit 10.1 contains the reference number for each of the exhibits where the data appeared. A quick glance at the reference numbers shows that households and nonprofit institutions covered in chapters 2 and 3 supplied the expenditures that make up over 70 percent of the sources of GDP.

Our examination of each of the four sectors included showing their sources and uses of current income and of their saving and investment. That information was summarized in two sets of tables. One set deals with sources and uses of current funds, namely, income and expenditure. The other set deals with saving and investment, namely, changes in net worth, liabilities, financial assets, and capital assets. Information from both sets is required to construct estimates for GDP.

### Households and Nonprofit Institutions

Details for *Wage and salary accruals*, *Other labor income*, *Proprietors' income with inventory valuation adjustment and capital consumption adjustment*, *Rental income of persons with capital consumption adjustment*, *Net interest*, and *Business transfer payments to persons* can be found in Exhibits 2.2, 2.3, 2.4, 2.5, 2.7, and 2.8. For the household and nonprofit institution sector, they appear as sources of funds. For GDP those same numbers appear as uses of funds.

In most instances the numbers in Exhibit 10.1 are shown in their reference tables. In a few they have to be derived in a fairly straightforward manner. For example, Exhibit 2.2 identifies explicitly *Wage and salary accruals*, \$4,475.1, and *Government* wage and salary accruals, \$724.4. *Private sector* wage and salary accruals have to be derived as the difference between the total and government wages and salaries or as the sum of the detail, including the rest of the world, which appears as a negative \$5.4 billion.

Just as sources of funds for the household and nonprofit institutions sector account for most of the uses of funds for GDP, its uses of funds account for most of GDP's sources of funds. Exhibit 3.3 showing *Personal consumption expenditures* by type of product constitutes the reference for \$6,268.7 billion of GDP's \$9.3 trillion total sources of funds. Expenditures for *Gross private domestic investment* in *Structures and producers' durable equipment* by *Nonprofit institutions* and in *Residential* structures by *Households* come from Exhibit 3.4 dealing with personal saving and investment.

### Federal, State, and Local Government

Our quest for the origins of other numbers for uses of funds then takes us to chapter 7. In Exhibit 7.10 we find *Employer contributions to social insurance* of

$323.6 billion and *Indirect business taxes and nontaxes* of $718.1. *Government consumption of fixed capital* takes us to Exhibit 7.12, the government sector's saving and investment summary for 1999. For GDP sources of funds, we turn to Exhibit 7.11 for government *Consumption expenditures* of $1,325.8 billion. For *Gross investment* of $308.7, the basis is once again Exhibit 7.12.

### Rest of the World

Exhibit 8.2 for the rest of the world provides information for both GDP sources and uses of funds. *Income from the rest of the world*, $305.9 billion, appears in Exhibit 10.1 as a negative number since we are concerned with deriving GDP uses of funds, and receipts are a form of negative uses. Income paid to the rest of the world, a use of funds, is a positive $316.9 billion—reminding us once again that, because we owe foreigners more than they owe us, we pay more income to those abroad than we receive. On the sources-of-funds side of GDP, we see that the figures for *Net exports of goods and services* are also derived from Exhibit 8.2. Here the $990.2 billion in *Exports* appears as a positive number; *Imports* of $1,244.2 billion as negative. Because in absolute terms imports are larger than exports, the net becomes a negative $254.0 billion.

### Business Sector

To fill in the rest of the blanks we turn chapter 9 and its treatment of the business sector. The underlying detail for *Corporate profits with inventory valuation adjustment and capital consumption adjustment* amounting to $856.0 billion are found in Exhibit 9.10. Entries in Exhibit 9.9 complete our quest for GDP uses of funds and provide the data for *Business transfer payments* of $39.7 billion, *Private consumption of fixed capital* of $961.4 billion, and a hefty but relatively insignificant *Statistical discrepancy* of $71.9 billion. *Private consumption of fixed capital* is calculated as the sum of consumption of fixed capital for corporate business, proprietorships and partnerships, and for other private business appearing in Exhibit 9.9.

To complete the entries for GDP sources of funds, we turn once again to Exhibit 9.10 for *Business sector* gross investment in *Structures and producers' durable equipment* of $1,144.4 billion and in *Residential* construction of $54.5 billion and for *Change in business inventories* of $43.3 billion.

That was not so hard after all, was it?

## THE USES-OF-FUNDS SIDE OF GROSS DOMESTIC PRODUCT

The left or income side of Exhibit 10.1 is subdivided into three major economic aggregates: *National Income*, *Gross National Income*, and *Gross Domestic Income*. They are the less well-known relatives of GDP.

### National Income

*National Income*, amounting to $7,469.7 billion, measures the earnings of factors of production *supplied* by the United States.[2] Note the word "supplied." If you own a bond issued by a foreign corporation, the interest paid on that bond appears as part of national income even though the business may carry out its entire operations outside the United States. Similarly, interest, dividends, and profits earned by a foreigner's investment in the United States would not appear as part of national income.

### Gross National Income

*Gross National Income* (GNI) includes national income plus

- *Business transfer payments,*
- *Indirect business taxes and nontax accruals,*
- *Subsidies less government enterprise surplus*, and
- *Consumption of fixed capital.*

So constituted, GNI provides an estimate of the total costs required and incomes received from sales of goods and services produced by labor and property *supplied* by the United States.[3]

Although business transfer payments and indirect business taxes and nontaxes do not contribute to production, they constitute business sector costs that are reflected in the market value of the output of goods and services.

The difference between the $15.6 billion current *Surplus of government enterprises* and $43.9 billion of *Government subsidies* is a negative $28.4 billion. Government largess in the form of subsidies exceeds government efficiency in the form of surpluses. Entities producing goods and services and receiving subsidies find their costs reduced. The effect of subsidies on individual entities parallels their effect on GNI.

### Gross Domestic Income

*Gross Domestic Income* (GDI) measures the "costs incurred and the incomes earned in the production of GDP," the market value of goods and services produced by factors of production *located* in the United States.[4] GNI provides an estimate of incomes received by factors of production *supplied* by the United States. Some of those factors of production are located in the rest of the world, and for them U.S. residents receive *Income from the rest of the world.* For factors of production located in the United States and owned by foreigners, we make payments. By deducting receipts of factor *Income from the rest of the world* and adding payments of factor *Income paid to the rest of the world*, we convert GNI into GDI. Although the distinction between income received by factors of production located in the United States and those supplied by the

United States may seem consequential, the difference is only $11.0 billion. A big concept with little net dollar effect.

The Bureau of Economic Analysis (BEA) of the Department of Commerce admits that the national income and product accounts (NIPA) contain errors, stating, "In theory, GDP should equal GDI, but in practice, they differ because their components are estimated using largely independent and less-than-perfect source data. This difference is termed the 'statistical discrepancy.'"[5] The *Statistical discrepancy*, a negative $71.9 billion, has been seen before in connection with the business sector. With that adjustment GDI becomes equal to GDP, $9,299.2 billion.

## THE SOURCES-OF-FUNDS SIDE OF GROSS DOMESTIC PRODUCT

Compared to derivation of the income side of GDP, construction of its sources side is relatively straightforward. Each economic sector is represented by expenditures for consumption and/or investment:

- *Personal consumption expenditures*,
- *Gross private domestic investment*,
- *Net exports of goods and services*, and
- *Government consumption & investment*.

At $6,268.7 billion, *Personal consumption expenditures* constitute by far the largest portion of GDP—about two-thirds of the $9,299.2 billion. *Gross private domestic investment*, $1,650.1 billion, relates primarily to the business sector and to the business-related activities of households and nonprofit institutions. Gross investment is synonymous with capital expenditures. *Gross private domestic investment* shown in Exhibit 10.1 is divided into two major components: *Fixed investment*, and *Change in business inventories*.

*Fixed investment*, the larger of the two at $1,606.8 billion, consists of *Structures and producers' durable equipment* and *Residential* construction. To *Structures and producers' durable equipment*, totaling $1,203.1 billion, *Nonprofit institutions*' gross investment contributes $58.7 billion and the *Business sector* the balance, $1,144.4 billion. *Households* investment in *Residential* construction accounts for $349.4 billion of the $403.8 billion total of *Residential* construction; the business sector accounts for the rest, $54.4 billion.

*Change in business inventories*, $43.3 billion, is the smaller of the two components of *Gross private domestic investment*.

Economic aspirations of the rest of the world interact with U.S. residents' world salesmanship and craving for foreign products in determining *Net exports of goods and services*—a minus $254.0 billion. *Government consumption and investment* constitute the fourth and last major category for the product side of GDP. At $1,634.4 billion it approximates *Gross private domestic investment* of $1,650.1 billion.

## ACCOUNTING RELATIONSHIPS FOR THE ENTIRE ECONOMY

Earlier—much earlier in chapter 3—we covered some accounting identities that express in formula terms the relationship between income, disbursements and saving, changes in net worth, in financial and tangible assets, and in liabilities. Those equations apply to a single entity or group of entities—such as economic sectors. To set the stage for how those equations are modified when applied to the total economy, we would do well to review them.

Of particular interest in this setting is the equation:

$$S = \Delta W = \Delta FA + \Delta TA - \Delta L$$

where

$S$ represents saving,
$\Delta W$ change in wealth,
$\Delta FA$ change in financial assets,
$\Delta TA$ change in tangible assets, and
$\Delta L$ change in liabilities (which are taken to include equity issued).

The change in tangible assets (such as producers' plant and equipment, residential construction, and change in inventories) is equivalent to investment (taken here to be net of capital consumption allowances). Using

$I$ to stand for investment,

the equation can be expressed:

$$S = \Delta W = \Delta FA + I - \Delta L .$$

That equation applies to all four economic sectors. Reference to Exhibits 3.4, 7.12, 8.2, and 9.10 shows that each sector generated savings and investment. Each sector's net worth or saving was accompanied by differing amounts of investment and changes in financial assets and liabilities.

For any entity or group of entities, a change in financial assets can differ from a change in liabilities. One entity's liabilities are others' financial assets, however, so for the economy as a whole total changes in all financial assets must equal total changes in all liabilities. Expressed as an identity:

$$\Delta FA = \Delta L$$

when all financial assets and all liabilities are included. Substituting that equality in the previous equation shows that in the aggregate

$$S = I .$$

That is, for the entire economy, saving occurring in any specified period is equal to the amount of capital formation.

### Equality of Total Changes in Financial Assets and Liabilities

So much for the concepts. Do the data confirm our findings? They are readily at hand in Exhibits 3.4, 7.12, 8.2, and 9.10. Exhibit 10.2 brings together *Change in Financial Assets* and *Change in Liabilities* for each of the four sectors and indicates that they do! Well, at least, almost.

**Exhibit 10.2**

**Reconciliation of Aggregate Changes in Financial Assets and in Liabilities and in Saving and Investment, 1999**

| | Change in Financial Assets | Change in Liabilities | Discrepancies & Adjustments | Discrepancies + Change in Liabilities (col 2 + col 3) | Net Change in Financial Assets (col 1 - col 4) | Change in Net Worth (Saving) | Investment |
|---|---|---|---|---|---|---|---|
| | 1 | 2 | 3 | 4 | 5 | 6 | 7 |
| **Sector** | | | | | | | |
| Households and Nonprofit Institutions | **$ 491.7** | $ 622.2 | $ (15.8) | **$ 606.4** | **$ (114.7)** | $ 147.6 | $ 262.4 |
| Government | **164.8** | 47.2 | 52.2 | **99.4** | **65.4** | 174.5 | 109.1 |
| Rest of the World | **714.0** | 394.1 | 6.8 | **400.9** | **313.1** | 313.1 | - |
| Business | **3,294.8** | 3,406.3 | 85.5 | **3,491.8** | **(197.0)** | 229.4 | 426.4 |
| **Adjustment:** Wage accruals less disbursements | | (5.2) | | **(5.2)** | **5.2** | 5.2 | |
| **TOTAL** | **$ 4,665.3** | **$ 4,464.6** | **$ 128.7** | **$ 4,593.3** | **$ 72.0** | **$ 869.8** | **$ 797.9** |

*Note*: Amounts in $ billions.

*Change in Financial Assets* and *Change in Liabilities* are obtained from flow-of-funds data gathered by the Board of Governors of the Federal Reserve System—or rather by their minions. While flow-of-funds data recognize accrued but unpaid wages as a liability, the NIPA do not. Since we are reconciling to the NIPA, *Wage accruals less disbursements*, $5.2 billion, are deducted from the *Change in Liabilities*. We first saw that number way back in chapter 2. Data sources are many, and the information is imperfect. Consequently, *Discrepancy and Adjustments* must be recognized in reconciling changes of total assets with changes in liabilities for the entire economy.

Exhibit 10.2 lists the changes in financial assets and in liabilities for each of the four sectors in 1999. In addition to liabilities it includes each sector's *Discrepancies and Adjustments*—a product of the construction of flow-of-funds data. *Discrepancies and Adjustments* include adjustments for differences in accounting treatment between the flow-of-funds data and the NIPA. The sum of the first column shows that in the aggregate, financial assets increased by $4,665.3 billion. Liabilities for all four sectors—the sum of the second column—increased $4,464.6 billion. Based on the sums of the two columns, total financial assets increased by $200.7 billion more than total liabilities. Either a lot of persons—folks and legal persons like corporations—are holding a large amount of worthless paper or something is wrong with the numbers.

Additional data from the Federal Reserve System and from the Department of Commerce indicate that the problem is with the numbers. Errors are introduced both by flow-of-funds accounts and by the NIPA. For each sector's flow of funds account, a discrepancy figure is required to balance changes in assets with changes in liabilities. If *Change in Financial Assets* matched *Change in Liabilities*, and discrepancies resulted only from errors in assigning assets and liabilities to their appropriate sectors, the total of *Discrepancies and Adjustments* for all sectors would net to zero. As the third column of Exhibit 10.2 shows, however, they don't. Discrepancies (adjustments sum to zero) add up to $128.7 billion, suggesting that some financial asset changes do not have liability mates because of flow-of-funds data imperfections.

The fourth column of Exhibit 10.2 adds Column 2 to Column 3. If discrepancies reflected only errors in accounting for financial flows, the sum of changes in financial assets minus the fourth column sum should net to zero for all sectors. However, as the $72.0 billion total for the table's fifth column, *Net Change in Financial Assets*, shows, they don't. Investment and changes in net worth—as well as changes in financial assets and in liabilities—must be taken into consideration when determining a discrepancy figure that balances *Change in Assets* with *Change in Liabilities* and *Change in Net Worth*.

The resemblance of the fifth column's $72.0 billion total to the statistical discrepancy for GDP of $71.9 billion can be taken to be more than just coincidence. Rounding error only accounts for the difference.

With an aggregate error of $128.7 billion in the flow-of-funds accounts and $71.9 billion in the NIPA, one should proceed with caution in drawing fine distinctions from the fifth column of Exhibit 10.2. The figures suggest, however, that *Households and Nonprofit Institutions*, and *Business* were net borrowers of funds. The *Government* sector and the *Rest of the World* were on balance suppliers of funds for 1999.

### Equality of Saving and Investment

How about saving and investment? Are they equal? Under the circumstances the questions do not generate much feeling of suspense. As the remaining two columns of Exhibit 10.2 show, saving and investment are not. The sixth column lists the *Change in Net Worth (Saving)* for each of the four sectors. With the adjustment for unpaid wage and salary accruals, it sums to $869.8 billion. *Investment*, the seventh column, sums to $797.9 billion. The difference, $71.9, is—rounding errors ignored—equal to the sum of the fifth column of Exhibit 10.2. Note that the differences between *Saving* and *Investment* for each sector correspond as well to the differences in the fifth column. Although for 1999 all sectors engaged in saving, the appetite of *Households and Nonprofit Institutions*, and *Business* for capital formation exceeded their self-financing capacities. The *Government*—thanks in large measure to the involuntary contributions of citizens and their employers to social insurance funds—and the *Rest of the World*—thanks to foreigners' willingness to hold as part of their portfolio of assets claims against the U.S. government and its residents—supplied the funding.

## ECONOMIC PERFORMANCE AND GROSS DOMESTIC PRODUCT

As a measure of the total output of final goods and services of the economy, GDP commonly is cited as an indicator of an economy's performance and as a basis for making comparisons among nations. Although construction of GDP is intricate, even the most enthusiastic of its knowledgeable users would maintain that it is only an estimate of what it purports to measure: the market value of goods and services produced by factors of production located within a country's boundary.

### Gross Domestic Product and Its Components over Time

In 1999 nominal GDP amounted to $9,299.2 billion—$9.3 trillion—an all time record. In 1959 it was equal to $507.2 billion. In those forty intervening years, GDP has increased eighteen-fold—an average annual rate of growth of 7.5 percent. At that rate, GDP has repeatedly doubled in intervals of less than ten years throughout the period.

*Nominal and Real Gross Domestic Product.* Exhibit 10.3 shows graphically what has happened to GDP for each of the forty years. The horizontal axis of the accompanying chart measures years; the vertical, the amount of GDP in trillions of dollars. It shows at a glance that GDP has risen every year. Not one but two lines appear on the graph, however! The line with the open data points, *Nominal GDP*, represents GDP expressed in terms of prices prevailing in the year that it

**Exhibit 10.3**
**Nominal and Real Gross Domestic Product, 1959 to 1999**

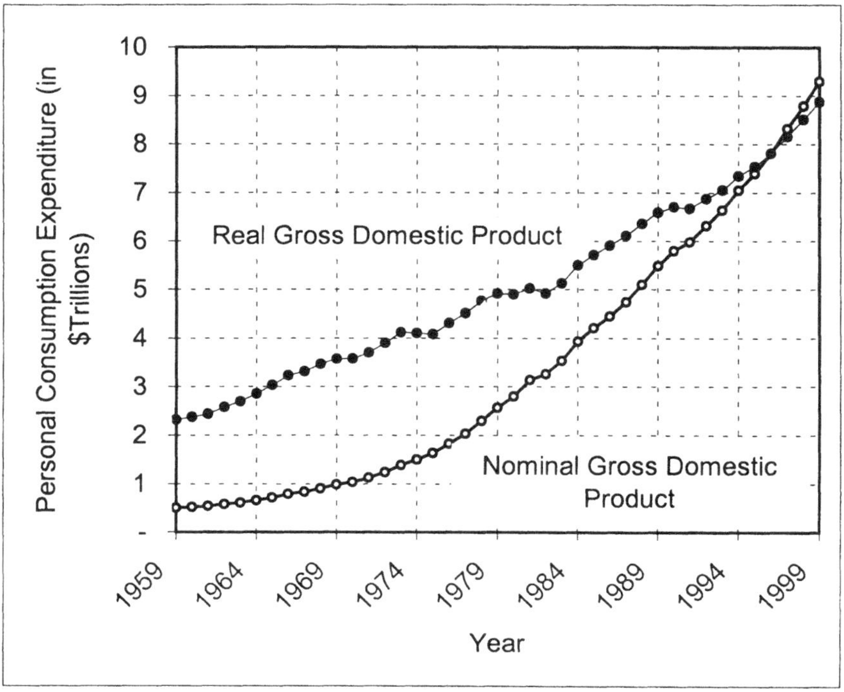


*Source* : U.S. Department of Commerce. Bureau of Economic Analysis. "Selected NIPA Tables." *National Accounts Data* . 8 Aug. 2000: Tables 1.1 & 1.2. 9 Sep. 2000. <http://www.bea.doc.gov/bea/dn1.htm>.

was recorded. A consistent rise in the general level of prices as well as increases in the amount of output of final goods and services contribute significantly to the apparent growth of GDP. Since both prices and output are changing, we cannot tell very well what really is happening.

The other line on the chart, *Real GDP*, attempts to dispel the confusion. It displays what the pattern of growth in output of goods and services would have been if prices had been constant. Note that for the year 1996, the "real" line crosses the "nominal" line. For price-level purposes 1996 is the base year. Prices prevailing in 1996 are used to value output for the preceding and following years. Prior to 1996, real GDP is calculated to be greater than nominal GDP, because output in those years was actually exchanged on the basis of lower prices then prevailing. Similarly, after 1996, real GDP is lower than nominal GDP because output is priced at the lower 1996 price level rather than at the more recent higher levels.

In a sense all GDP numbers are artificial. They all are made up as a result of certain conventions, practices, and estimates that in varying degrees are arbitrary. Of the two GDP estimates, however, nominal and real, "real" GDP is more artificial than "nominal" GDP. Calculation of real GDP involves one additional arbitrary calculation of applying prices and weights existing in a base period to output produced in other periods. Nominal GDP is a little closer to being the sum of market transactions involving exchanges of goods and services among buyers and sellers. Only for the base period does real GDP have grounding in that reality. Despite its artificiality, real GDP reveals information that otherwise would be obscured. It provides an indication of by how much the physical output of goods and services really increased from 1959 to 1999.

The pattern of increase in real GDP shown in Exhibit 10.3 is a bit more interesting than for that of nominal GDP. Nominal GDP is monotonic—always increasing. Real GDP, on the other hand, wiggles around a little. The curve dips downward in 1974 and 1975. It drops slightly in 1980 and then perceptibly in 1982. The last dip occurred in 1991.

Nominal GDP, we observed, has increased eighteen fold. Not so for real GDP. It starts higher at $2.3 trillion in 1959 and ends lower at $8.9 trillion in 1999—an increase of 3.8 times—more than tripling, almost quadrupling. That increase reflects an average annual compound growth rate of 3.4 percent. During the same period of time, the population of the United States has increased from 178 million to 273 million persons. In 1959 real GDP per person, therefore, equaled $13,000; in 1999 $32,500—2.5 times greater—not a bad performance for the effort of nearly two generations.

*Productivity.* Although often taken for granted in a market-oriented capitalist economy, increases in the amount of goods and services available to people are not inevitable. A large portion of the world's population lives at a subsistence level. A subsistence level must not be confused with definitions of poverty in the United States. A subsistence level means having just enough to survive. Any amount below subsistence means you disappear, become extinct, turn to dust. Prehistoric hunting and gathering tribes of human beings started with their per capita GDP close to or at such a level. For many of the world's people, not much economic progress has occurred since then.

As the U.S. population increased, so did output. A larger population suggests a larger labor force. With more workers and more effort devoted to producing goods and services, output should increase. Between 1959 and 1999 the labor force not only increased, but it increased more than in proportion with population. Two factors contributed to the more rapid growth in the labor force: aging of the population and greater participation of women.

The four charts in Exhibit 10.4 illustrate those phenomena. The charts show the *Population sixteen years of age or older*, the *Total labor force*, and *Women* and *Men in the labor force* as percents of the total U.S. population from 1959 to 1999. The horizontal axis measures years and the vertical axis measures percentages of total population. The scales of the top two charts differ but their spread is the same: twenty percentage points. Similarly, vertical axes of the bottom two charts have differing ranges but the same fifteen-percentage point spread.

**Exhibit 10.4**

**Labor Force Statistics as Percent of Total Population, 1959 to 1999**

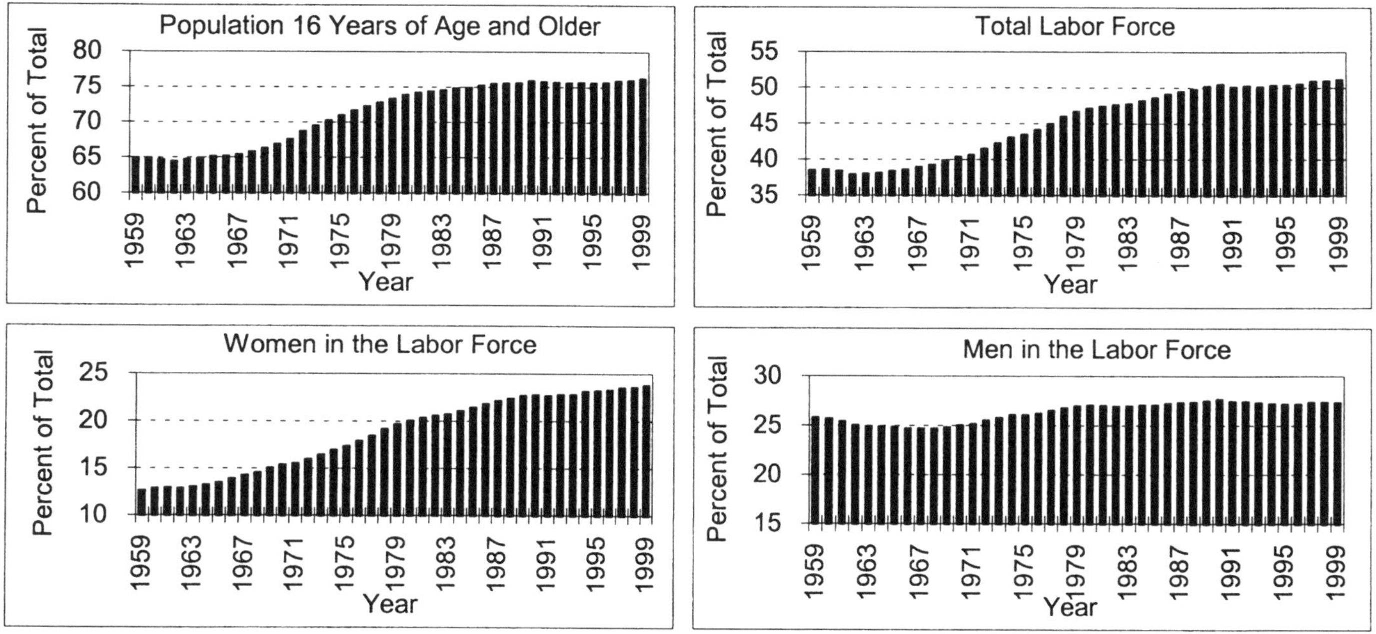


*Source*: U.S. Department of Commerce. Bureau of the Census. "Historical National Population Estimates." *National Population Estimates*. 28 Jun. 2000: Series P-15, Nos. 311, 917, 1095. 29 Sep. 2000. <http://www.census.gov/population/www/estimates/uspop.html> and U.S. Department of Labor. Bureau of Labor Statistics. "Employment status of the civilian population by sex and age." *Labor Force Statistics from the Current Population Survey*. 4 Feb 2000: Table A-1 29 Sep. 2000. <http://stats.bls.gov/webapps/legacy/epsatab1.htm>.

In 1959, 65 percent of the population was sixteen years of age or older. By the end of the period, that percentage had risen to 76 percent. Out of the total population, more people were eligible to participate in the *Labor Force*. With greater eligibility, the *Labor Force* as a percentage of the total population rose. From 38 percent in 1959, it climbed to 51 percent.

If the only factor influencing the relative growth in the labor force had been population aging, however, an increase in the neighborhood of 44 percent would have been expected. But something else was going on as well: more women working outside the home. In 1959 women in the labor force accounted for 13 percent of the total population; by 1999 that percentage approached 24 percent—a substantial change! During the same period the percentage of population consisting of men in the labor force began at a little less than 26 percent and ended at a little over 27 percent—very little change. In 1959 women made up about one-third of the labor force; forty years later they account for over 46 percent.

As a result of those two factors, the labor force in the United States rose from 68 million persons to 139 million—a doubling from 1959 to 1999. The total population, on the other hand, increased a little over 50 percent.

By itself a doubling of the labor force does not explain fully the increase in output of goods and services. Real GDP more than tripled. By the end of the period, each worker produced more goods and services than he or she had at the beginning of the period. How much more? Exhibit 10.5 provides an answer.

The chart displays *Real GDP per Worker* from 1959 to 1999. Worker is defined as a full-time equivalent employee. Full-time equivalent employees include only those members of the labor force who are employed. That makes sense since only employed members of the labor force contribute to production of goods and services. A number for full-time equivalent employees is calculated by industry and then summed. For each industry the total number of employee hours is divided by the average number of hours worked by full-time employees to calculate full-time equivalent employees. Dividing real GDP by employed workers produces *Real GDP per Worker* in thousands of dollars. From the chart we can see that output per worker has risen from $41,700 at the beginning of the period to $72,700 by the end of the period. On average each worker produces 74 percent more goods and services in 1999 than in 1959.

On the graph a least-squares trend line passes through the points representing average real GDP for each year. The slope of the trend line suggests that output per worker increases over $700 per year. That is phenomenal! Anyone who has ever cultivated a vegetable garden on the same plot of ground knows that producing additional produce each year at best is difficult and generally impossible. Take almost any task we perform as individuals and ask how much more efficient we have become at performing it this year as compared to last. The usual answer is, "Not much." Despite our limitations as individuals, collectively in the market economy, our output per worker has been increasing over forty years and shows no sign of diminution.

**Exhibit 10.5**
**Real Gross Domestic Product per Full-Time Equivalent Employee, 1959 to 1999**

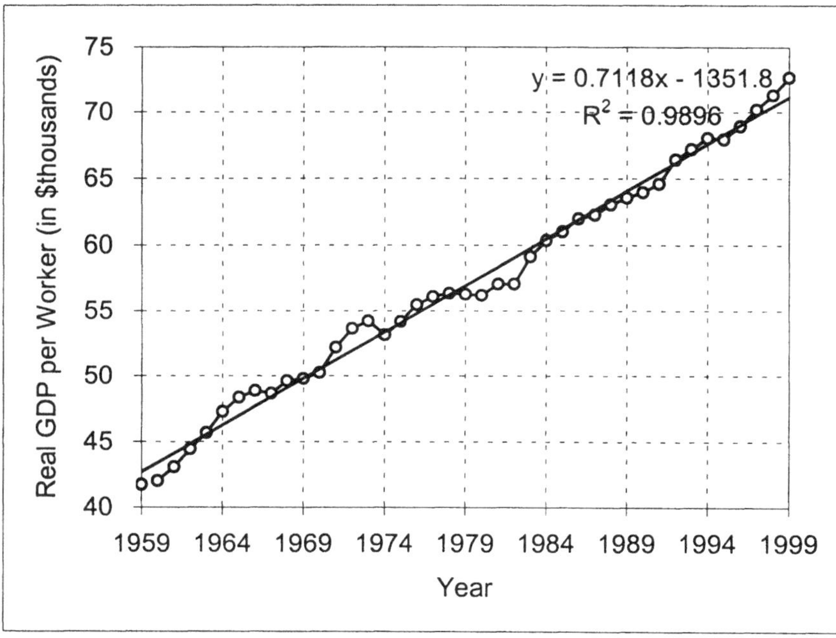


*Source* : U.S. Department of Commerce. Bureau of Economic Analysis. "Selected NIPA Tables." *National Accounts Data* . 8 Aug. 2000: Table 1.2. 9 Sep. 2000. <http://www.bea.doc.gov/bea/dn1.htm>. and "'Annual Only' NIPA Tables." *National Accounts Data* . 30 Aug 2000: Table 6.5B. 5 Sep. 2000. <http://www.bea.doc.gov/bea/dn1.htm>.

Even cows cooperate to increase productivity in a market economy. In 1959, 20.1 million milk cows—about the same number as the current people population of the state of Texas—produced 122 billion pounds of milk. In 1998, 9.2 million cows produced 157 billions pounds of milk.[6] Each cow produces almost 2.8 times more milk than her 1959 foremother. That's no bull! Behind the placid expression of Sadie, Bessie, Daisy, and all the other milk cows lies an appreciation of the market system and a fierce determination to forestall the day when their last remains unceremoniously are carted off in a bun to someone's bottomless pit beneath the golden arches.

At times productivity per worker is greater than the trend line. At other times it is less. It begins the period below the trend line. Rising rapidly in the early 1960s through 1965, productivity per worker reaches the trend line in 1963 and then surpasses it. Per worker productivity rides along above the trend line until 1969 and 1970 when it falls back to the line. Spurts in productivity in 1971, 1972, and 1973 send it well above the line, but a sharp fall in 1974 sends it back. Then until 1979 real GDP per worker follows the trend line closely.

Next come five years of productivity below the line. From 1984 to 1996 productivity growth per worker has followed the line fairly closely. From 1997 to 1999 productivity has moved decidedly above the line.

Attributing increased productivity of workers to innate improvements in their intelligence, strength, endurance, diligence, and other characteristics employers laud as a result of biological evolution appears unpromising since evolution is a somewhat slow (and, in some circles, suspect) process. Improved education offers a more likely explanation. In 1960, 41 percent of the population twenty-five years of age and older had a high school education; for 1999 the percentage is above 80 percent. The percentage of the population with four or more years of college grew from 8 to 24 percent.[7] Pointing to such statistics, ambitious school and college administrators may wish to take credit for productivity growth. It does represent an investment in human capital, but attributing all the growth to education overlooks other inputs to productive processes.

Two inputs—fixed capital and energy—merit examination. For our purposes consumption of fixed capital (CFC) by the private sector and government will represent plant and equipment employed in producing goods and services. Private and government fixed investment price indexes are used to adjust for price inflation and express capital consumption in constant value dollars. Dividing the sum of the two time series by each year's full-time equivalent employment produces figures for capital consumption per worker.

According to the Department of Energy, the United States consumed 43.5 million quadrillion (a million billion) British thermal units (BTUs) in 1959. By 1999 energy consumed amounted to 96.6 million quadrillion BTUs. Dividing those figures—and those of the years in between—by full-time equivalent employment generates estimates of energy consumption per worker. Although not all energy is used for production purposes, we assume that the proportion used for other purposes remains relatively constant throughout the period.

The results of those calculations appear in Exhibit 10.6. As in Exhibit 10.5, *Real GDP per Worker* is expressed in thousands of dollars and is measured along the vertical axis. *Real CFC per Worker* is expressed in hundreds of dollars along the horizontal. Capital consumed per worker, represented by the white dots, ranges from \$3,670 in 1959 to \$9,540 in 1999. With few exceptions the amount of capital employed per worker steadily increases, so that by the end of the period, capital used per worker has more than doubled.

The white dots in Exhibit 10.6 show the relationship between capital consumption per worker and real GDP per worker. Not surprisingly, worker productivity increases as the amount of capital available increases, and the dots arrange themselves in a roughly linear fashion. A least-squares regression line suggests that every \$100 dollars in *Real CFC per Worker* generates almost \$500 in *Real GDP per Worker*. The coefficient of determination ($R^2$) indicates that the association between the two variables accounts for about 96 percent of their variance.

White dots tend to cluster about the line but rarely fall exactly on it. When they are above the line, a given amount of capital consumption per worker gen-

**Exhibit 10.6**
**Real Gross Domestic Product, Real Consumption of Fixed Capital, and Energy Consumption per Full-time Equivalent Employee, 1959 to 1999**

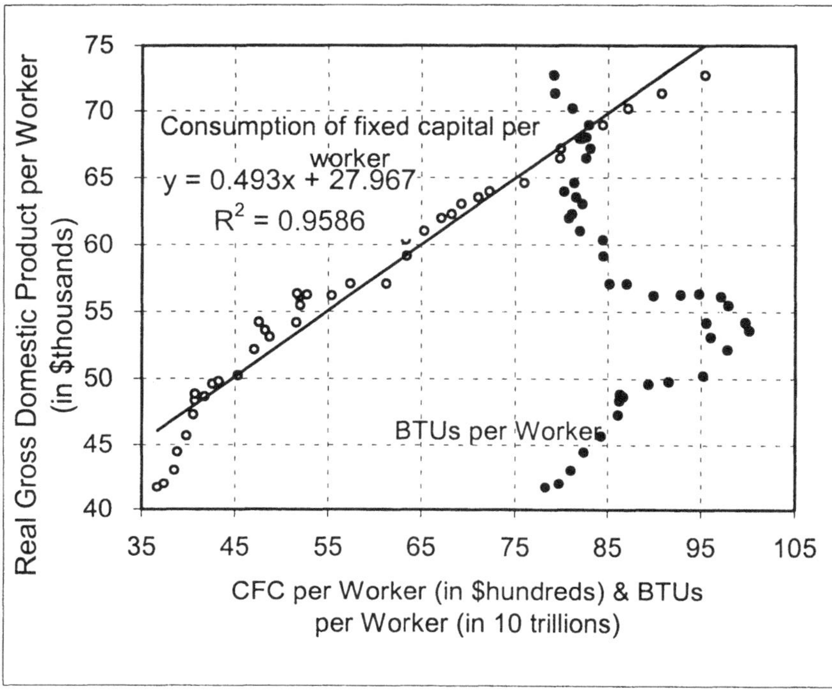


*Sources* : U.S. Department of Commerce. Bureau of Economic Analysis. "Selected NIPA Tables." *National Accounts Data* : Table 1.2. 8 Aug. 2000. 9 Sep. 2000. <http://www.bea.doc.gov/bea/dn1.htm>; "'Annual Only' NIPA Tables." *National Accounts Data* . 30 Aug 2000: Tables 6.5B, 7.1, 7.13 & 8.14. 5 Sep. 2000. <http://www.bea.doc.gov/bea/dn1.htm>; U. S. Department of Energy. Energy Information Agency. "Energy Consumption by *Source* ." *Annual Energy Review* . Sep. 2000: Table 1.3. 04 Dec. 2000. <http://www.eia.doe.gov/emeu/aer/overview.html>.

erates more output than indicated by the line. When they are below it, the output of goods and services falls short of the trend line. The amount of energy consumed per worker tends to relate to those fluctuations above and below the line.

*BTUs per Worker* are measured along the horizontal axis of Exhibit 10.6 in units of 10 trillion and are represented by the black dots. Unlike CFC per worker, they do not invariably increase with passage of time. The 1999 figure of 791 trillion BTUs per worker (which appears in units of 10 trillion as 79.1 to make the units suited for graphic presentation) exceeds BTUs for 1959 but does not represent the largest number in the series. Indeed, energy consumption per worker exceeded the 1999 figure throughout the period from 1960 to 1998. The successes and excesses of the Organization of Petroleum Exporting Countries (OPEC) and fluctuations in the price of petroleum and other energy sources made their impact on combinations of labor, capital, and energy used to produce goods and services in the United States.

In the accompanying graph the black dots represent the relationship between energy consumption and output per worker. The relationship clearly is not linear. However, the black dots do provide a useful reference. As the black dots move to the right, the white dots tend to be above their trend line. A move of the black dots to the left seems to push the white dots down and below their trend line. In other words, greater energy consumption per worker increases output per worker for a given amount of capital.

The combined effects of capital and energy consumption per worker on worker productivity can be expressed as an equation. For that purpose, we define a production function of the form:

$$Q = \alpha \cdot K^{\beta} \cdot E^{\gamma}$$

where

$Q$ represents output per worker,
$K$ consumption of fixed capita per worker,
$E$ consumption of energy per worker, and
$\alpha$, $\beta$, and $\gamma$ stand for parameters of the production function.

Expressing the values for the variables as logarithms and applying least-squares regression analysis produces the following empirical form for the production function:

$$Q = 0.23 \cdot K^{0.56} E^{0.34} .$$

A coefficient of determination of 0.99 for the equation suggests that those differences are relatively small and that capital and energy consumption account for virtually all of the variance in output per worker for the observed period. The results also suggest that a 1 percent increase in capital consumption per worker generates a 56/100 of 1 percent increase in real GDP per worker and that 1 percent increase in energy consumption increases output by 34/100 of 1 percent.

In 1999 per worker consumption of fixed capita was 2.6 times greater than in 1959; per worker energy consumption was 1.01 times greater than in 1959. Applying to each their respective exponents of 0.56 and 0.34 and multiplying them together produces 1.71. That figure suggests that worker productivity would be 71 percent greater in 1999 than in 1959. It approximates nicely the observed productivity increase of 74 percent. During the same period of time, full-time equivalent employment grew from 55.6 million to 122.1 million, an increase of 2.2 times. Multiplying 1.7 by 2.2 produces 3.7, an estimate that once again approximates observed growth in real GDP of 3.8 times.

The above exercise reveals that over the past forty years, capital consumption has contributed more to worker productivity than energy consumption. Even if both had increased in the same proportions, the production function's exponents indicate capital is decidedly the more important. Continued enhancement of worker productivity requires continued capital formation. As has been demonstrated, continued capital formation, in turn, requires continued saving. Not all the credit for improved productivity per worker should be ascribed to growth in plant and equipment, however. Advancement in worker education and training and in technological innovation has paralleled increased investment in fixed capital; they deserve part of the credit, too. Investment in people and encouragement of technology are essential ingredients in the recipe for economic progress.

*Components of Gross Domestic Product.* As presented in Exhibit 10.1, we saw that the sources-of-funds side of GDP is composed of four components. Exhibit 10.7 shows those components of nominal GDP as percentages of total GDP for 1959 and for 1999, with the defense and nondefense components of federal government consumption and investment expenditures shown separately. *Personal consumption* expenditure has increased its share of GDP over the forty-year period—from 63 percent in 1959 to 67 percent in 1999. Not all forms of personal consumption expenditure enjoyed the same robust growth, however. As a share of GDP, personal consumption expenditures for *Durable goods* held their own at 8 percent of the total. *Nondurable goods* dropped from 29 to 20 percent. *Services* rose from 25 percent to a phenomenal 39 percent.

*Net exports* have changed from a diminutive negative number to a negative 3 percent of GDP. The net percentages fail to show imports and exports separately. In 1959 exports accounted for 4 percent of U.S. output of goods and services; forty years later they accounted for 11 percent. In 1959 one dollar in twenty-five came from sales of U.S. products abroad; in 1999 one dollar in nine came from sales of U.S. products to the rest of the world. Imports of goods and services more than kept pace with U.S. exports. Relative to GDP their 1999 percentage is a negative 13 percent, up from a negative 4 percent in 1959.

Unlike *Gross private domestic investment*, whose growth has more than kept pace with overall GDP and which increased from 15 percent to 18 percent, *Government consumption and investment* expenditures have experienced a relative decline from 22 to 18 percent. That five-percentage point decline is more than accounted for by the relative decline in *Federal defense* expenditure from 11 percent in 1959 to 4 percent in 1999. *Federal nondefense* expenditure has held its own at 2 percent. State and local government increased its expenditure share of GDP by two percentage points, from 9 percent in 1959 to 11 percent in 1999. In terms of final goods and services, state and local governments now overshadow the federal government.

## Gross Domestic Income

With perfectly accurate data and access to all data sources, gross domestic income would be equal to GDP. However, the real world is not that perfect. For 1999 gross domestic income equals $9,371.1 billion, and GDP equals $9,299.2 billion. The difference, $71.8 billion, amounts to eight-tenths of 1 percent of gross domestic income. Although even $1 billion is a large amount of money, relative to the aggregates being estimated, the discrepancy is pretty small. If GDP is perfectly accurate, we can say the gross national income is eight-tenths

**Exhibit 10.7**

**Comparison of Components of Gross Domestic Product as Percents of Total Gross Domestic Product, 1959 and 1999**

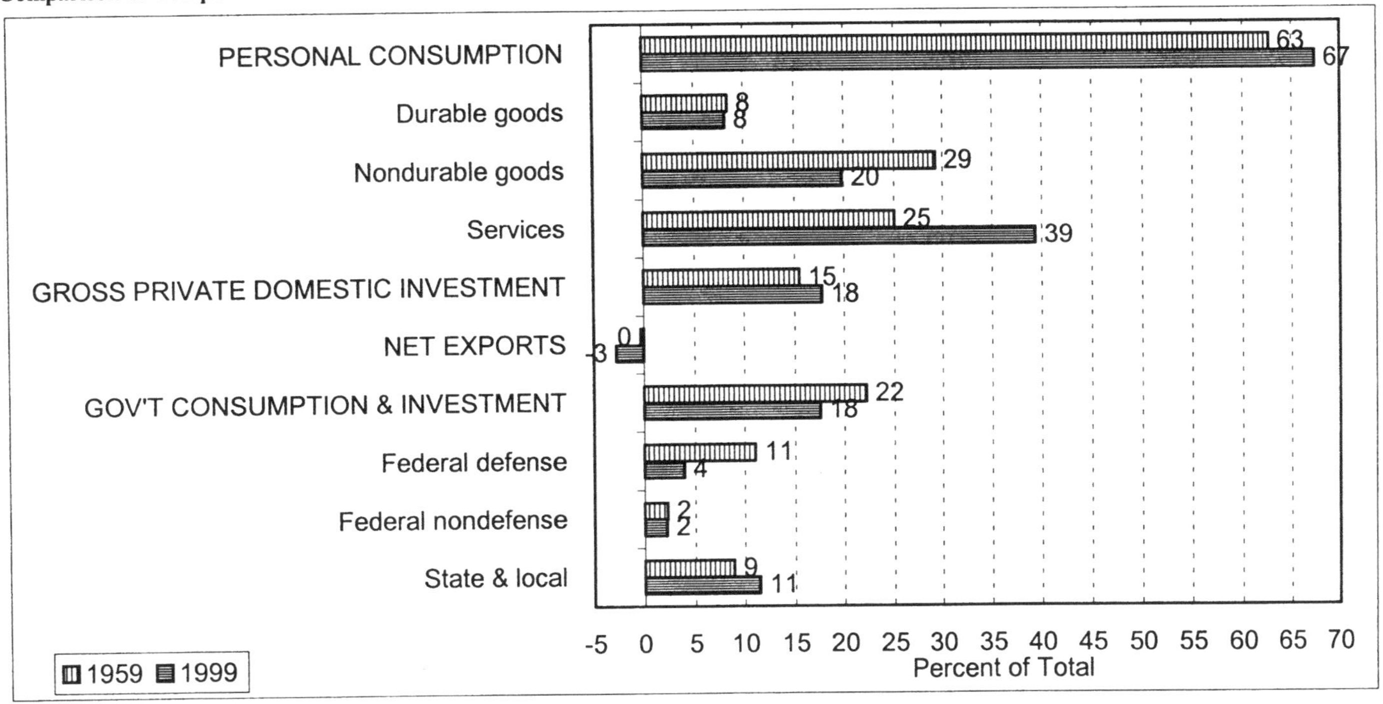


*Source* : U.S. Department of Commerce. Bureau of Economic Analysis. "Selected NIPA Tables." *National Accounts Data* . 8 Aug. 2000: Table 1.1. 9 Sep. 2000. <http://www.bea.doc.gov/bea/dn1.htm>.

of 1 percent away from perfection. For purposes of the following presentation, gross domestic income will be treated as equivalent of GDP.

*Changes in the Components of Gross Domestic Income.* Gross domestic income represents the uses-of-funds side of the GDP account. In the great recycling of funds that occurs with economic transactions, personal consumption expenditures, investment in structures and equipment, net exports of goods and services, and government expenditures for consumption and investment supply funds for output-producing institutions. Gross domestic income describes what those institutions do with the funds they receive from sales of their output. They pay the factors of production that have been used as inputs in the productive process, pay taxes, and cover other costs.

Exhibit 10.8 displays some of the components of gross domestic income presented on the left-hand side of Exhibit 10.1. For each of the components, their share of GDP is shown as a percentage for 1959 and 1999. Since some of the changes in relative shares occurring among the components of gross domestic income will be familiar from our earlier examination of the four economic sectors, we will cover only the highlights.

*Net receipts from rest of world* post a shift from positive to negative, from 1 percent in 1959 to a slightly negative percentage. Behind net percents lie payments and receipts. From an insignificant amount, payments to the rest of the world have risen to 3 percent of GDP. In 1959 U.S. residents received more in income than they paid to foreigners. Now they pay more than they receive.

The share of *Consumption of fixed capital* has risen slightly, from 11 percent to 12 percent, and *Indirect business taxes and nontaxes* has held its own at 8 percent. None of those components involve national income: payments to the factors of production, which accounts for most of GDP. *Supplements to wages and salaries* increased their share substantially, from 4 percent in 1959 to 9 percent by 1999. That gain is offset in part by the drop in the share of *Wage and salary accruals* from 51 percent to 48 percent. A larger portion of employee compensation now consists of wage and salary supplements that tend to limit the discretion of households and individuals in how they spend their income. Despite the slower growth of wages and salaries, employee compensation accounts for a larger share of gross national income in 1999 than in 1959, 57 percent versus 55 percent.

With one exception, shares of gross national income received by property ownership of the factors of production declined. The percent of the total accounted for by *Proprietors' income* dropped from 10 percent to 7 percent and by *Rental income*, from 3 to 2 percent. *Corporate profits* with inventory valuation and capital consumption adjustments witnessed a drop as well, from 11 percent in 1959 to 9 percent in 1999.

Only *Net interest* among the forms of property income grew sufficiently to increase its share from 2 percent to 5 percent during the forty-year period. Two factors account for that growth: relatively greater reliance on debt financing and higher interest rates. In 1962, for instance, the rate of interest on ten-year U.S.

**Exhibit 10.8**

**Uses of Gross Domestic Product as Percents of Total Gross Domestic Product, 1959 and 1999**

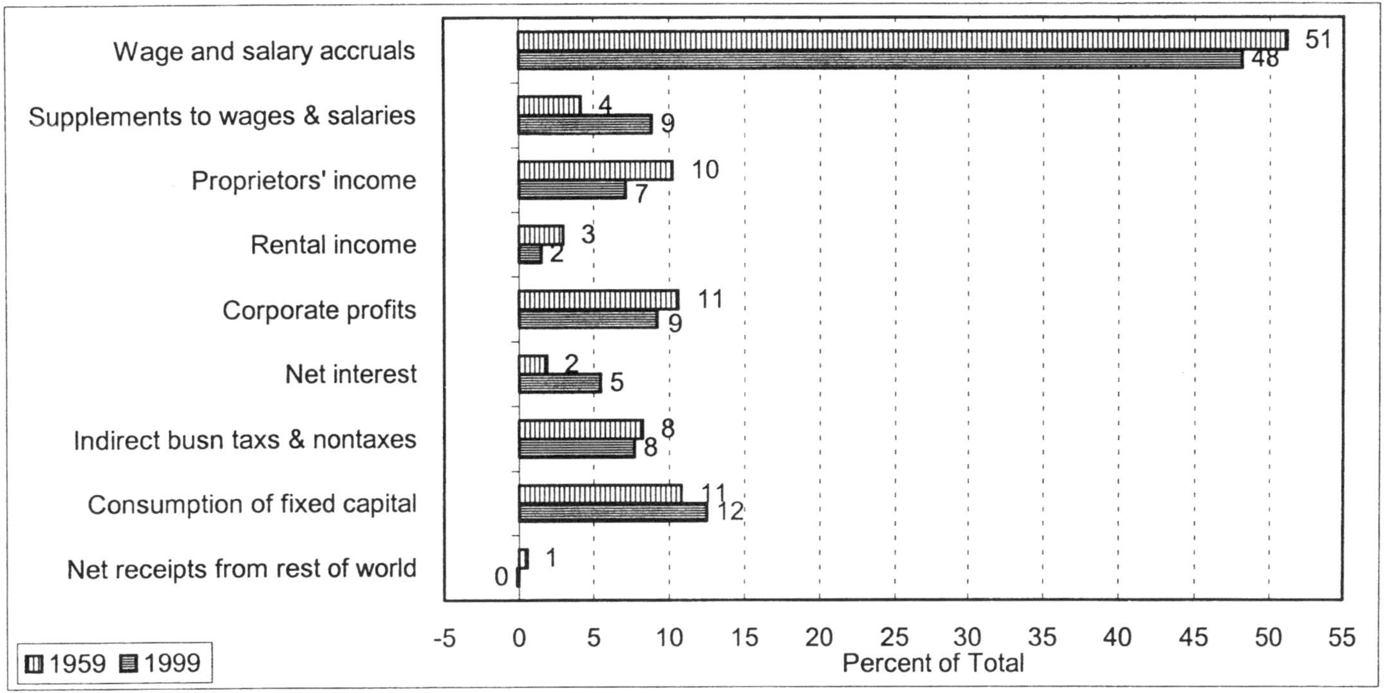


*Sources* : U.S. Department of Commerce. Bureau of Economic Analysis. "Selected NIPA Tables." *National Accounts Data* . 8 Aug. 2000: Table 1.9 & 1.14. 9 Sep 2000. <http://www.bea.doc.gov/bea/dn1.htm>.

Government Treasury bonds averaged 4.0 percent for the year; in 1999, 5.6 percent.

## GROSS STATE PRODUCT

The factors of production located within the United States produce the goods and services whose market value is estimated as GDP. Conceptually, then, it should be possible to extend and contract the concept to measure the output produced by factors of production located within any larger or smaller geographic boundary. And it is! The BEA produces gross state product statistics that measure the market value of the output of goods and services produced within each of the fifty states and the District of Columbia. In addition, for each state and the District of Columbia, gross state product is broken down into sixty-three industries, and time series estimates are available in current and constant dollars. Current dollar estimates by state and by industry date back to 1977. Constant dollar estimates date back only to 1982 since adjusting for price changes using chain-type indexes produces a discrepancy between the parts and the aggregate that tends to grow as the number of years from the base period lengthens.

Gross state product data are published in the *Survey of Current Business*.[8] They also may be obtained from the Department of Commerce in the form of a CD-ROM and can be accessed through the Internet on the BEA Web site, *www.bea.doc.gov*.

### Gross State Product by State

Exhibit 10.9 displays *Gross State Product* for 1977 and 1998. Note that total *Gross State Product* for 1998, $8,745.2 billion, does not equal GDP for that year, $8,790.2 billion. In 1998 the statistical discrepancy amounted to $24.8 billion. For gross state product "insufficient information is available to allocate the statistical discrepancy to states."[9] Without the adjustment for the statistical discrepancy, we might expect the bottom line figure for 1998 gross state product to equal 1998's gross domestic income, $8,815.0 billion. However, it does not. Gross state product excludes employee compensation earned by federal civilian and military personnel stationed abroad and consumption of fixed capital for military equipment and structures located abroad.[10] When those exclusions are deducted from gross national income, they reconcile to the sum of gross state products (approximately).

In 1977, twenty-one years earlier, *Gross State Product* totaled $1,985.7 billion. Over that interval of time, gross state product has more than quadrupled. Of course, we are not making an adjustment for price inflation, but such an adjustment seems unnecessary here. As the last number in the last column of Exhibit 10.9 shows, total gross state product increased at an average annual rate of 7.3 percent.

A check up and down that column shows that rates of growth in gross state product differed markedly among states. Nevada enjoyed the most rapid growth, averaging almost 11 percent. West Virginia suffered the slowest growth, less than 5 percent a year. The difference between 5 and 11 is not trivial, particularly when we are dealing with an average growth rate extending over twenty-one years. As a consequence Nevada's gross state product increased 8.4 times while West Virginia's increased 2.7 times.

Four other states enjoyed annual average rates of growth exceeding 9 percent: Arizona, Florida, Georgia, and New Hampshire. Seven other states experienced growth rates averaging less than 6 percent: Alaska, Iowa, Louisiana, Michigan, Montana, North Dakota, and Wyoming. What accounts for the differences? Each state undoubtedly has a different story. Given the geographic dispersion, however, giving credit to (or blaming) the climate and topography for the good or poor economic performance of those states does not offer much prospect of credibility.

Past performance does not assure future success. Accompanying gross state product for 1977 and 1999 are columns signifying each state's ranking from smallest to largest. For certain states the ranking for 1977 appears in bold type. For those states their rank fell from 1977 to 1999. For states whose ranking increased, the 1999 rank appears in bold type. Ranking deteriorated for twenty-three states; sixteen states improved their ranking. What happened to the other twelve regions? They maintained their relative position.

In the ranking for 1999 we see that Vermont is number one; that is, its $16.3 billion gross state product is the smallest among the states. It held that dubious distinction in 1977 as well. It is trying, however. Vermont's 7.8 percent annual rate of growth surpasses the national average. If its strong performance continues over the next twenty-one years—and if North Dakota's does not improve—it will have passed its closest competitor by a wide margin. California's ranking, fifty-one, identifies the state with the largest gross state product, $1,118.9 billion—over $1.1 trillion—and nearly sixty-nine times greater than that of Vermont. Such a disparity leads us to wonder about the distribution for gross state product among the states.

### Distribution of Gross State Product

Using 1998 data, the chart in Exhibit 10.10 plots the accumulative amount of each state's percentage of gross state product beginning with the smallest and proceeding to the largest. We start with Vermont and end with California. Although we know better, with fifty states and the District of Columbia, a naive mathematician from another planet might expect that each state's share of gross state product would average a little less than 2 percent of the total. Vermont's share is about one-tenth of that expectation—a situation shared by the next four states on the list. Iowa—whose gross state product ranks twenty-third—has a gross state product that equals 1 percent of the total—just one-half the ex-

**Exhibit 10.9**
**Gross State Product, 1977 and 1998**

| State | 1977 Amount in $ Billions | Rank | 1998 Amount in $ Billions | Rank | Average Annual Growth Rate |
|---|---|---|---|---|---|
| Alabama | $ 26.5 | **28** | $ 109.8 | 27 | 7.0 |
| Alaska | 7.5 | **10** | 24.2 | 6 | 5.8 |
| Arizona | 19.2 | 21 | 133.8 | **29** | 9.7 |
| Arkansas | 15.0 | 18 | 61.6 | 18 | 7.0 |
| California | 229.3 | 51 | 1,118.9 | 51 | 7.8 |
| Colorado | 25.2 | 26 | 141.8 | **30** | 8.6 |
| Connecticut | 29.4 | 30 | 142.1 | **31** | 7.8 |
| Delaware | 6.0 | 5 | 33.7 | **10** | 8.6 |
| District of Columbia | 15.2 | **19** | 54.1 | 16 | 6.2 |
| Florida | 66.3 | 43 | 418.9 | **47** | 9.2 |
| Georgia | 41.2 | 37 | 253.8 | **42** | 9.0 |
| Hawaii | 9.4 | **13** | 39.7 | 11 | 7.1 |
| Idaho | 7.0 | 8 | 30.9 | 8 | 7.3 |
| Illinois | 115.5 | 48 | 425.7 | 48 | 6.4 |
| Indiana | 47.4 | **41** | 174.4 | 37 | 6.4 |
| Iowa | 26.4 | **27** | 84.6 | 23 | 5.7 |
| Kansas | 20.4 | **23** | 77.0 | 21 | 6.5 |
| Kentucky | 28.5 | **29** | 107.2 | 26 | 6.5 |
| Louisiana | 39.4 | **35** | 129.3 | 28 | 5.8 |
| Maine | 7.6 | **12** | 32.3 | 9 | 7.2 |
| Maryland | 35.5 | 32 | 164.8 | **36** | 7.6 |
| Massachusetts | 49.7 | **42** | 239.4 | 41 | 7.8 |
| Michigan | 88.1 | **45** | 294.5 | 43 | 5.9 |
| Minnesota | 36.3 | 34 | 161.4 | 34 | 7.4 |
| Mississippi | 16.0 | **20** | 62.2 | 19 | 6.7 |
| Missouri | 41.8 | 38 | 162.8 | **35** | 6.7 |

*Source*: U.S. Department of Commerce. Bureau of Economic Analysis. "Gross state product (GSP)." *Regional Accounts Data*. 25 Oct. 2000. 5 Dec. 2000.

pectation. Not until we get to Indiana—thirty-seventh on the list—does a state's gross state product equal the expected average of around 2 percent.

The sum of the gross state products of the five states with the smallest amounts of gross state product—Vermont, North Dakota, Wyoming, Montana, and South Dakota (ten percent of the total number of states)—is required to equal just 1 percent of total gross state product. Gross state products of fifteen

**Exhibit 10.9 (continued)**
**Gross State Product, 1977 and 1998**

| State | 1977 Amount in $ Billions | Rank | 1998 Amount in $ Billions | Rank | Average Annual Growth Rate |
|---|---|---|---|---|---|
| Montana | 6.4 | **7** | 19.9 | 4 | 5.6 |
| Nebraska | 13.6 | **16** | 51.7 | 15 | 6.6 |
| Nevada | 7.5 | 11 | 63.0 | **20** | 10.7 |
| New Hampshire | 6.3 | 6 | 41.3 | **13** | 9.3 |
| New Jersey | 66.8 | 44 | 319.2 | 44 | 7.7 |
| New Mexico | 10.4 | 14 | 47.7 | 14 | 7.5 |
| New York | 178.0 | 50 | 706.9 | 50 | 6.8 |
| North Carolina | 44.1 | 40 | 235.8 | 40 | 8.3 |
| North Dakota | 5.3 | **3** | 17.2 | 2 | 5.7 |
| Ohio | 98.1 | **46** | 341.1 | 45 | 6.1 |
| Oklahoma | 23.9 | **25** | 81.7 | 22 | 6.0 |
| Oregon | 22.3 | 24 | 104.8 | **25** | 7.6 |
| Pennsylvania | 100.5 | **47** | 364.0 | 46 | 6.3 |
| Rhode Island | 7.3 | **9** | 30.4 | 7 | 7.1 |
| South Carolina | 20.3 | 22 | 100.4 | **24** | 7.9 |
| South Dakota | 5.1 | 2 | 21.2 | **5** | 7.0 |
| Tennessee | 33.5 | 31 | 159.6 | **33** | 7.7 |
| Texas | 131.7 | 49 | 645.6 | 49 | 7.9 |
| Utah | 10.4 | 15 | 59.6 | **17** | 8.7 |
| Vermont | 3.4 | 1 | 16.3 | 1 | 7.8 |
| Virginia | 44.0 | 39 | 230.8 | 39 | 8.2 |
| Washington | 36.0 | 33 | 192.9 | **38** | 8.3 |
| West Virginia | 14.7 | **17** | 39.9 | 12 | 4.9 |
| Wisconsin | 40.8 | **36** | 157.8 | 32 | 6.7 |
| Wyoming | 5.7 | **4** | 17.5 | 3 | 5.5 |
| **TOTAL United States** | $ 1,985.7 | | $ 8,745.2 | | 7.3 |

<http://www.bea.doc.gov/bea/regional/data.htm>.

of the smallest states—30 percent of the total number of states—are needed to account for 5 percent of total gross state product. Only when we get to Oklahoma—rank twenty-two—does the accumulation of gross state products of the preceding states amount to at least 10 percent of the total.

For the largest states the situation is much different. California's gross state product accounts for about one-eighth of total gross state product. Its output of final goods and services approximates that of the twenty-four smallest states.

**Exhibit 10.10**
**Distribution of Gross State Product among States, 1998**

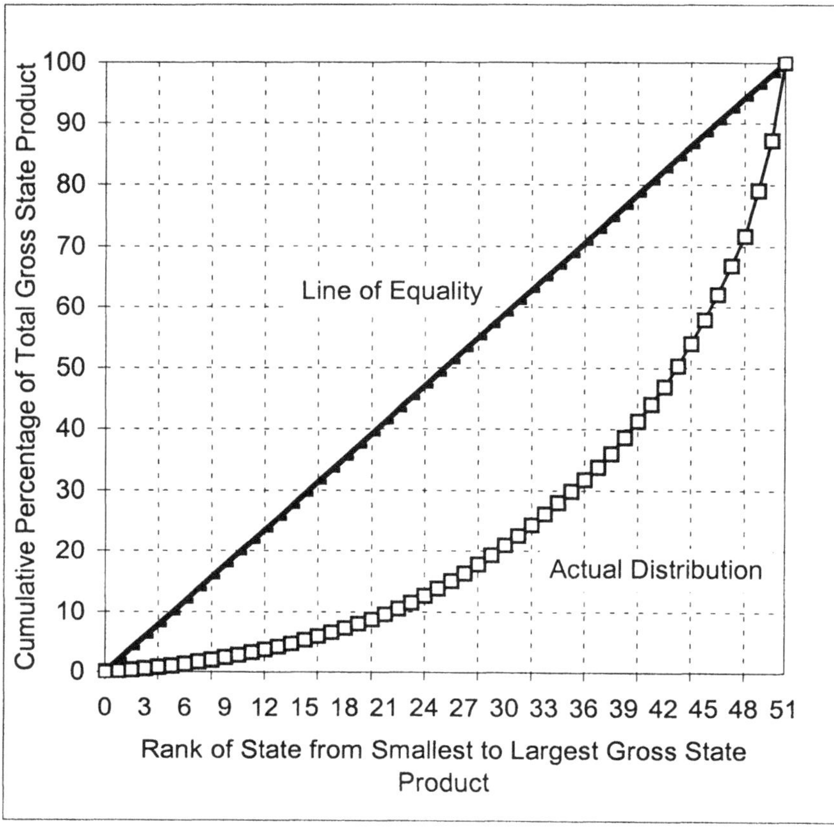


In terms of gross state product, the four largest states—California, New York, Texas, and Illinois—account for about one-third of total gross state product—an output equivalent to that of the smallest thirty-seven states. Adding another four of the largest states—Florida, Pennsylvania, Ohio, and New Jersey—brings us to nearly half of the total output. Although all states are equally represented in the U.S. Senate, they clearly are not equal in the nation's economic market place.

In one of the world's largest free market areas, however, size of gross state product appears to be no guarantee of strong economic performance. Exhibit 10.9 shows that of the eight states with the largest *Gross State Product*, the growth rates of four have exceeded the national average and four have not. Having a small gross state product confers no advantage. Of the five smallest, only Vermont managed a growth rate above the national average during the 1977 to 1998 period.

The horizontal axis of Exhibit 10.10 ranks the states from smallest to largest in terms of gross state product. The vertical axis measures the accumulative percentage of gross state product. The curved line emanating from the lower left-hand corner and proceeding to the upper right-hand corner traces the distribution. If our extraterrestrial visitor had been correct in its (with such visitors, it's hard to tell their gender, if any) supposition, and all states had an equal share of the total, the distribution would have been represented by the straight diagonal line—the line of equality. Such may be the prevailing situation in our visitor's home planet, but not in this United States.

The variation of the actual distribution from perfect equality can be quantified by using a modified version of the Gini coefficient. The coefficient indexes the degree of inequality from zero to one. On the chart the area between the actual distribution and the line of perfect represents the extent of inequality. In this case, the Gini coefficient equals 0.48—just about halfway between the two extremes.

Differences in geographic and economic size among states are not causes for great concern within the United States. Oklahoma does not feel threatened by its larger and economically more significant neighbor to the south. Nevada does not fear an invasion from California—except on weekends when its casinos will welcome visitors from the west. Rhode Island does not feel compelled to protect its borders by alliances with Pennsylvania to thwart New York's expansionist designs. So great are the blessings of a property system, rule of law, and market economy that such ideas seem absurd. We live in an idyllic world envisioned by Ludwig von Mises:

> When there is private ownership of the means of production everywhere and when the laws, the tribunals, and the administration treat foreigners and citizens on equal terms, it is of little importance where a country's frontiers are drawn. Nobody can derive any profit from conquest, but many can suffer losses from fighting. War no longer pays . . .. All nations can coexist peacefully, because no nation is concerned about the size of its state.[11]

Rejoice and be glad! We are fortunate indeed. Even a cursory awareness of what has gone and is going on shows that the rest of the world does not enjoy such a happy arrangement.

## CONCLUDING OBSERVATIONS

Gross domestic product measures the market value of goods and services produced by factors of production located in the United States. It represents the most widely accepted measure of economic activity and the economic value of output available for consumption and investment. Over the forty-year period from 1959 to 1999 we have seen that GDP has grown substantially. In terms of price levels prevailing in each of the years, it has risen from $507 billion to $9.3 trillion, an eighteen-fold increase. When adjusted for inflation and expressed in terms of prices in 1996, it has grown from $2.3 trillion to $8.9 trillion, a nearly four-fold increase sufficient to permit real goods and services per capita to increase 2.5 times.

Our analysis suggests that investment in productive capital—human as well as inanimate—enhances the productivity that has made an improved standard of living possible. The promise of investment today is a better tomorrow.

Inspection of detailed GDP statistics and economic performance on a year-by-year basis shows that growth has neither been continuous nor uniform either among the components or among regions of the country. Personal consumption and Gross private investment have increased their shares of GDP. In relative terms government sector consumption expenditures and investment have contracted. Nearly half of total gross state product is produced in just eight states. Only 10 percent of gross state product is produced in the smallest twenty-two states.

## NOTES

1. U.S. Department of Commerce, Bureau of Economic Analysis, *National Income and Product Accounts of the United States, 1929-94*, vol. 1 (Washington, DC: U.S. Government Printing Office, Apr. 1998) M-1.
2. *National Income and Product Accounts of the United States* M-2.
3. *National Income and Product Accounts of the United States* M-2.
4. *National Income and Product Accounts of the United States* M-1.
5. *National Income and Product Accounts of the United States* M-1.
6. U.S. Department of Commerce, Bureau of the Census, *Statistical Abstract of the United States: 1999* (Washington, DC: U.S. Government Printing Office, 1999) 963.
7. *Statistical Abstract of the United States: 1999* 169.
8. Richard M. Beemiller and Clifford H. Woodruff III, "Gross State Product by Industry, 1977-98," *Survey of Current Business* (Oct. 2000): 69–90.
9. Beemiller: 24–45.
10. Beemiller: 35.
11. Ludwig von Mises, *Omnipotent Government, The Rise of the Total State and Total War* (New Haven: Yale University Press, 1944) 50.

# 11

# A Glance Behind

What events happened in the United States to significantly shape data reported in the national income and product accounts (NIPA)? It could be argued that every event alters production and consumption of goods and services and the distribution of income to some degree. But "significantly" narrows the choices considerably, and a quantitative basis exists for choosing among suggestions. In the course of our review of the NIPA, of other national accounting systems, and of the data they produce, those major events have been identified. Their importance may have been lost in the detail, however. With gross domestic product (GDP) having been defined and examined, now is a good time to make sure they are not overlooked.

Our analysis has covered four decades. Significant changes mark each decade. Some changes reflect the growth of a trend to a critical and noticeable size. Other changes represent a move in a new direction. Some changes have brought about a continuing change in the patterns observed in the national income and product data—changes that are likely (or liable) to persist into the future. Other changes made impacts on the composition and distribution of national output that have subsequently—but perhaps not permanently—been reversed.

## MAJOR EVENTS, 1959 TO 1999

Although limited to changes that have made their mark on the NIPA, selection involves judgment calls. My nominations for key events include:

In the 1960s:

- Passage of legislation establishing the Medicare and Medicaid programs, and
- Increasing participation of women in the labor force.

In the 1970s:

- Break with the Bretton Woods agreement, abandonment of the pegged exchange rates, and adoption of managed floating exchange rates,
- OPEC and rise of petroleum prices, and
- Stagflation.

In the 1980s:

- Central bank adoption of monetarist approach to money management,
- Federal government tax cuts and massive budget deficits,
- Declining trend in interest rates and price inflation,
- Continuous balance of payments deficits, and
- Glut of oil on world petroleum markets.

In the 1990s:

- Stock market boom,
- Declining personal saving, and
- Federal government budget surplus.

### Medicare and Medicaid

In the 1960s two events stand out. For one a defining moment exists. For the other continuation and intensification of a trend. The passage of legislation enabling Medicare and Medicaid in 1965 represents the defining moment. As we have seen, that legislation has had a significant impact on the tax burden of wage and salary earners, on government receipts and disbursements, on employee compensation that businesses pay, on the cost of medical care for all citizens, and on the growth of the medical services industry. After the passage of more than three decades, escalation of medical care costs continues at an unsustainable pace as a consequence of that legislative action.

### Labor Force

A change in the composition of the labor force constitutes the second event of the 1960s: increasing participation of women. In 1959 women made up about one-third of the labor force. By 1998 the percentage had risen to over 46 percent and may be approaching its limit of maximum participation. From 1959 to 1969 participation rose almost five percentage points. The ten years from 1969 to 1979 added another four percentage points, bringing the percent of the labor force accounted for by women to 42 percent. Ten years later, by 1989, three more percentage points were added, and the figure stood at 45 percent. A gain of 1 percent from 1989 to 1999 suggests the transition is nearing completion.

The widespread participation of women in the paid labor force has resulted in a rapid growth in the labor force. From 1959 to 1999 the labor force more than doubled from 68.4 million to 139.4 million. During the same period of time, the population of individuals over sixteen years of age increased 81 percent from 115.3 million to 208.8 million. Participation of the working-age population in the labor force grew from 59 percent to 67 percent. The infusion of women into the labor force has caused the annual rate of growth in the labor force from 1959 to 1998 to exceed the annual rate of growth in working-age population.

What caused the transition? Many factors undoubtedly contributed. Economic factors played a role, aided and abetted by the rising costs of Medicare, Medicaid, and social insurance. As we have seen, the take-home portion of wage and salary income as a percentage of personal income has declined during the period from 64 percent of personal income to 53 percent. As households struggled to maintain their standard of living, many people concluded that two sources of labor income were not only better but also necessary. Growth in final output of goods and services expressed in terms of GDP expressed in 1996 prices has outstripped growth in labor input. While the labor force doubled, real GDP increased by a factor of 3.8—almost quadrupling—from $2,319.0 billion in 1959 to $8,875.8 billion in 1999. Workers in 1999 produced 74 percent more than their counterparts forty years earlier.

### Foreign Exchange Rates

Along with abandonment of budget discipline came a break with the Bretton Woods agreement and fixed exchange rates in 1971. Budget discipline and fixed rates are not unrelated. Fixed exchange rates require a country to adopt monetary and fiscal policies that maintain its foreign currency reserves. Under fixed exchange rates an excess of imports of goods and services over exports requires measures to raise interest rates, curb inflation, reduce employment, and slow economic growth. Such policies seem appropriate and prudent for other countries, but they were not welcome in the United States.

Relaxation of constraints posed by a fixed exchange standard seems to have strengthened rather than weakened the position of the U.S. dollar as an international medium of exchange. Gold had served as the ultimate means of settling claims among countries prior to desertion of the U.S. dollar's valuation in terms of gold. Thereafter, the dollar replaced gold as a means of international settlement. Special drawing rights and other schemes for an international currency did not emerge as major players. That outcome has made possible the United States' substantial balance of payments deficits. Growth in trade among nations has created a demand for an international currency, and this country's balance-of-payments deficits produce an ample supply.

### Crude Oil Prices

The Organization of Petroleum Exporting Countries (OPEC) emerged as a force to be reckoned with in determining world prices in the 1970s. The consequences of shifts in oil prices and supplies rocked the U.S. economy during the 1970s and 1980s. OPEC's actions were not unrelated to the move to floating exchange rates. World crude oil prices were and still are denominated in terms of U.S. dollars. When the value of the dollar no longer was fixed, it floated downward. With 1971 crude oil prices at $2.55 per barrel, OPEC member countries, already unhappy, became even unhappier and less accommodating suppliers. Price increases and nationalization of oil concessions granted to Western oil companies occurred during the 1970s, but two events—jolts, really—stand out. The United States supported Israel during the fourth Arab-Israeli war that broke out in early October 1973. Annoyed, OPEC members imposed an embargo on oil exports to the United States that lasted until early March 1974. The immediate shortages and rising costs of energy in the United States rippled through its economy, affecting both the output of goods and services and the manner of their production.

The second jolt came in 1980. By early 1979 crude oil prices stood at $14.56 per barrel. In May 1980 crude oil prices were raised to $28.00 a barrel, retroactive to April 1. It was no April fool's joke. By the end of the year, prices exceeded $30 a barrel. That proved to be the high water—high oil price, rather—mark. Over the long term the forces of greed on the part of producing nations and self-preservation on the part of consuming countries prevailed. Fudging on oil production quotas by OPEC members became widespread, and conservation and development of alternative supply sources by consumers began to have an effect. Supply started to meet and then exceed demand. Prices retreated to $28 per barrel by 1985, and in 1986 they dropped 50 percent. Both the price upswing and downward plunge impacted and continue to affect the U.S. economy.

### Stagflation

A new phenomenon in the 1970s generated a new term: stagflation. Conventional (Keynesian) wisdom held that falling prices and rising unemployment accompanied one another. Although consumers seek bargains, benefits from falling prices are lost on those without income. The evil consequences of unemployment called for corrective monetary and fiscal actions. Increases in the money supply, easing of credit, increases in government spending, and tax cuts comprised the medicine prescribed to gain back robust economic health.

Exhibit 11.1 displays the pattern of the *Unemployment rate* and of *Price inflation* measured by the consumer price index from 1959 to 1999. The vertical axis measures *Unemployment rate* and *Price inflation* rates, and the horizontal axis measures years. The vertical bars represent the *Unemployment rate* and *Price inflation*. The *Misery index* is simply the sum of unemployment rates and price inflation rates for each year from 1959 to 1999. It summarizes very nicely economic conditions during the forty-year period. The line above the vertical bars represents the *Misery index*.

During the 1960s conventional wisdom seemed to correspond to the way the economy behaved. Inflation was low, but unemployment was high. With increases in rates of price inflation, unemployment rates declined, but over the decade the misery index rose. In the 1970s the handy association between inflation and unemployment changed. Rising prices accompanied rising unem-

**Exhibit 11.1**
**Unemployment, Price Inflation, and the Misery Index, 1959 to 1999**

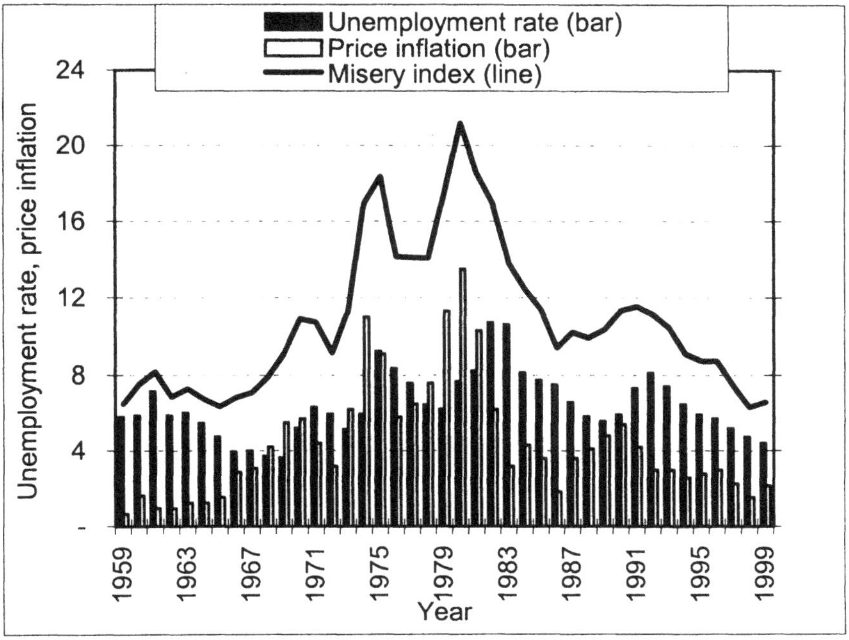


*Source* : U.S. Department of Labor. Bureau of Labor Statistics. "Table Containing History of CPI -U U.S." *Consumer Price Indexes* . 28 Sep. 2000. 9 Dec. 2000. <http://www.bls.gov/cpihome.htm> And: "Employment status of the civilian population by sex and age." *Labor Force Statistics from the Current Population Survey* . 4 Feb 2000: Table A-1 29 Sep 2000. <http://stats.bls.gov/webapps/legacy/epsatab1.htm>.

ployment. As inflation declined so did unemployment. The misery index indicates that the 1970s was a miserable decade.

Exhibit 11.2, a scatter diagram with inflation rates on the vertical axis and unemployment rates on the horizontal, shows more clearly the fundamental shift in macroeconomic behavior. The white dots represent inflation and unemployment rates from 1959 to 1969; the black dots, inflation and unemployment rates from 1970 to 1980. In the 1960s, not only were inflation and unemployment rates lower than in the 1970s, but also the relationship between them tended to be inverse. That is, low inflation was associated with high unemployment, and vice versa. A least-squares regression line confirms the visual impression. It slopes in a downward direction from left to right.

Relative to the 1960s, higher inflation and unemployment rates characterized the 1970s. More importantly, as the arrangement of the black dots and their accompanying least-squares regression line on Exhibit 11.2 suggest, the relationship between the two rates changed from inverse to positive. Stagflation had arrived and confounded the old remedies. Rising prices accompanied rising unemployment. The economy had caught a new disease, and new cures were

**Exhibit 11.2**
**Relationship between Price Inflation and Unemployment in the 1960s and 1970s**

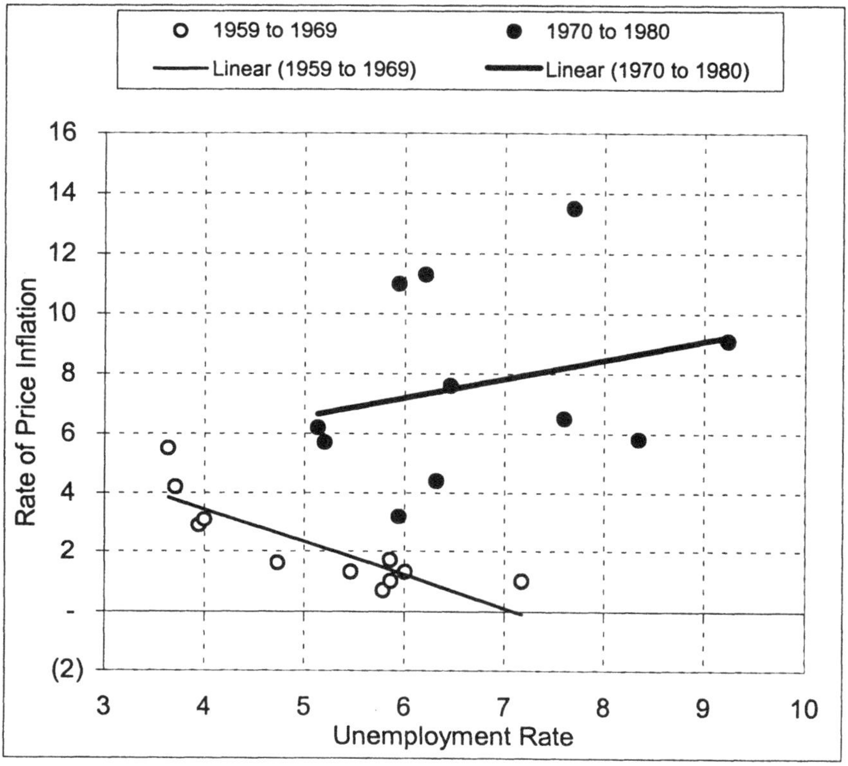


*Source* : U.S. Department of Labor. Bureau of Labor Statistics. "Table Containing History of CPI-U U.S." *Consumer Price Indexes* . 28 Sep. 2000. 9 Dec. 2000. <http://www.bls.gov/cpihome.htm> And: "Employment status of the civilian population by sex and age." *Labor Force Statistics from the Current Population Survey* . 4 Feb 2000: Table A-1 29 Sep 2000. <http://stats.bls.gov/webapps/legacy/epsatab1.htm>.

needed. The Keynesian economic physicians were ushered out, and with the 1980s the monetarists came marching into the Federal Reserve System.

## Monetary Policy

As Exhibit 11.1 shows, the rate of price inflation peaked in 1980, and since then it has trended downward. Unemployment, growing in 1980, continued to rise and reached a peak in the 10 percent to 11 percent range in 1982 and 1983. Since then, *mirabile dictu*, it too, like inflation, has undulated downward. The misery index declined. What did the monetarists do that the Keynesians did not? Do they deserve credit for the greater stability that has transpired in the 1980s and 1990s? Has a prescription been found that assures a healthy economy in the future? Or are the two groups of physicians of economics like doctors before scientific medicine? One called for enemas; the other, for purgatives. Sometimes the patient recovered; sometimes not.

The Federal Reserve System does its work by influencing the money supply and credit conditions. Everyone knows what money is. Even small children learn to prefer a small dime to a larger nickel out of respect for the greater purchasing power of the former. However, our central bankers are not so sure. The definition of the money supply becomes more complicated. Not one but three definitions of money exist. The narrowest definition, called M1, relates most closely to money's function in facilitating transactions. It consists of currency, traveler's checks, demand deposits, and other checkable deposits. In 1999 the average amount of M1 money in circulation amounted to $1.1 trillion.

An intermediate definition of money, M2, includes M1 plus retail money market funds, saving deposits, and small time deposits. Although money market funds and savings and time deposits cannot be used to conduct transactions, they usually can be converted to cash quickly with little cost or risk and better serve money's other function of providing a store of value. Those additions bring the 1999 money supply to $4.5 trillion. The broadest definition of money, not surprisingly labeled M3 and amounting to $6.2 trillion, includes M2 plus business time deposits, repurchase agreements, Euro dollars, and institution only money market funds.

The volume of transactions makes up one of the factors determining the demand for money. Transactions influencing the demand for money include purchases and sales of intermediate products and of existing real and financial assets as well as of final goods and services. Absence of estimates of those other transactions necessitates using GDP as a proxy of all transactions conducted with exchange of money. Note that the volume of transactions is but one factor determining the demand for money. In a market economy innovation is not confined to manufacturing goods and delivering services. Innovations occur in financial institutions and practices as well. Increasing use of credit cards, for example, economizes on the use of money for transaction purposes. The emergence of new financial instruments blurs the distinction between money and other financial assets.

By influencing credit conditions the central bank seeks to maintain low unemployment rates, growth in real GDP, and stable prices and interest rates. By buying or selling U.S. government securities from the private sector, the Federal Reserve can increase or decrease the money supply. A purchase of U.S. Treasury bonds by the Federal Reserve System from commercial banks, for example, leaves the banks holding cash reserves available to lend to private borrowers. Increasingly, the Federal Reserve has relied on changes in the Federal Funds rate—the rate at which banks borrow from one another—to change credit conditions. In either event, sooner or later, Federal Reserve policy is reflected in changes in the money supply.

Since 1980 fluctuations in price inflation, interest rates, and unemployment have been dampened. Price inflation, interest rates, and unemployment have declined. Real GDP has grown continuously since 1991. Do monetarists manage the money supply differently than Keynesians, or has accomplishment of the policy objectives been a result of the luck of the draw?

Examination of the data suggests that Keynesian and monetarist money management does differ. The difference does not necessarily preclude attribution of luck to the good performance.

*Money Supply Change Relative to Gross Domestic Product.* We will begin our examination with a look at changes in the money supply and in nominal gross domestic product (a crude indicator of demand for money). For the money supply we shall use the intermediate series, M2. Gross domestic product rose from $507.4 billion in 1959 to $9,299.2 billion in 1999—an eighteen-fold increase. The money supply grew to over fifteen times its 1959 amount, $293.2 billion, to $4,525.3 billion in 1999. We already have seen that rates of growth in GDP were not constant over the forty-year period. Not surprisingly, neither were the money supply growth rates.

Exhibit 11.3 contains four charts. The top two show on the vertical axis year-to-year percentage growth rates for *Nominal GDP* and the *Money Supply* from 1959 to 1999. Comparison of percentages shows that for some years the rate of change in the *Money Supply* exceeds that for GDP. In others the reverse is true. The largest single-year rate-of-change in the *Money Supply* occurs in 1976 when it reaches 12.8 percent. *Nominal GDP* more than matches that single-year change rate with 13.0 percent in 1978. In 1976, however, the high rate of change in the *Money Supply* is accompanied by a high rate of change in *Nominal GDP*, 11.5 percent. Only 1.3 percentage points separate the two rates. In 1978, on the other hand, the high rate of change in *Nominal GDP* exceeds the growth in the *Money Supply* by a wide margin. Its 13.0 percent change is accompanied by an 8.3 percent change in the money supply. What significance, if any, can be attached to differences in the two percentages?

Money is a stock; it exists at a point in time. Gross domestic product measures the flow of output of goods and services measured in terms of money values over a period of time, in our case, a year. The two can be related to one another through an equation of the form:

$$M \cdot V = GDP$$

where

$M$ is the money supply;

$V$ is the velocity of money, that is the number of times a year inventory of money turns over or is spent for final goods and services; and

$GDP$ is gross domestic product.

This identity, sometimes referred to as the money supply equation, has been around a long time.

For 1999, as we already have observed, the *Money Supply* over the year's twelve months averages $4,525.3 billion, and *Nominal GDP* amounts to $9,299.2 billion. Division of GDP by the money supply produces a figure for *Velocity of Money* of 2.05. Similar feats of arithmetic for other years are displayed in the lower-left chart in Exhibit 11.3. It shows that velocity ranged from

**Exhibit 11.3**

**Change in the Money Supply Relative to Change in Nominal Gross Domestic Product, 1959 to 1999**

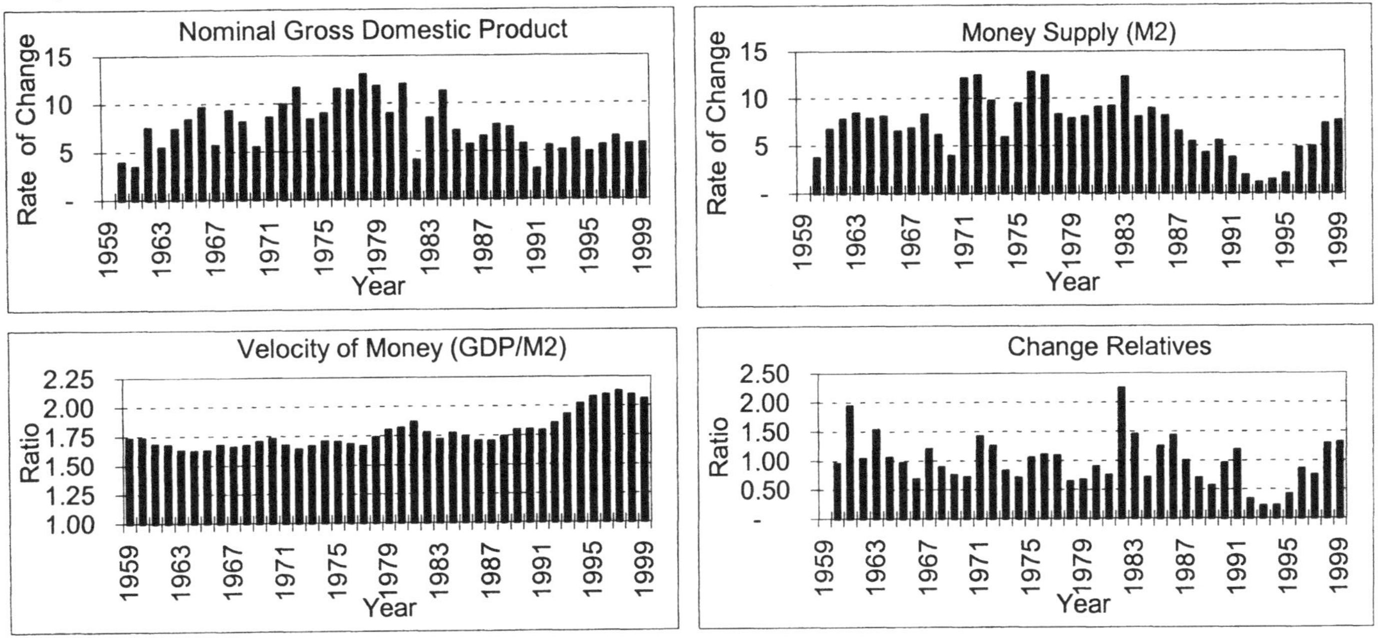


*Source*: Board of Governors of the Federal Reserve System. "Monthly Historical Money Stock Tables." *H.6 Money Stock and Debt Measures*. 7 Dec. 2000: Table 1. 9 Dec. 2000. <http://www.federalreserve.gov/releases/H6/hist/> And: U.S. Department of Commerce. Bureau of Economic Analysis. " "Selected NIPA Tables." *National Accounts Data*. 8 Aug. 2000: Table 1.1. 9 Sep. 2000. <http://www.bea.doc.gov/bea/dn1.htm>.

a low of 1.62 in 1964 to a high of 2.12 in 1997. Clearly, velocity is not constant through time. Changes in technology and communication, new financial instruments, and adoption of new ways of doing business assure that it changes over time. However, the velocity of money is not volatile. In twenty-four of the forty years, year-to-year velocity changes less than 1 percent. For twenty-eight of the years, less than 2 percent; for thirty-three, less than 3 percent. The maximum year-to-year percentage change is less than 5 percent. Considering institutional and technological changes in processing transactions and the eighteen- and fifteen-fold increases in *Nominal GDP* and the *Money Supply* that have transpired from 1959 to 1999, the *Velocity of Money* seems to standing still.

With *Velocity of Money* relatively constant, by the money supply equation we can expect that percentage changes in GDP will match changes in the money supply, and vice versa. If *r* represents a percentage change GDP, then the money supply must also change by *r* percent in order for velocity to remain constant since by the identity:

$$M \cdot (1 + r / 100) \cdot V = GDP \cdot (1 + r / 100)\,.$$

A check with Exhibit 11.3 shows that such correspondence is a rare occurrence. But the difference should be celebrated. It may serve to tell us about the policy directions of the Federal Reserve System.

Presumably, if economic conditions are rolling along smoothly, and if, in fact, central banks do influence the money supply and financial liquidity generally, the Federal Reserve would increase the money supply at the same rate as GDP. If, however, growth in output of goods and services is low or falling, an increase in the money supply at a rate greater than that for GDP seems prudent to ease credit conditions and stimulate spending. A similar course of action appears warranted when unemployment and interest rates are high. High rates of price inflation, on the other hand, would call for policies that lower growth rates in the money supply relative to those for GDP.

The lower-right chart in Exhibit 11.3 displays *Change Relatives*. They will serve as our indicator of Federal Reserve System policies. Change relatives are computed as the ratio of the percentage change in the money supply divided by the percentage change in nominal GDP for each of the years from 1960 to 1999. For example, in 1999 nominal GDP increased 5.8 percent, and the money supply increased 7.6 percent. To compute the change relative value for that year, we divide 7.6 percent by 5.8 percent. The resulting quotient, 1.3, is our change relative for 1999. It determines the height of the bar for 1999 in the lower-right chart of Exhibit 11.3. *Change Relatives* range from a low of 0.21 in 1993 to a high of 2.24 in 1982. Both of those extremes are realized during the reign of the monetarists.

Although the money supply equation suggests that a *Change Relative* of 1.00 represents a money supply policy that is neither expansionary nor constricting, the world is not so simple. Gross domestic product increases relatively more than the money supply over the forty years from 1959 to 1999. On balance over the period, therefore, *Change Relatives* average less than unity. However, they still could be expansionary if institutional and technological innovations and peoples' preferences enabled a secular increase in the velocity of money. Fortunately, determining a neutral value for *Change Relatives* is not necessary for our purposes. An interpretation that *Change Relatives* with higher values than others represent more expansionary policy actions will suffice.

The mild undulations in the *Velocity of Money* and the more discernable fluctuations in *Change Relatives* tell an interesting story. Note that in 1981 the *Velocity of Money* peaks at around 1.9. In 1981 the *Change Relative* is low and is preceded by three years of relatively low *Change Relatives*. With robust forces for nominal GDP growth—either from real economic growth or price inflation—such rise in the *Velocity of Money* is to be expected when the monetary authority limits increases in the money supply. Beginning in 1994 the *Velocity of Money* exceeds 2.0. Once again its rise is preceded by a period of low *Change Relatives* extending back to 1992 and continuing until 1997.

*Real Gross Domestic Product.* Real GDP serves as our measure of the output of goods and services and the level of economic activity. From 1959 to 1999 real GDP generally moved upward, but occasionally it fell. Did fluctuations in *Change Relatives* relate to fluctuations in real GDP? The answer, as we shall see, is yes and no, depending on the time period selected.

Year-to-year percentage changes in real GDP range from a drop of 2.0 percent in 1982 to a rise of 7.3 percent 1984. In both years change relatives respond appropriately: high in 1982 when the change in real GDP was low and low in 1984 when the change in real GDP was high. Quite often change relative values and ups and downs in real GDP are not so well behaved. Exceptions occur. In 1970 and 1974, for example, low and negative percentage changes in GDP correspond with low values for the change relatives. High change relative values in 1971 and 1986 coincide with high growth rates in GDP.

Exhibit 11.4 offers a display of the relationship between rates of change in real GDP and change relatives, and addresses the question concerning differences in the performance of Keynesian and monetarist policy makers. Percentage change rates in real GDP appear along the vertical axis, and change relative values appear on the horizontal axis. The white dots appearing on the graph represent value and rate pairs for each of the years from 1960 to 1979; the black dots, for each of the years from 1980 to 1999.

Conspicuous among the dots are two lines. The top and nearly horizontal line represents the least-squares regression relationship between change relatives and annual percent changes in real GDP for the white dots. The lower line with a negative slope represents the relationship for the black dots. Those results indicate the existence of a difference between Keynesian and monetarist money managers. The top nearly horizontal line shows an absence of a relationship between change relatives and fluctuations in real GDP during the period from 1959 to 1979. The lower line with the distinctly downward slope suggests the existence of an appropriate association between the two variables from 1980 to 1999. With a coefficient of determination of 0.1417 (designated by $R^2$), the equation for the lower line explains only 14 percent of the variance between the

**Exhibit 11.4**
**Relationship between Change Relatives and Changes in Real Gross Domestic Product, 1959 to 1979 and 1980 to 1999**

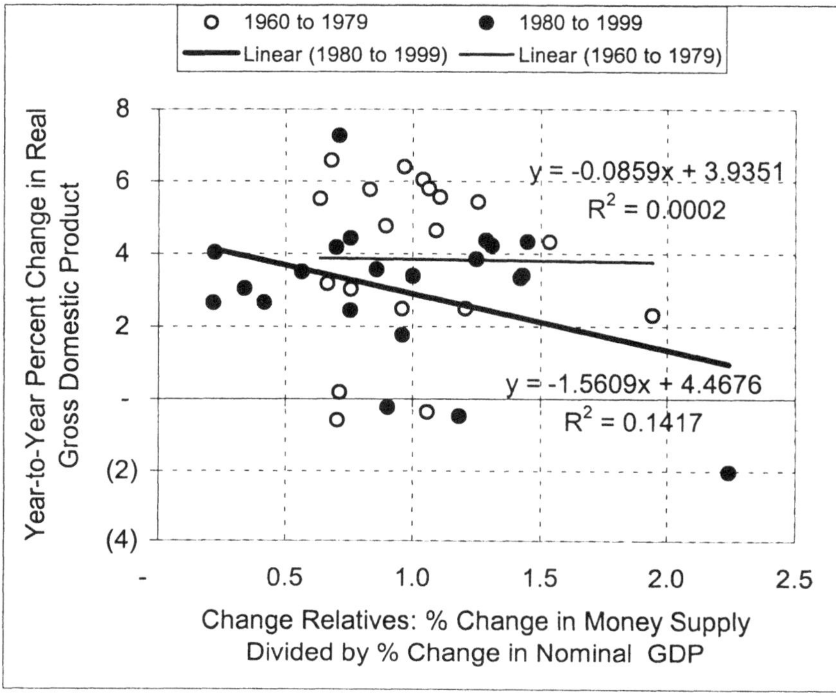


*Source* : Board of Governors of the Federal Reserve System. "Monthly Historical Money Stock Tables." *H.6 Money Stock and Debt Measures* . 7 Dec. 2000: Table 1. 9 Dec. 2000. <http://www.federalreserve.gov/releases/H6/hist/> And: U.S. Department of Commerce. Bureau of Economic Analysis. "Selected NIPA Tables." *National Accounts Data* . 8 Aug. 2000: Table 1.1. 9 Sep. 2000. <http://www.bea.doc.gov/bea/dn1.htm>.

variables, but, hey, a lot is going on. The data used are really crude. The money supply definition, use of annual rather than quarterly or monthly time series, no allowance for lag time between policy implementation and its effects, and nominal GDP as a proxy for all transactions constitute just a few of the shortcomings of the data. Nonetheless, the relationship seems sufficiently robust to shine through those and undoubtedly other sources of error and distortion.

### National Government Deficits

With respect to fiscal policy, the 1980s did not open auspiciously for economic stability. With the Reagan administration came substantial tax cuts and increases in the national government deficit. In chapter 5 we saw that as a percentage of personal income, federal personal income tax declined from 11.2 percent in 1981 to 9.2 percent in 1984. Expenditures of the national government, however, did not contract accordingly.

Annual national government deficits were not new. Balanced budget discipline had been abandoned in 1970. For the next twenty-seven years, national government current expenditure exceeded its current revenues. Deficits avoided the test of weighing the political cost of tax hikes against the political benefit of additional spending.

Consecutive deficits marked the 1970s, but they had been held to double-digit figures (billion-dollar digits, that is). Then, from 1981 to 1982, the annual deficit more than doubled from $53.7 billion to $132.6 billion. By 1984 it had reached $168.1 billion and continued upward until peaking in 1986 at $192.1 billion. The lull following that peak was temporary, however. For 1992 the national government posted a $297.5 billion deficit—the all-time high. From 1984 to 1999 national government deficits totaled over $2.5 trillion.

Reliance on deficit financing produced federal debt outstanding of $5.6 trillion by 1999, nineteen times greater than the amount in 1959.[1] Congressional and Executive yearning to do good by spending beyond current revenues produces its own self-fulfillment through added debt maintenance costs. Interest payments have risen from 7 percent to 14 percent of federal government current expenditures. However, growth in national government debt outstanding becomes less impressive (and less alarming) when compared with GDP. In 1959 national debt amounted to 58 percent of GDP; in 1999 to 62 percent. From 1944 to 1947 national government debt exceeded GDP. Rather than repayment, private sector growth in output of goods and services (and price inflation) has come to the rescue and reduced the percentage of debt relative to GDP.

Over the forty years after 1959, growth in federal government debt relative to GDP occurred after 1981. In 1981 it reached a low point of 33 percent. An increase in national debt outstanding as a percentage of GDP during World War II and other periods of crisis is understandable. But what crises beset us during the 1980s and 1990s—other than ones manufactured in Washington, DC?

Increases in government debt during the 1980s might have been expected to fuel inflationary pressures. But inflation did not materialize in part due to Federal Reserve policies to offset debt growth. During the period Federal Reserve banks increased their holdings of U.S. Government securities by $319 billion.[2] Federal Reserve efforts hardly would have been sufficient, but they were helped along by two other developments that produced a market for U.S. Government securities. As shown in Exhibit 7.7, in 1984, while the rest of the national government was going into deep deficit territory, social insurance funds began to accumulate surpluses. From 1984 to 1999 those surpluses amounted to $439 billion and are held largely in the form of debt issued by the federal government.

### Balance of Payments Deficits

A substantial increase in U.S. balance-of-payments deficits created another major demand for U.S. government securities. In 1984 the U.S. balance-of-payments deficit on current account set a new record of $91.5 billion. That record was quickly surpassed in succeeding years when deficits in excess of $100 billion have been routine. Given a choice, foreigners seem to prefer holding U.S. Government securities rather than buying our automobiles, appliances, and other tangible goods and services. During the seventeen-year period starting in 1982, they acquired almost $1.5 trillion of U.S. Government securities.[3] Their bond-holding proclivities plus monetary authority intervention and social insurance fund surpluses absorbed around 88 percent of the increase in federal government debt. The story might be very different had those sponges been absent. With a decline in federal government deficits in the late 1990s and prospects for a move toward surpluses emerging, a time may come to wring them out.

### Decline in Personal Saving and the Stock Market

Just as the national government's budget climbs into surplus territory as the decade of the 1990s concludes, the household and nonprofit institution sector appears about to slide into deficit. As already observed in chapter 5, personal saving as a percent of personal income has declined. In 1981 people saved over 9 percent of their personal income. From there it moved downward into the 6 percent to 8 percent range. From 8 percent in 1992, the saving rate has fallen each year and had dropped to 1.9 percent by 1999. The trends shown in Exhibit 5.1 presaged a move into negative territory.

The credit (or blame) for the decline in personal saving can be attributed to the rise in prices of corporate stock traded in the organized markets. The rise in value of stock portfolios held directly by persons and indirectly in mutual and pension funds has produced a perception of increased wealth. With increased wealth comes a disinclination to save. In the nineteen years since 1980, the Dow-Jones industrial stock average has increased almost twelve fold—from 964 to 11,497—an average annual increase of 14 percent. Since 1990 the pace has averaged 17.8 percent increase each year! A stock market boom! But will it last? Is a collapse around the corner that will reverse people's improvidence and return them to the slow and painful process of saving out of income? Despite stock-market declines registered in early 2001, consumer spending remained strong.

Few considered the stock market to be overvalued in 1980. The Dow-Jones index was only 285 points above the 1959 index of 679. Appreciation had averaged only 1.6 percent a year over the twenty-one-year period. How can we tell if the stock market today is more or less overvalued than in 1980? Information presented in Exhibit 11.5 offers an approach to answering the question.

In 1980 corporate profits with inventory valuation and capital consumption adjustments amounted to $251.4 billion; in 1999, to $823.0 billion. In 19 years, corporate profits had grown over three times. During the same period, the stock market index increased over eleven times. Bad news for the Wall Street bulls? No and yes. No, not as early as some claimed. Yes, eventually. Falling interest rates provided a grace period.

**Exhibit 11.5**
**Comparison of Indexes of Present Value of Corporate Profits and Dow-Jones Industrial Average, 1980 to 1999**

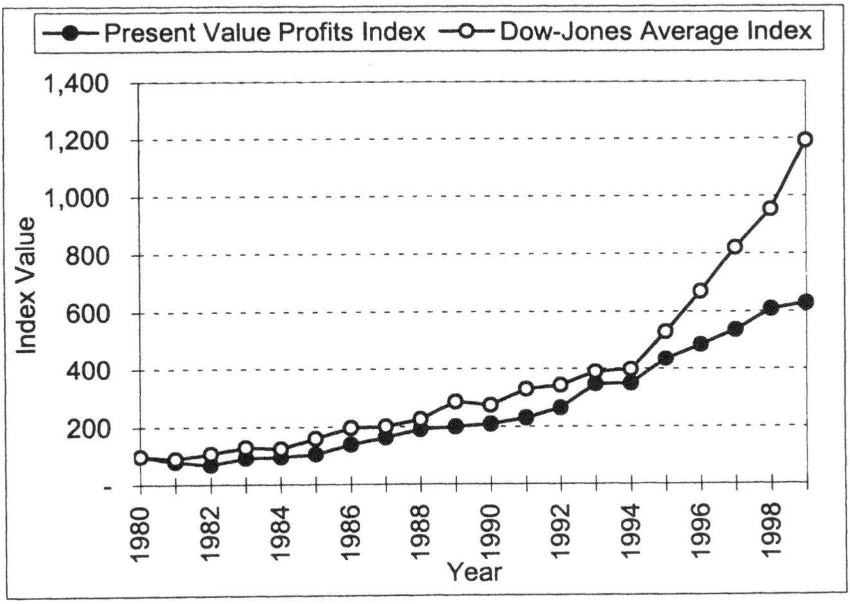


*Source* : U.S. Department of Commerce. Bureau of Economic Analysis. "Selected NIPA Tables." *National Accounts Data* . 8 Aug. 2000: Table 1.14. 9 Sep. 2000. <http://www.bea.doc.gov/bea/dn1.htm>. And: Board of Governors of the Federal Reserve System. "U.S. Government Securities: Treasury constant maturity 30-year." *H.15 Selected Interest Rates* . 4 Dec. 2000. 9 Dec. 2000. <http://www.federalreserve.gov/releases/H15/ data/htm> And: Dow Jones & Company. "Dow Jones Industrial Average." *Dow Jones Averages The Markets' Measure* . 3 August 2000 <http://averages.dowjones.com/dija_ year_close.html>.

How much is $251.4 billion worth in terms of earnings into the indefinite but infinite future? That question is not as absurd as it may seem. After all, conservative investment advisers recommend holding stocks for the long term. Even if you do not, someone has to hold them, so for the economy as a whole, the question makes sense. What that stream is worth depends on the rate at which future income is discounted. Since gyrations in the interest on thirty-year U.S. Government bonds sends the stock market up or down, it appears to provide a reasonable approximation to an appropriate interest rate.

The interest rate on U.S. government long-term bonds in 1980 was 11.3 percent. The present value of an indefinitely long stream of income in the amount of $251.4 billion per year discounted at 11.3 percent is $2,230.7 billion. Computing that value involves merely dividing 0.1127 into $188.3 billion. Price inflation as well as real economic growth can be expected to cause the $251.4 billion figure to increase in successive years. Expectations of inflation presumably already are built into the long-term interest rate. Given the high and rising rates of inflation experienced during the 1970s, the long-term interest rate in 1980 probably contained a hefty allowance for future price increases. The present value of future corporate earnings, therefore, can be considered a conservative figure.

For 1999 $823.0 billion in corporate profits discounted at the then prevailing long-term government bond interest rate of 5.9 percent produces a present value of $14.0 trillion. In Exhibit 11.5, present value corporate profits and the Dow-Jones industrial average index are indexed with 1980 equal to 100 and plotted in the chart that measures years on the horizontal axis and index values on the vertical. The two lines begin the period exactly at the same point and follow along closely until 1995. They then diverge and conclude the period with the stock market index about 90 percent greater than our present value calculation. The results suggest more than just a possibility of overvaluation. Eventually, Cassandra was right. On the other hand, a stock market investor employing this analysis and heeding it in the mid 1990s would have missed quite a party. Who knows? If inflation remains low and if long-term interest rates trend downward, the party may not be over yet. Despite rising energy prices and slowdowns in economic activity in 2000 and early 2001, the stock market continued to respond favorably to Federal Reserve cuts in the Federal Funds rate.

## MAJOR TRENDS

A decline in personal saving as a share of personal income is not the only shift in the composition of personal income that we observed from our examination of national income and product statistics from 1959 to 1999. Other major components with declining shares include salaries and wages and disposable personal income. Salaries and wages' share faded from 66 percent at the beginning to 57 percent at the end. Disposable personal income, from 89 percent to 85 percent. When some elements' shares drop, others gain. Gainers include other labor income (up from 3 percent to 6 percent), transfer payments (up from 6 percent to 13 percent), and social insurance contributions (up from 2 percent to 4 percent).

Like households (and nonprofit institutions), other sectors experienced changes in the composition of their sources and uses of funds. For national, state, and local units of government, taken as a whole, the relative contributions of property taxes, corporate profits taxes, and indirect business taxes waned while personal taxes and nontaxes and contributions for social insurance waxed. The shares of personal taxes and nontaxes rose from 35 percent to 41 percent of government current receipts, and social insurance contributions climbed from 11 percent to 24 percent. Changes in uses of funds reflect changes on the sources side of the income and expense statement. Transfer payments to persons grew from 20 percent of total uses of current funds to 37 percent while consumption expenditures shrank from 68 percent to 48 percent.

A deficit in the U.S. balance of payments persisted throughout the period. Our sources of funds from foreigners were less than the funds we used to buy things from them. As a source of funds from the rest of the world, the relative importance of exports of goods declined while our exports of services and of income receipts increased from 1959 to 1999. In looking at how the United States used those funds (and some additional borrowed funds), we found that imports of durable goods rose from 25 percent to 44 percent and payments for factor income grew from 6 percent to 20 percent. On the other hand, imports of nondurable goods, services, and transfer payments declined in importance.

Within the business sector we find that not all industries participated equally in U.S. productivity increases. Relative to the total, the output of agriculture, mining, construction, and manufacturing fell. Their collective shares declined from 39 percent in 1959 to 22 percent in 1999. Finance, insurance, and real estate and Services took their place, rising from 23 percent to 40 percent.

## WHAT IF

Some trends, like shifts in the composition of goods and services purchased for personal consumption, reflect largely independent decisions of numerous individuals and households attempting to maximize satisfaction from their income. In a market-oriented economy where consumer choice reigns, such trends can be taken as given. Other trends reflect collective decisions, and their satisfaction-maximizing potential is less certain.

No collective decision taken over the past forty years has had a greater impact on the current distribution of income than the adoption of the Medicare and Medicaid programs in the mid 1960s. In 1999 employer and employee payments for Medicaid amounted to $62.1 billion and $63.5 billion, respectively. Self-employed persons made $32.7 billion in social insurance payments of which between 20 percent and 25 percent is allocable for Medicare. Medicaid disbursements, $183.9 billion, came from tax dollars. In total the cost of the two programs amounted to around $320 billion.

In 1959 disposable personal income was 89 percent of personal income. In 1999 it was 85 percent, the lowest percentage for the entire forty years. Although its percentages have undulated over the period, the trend has been downward. At the same time, Medicare and Medicaid costs as percentages of personal income have increased.

Assuming that employers would have paid to employees in the form of wages and salaries the $62.1 billion they paid for Medicare and that Medicaid disbursements of $183.9 billion would have taken the form of a reduced tax burden, disposable personal income in 1999 would have been 89 percent of personal income—the same as in 1959. Disposable personal income as a percent of personal income would have fluctuated, but no downward trend would have been present. The promise of collective provision of medical care carries with it the peril of less individual discretion on how income is spent. For some the promise is more important than the peril; for others the peril is a greater concern.

## NOTES

1. U.S. Executive Office of the President, Council of Economic Advisers, "Table B-76," *Economic Report of the President* (Washington, DC: U.S. Government Printing Office, 2000), 12 Dec. 2000 <http://w3.access. gpo.gov/eop/>.

2. Board of Governors, Federal Reserve System, "Z.1 Historical data," *Flow of Funds Accounts of the United States*, 15 Sep. 2000: Table F.108, 18 Sep. 2000 <http://www.bog.frb.us/releases/z1/current/data.htm>.

3. Board of Governors, Federal Reserve System, "Z.1 Historical data": Table F.107.

# 12

# A Look Ahead

To what extent will the past be a prologue to the future? Which of the trends will be sustained? Which ones will be reversed? What will our charts look like forty years from now?

## A LOOK AHEAD

A person seeking answers to such questions in 1959 would not have had access to the forty years of prior national economic statistics available to an individual with similar curiosities at the turn of the century. Such lengthy time series of consistent data for our exhibits did not exist. Neither were they initially integrated with the flow-of-funds accounts of the Federal Reserve System, the balance-of-payments accounts, and input-output analysis. A complete picture of the economy requires all those essential elements of information plus data on such items as population, the labor force and its composition, employment and unemployment rates, the money supply and other indicators of financial market conditions, interest rates, and foreign exchange rates. Even if all that information had been available to our hypothetical forecaster, absence of electronic data access and processing would have presented an insurmountable obstacle. A lifetime of calculation would have been required to conduct analyses that now can be performed in a matter of minutes. After a lifetime of calculation, the future would have become history.

We have no such reasons for failing to use existing information as a basis for attempting to peer into the future. So let us shine up our crystal balls and look ahead.

**Some Existing Projections**

In anticipating the future, others have preceded us. In 1994 a bipartisan commission submitted an interim report to the President of the United States on dealing with government spending policy and taxation as far ahead as the year 2030.[1] Regularly, the Congressional Budget Office prepares forecasts on economic conditions and the national government budget ten years in advance. Its most recent predictions cover the period from the year 2000 to 2010.[2] Annual reports of the Board of Trustees of the Federal Old-Age and Survivors Insurance and Disability Insurance Funds (OASDI) also contain forecasts. Their most recent attempt extends to the year 2075.[3] (Given that many of those receiving social security checks in 2075 have not been born yet, such forecasts must involve big crystal balls.) Because of general concerns about the financial soundness of the social insurance programs, this third forecast will inform our journey into the future.

The 2000 OASDI Trustees report provides a long-range projection of social insurance fund balances based on actuarial estimates. The actuaries base their projections on three sets of alternative economic and demographic assumptions: low-cost or optimistic (alternative I), intermediate-cost (alternative II), and high-cost or conservative (alternative III): "The intermediate set, alternative II, represents the Board's best estimate of the future course of the population and the economy."[4] Annual rates of growth in real GDP are projected to decline from 3.5 percent in year 2000 to 1.5 percent by 2075. For most of the period the consumer price index rises 3.3 percent a year; lower rates prevail until 2005. Annual rates of increase in the labor force range from over 1.3 percent at the beginning of the period to 0.2 percent by the end. From 2005 onward 5.5 percent unemployment rates are assumed.[5]

Those assumptions together with demographic ones underlie projections of fund balances for OASDI and health insurance. Initially the OASDI funds' total income is greater than its outgo. Moreover, its accumulation of prior surpluses plus the 1999 surplus produces an end-of-year 2000 balance of $896 billion. That balance continues to grow and reaches a maximum in 2024 at $6.0 trillion. Thereafter outlays exceed income; the balance declines; 2037 marks the last year with a positive balance. By 2040 OASDI's annual deficit approximates $1.2 trillion. By 2050, $1.9 trillion. By 2060, $3.3 trillion. By 2075, $7.4 trillion in just that year!.[6]

Like OASDI, the Board of Trustees of the Federal Hospital Insurance (HI) and Supplementary Medical Insurance (SMI) Trust Funds report that the Health Insurance Fund begins the period with income exceeding outgo. That surplus and prior accumulations result in a 1999 year-end asset balance of $141.4 billion[7]. Continued surpluses further increase the balance to 2017. Thereafter outgo exceeds income; asset balances shrink and drop to zero by 2025. In 2025 a projected $154 billion deficit is not funded. For 2030 the projected deficit amounts to $289 billion.[8] The HI deficits continue to increase gradually until in 2036 they reach $505 billion. Then OASDI assets are exhausted, its deficits are combined with health insurance deficits. The addition of the OASDI annual deficit in 2037, $1,047, causes a jump in unfunded outlays to $1.6 trillion. Together, hand in hand as it were, the two entitlement programs begin their orderly march to greater deficits. By 2075 the combined OASDI and HI *annual* deficits equal $12.2 TRILLION.

For someone old enough to read this text, becoming concerned about a deficit liable to occur in 2075—even one of $12.2 trillion in a single year—takes real effort and imagination. Unless one leads a very placid life, the deficit is not likely to be the first thing a person thinks of upon waking in the morning. Even if we were sure that the $12.2 trillion deficit would materialize in 2075, it is hard to get excited. We discount the future so the present value of even such a huge amount does not appear to be very important. A dental appointment six months from now does not cause nearly as much anxiety as the one we are proceeding to this afternoon.

How important $12.2 trillion is today can be quantitatively estimated—with acceptance of certain assumptions, of course. In 2025 the first deficit materializes at $154 billion. How much would you have to have in 2000 to prepare for that eventually twenty-five years later if you were able to invest the amount and its subsequent earnings and earn 6 percent a year—a rough approximation to the current interest rate on long term government bonds? If

$X$ is the amount,

its value can be calculated as

$$X \cdot (1.06)^{25} = \$154{,}000{,}000{,}000$$

or solving for $X$

$$X = \$154{,}000{,}000{,}000 \cdot 1.06^{-25} = \$35{,}881{,}789{,}097.60$$

to be absurdly precise. In other words, or numbers, to meet each dollar obligation due in 2025 requires that just a little over 23 cents be set aside now to earn a return of 6 percent a year. Similar present value calculations can be performed for each of the following year's deficits. That horrendous year 2075 $12.2 trillion deficit in present value terms becomes a measly $155 billion.

A single deficit of $12.2 trillion in 2075 seems manageable today, but it is but one of a series of fifty-one deficits. With the present value of each of them having been calculated, they can be added together to determine the total obligation in today's terms of the two programs. In the year 2000 the cumulative present value of those deficits from 2025 to 2075 is $7.1 trillion—an amount equal to about 76 percent of the entire GDP in 1999. Talk about mortgaging the future!

Before becoming hysterical about social security and Medicare deficits, we should recognize that they are projections. The projections are based on assumptions that the actuaries feel are most likely to prevail—the intermediate assumptions between possible (optimistic) conditions that increase revenues to the social insurance funds and that reduce their outlays and those (pessimistic) conditions that reduce their inflows of funds and increase their outlays. Probabilities that all the optimistic assumptions occur may be small, but some of them may come to pass and ameliorate the looming deficit. Indeed, D- (Deficit) day for the social insurance funds keeps receding into the future. Earlier reports of the financial conditions of the funds were more pessimistic. According to the OASDI fund Board of Trustees, "In 1996, by contrast, the Hospital Insurance trust fund was projected to be exhausted in early 2001—just over 4 years away! And the exhaustion date for the Social Security funds was continuing to creep closer each year."[9]

### Another Perspective on the Future

To peer into the future, we will take the intermediate road (neither optimistic nor pessimistic), assume deficits do come to pass, and broaden our perspective to see what the rest of the economy may look like under such circumstances. OASDI and Health Insurance constitute but two of a large number of entitlement programs promoted by the national government. In addition to Hospital Insurance, the Medicare program also includes Supplementary Medical Insurance. Medicare promises to be a major consideration in the future. The list of other transfer programs of lesser magnitude goes on and on. We need to broaden our perspective to determine the size of the future possible train wreck imposed by Washington's generosity with taxpayer money and to look for evidence of resolution of whatever problems may arise.

Our examination of the past covered forty years. Our look into the future will extend to 2040. From 2000 that is another forty years. Symmetry recommends the time interval. It also picks up the first year in which deficits begin for the OASDHI program. The OASDHI reports express their projections as percentages of GDP. Initially, we will follow their lead.

*Government Current Income and Expenditures.* The annual report of the Board of Trustees of the Federal OASDI Funds provides projections of transfers to persons through the OASDI and Medicare (OASDHI) programs as percentages of GDP. The share of GDP going for OASDI transfers to persons increases from 4.2 percent in 2000 to 6.7 percent in 2040. During the same period Medicare (Hospital Insurance, HI) and Supplementary Medical Insurance (SMI) percentages increase from 2.4 to 4.7. Outlays for Medicare and Medicaid have tended to increase in proportion, with Medicaid outlays being about 82 percent of Medicare. Accordingly, our projections of Medicaid as a percent of GDP are calculated at 0.824 of the percentages for HI and SMI. They range from 1.9 percent of GDP in 2000 to 3.9 percent in 2040.

OASDI, Medicare, and Medicaid account for about two-thirds of government transfer payments to persons in 1999. The remaining one-third—all other government transfers to persons—as a percent of GDP from 1959 to 1999 has ranged from a low of 1.9 percent in 1966 to a high of 4.1 percent in 1975 and stands at 2.3 percent in 1999. Over the entire period all the other transfer programs to persons collectively have averaged a little more 2.7 percent, but the percentage has been a little less than 2.7 in the past 10 years. Accordingly, a constant percentage of 2.7 percent is assumed for other transfers.

The projections of those government transfer programs to persons as a percentage of GDP sum to a total percent of government outlays for transfer payments to persons. The projections indicate that they will rise from 11 percent of GDP in 2000 to 18 percent by 2040.

Social insurance contributions, indirect business tax and nontax receipts, corporate profits taxes, and personal tax and nontax receipts pay for transfer payments and other outlays of the state and local as well as national governments. Social security and Medicare contributions already have been projected in the Trustees' annual report. They do not account for all social insurance contributions, however. From 1959 to 1999 the other contributions to social insurance by persons have ranged from 0.7 percent to 1.0 percent of GDP. In 1999 they stood at 0.5 percent and averaged 0.7 percent over the past ten years. We will adopt the average.

From 1959 to 1999 both indirect business tax and nontax receipts and corporate profit taxes have declined as a percentage of GDP. In 1959 corporate profits taxes were 4.7 percent of GDP; in 1999 they amounted to 2.8 percent, up from a 1982 low of 2.0 percent. Indirect business tax and nontax receipts reached their peak of 9.2 percent in 1971. The year 1979 marked a low of 7.4 percent. Most recently their percentage stood at 7.7 percent. Increases and decreases seeming equally likely, 3.0 percent of GDP for corporate profits taxes and 8.0 percent for indirect business tax and nontax receipts will be adopted for projection purposes.

Unlike indirect business tax and nontax receipts and corporate profit taxes, personal tax and nontax receipts show a rising trend during the historical period. Fluctuations up and down have occurred, but 1999 marks the highest percentage, 12.4 percent. As a baseline for projection, a constant 12.0 percent of projected GDP will be used to compute Personal tax and nontax receipts.

All of the above items have been expressed in terms of *percentages* of GDP. For projections of dollar amounts, we need *estimates* of GDP. They have been taken from the 2000 OASDI Trustees annual report and appear in Exhibit 12.1. The estimates and projections are shown at five-year intervals starting with year 2000 and proceeding to 2035. Each year is shown from 2035 to 2040.

Projections of national, state, and local government income follow from projected GDP. *Social Insurance Contributions* are calculated as *GDP* times the sum of the percentages for OASDHI contributions and Other social insurance. Projections for *Indirect Business Tax and Nontax Receipts*, *Corporate Profits Taxes*, and *Personal Tax and Nontax Receipts* are produced by multiplying their respective percentages by *GDP*. The final source of government income, *OASDHI Deficit Coverage* is taken from the OASDHI projections.

I am assuming that the deficits of social security and Medicare will be covered each year from current receipts by raising one or more taxes. The declining importance of corporate profits taxes and indirect business taxes and nontaxes makes them unlikely candidates for hikes to meet those deficits. The regressive nature of social insurance contributions suggests that current reluctance to raise contribution rates will continue into the future. By a process of elimination, per-

**Exhibit 12.1**

**Government Receipts and Outlays, 2000 to 2040**

| | Amounts in $ Billions | | | | | | | | |
|---|---|---|---|---|---|---|---|---|---|
| | | Government Income | | | | | | Government Outlays | |
| Year | Gross Domestic Product | Social Insurance Contributions | Indirect Busn Tax & NonTax Recepts | Corporate Profits Taxes | Personal Tax & Nontax Receipts | OASDHI Deficit Coverage | Total Income Total Outlays | Transfer Payments to Persons | Other Outlays |
| 2000 | 9,781 | 714 | 782 | 293 | 1,174 | | 2,964 | 1,090 | 1,874 |
| 2005 | 12,524 | 908 | 1,002 | 376 | 1,503 | | 3,789 | 1,452 | 2,336 |
| 2010 | 16,141 | 1,162 | 1,291 | 484 | 1,937 | | 4,875 | 1,983 | 2,892 |
| 2015 | 20,641 | 1,484 | 1,651 | 619 | 2,477 | | 6,232 | 2,769 | 3,463 |
| 2020 | 26,169 | 1,882 | 2,094 | 785 | 3,140 | | 7,901 | 3,869 | 4,032 |
| 2025 | 33,022 | 2,375 | 2,642 | 991 | 3,963 | 154 | 10,124 | 5,338 | 4,786 |
| 2030 | 41,741 | 2,998 | 3,339 | 1,252 | 5,009 | 289 | 12,887 | 7,210 | 5,677 |
| 2035 | 52,936 | 3,786 | 4,235 | 1,588 | 6,352 | 465 | 16,426 | 9,483 | 6,944 |
| 2036 | 55,523 | 3,965 | 4,442 | 1,666 | 6,663 | 505 | 17,241 | 9,971 | 7,270 |
| 2037 | 58,236 | 4,153 | 4,659 | 1,747 | 6,988 | 1,592 | 19,140 | 10,473 | 8,666 |
| 2038 | 61,076 | 4,356 | 4,886 | 1,832 | 7,329 | 1,681 | 20,084 | 11,012 | 9,073 |
| 2039 | 64,050 | 4,562 | 5,124 | 1,922 | 7,686 | 1,771 | 21,064 | 11,558 | 9,506 |
| 2040 | 67,157 | 4,776 | 5,373 | 2,015 | 8,059 | 1,863 | 22,085 | 12,137 | 9,948 |

**Exhibit 12.2**
**Components of Government Receipts and Outlays as Percents of Total Receipts & Outlays, 1959, 1999, and 2040**

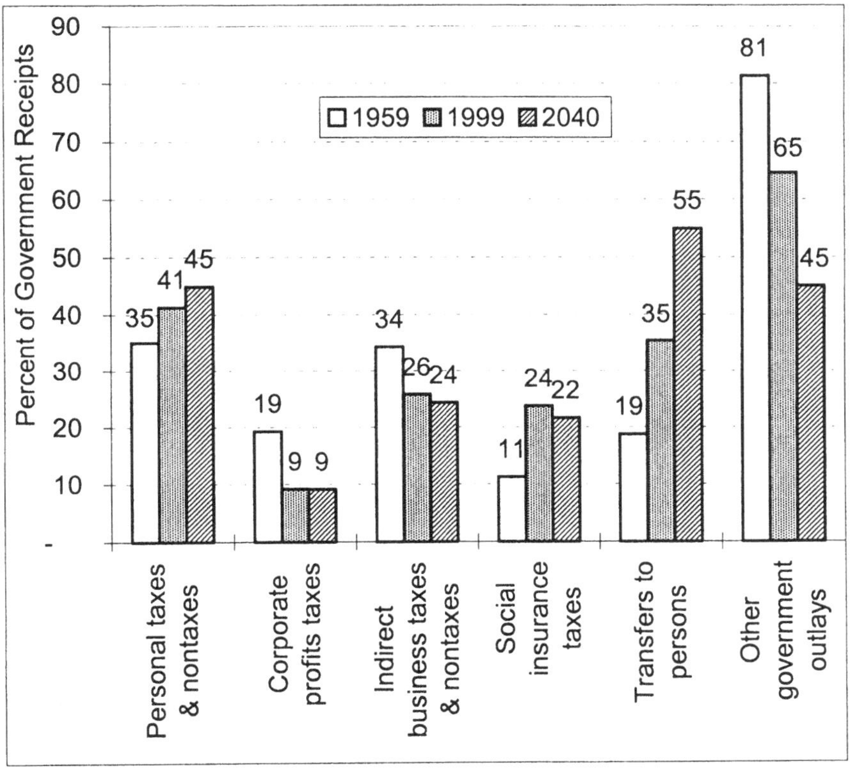


sonal income taxes become the most likely candidate, and subsequently will be adjusted upward in our projections to cover the deficit.

The sum of those five revenue sources produces a total for government receipts that are taken to be equal to government outlays. *Transfer Payments to Persons* constitute the most important of those outlays—by between 2020 and 2025, at any rate—and their projections are calculated by multiplying their percentage by *GDP*. *Other Outlays* are calculated as a residual by subtracting *Transfer Payments to Persons* from *Total Income/Total outlays*.

How government receipts and outlays in the world of 2040 differ from those with which we are familiar is displayed in Exhibit 12.2 and 12.3. In Exhibit 12.2 bar graphs show each component as percentages of total government receipts for 1959, 1999, and 2040. *Personal taxes and nontaxes* make up 45 percent of government revenue in 2040, up four percentage points from 1999's 41 percent and six points from 1959's 35 percent. The 2040 percentage includes the entire projected OASDHI deficit. While increases in personal taxes are unlikely to be welcome, the level of increase does not appear to be unreasonable.

*Corporate profits taxes*, down from 1959's 19 percent of government receipts, hold steady at 9 percent. *Indirect business taxes and nontaxes* continue their downward direction. *Social insurance taxes*, having risen as a source of government receipts from 11 to 24 percent from 1959 to 1999, decline slightly from their 1999 level to 22 percent by 2040. That reduction presumably results from a lower growth rate in the labor force.

On the outlay side of the income and expense statement, the share of *Transfers to persons* as a percent of total receipts continues its rise. From 19 percent in 1959 to 35 percent in 1999, it is projected to grow to 55 percent by 2040. Such growth appears to be entirely within the realm of possibility. The past forty years have seen an increase of sixteen percentage points in its relative importance. A twenty percentage point increase—now from a much larger base—may seem less dramatic over the next forty years. As transfers grow, the relative share of whatever else the government spends goes down—given our assumption of a balanced budget. By 2040 government will be more in the business of redistributing income than providing public goods and services. In 1999 the *Transfers to persons* rather than output of public goods and services already constitute its most important single activity. Has anyone noticed?

Exhibit 12.3 provides a perspective on growth of government relative to total economic activity as measured by GDP. The projections for 2040 indicate that *Government outlays* will equal 33 percent of GDP. In 1999 it stands at 30 percent. Having survived a five-percentage-point increase from 1959's 25 percent, another three points over forty years appears relatively modest. Of equal or greater importance are changes in the composition of government outlays. The rise of government *Transfers to persons* from 5 percent to 11 percent to 18 percent squeezes *Other government outlays* down from 20 percent to 19 percent to 15 percent. Relatively, government direct consumption of real goods and services can be expected to diminish. More of the nation's output pie will be left over for private use. Comparison of the quality and cost of government goods and services with those provided by the private sector suggests that such a development is not necessarily a bad thing.

*Personal Income*. What will the world of 2040 be like for individuals and households? To answer that question we take a look at personal income and its components.

Exhibit 12.4 contains the ingredients needed to project personal income and its components. We begin with *Wage, Salary, and Other Labor Income*. Although wages and salaries have tended to decline relatively, other labor income has increased. Together, *Wage, Salary, and Other Labor Income* have equaled about 54 percent of GDP from 1959 to 1999. They began the period a little less than 54 percent and end it very little changed. In 1970 they reached a maximum of 57.1 percent; in 1997, a low of 52.5 percent. The absence of any discernible trend up or down suggests using 54 percent for our projections.

Similarly, *Property Income*—the sum of proprietors' income, rent, interest, and dividends received by persons—shows no tendency to rise or fall. It begins the period at a little over 20 percent and ends the period at 23 percent. Its

**Exhibit 12.3**
**Government Expenditures as Percents of Gross Domestic Product, 1959, 1999, and Projected 2040**

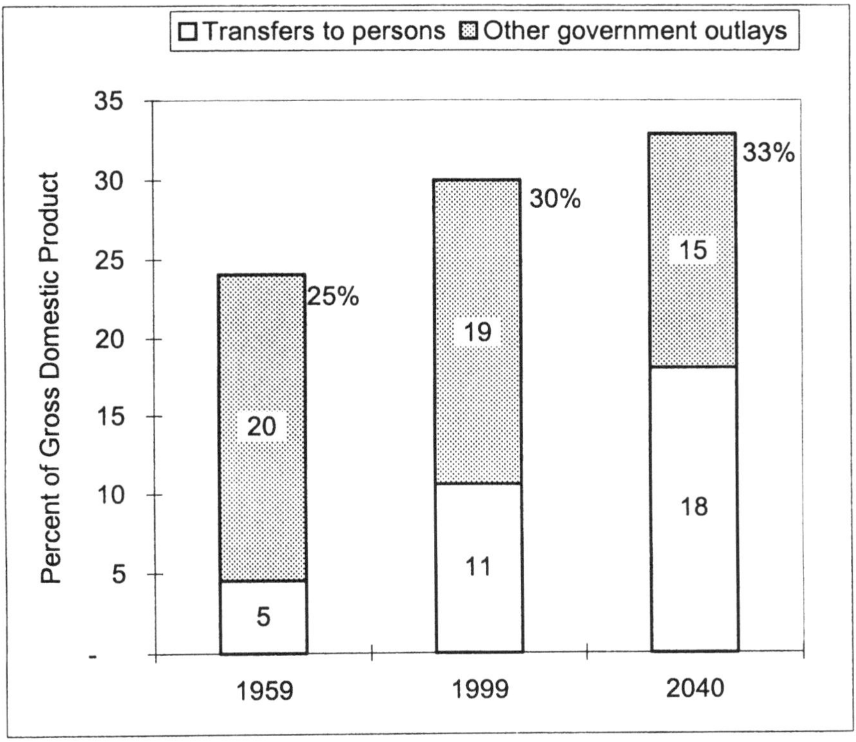


*Source* : U.S. Department of Commerce. Bureau of Economic Analysis. "Selected NIPA Tables." *National Accounts Data* : Tables 3.1 and 1.1. 8 Aug. 2000. 9 Sep. 2000. <http://www.bea.doc.gov/bea/dn1.htm>.

maximum, 23.6 percent, occurs in 1989 and 1990. The year 1976 marks its minimum, 18.4 percent. Over the entire period its share of GDP averages to 21 percent. We shall use 21 percent to project *Property income*.

The OASDI Trustees 2000 annual report provides us with projections of OASDHI contributions. Over the past forty years, employees have been taxed for about 48 percent of total OASDHI contributions. In 1959 the percentage was a shade over 40 percent; in 1999 it stands at 50 percent, so we will apply 50 percent to the percentages of GDP the Trustees' report provides for total OASDHI contributions to compute employees OASDHI contribution share as a percentage of GDP.

Most recently employee payments for other social insurance contributions have constituted about 37 percent of the total. Accordingly 37 percent of other social insurance contributions will be added to employees OASDHI contribution share to compute personal *Social Insurance Contributions*.

**Exhibit 12.4**

**Personal Income and Disposable Personal Income, 2000 to 2040**

| | Amounts in $ Billions | | | | | | | |
|---|---|---|---|---|---|---|---|---|
| Year | Wage, Salary & Other Labor Income | Property Income | Transfer Payments | Social Insurance Contributions | Personal Income | Personal Taxes & Nontaxes | OASDHI Deficit Coverage | Disposable Personal Income |
| 2000 | 5,282 | 2,054 | 1,090 | 349 | 8,077 | 1,174 | - | 6,903 |
| 2005 | 6,763 | 2,630 | 1,452 | 443 | 10,402 | 1,503 | - | 8,899 |
| 2010 | 8,716 | 3,390 | 1,983 | 567 | 13,521 | 1,937 | - | 11,585 |
| 2015 | 11,146 | 4,335 | 2,769 | 724 | 17,525 | 2,477 | - | 15,048 |
| 2020 | 14,131 | 5,495 | 3,869 | 918 | 22,577 | 3,140 | - | 19,437 |
| 2025 | 17,832 | 6,935 | 5,338 | 1,159 | 28,945 | 3,963 | 154 | 24,829 |
| 2030 | 22,540 | 8,766 | 7,210 | 1,463 | 37,053 | 5,009 | 289 | 31,755 |
| 2031 | 23,633 | 9,191 | 7,623 | 1,532 | 38,915 | 5,252 | 320 | 33,343 |
| 2032 | 24,781 | 9,637 | 8,060 | 1,606 | 40,873 | 5,507 | 354 | 35,012 |
| 2033 | 25,986 | 10,106 | 8,518 | 1,682 | 42,928 | 5,775 | 389 | 36,764 |
| 2034 | 27,254 | 10,599 | 8,992 | 1,764 | 45,080 | 6,056 | 426 | 38,598 |
| 2035 | 28,585 | 11,117 | 9,483 | 1,847 | 47,337 | 6,352 | 465 | 40,520 |
| 2036 | 29,982 | 11,660 | 9,971 | 1,935 | 49,678 | 6,663 | 505 | 42,510 |
| 2037 | 31,447 | 12,230 | 10,473 | 2,027 | 52,124 | 6,988 | 1,592 | 43,544 |
| 2038 | 32,981 | 12,826 | 11,012 | 2,125 | 54,693 | 7,329 | 1,681 | 45,683 |
| 2039 | 34,587 | 13,451 | 11,558 | 2,226 | 57,370 | 7,686 | 1,771 | 47,913 |
| 2040 | 36,265 | 14,103 | 12,137 | 2,330 | 60,174 | 8,059 | 1,863 | 50,252 |

**Exhibit 12.5**
**Components of Personal Income as Percents of Personal Income, 1959, 1999, and Projected 2040**

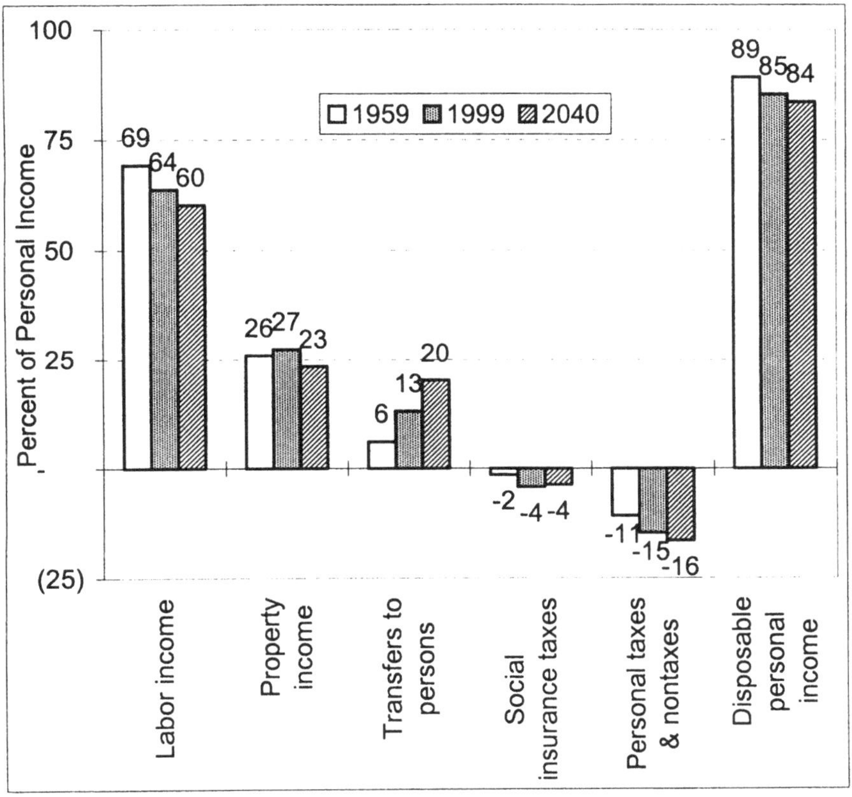


With those percentages in place, projections of personal income and its components become possible. *Wage, Salary, and Other Labor Income* and *Property Income* are computed by multiplying their respective percentages, 54 percent and 21 percent, by the GDP figures appearing in Exhibit 12.1. *Transfer Payments* are transferred from Exhibit 12.1. Employees' share of OASDHI contribution and of other social insurance contributions produces projections for *Social Insurance Contributions.* The sum of the three income items less *Social Insurance Contributions* generates *Personal Income. Personal Taxes and Nontaxes* and *OASDHI Deficit Coverage* are brought forward from Exhibit 12.1. Subtracting them from *Personal Income* produces *Disposable Personal Income.*

Exhibit 12.5 provides a display of the results of our projections and compares them with historical data. Shares of personal income accounted for by *Labor income*—wages, salaries, and other labor income—declines from 69 percent in 1959, to 64 percent in 1999, to a projected 60 percent in 2040. The pattern for property income is somewhat more complex, rising from 26 percent in

1959 to 27 percent in 1999 to 23 percent in 2040. In the aggregate, productive activity yielded 95 percent of personal income at the beginning of the period. In 1999 that percentage has fallen to 91 percent. By 2040 it will have fallen to 83 percent.

Government transfers to persons account for the change. In 1959 people received one dollar in seventeen in the form of transfers. By 1999 one dollar in eight took the form of a government handout. By 2040 one dollar in five may take that form. What effects will the dependency on government entitlements of so many for so much have in a democratic form of government? What aspiring elected official can resist appealing to the masses craving for more and more generously designed programs moving economic wherewithal from workers to the idle, from the young and able to old and infirm, and from the well to the ill? To what extent will people trade independence, freedom, and the perils of risk taking for the illusion of security, comfort, and something for nothing?

While the relative importance of income paid for current production of goods and services declines, the bite taken in the form of taxes increases. In 1959 *Social insurance taxes* and *Personal taxes and nontaxes* amounted to 13 percent of personal income; in 1999, 19 percent; in 2040 they gobble up a projected 20 percent. Projected to 2040, a coincidental symmetry is established between what government social insurance and welfare programs give and take away. One dollar in five out of personal income is given to the entitled in the form of transfers. One dollar in five is taken away from the producers of goods and services. Incentives receive a one-two punch.

What is left, *Disposable personal income* as a percent of personal income, drops from 1959's 89 percent to 85 percent in 1999, and then in 2040 to 84 percent. While the prospects in view are not entirely welcome, they hardly appear catastrophic. The greater relative change in transfer payments as a share of personal income occurred in the past forty years. An increase from 6 percent to 13 percent seems far more striking than one from 13 percent to 20 percent. Lower retirement ages and reduced personal saving rates may be taken as evidence of detrimental effects on productive effort of increased availability of transfer payments. However, modest modifications to qualifying retirement ages for social security address the first effect, and a host of other variables influence personal saving. Rising taxes and declining disposable personal income also dampen incentives. A one-percentage-point drop in disposable personal income over forty years hardly seems perceptible, but somewhere along the spectrum of what one earns and what one keeps surely comes a perceptible impact on people's behavior.

Based on the assumptions of the 2000 OASDI Trustees annual report, in 2040 real GDP (expressed in 1996 prices) calculates to $18.8 trillion dollars.[10] From 1999's real GDP of $8.9 trillion, that represents a 112 percent increase—more than double. Population will be larger too. From 273 million persons in 1999, based on intermediate range projections, U. S. residents in 2040 will number 377 million souls, a 38 percent increase.[11] Thus, per capita GDP of $49,900 in 2040 will be up 53 percent from 1999's figure of $32,500. Such additional affluence will undoubtedly alter people's views about society's condition. With their additional resources, they may wish to purchase for others a reduction of poverty and widespread access to health care. High tax burdens and transfers of income from young to old, from able to disabled, and from healthy to sick may not be begrudged. Then again, they may be.

## Comparison of the Known Past and Possible Future

An inchworm inches along at a slow pace. When it arrives at its destination, however, many inches have been covered, and the distance is many times its incremental progress. So also, our day-to-day, month-to-month, and year-to-year economic progress seems modest and tentative. Nevertheless, looked at over the past forty years, our accomplishment in economic terms is impressive. How do the economic conditions that have prevailed over the past forty years compare with those that are envisioned for the future?

Our vision for the future is based on economic and demographic assumptions adopted by the actuaries of the Social Security Administration. Among the economic factors they consider are:

- Annual percent rate of growth in real gross domestic product;
- Annual percent rate of growth in the wage rate of employees covered by social security;
- Annual percent change in the consumer price index for urban wage earners and clerical workers;
- Real wage rate differential, the difference between percentage increases in the wage rate of employees covered by social security and the consumer price index;
- The average annual interest rate for special public-debt obligations issued to the trust funds in each of the twelve months of the year;
- The unemployment rate of civilian labor force expressed as a percentage;
- Annual percent change in the civilian labor force; and
- The increase in productivity per worker expressed as a percentage.

For each of those factors, low (optimistic), intermediate, and high (pessimistic) cost values have been assigned.

Exhibit 12.6 displays those values along with the actual values that have been experienced over the past forty years. Since values for both the actual and projected factors vary from year to year, they are shown as averages. The average percentages for *Real GDP growth*, *Wage rate increase*, *Consumer price index*, and *Productivity per worker* have been calculated as geometric means. The *Real wage rate differential* is the difference between the average *Wage rate increase* and *Consumer price index*. The *Interest rate* and *Increase in labor force* percentages are calculated as arithmetic averages.

Over the past forty years, *Real GDP growth* has averaged 3.2 percent a year, and is represented in Exhibit 12.6 as the solid black dot in the first column. A high rate of *Real GDP growth* is good for the long-term financial viability of the

**Exhibit 12.6**

**Comparison of Actual Experience 1960 to 1999, with Actuarial Assumptions: Optimistic, Intermediate, and Pessimistic, 2000 to 2040**

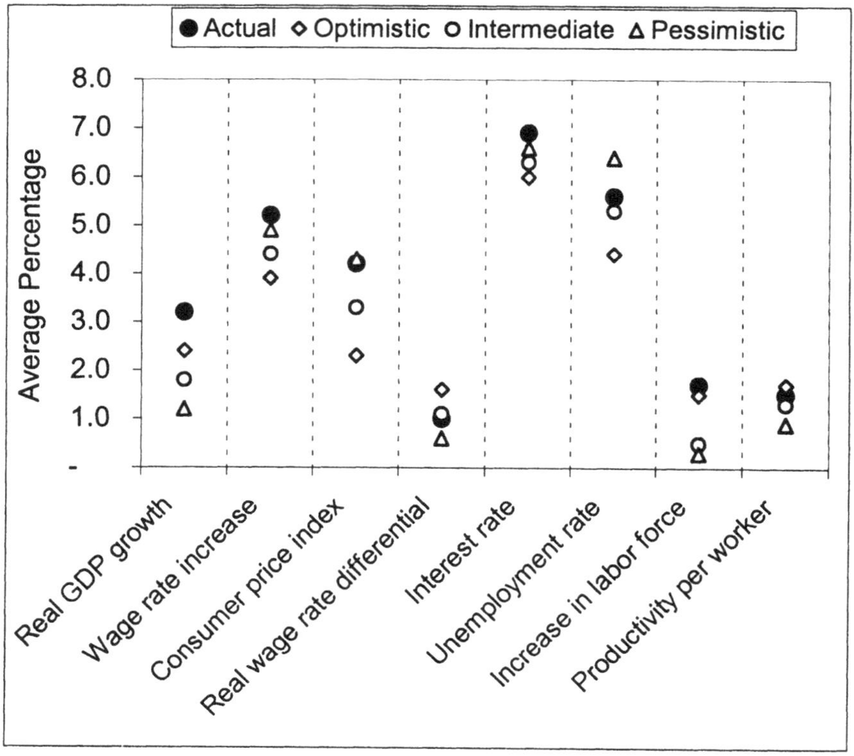


*Source* : Board of Trustees of the Federal Old-Age and Survivors Insurance and Disability Insurance Trust Funds. *2000 Annual Report of the Board of Trustees of the Federal Old-Age and Survivors Trust Fund and the Federal Disability Insurance Trust Fund*. Washington, DC: U.S. Government Printing Office, 2000) 58.

social insurance programs. The optimistic-assumption *Real GDP growth* rate for the next forty years, represented by the open diamond, is only 2.4 percent. The pessimistic assumption, shown as the open triangle, is 1.2 percent. In between is the white dot, at 1.8 percent, the intermediate assumption.

Why is *Real GDP growth* expected to be less in the future than in the past? The *Increase in labor force* provides an answer. The labor force is expected to increase less rapidly in the next forty years than it has in the past forty because we are running out of women shifting from homemaking to paid employment. Labor is an important input in the production of goods and services. Entrants to the labor force from the domestic population for the next sixteen years or more years has been determined thanks to a lot of unskilled reproductive activity. What happens beyond that point depends on fertility rates. Only under the optimistic scenario are they expected to increase over current levels. Immigration also can contribute to the labor force. In 1996, 1997, and 1998, it was in excess of 900,000 persons annually.[12] The OASDI Board of Trustees report, however, states, "total net immigration is assumed to be 900,000 persons per year for the intermediate projection."[13] Add 310,000 to that figure for the optimistic assumption, and subtract 140,000 for the pessimistic assumption. The consequences of the fertility and immigration assumptions account for the *Increase in labor force* in Exhibit 12.6. The 1.7 percent average annual increase of the past forty years surpasses the optimistic, intermediate, and pessimistic increases of 1.5 percent, 0.5 percent, and 0.3 percent, respectively.

Average percents for the *Wage rate increase*, the *Consumer price index*, and the *Interest rate* are related to one another. Rapid increases in wages and high inflation often accompany one another. Both are bad news for the solvency of the social insurance funds. Interest rates tend to be high in inflationary times as well. The forty-year experience of 5.2 percent for the wage rate surpasses even the pessimistic assumption of 4.9 percent. The intermediate and optimistic assumptions come in at 4.9 percent and 3.9 percent. For inflation, the 4.2 percent *Consumer price index* inflation actually experienced is outdistanced by the pessimistic assumption of 4.3 percent. The intermediate-assumption comes in at 3.3 percent; the optimistic, at 2.3 percent.

The higher the *Real wage rate differential*, the better are the prospects for social insurance fund financial viability. The intermediate assumption's 1.1 percent approximates very closely our forty-year experience of 1.0 percent. An optimistic assumption of 1.6 percent and the pessimistic assumption of 0.6 percent bracket them.

High unemployment is bad news. Accordingly, the pessimistic-assumption *Unemployment rate* is set at 6.4 percent, higher than the forty-year average of 5.6 percent. The intermediate assumption is a bit more favorable than actual with a 6.3 percent. The optimistic alternative comes in at 4.4 percent.

An optimistic forecast for increases in *Productivity per worker* averaging 1.7 percent over the next forty years is a bit more than actual experience of 1.5 percent. The intermediate cost is a bit less at 1.3 percent. The pessimistic assumption comes in at 0.9 percent.

A tenth of a percent here, a tenth of a percent there: over forty years they can have an enormous impact. While the intermediate assumptions, being in the middle, are considered more likely to occur than either the optimistic or pessimistic scenarios, any of the three or some blend is possible. According to the combined report of the OASDI and medical insurance funds boards of trustees on the status of the social security and Medicare programs, deficits disappear when optimistic assumptions are invoked! Deficits DO NOT occur![14] Future economic conditions are not like floods, hurricanes, earthquakes, and other natural disasters, because they are subject to human influence. Can we not limit inflation through sound monetary policy? Can we not choose to increase investment and thereby increase worker productivity? If fertility rates fall, cannot the labor force be augmented through immigration? The United States hardly needs to beg people to enter its borders and become citizens. Certainly more constructive options exist than maintaining currently high rates of taxation to finance possible social insurance fund deficits. Wouldn't it be great if in 2040 citizens enjoyed higher per capita real gross domestic product and a soundly financed social insurance fund! The choice is ours.

## THE PAST AS PROLOGUE

New Frontier. Great Society. New Federalism. Chewing gum and walking at the same time. Iran crisis. Supply-side economics. Thousand points of light. Whitewater. Once familiar words since 1959, some already become difficult to recall. Not many had a lasting impact on the nation's economy.

While words and phrases came and went, the economy moved forward. By 1999 its total output of goods and services for consumption and investment was more than triple and closer to four times its output in 1959. Output per person had more than doubled.

While past performance does not necessarily guarantee future success, neither does it portend disaster. Although real GDP forecast for 2040 is projected to more than double, its growth over the next forty years falls far short of growth rates experienced over the past forty years. Nevertheless, the results indicate that the forecasted amount should be sufficient to satisfy future and current obligations. Reasons for such a conservative view of the future are unclear. Scientific discovery, technological development, and innovation show no signs of slowing down. Our analysis suggests that availability of productive capital per worker is a major contributor to productivity. Capital formation is a consequence of economic choice—an interaction of incentives to save out of current income and to engage in entrepreneurial activity. Preservation of an environment that nurtures such incentives and facilitates their realization is perhaps the most important key to future prosperity and insurance against calamity.

Although a conservative projection of future economic growth may seem prudent and may be soundly based, it can also stem from an instinctive underestimate of the power of the market system when coupled with political stability, respect for private property, and equal treatment for all individuals under the law. After all, the projections originate not so much from the private sector as from the public. In the public sector, the order of business is legislation, administration, and interpretation, not innovation, production, and creation. Moreover, the prospect of future prosperity equal to the past dispels the perceived crises surrounding the social and medical insurance programs and undermines a rationale for continued high levels of taxation.

Forecasts that do not spell out dire warnings of impending calamity, catastrophe, cataclysm, and collapse do not seem to be fashionable. Perhaps optimistic forecasts do not appear helpful or influential. Weather warnings of possible tornadoes tend to get more attention than those predicting sunny skies and warm breezes. For the U.S. economy, however, such storms do not appear to be brewing over the horizon. Sufficient numbers of unanticipated threats, challenges, and problems undoubtedly will arise to make the new millennium exciting. Proposing problematic adversities hardly seems helpful

## BIG PICTURE, LONG VIEW

In 1999 25 million U.S. residents were seventy years of age and older. In their lifetimes they have seen the nation's output of final goods and services available per person increase almost fivefold. They also have seen an economic collapse (the Great Depression), World War II, a world on the brink of mutually assured destruction, limited warfare, stagflation, and bungee jumping. But despite all those challenges, the United States' engine of productivity has been churning away, producing a cornucopia of goods and services to make life, liberty, and the pursuit of happiness more pleasant.

For reasons of data availability and historical circumstance, our analysis of national income and product statistics has been limited to the forty-year period from 1959 to 1999. But comparable gross domestic product estimates date back to 1929. In 1929 gross domestic product expressed in 1996 prices amounted to \$822.2 billion.[15] Since then *real* gross domestic product has increased almost eleven times. Population has more than doubled, so that over seventy years gross domestic product per person has just about quintupled.

The enormity of the success of the enterprise beggars the imagination. We know, but we hardly appreciate its implications. The gross domestic product of the United States, with 5 percent of the world's population, accounts for 22 percent of the gross domestic product of all nations. The combined gross domestic product of the nations comprising the European Monetary Union is not quite three-fourths that of the United States. China, with 21 percent of the world's population, ranks second after the United States in terms of gross domestic product. Its gross domestic product is less than half that of the United States. Even in terms of population, the United States stands tall. Only China and India have larger populations.[16]

The gross state product of California is greater than that of all other nations except China, Japan, India, Germany, France, the United Kingdom, Italy, and Brazil. The combined gross state product of California, New York, and Texas exceeds the gross domestic product of all nations but China and Japan.

Canada and Mexico are the two most important trading partners of the United States. Of total U.S. exports in 1999, 24 percent went to Canada and 13 percent went to Mexico. Twenty percent of U.S. total imports came from Canada, and 11 percent came from Mexico. U.S. exports to Canada, 1.8 percent of U.S. GDP, amount to 20 percent of Canada's gross domestic product, and Canada exports 24 percent of its gross domestic product to the United States. U.S. exports to Mexico amount to 10 percent of Mexico's gross domestic product, and it exports 13 percent of its gross domestic product to the United States. Merely by virtue of the size of its economy, the United States has a far greater impact on its neighbors to the north and south than they do on it.

How has this achievement of economic productivity come about? Do not all persons of the world look after their self-interest? Does not everyone aspire to improve the well-being of self and family? Clearly, many find themselves in circumstances that do not permit or encourage accomplishing that basic objective. Here in the United States, as previously observed, the market mechanism operating in a context of individual equality under the law, respect for private property, and political stability provides an environment that encourages entrepreneurship. Opportunity for profit and rich rewards beckons to all, but success is not guaranteed. In the U.S. business sector, we found that less than 70 percent of profit-seeking business firms reported net income in 1996. Fortunately, rewards of success outweigh the costs of failure and lead to economic progress.

Alexis de Tocqueville came to the United States 170 years ago when our government and economic system was considered an experiment of uncertain outcome. Many of his observations then serve us well today. In their private lives he observed that "there is perhaps no country on earth where fewer idle people are encountered than in America, and where all those who work are more inflamed by the search for well being."[17] That strenuous lifestyle continues to this day. Despite Americans' intense pursuit of self-interest, Tocqueville found that they often engaged in public affairs with equal vigor "to secure by themselves a government that permits them to acquire the goods they desire and that does not prevent them from enjoying in peace those they have acquired."[18]

What could bring an end to individual striving that has served the entire nation well for over 200 years? Once again Tocqueville has an observation and a message relevant to this day. People

> feel the need to be led and the wish to remain free. Not being able to destroy either one of these contrary instincts, they strive to satisfy both at the same time. They imagine a unique power, tutelary, all powerful, but elected by citizens. . . . They console themselves for being in tutelage by thinking that they themselves have chosen their school masters.[19]

From that compromise of two opposed yearnings comes the possibility of despotism of the people, by the people, and for the people: a powerful central government "absolute, detailed, regular, far-seeing, and mild."[20] With its powers derived from the people, it "willingly works for their happiness . . . provides for their security, foresees and secures their needs, facilitates their pleasures, conducts their principal affairs, directs their industry."[21] As a result society finds itself covered "with a network of small, complicated, painstaking, uniform rules through which the most original minds and the most vigorous souls cannot clear a way to surpass the crowd." The central government "rarely forces one to act, but it constantly opposes itself to one's acting; it does not destroy, it prevents things from being born; it does not tyrannize, it hinders, compromises, enervates, extinguishes, dazes."[22]

Those admonitions suggest that the menace to the future growth and prosperity of the United States may not come from without but from within. Unintended consequences of central government actions undertaken with good intentions may threaten to lead people to trade independence for dependence, individual initiative for conformity, risk taking for security, and restlessness for resignation. Institutional arrangements that confer privileged status to certain types of collective activity, that create a sense of dependency, and that preclude or bias individual choice should be viewed with a sense of wariness.

Disruptions experienced in the past will visit the future. Terrors imaginable and unimaginable will occur. But those calamities and disasters may not threaten the long-term future of the United States as much as a failure to press on, seek out new opportunities, and move beyond current horizons. The promises outweigh the perils.

## NOTES

1. United States, Bipartisan Commission on Entitlement and Tax Reform, *Interim Report to the President / Bipartisan Commission on Entitlement and Tax Reform* (Washington, DC: Superintendent of Documents, 1994).

2. United States, Congress of the United States, Congressional Budget Office, *The Budget and Economic Outlook: An Update* (Washington, DC: The Congressional Budget Office, 18 Jul. 2000) 13 Dec. 2000 <http://www.cbo.gov/>.

3. U.S. Board of Trustees, Federal Old-Age and Survivors Insurance and Disability Insurance Funds, *The 2000 Annual Report of the Board of Trustees of the Federal Old-Age and Survivors and Disability Insurance Trust Funds* (Washington, DC: U.S. Government Printing Office, 30 Mar. 2000) 10 Dec. 2000.

4. *The 2000 Annual Report of the Board of Trustees of the Federal Old-Age and Survivors and Disability Insurance Trust Funds*, Section II, Subsection D, 1.

5. *The 2000 Annual Report of the Board of Trustees of the Federal Old-Age and Survivors and Disability Insurance Trust Funds*, Table II.D.1.

6. *The 2000 Annual Report of the Board of Trustees of the Federal Old-Age and Survivors and Disability Insurance Trust Funds*, Tables III.B3 and III.B4.

7. *The 2000 Annual Report of the Board of Trustees of the Federal Old-Age and Survivors and Disability Insurance Trust Funds*, Table I.E1.

8. *The 2000 Annual Report of the Board of Trustees of the Federal Old-Age and Survivors and Disability Insurance Trust Funds*, Table III.B4.

9. U.S. Board of Trustees, Federal Old-Age and Survivors Insurance and Disability Insurance Funds and Board of Trustees, Federal Hospital Insurance and Supplementary Medical Insurance Trust Funds, *Status of the Social Security and Medicare Programs, A Summary of the 2000 Annual Reports* (Revised Apr. 2000), 24 Apr. 2000: 11, 10 Dec. 2000 <http://www.ssa.gov/OACT/TRSUM/trsummary.html>.

10. *The 2000 Annual Report of the Board of Trustees of the Federal Old-Age and Survivors and Disability Insurance Trust Funds*, Table II.D1.

11. U.S. Department of Commerce, Census Bureau, *Population Projections: National*, 7 Sep. 2000, 14 Dec. 2000 <http://www.census.gov/>.

12. U.S. Department of Commerce, Bureau of the Census, "No. 4. Components of Population Change, 1980 to 1998, and Projections, 1999 to 2050," *Statistical Abstract of the United States: 1999* (Washington, DC: U.S. Government Printing Office, 2000) 9.

13. *The 2000 Annual Report of the Board of Trustees of the Federal Old-Age and Survivors and Disability Insurance Trust Funds* 62.

14. *Status of the Social Security and Medicare Programs* 8.

15. U.S. Department of Commerce, Bureau of Economic Analysis, "Gross domestic product in current dollars and in chained (1996) dollars." *National Income and Product Accounts*. 31 Jan. 2001. 15 Feb. 2001 <http://www.bea.doc.gov>.

16. World Bank Group, "Data by Topic," *Data and Maps*, 2 Aug. 2000, 16 Feb. 2001 <http://www.worldbank.org/data/databytopic.htm>.

17. Alexis de Tocqueville, *Democracy in America*, trans. & ed. Harvey C. Mansfield and Delba Winthrop (Chicago: University of Chicago Press: 2000) 516.

18. De Tocqueville 517.

19. De Tocqueville 664.

20. De Tocqueville 663.

21. De Tocqueville 663.

22. De Tocqueville 663.

# Selected Bibliography


Adams, Charles. *Those Dirty Rotten Taxes: The Tax Revolts that Built America.* New York: Free Press, 1998.

Advisory Commission on Intergovernmental Relations. "Public Attitudes on Government and Taxes." *Intergovernmental Perspectives* 20.3 (Summer/Fall 1994): 29–30.

Anderson, Victor. *Alternative Economic Indicators.* London, New York: Rutledge, 1991.

Appleyard, Dennis R. and Alfred J. Field, Jr. *International Economics: Payments, Exchange Rates, and Macro Policy.* Chicago: Richard D. Irwin, 1993.

Bailey, Stephen J. *Business Sector Economics: Theory, Policy, and Practice.* Houndmills, Basingstroke, England: MacMillan, 1995.

Barshefsky Charlene. "Prospering in the High Risk Food Economy." *Farm Journal* Forum. Washington, DC. 14 Nov. 1997.

Beemiller, Richard M. and Michael T. Wells. "Gross State Product by Industry, 1995–97." *Survey of Current Business.* Jun. 1999: 24–45.

Beran, Michael J., Duane M. Rumbaugh, and E. Sue Savage-Rumbaugh. "Chimpanzee (Pan troglodytes) counting in a computerized testing paradigm." *Psychological Record.* 48.1 (Winter, 1998): 3–19.

Bethell, Tom. *The Noblest Triumph: Property and Prosperity through the Ages.* New York: St. Martin's Press, 1998.

Board of Governors of the Federal Reserve System. "Treasury constant maturities, 10-year." *Historical Data.* 18 Sep. 2000: H.15. 29 Sep. 2000. <http://www.bog.frb.us/releases/h15/data.htm>.

———. *Guide to the Flow of Funds Accounts.* Washington, DC: Board of Governors of the Federal Reserve System, 1993.

———. *Flow of Funds Accounts of the United States.* 9 Jun. 2000. 19 Jun. 2000 <http://bog.frb.fed.us/z1/current/ coded>.

Brownlee, W. Elliott. *Federal Taxation in America: A Short History.* Washington, DC: Woodrow Wilson Center Press, 1996.

Bryant, W. Keith. *The Economic Organization of the Household.* New York: Cambridge University Press, 1990.

Carson, Carol S. "The History of the United States National Income and Product Accounts: The Development of an Analytical Tool." *The Review of Income and*

*Wealth*. 21. 2 (June, 1975): 153–81.

Carter, Anne P. *Structural Change in the American Economy*. Cambridge: Harvard University, 1970.

Cimons, Marlene. "Are You Overweight?" *Runner's World*. Jan. 1999: 36–37.

Clotfelter, Charles T. and Phillip T. Cook. *Selling Hope, State Lotteries in America*. Cambridge, MA: Harvard University Press, 1963.

Conable, Barber B. *Congress and the Income Tax*. (with A. L. Singleton). Norman: University of Oklahoma Press, 1989.

DeRosa, David F. In Defense of Free Capital Markets: The Case Against a New International Financial Architecture. Princeton: Bloomberg Press, 2001.

Dewey, Donald. *The Antitrust Experiment in America*. New York: Columbia University Press, 1990.

Fisher, Irving. *The Making of Index Numbers, A Study of Their Varieties, Tests, and Reliability*. 3rd ed. Revised. 1927. New York: August M. Kelley, 1967.

Franklin, Benjamin. "Letter to Jean Baptiste LeRoy." 13 Nov. 1789. *The Writings of Benjamin Franklin*. vol. 10. 1789–90. Ed. Albert Henry Smyth. New York: Macmillan Co., 1907: 68–69.

Herber, Bernard P. *Modern Public Finance, The Study of Public Sector Economics*. Homewood, IL: Richard D. Irwin, Inc., 1975.

Horowitz, Michael. "What do we do about Medicare?" *The American Enterprise*. Jan./Feb. 1997: 21–22.

Ignatius, David. "The Oil Game Turns Cutthroat." *Houston Chronicle*. 14 Feb. 1999: 1C and 4C.

Jah, Raghbendra. Modern Public Economics. London and New York: Routledge, 1998.

Jefferson, Thomas, *Notes on the State of Virginia* written in the year 1781; somewhat corrected and enlarged in the winter of 1782, for the use of a foreigner of distinction, in answer to certain queries proposed by him. 2nd ed. Philadelphia: 1794. American Antiquarian Society. *Early American Imprints* 1639–1800 (Worchester, MA: Readex Microprint, 1960) Evans number 27162.

Johnson, Peter A. *The Government of Money, Monetarism in Germany and the United States*. Ithaca and London: Cornell University Press, 1998.

Keynes, John Maynard. *The General Theory of Employment, Interest, and Money*. New York: Harcourt, Brace and Company, 1936.

Kiefer, Donald W. *Tax Cuts and Rebates for Economic Stimulus: the Historical Record*. 2 Jan. 1992. *Major Studies and Issue Briefs of the Congressional Research Service*. Washington, DC: Congressional Research Service, Library of Congress, 1992: microfilm 92-20 S, reel 1, fr. 00661.

Leahy, Michael P. "New Summary Measures of the Foreign Exchange Value of the Dollar." *Federal Reserve Bulletin*. Washington, DC: Board of Governors of the Federal Reserve System, Oct. 1998: 811–18.

Leontief, Wassily. *Input-Output Economics*. 2nd ed. New York, Oxford: Oxford University Press, 1986.

Locke, John. *Two Treatises on Government*. 3rd ed. London: 1698. Book 2, Chapter 5, 185. *Early English Books*. Ann Arbor, MI: University Microforms International, 1978. 793:25.

Marx, Karl. "Critique of the Gotha Program." 1891. *The Marx-Engels Reader*. 2nd ed. Ed. Richard Tucker. New York: W. W. Norton Company, 1978.

McMickle, Peter L. and Richard G. Vangermeersch. *The Origins of a Great Profession*. Memphis: The Academy of Accounting Historians, 1987.

Miller, Ronald E., and Peter D. Blair. *Input-Output Analysis: Foundations and Extensions*. Englewood Cliffs, NJ: Prentice Hall, Inc., 1985.

Mises, Ludwig von. *Omnipotent Government, The Rise of the Total State and Total War.* New Haven: Yale University Press, 1944.

———. *Planned Chaos.* Irvington-on-Hudson, NY: The Foundation for Economic Education, Inc., 1947.

Moulton, Brent R. and David F. Sullivan. "A Preview of the 1999 Comprehensive Revision of the National Income and Product Accounts: New and Redesigned Tables." *Survey of Current Business.* Sep. 1999: 15–28.

Moulton, Brent R., Robert P. Parker, and Eugene Seskin. "A Preview of the 1999 Comprehensive Revision of the National Income and Product Accounts: Definitional and Classificational Changes." *Survey of Current Business* Aug. 1999: 7–20.

Musgrave, Richard A., and Peggy B. Musgrave. *Public Finance in Theory and Practice.* 5th ed. New York: McGraw-Hill Company, 1989.

Okubo, Sumiye O., Ann M. Lawson, and Mark A. Planting. "Annual Input-Output Accounts of the U.S. Economy, 1996." *Survey of Current Business* Jan. 2000: 37–46.

Otis, James. *The Rights of the British Colonies Asserted and Proved.* Boston: Edes and Gill, 1764. *Early American Imprints, First Series.* Worcester, Massachusetts: American Antiquarian Society, 1955–83. Microopaque number 9773.

Park, Thae S. "Comparison of BEA Estimates of Personal Income and IRS Estimates of Adjusted Gross Income: New Estimates for 1997 and Revised Estimates 1959–96." *Survey of Current Business.* Feb. 2000: 12–22.

Pechman, Joseph A. *Federal Tax Policy.* 5th ed. Washington, DC: The Brookings Institution, 1987.

Raghbendra, Jah. *Modern Public Economics.* London and New York: Routledge, 1998.

Ricardo, David. *Principles of Political Economy and Taxation.* 1st American ed. Georgetown, DC: 1819. American Antiquarian Society. *Early American Reprints.* 2nd Series. New York: Readex Microprint, 1981. 49280.

Rousslang, Donald J., *et. al. The Economic Effects of Significant U.S. Import Restraints, Phase 1: Manufacturing: Report to the Committee on Finance of the United States Senate on Investigation No. 322–262 under Section 332 of the Tariff Act of 1930. USITC Publication, no 2222.* Washington, DC: U.S. International Trade Commission, 1989.

Ruggles, Richard. "National Income Accounting." *The History of Accounting, An International Encyclopedia.* Ed. Michael Chatfield and Richard Vangermeersch. New York and London: Garland Publishing, Inc., 1996.

Sacco, Ralph L., Mitchell Elkind, Bernadette Boden-Albada, I-Feng Lin, Douglas E. Kergman, W. Allen Hauser, Steven Shea, and Myunghee C. Palk, "The Protective Effect of Moderate Alcohol Consumption on Ischemic Stroke," *The Journal of the American Medical Association,* 281.1 (6 Jan. 1999) 53–60, 22 Dec. 2000 <http://jama.ama-assn.org/issues/v281n1/toc.html>.

Seskin, Eugene P. "Improved Estimates of the National Income and Product Accounts for 1959–98: Results of the Comprehensive Revision." *Survey of Current Business.* Dec. 1999: 15–43.

Simmons, Kennett Lynn. *Managed Health Care: right idea—wrong rules.* Diss. University of Texas at Austin, 1992.

Simon, James, and Christopher Nobes. *The Economics of Taxation.* 4th ed. New York: Prentice Hall, 1992.

Skidmore, Max J. "Social Security in the United States." *Social Security Programs: A Cross-Cultural Comparative Perspective.* Eds. Dixon, John and Robert P. Scheurell. Westport, CT: Greenwood Press, 1995.

Smith, Adam. *An Inquiry into the Nature and Causes of the Wealth of Nations.* Hartford, 1818: Book IV, Chapter 2, p. 319, American Antiquarian Society, *Early American*

*Reprints*, 2nd series. New York: Readex Microprint, 1980. 45724.
Stone, Richard. "Definition and Measurement of the National Income and Related Totals." Appendix to *Measurement of National Income and the Construction of Social Accounts*, Studies and Reports on Statistical Methods, no. 7. Geneva: United Nations, 1947.
Sweeney, John J. "The Gap between the Rich and Everyone Else: Honest Labor and the Standard of Living." The City Club, Forum Foundation, Cleveland, Ohio, 7 Jun 1996. *Vital Speeches of the Day*. 62.18 1 Jul. 1996: 549–51.
Tocqueville, Alexis de. *Democracy in America*. trans. & eds. Harvey C. Mansfield and Delba Winthrop. Chicago: University of Chicago Press: 2000.
United Nations. *A System of National Accounts and Supporting Tables*. New York: United Nations, 1952 and 1953.
———. *A System of National Accounts and Supporting Tables*, Studies in Methods, Series F, no. 2, Revision 3. New York: United Nations, 1968.
United States. Bipartisan Commission on Entitlement and Tax Reform. *Interim Report to the President / Bipartisan Commission on Entitlement and Tax Reform*. Washington, DC: Superintendent of Documents, 1994.
United States. Board of Trustees, Federal Old-Age and Survivors Insurance and Disability Insurance Funds. *The 1997 Annual Report of the Board of Trustees of the Federal Old-Age and Survivors Insurance and Disability Insurance Trust Funds*. Washington, DC: US Government Printing Office, 1997.
———. *The 1999 Annual Report of the Board of Trustees of the Federal Old-Age and Survivors and Disability Insurance Trust Funds*. Washington, DC: U.S. Government Printing Office, 1999.
———. *The 2000 Annual Report of the Board of Trustees of the Federal Old-Age and Survivors and Disability Insurance Trust Funds*. Washington, DC: U.S. Government Printing Office, 2000.
United States. Board of Trustees, Federal Hospital Insurance and Supplementary Medical Insurance Trust Funds. *1999 Annual Reports of the Board of Trustees of the Federal Hospital Insurance and Supplementary Medical Insurance Trust Funds*. Washington, DC: U.S. Government Printing Office, 1999.
United States. Board of Trustees, Federal Old-Age and Survivors Insurance and Disability Insurance Funds and Board of Trustees, Federal Hospital Insurance and Supplementary Medical Insurance Trust Funds. *Status of the Social Security and Medicare Programs,* A Summary of the 1999 Annual Reports. Washington, DC: U.S. Government Printing Office, Apr. 2000.
United States. Congress of the United States, Congressional Budget Office. *The Budget and Economic Outlook: An Update*. Washington, DC: The Congressional Budget Office, 18 Jul. 2000. 13 Dec. 2000 <http://www.cbo.gov/>.
United States. Department of Commerce. Bureau of the Census. *1992 Census of Governments, Government Finances, Compendium of Government Finances*. Vol. 4, No. 5. Washington, DC: U.S. Government Printing Office, Feb. 1997.
———. "Historical National Population Estimates." *National Population Estimates*. 28 Jun. 2000: Series P–15, Nos. 311, 917, 1095. 29 Sep. 2000. <http://www.census.gov/population/www/estimates/uspop.html>
———. *Population Projections: National*. 7 Sep. 2000. 14 Dec. 2000. <http://www.census.gov/>
———. *Statistical Abstract of the United States*. Washington, DC: U.S. Government Printing Office, 1982.
———. *Statistical Abstract of the United States*. Washington, DC: U.S. Government Printing Office, 1998.

———. *Statistical Abstract of the United States*. Washington, DC: U.S. Government Printing Office, 1999.

United States. Department of Commerce. Bureau of Economic Analysis. *The Balance of Payments of the United States: Concepts, Data Sources, and Estimating Procedures*. Washington, DC: U.S. Government Printing Office, May 1990.

———. "Benchmark Input-Output Accounts for the U.S. Economy, 1992." *Survey of Current Business*. Nov. 1997: M-13.

———. *Corporate Profits: Profits Before Tax, Profits Tax Liability, and Dividends*. Methodology Paper No. 2. Washington, DC: U.S. Government Printing Office, 1985.

———. *Foreign Transactions*. Methodology Paper No. 3. Series MP-3. Washington, DC: U.S. Government Printing Office, May 1987.

———. "'Annual Only' NIPA Tables." *National Accounts Data*. 30 Aug 2000. 5 Sep. 2000. <http://www.bea. doc.gov/bea/dn1.htm>.

———. "GDP: One of the Great Inventions of the 20th Century." *Survey of Current Business*. Jan 2000: 6–14.

———. *GNP: An Overview of Source Data and Estimating Methods*. Methodology Paper No. 4. Washington, DC: U.S. Government Printing Office, Sep. 1987.

———. *Government Transactions*. Methodology Paper Series MP-5. Washington, DC: U.S. Government Printing Office, November 1988.

———. *An Introduction to National Economic Accounting*. Methodology Paper No. 1. Washington, DC: U.S. Government Printing Office, 1985.

———. *National Income and Product Accounts of the United States, 1929–94*: Vol. 1. Washington, DC: U.S. Government Printing Office, April 1998.

———. *Personal Consumption Expenditures*. Methodology Paper Series No. 6. Washington, DC: U.S. Government Printing Office, 1990.

———. "Selected NIPA Tables." *National Accounts Data*. 21 Apr. 2000: Table 2.1. 6 May 2000. And 8 Aug. 2000: Table 2.1. 9 Sep. 2000:. <http://www.bea.doc.gov/bea/dn1.htm>.

———. "Underlying detail estimates for PCE, historical file." *State of the Nation Library*. 8 Sep. 2000: Table 206U. 8 Oct. 2000 <http://www.stat-usa.gov/online.nsf/NIPANav?OpenNavigator>.

———. "Updated Summary of NIPA Methodologies." *Survey of Current Business*. Sep. 1998: 14–35.

———. "Wassily Leontief and His Contributions to Economic Accounting." *Survey of Current Business*. Mar. 1999: 9.

United States. Department of Health and Human Services. Office of the Assistant Secretary for Planning and Evaluation. "93-774: Medicare: Supplementary Medical Insurance." *Catalog of Federal Domestic Assistance*. 8 Nov. 2000. <http://aspe.os.dhhs.gov/afda/P93774.htm>.

United States. Department of Labor. Bureau of Labor Statistics. "Employment status of the civilian population by sex and age." *Labor Force Statistics from the Current Population Survey*. 4 Feb 2000: Table A-1. 29 Sep. 2000. <http://stats.bls.gov/webapps/legacy/epsatab1.htm>

United States. Department of Transportation. Maritime Administration. *Merchant Fleets of the World: Oceangoing Steam and Motor Ships of 1,000 Tons and Over as of October 1, 1998*. Washington, DC: U.S. Department of Transportation, Oct. 1998.

United States. Department of the Treasury. Internal Revenue Service. *Publication 596 Earned Income Tax Credit for Use in preparing 1999 Returns*. 12 Apr. 2000. 8 Oct. 2000. <http://ftp.fedworld.gov/pub/irs-pdf/p596pdf>.

———. *1995 Instructions for Form 1040 and Schedules A, B, C, D, E, EIC, and SE.* Washington, DC: U.S. Government Printing Office, 1994.

———. *1995 Instructions for Form 1065.* Washington, DC: U.S. Government Printing Office, 1994.

———. *Statistics of Income—1996: Corporation Income Tax Returns.* IRS Publication 16 (Revised 9-99) 17 Nov. 2000 <http://www.irs.ustreas.gov/plain/tax_stats/soi/corp-complete.html/>

———. "Table 3. Balance Sheets and Related Income Statements, by Major Industrial Group." *Statistics of Income, 1958–59, Corporation Income Tax Returns.* Publication No. 16 (1-61) Washington, DC: U.S. Government Printing Office, 1961.

———. "Table 3. Balance Sheet, Income Statement, and Selected Items, by Minor Industry, by Size of Total Assets." *1995 Source Book of Statistics of Income, Corporation Income Tax Returns.* (Publication No. 1053 (3-98)) Washington, DC: U.S. Government Printing Office, 1998.

United States. Executive Office of the President. Office of Management and Budget. *Analytical Perspectives, Budget of the United States Government, Fiscal Year 2001.* Washington, DC: U.S. Government Printing Office, 1999. 9 Nov. 2000 <http://frwebgate.access.gpo.gov/cigbin/waisgate.cgi?WAISdocID=9398117137+0+0+0&WAISaction=retrieve>.

———. *Economic Report of the President, 1999.* Washington, DC: U. S. Government Printing Office, 1999.

———. *Economic Report of the President, 2000.* Washington, DC: U. S. Government Printing Office, 2000. 12 Dec. 2000 <http://w3/.access.gpo.gov/eop/>

United States. Social Security Administration. *Annual Statistical Supplement to the Social Security Bulletin, 1996.* Washington, DC: U. S. Government Printing Office, 1996.

———. *Annual Statistical Supplement to the Social Security Bulletin, 1997.* Washington, DC: U.S. Government Printing Office, 1998.

———. *Annual Statistical Supplement to the Social Security Bulletin, 1998.* Washington, DC: U. S. Government Printing Office, 1998.

———. *Annual Statistical Supplement to the Social Security Bulletin, 1999.* Washington, DC: U. S. Government Printing Office, 1999.

White, Lawrence J. *International Trade in Ocean Shipping Services: the United States and the World.* Cambridge, MA: Ballinger, 1988.

Williams, John J. "A New Perspective on the Evolution of Double-Entry Bookkeeping." *The Development of Double-Entry: Selected Essays.* Ed. Christopher Nobes. New York and London: Garland Publishing, Inc., 1984.

Williamson, John B. and Fred C. Pampel. *Old-Age Security in Comparative Perspective.* New York: Oxford University Press, 1993.

Wilson, Arlene. *The Exchange Stabilization Fund.* Washington, DC: Congressional Research Service, Library of Congress, 1995. *Major studies and issue briefs of the Congressional Research Service, Supplement, 1995.* Arlington, VA: University Publications of America, 1996: reel 9, fr. 00475.

World Bank Group. "Data by Topic." *Data and Maps.* 2 Aug. 2000. 16 Feb. 2001. <http://www.worldbank.org/data/databytopic.htm>.

# Index

**About the Author**

EDWARD L. WHALEN holds a doctorate in economics from Princeton University and served most of his career as a faculty member in the economics department of Indiana University and as the University's Director of Budgeting. More recent assignments include appointments as chief financial officer at the University of Houston System, interim vice president of administration and finance at Clarke College, and consultant to the National Association of College and University Business Officers. He also has served as an economic consultant to the Agency for International Development and the U.S. Office of Management and Budget. Now retired, Dr. Whalen is author of one previous book, co-editor of another, and has contributed articles to journals in his field.

www.ingramcontent.com/pod-product-compliance
Lightning Source LLC
Chambersburg PA
CBHW071352220926
51613CB00008B/123
*9781567204261*